ONE WEEK LOAN

Renew Books on PHONE-it: 01443 654456

Books are to be returned on or before the last date below

D1345397

POLICING THE CARIBBEAN

CLARENDON STUDIES IN CRIMINOLOGY

Published under the auspices of the Institute of Criminology, University of Cambridge; the Mannheim Centre, London School of Economics; and the Centre for Criminological Research, University of Oxford.

General Editor: Ian Loader
(*University of Oxford*)

Editors: Manuel Eisner, Alison Liebling, and Per-Olof Wikström
(*University of Cambridge*)

Robert Reiner, Jill Peay, and Tim Newburn
(*London School of Economics*)

Lucia Zedner and Julian Roberts
(*University of Oxford*)

RECENT TITLES IN THIS SERIES:

Police Culture in a Changing World
Loftus

Social Order and the Fear of Crime in Contemporary Times
Farrall, Jackson, and Gray

Black Police Associations: An Analysis of Race and Ethnicity within Constabularies
Holdaway

The Prisoner Society: Power, Adaptation, and Social Life in an English Prison
Crewe

Making Sense of Penal Change
Daems

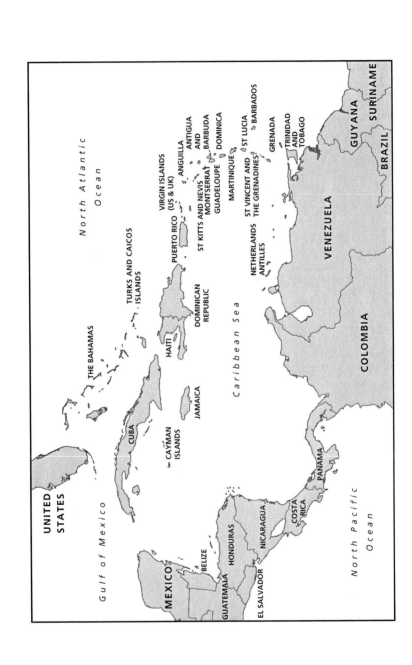

Policing the Caribbean

Transnational Security Cooperation in Practice

BEN BOWLING

OXFORD
UNIVERSITY PRESS

OXFORD

UNIVERSITY PRESS

Great Clarendon Street, Oxford OX2 6DP

Oxford University Press is a department of the University of Oxford.
It furthers the University's objective of excellence in research, scholarship,
and education by publishing worldwide in

Oxford New York

Auckland Cape Town Dar es Salaam Hong Kong Karachi
Kuala Lumpur Madrid Melbourne Mexico City Nairobi
New Delhi Shanghai Taipei Toronto

With offices in

Argentina Austria Brazil Chile Czech Republic France Greece
Guatemala Hungary Italy Japan Poland Portugal Singapore
South Korea Switzerland Thailand Turkey Ukraine Vietnam

Oxford is a registered trade mark of Oxford University Press
in the UK and in certain other countries

Published in the United States
by Oxford University Press Inc., New York

© Ben Bowling 2010

The moral rights of the author have been asserted
Database right Oxford University Press (maker)

Crown copyright material is reproduced under Class Licence
Number C01P0000148 with the permission of OPSI
and the Queen's Printer for Scotland

First published 2010

British Library Cataloguing in Publication Data

Data available

Library of Congress Cataloging-in-Publication Data
Bowling, Benjamin.
 Policing the Caribbean / Ben Bowling.
 p. cm.
 Includes bibliographical references and index.
 ISBN 978-0-19-957769-9 (hardback)
 1. Police—West Indies. 2. Police—International cooperation. 3. Security,
International—West Indies. 4. Law enforcement—West Indies. I. Title.
 HV7921.B65 2010
 363 . 2 ' 309729—dc22

2010012137

Typeset by MPS Limited, A Macmillan Company
Printed in the UK by CPI Antony Rowe, Chippenham, Wiltshire

ISBN 978-0-19-957769-9

3 5 7 9 10 8 6 4 2

General Editor's Introduction

Clarendon Studies in Criminology aims to provide a forum for outstanding empirical and theoretical work in all aspects of criminology and criminal justice, broadly understood. The Editors welcome submissions from established scholars, as well as excellent PhD work. The Series was inaugurated in 1994, with Roger Hood as its first General Editor, following discussions between Oxford University Press and three criminology centres. It is edited under the auspices of these three criminological centres: the Cambridge Institute of Criminology, the Mannheim Centre for Criminology at the London School of Economics, and the Centre for Criminology at the University of Oxford. Each supplies members of the Editorial Board and, in turn, the Series Editor.

In this book, Ben Bowling offers a rich, detailed case study of transnational police cooperation in the Caribbean region. The book is a significant addition to the growing literature on transnational policing for several reasons. The first is its focus on the Caribbean. This region, Bowling points out, has for several decades been at the frontline of the 'war on drugs' and the illicit drugs trade has produced huge spill-over effects in terms of violent crime and political corruption, as well as on the economies of Caribbean islands. In a field of study dominated by work on Europe, this is a welcome change of empirical tack. Secondly, Bowling pays careful attention to two different senses in which policing activity is crossing borders—in terms of both collaboration between police actors from different national jurisdictions and the involvement in law enforcement of a plurality of 'policing' agencies. The book is notable, thirdly, for the extent and depth of the empirical research on which it is based; research comprising close observation and in-depth interviews with those responsible for policing the Caribbean. In a field of study that remains relatively short of high-quality empirical enquiries into policing practices, Bowling's contribution is especially significant.

What follows in this book is a fine-grained account of the activities and outlooks of those who are engaged in a daily struggle to control the drugs trade and the problems that it brings to a region of the world unhappily caught in the path between drug producers and consumers. Some of these actors will be well-known to any reader versed in the sociology of policing—Police Commissioners, detectives, and intelligence officers. Others—the military, agents of border protection and maritime patrol, overseas liaison officers—are much less familiar, and it is to Bowling's credit that their role is given such a central place in his story. But if this book is valuable for the richness of its empirical narrative, this is not all that it offers. Bowling also uses his research to pose—and begin to answer—some large and troubling questions about police accountability and effectiveness in this terrain: how can one ensure that these new forms of police collaboration offer adequate forms of responsiveness to and redress for citizens? Might the proliferation of security activity in the Caribbean region have not only failed to alleviate the harm that the drugs trade and its attendant ills produce, but actually made a bad situation worse? The answers that Ben Bowling's important study supplies to these questions command both our attention and further work.

The Editors welcome this important edition to the Clarendon Studies.

Ian Loader
Oxford
December 2009

Preface

Policing the Caribbean explores policing practices that extend beyond the boundaries of the nation state. It examines inter-island, regional, and transatlantic collaborations in criminal investigation, above all in responding to the clandestine trade in cocaine and ganja that flows through the region. Transnational policing is one of the most significant recent developments in the policing field and heralds a number of changes in the organization of security in the Caribbean and other parts of the world.[1] Most obviously, and by definition, it has entailed a greater degree of communication, cooperation, and collaboration with officers from elsewhere. Many of the people described in this book spend their working lives speaking on the phone or emailing their 'opposite numbers' on other islands or meeting with overseas liaison officers from Britain or America. Some facets of local policing—the work of the Interpol officer, Special Branch, and Drug Squad—are intrinsically transnational. Most obviously, the overseas liaison officer, who is stationed on the islands for three or four years at a time, is a fully-fledged globally mobile kind of police officer. This specialism has emerged relatively recently, but seems set to play a very significant role in the future of policing.

Transnational policing is by no means the exclusive preserve of the police and herein lies a major dissolving of the boundaries of the discipline of police research. The idea that the police are part of an 'extended family' of related occupations has been recognized in academic literature and police policy-making. The present work extends the police family tree into the transnational realm and to relatives elsewhere in the 'security sector'. Until recently, UK overseas policing was led not by the Police, but by what was Her Majesty's Customs & Excise. Policing the Caribbean is a job for the armed forces as much as it is for the Police. In the absence of a credible military threat from a foreign state, Caribbean defence forces have become de facto armed police, supporting their constabulary

---

[1] Andrew Goldsmith and James Sheptycki (eds) (2007), *Crafting Transnational Policing: State-building and Police Reform Across Borders*. Oxford: Hart.

colleagues in drug enforcement and order maintenance. It now seems clear that military force is a major component in policing elsewhere in the world. The Caribbean is, of course, comprised almost entirely of water, blending seamlessly into the great Atlantic Ocean. Therefore, marine police and coastguards are required to patrol shorelines, harbours, territorial waters, and open seas. Maritime police—neglected cousins of the terrestrial patrol officer—work at and beyond the watery limits of the nation state. Other agencies with a major law enforcement function—Customs, immigration, airport security, port authorities, the post office, private security firms, secret intelligence, and security services—all have a role in transnational policing, supported by ministries of national security, defence, foreign, and home affairs. The family resemblances among the new security sector include possession of intrusive and coercive powers, working practices such as surveillance of suspect populations, stop and search, intelligence-gathering, interrogation, and a pervasive occupational culture of control. Policing the Caribbean involves literally dozens of separate organizations with overlapping roles, responsibilities, and jurisdictions. In addition to the major players on each island, there are regional associations among police, military, and Customs. There is a Regional Security System and committees of security ministers; transnational civil servants and security advisors from the United States, United Kingdom, and United Nations, all trying to stitch together a complex multi-layered 'patchwork quilt' of security.[2]

Numerous problems arise from the security archipelago that has grown organically over the four decades since the formal end of British colonial government. First, it doesn't work very well. It is inefficient, based largely on poorly equipped and under-resourced units, the organization of which would defy the combined strategic skills of von Clausewitz and Sun Tzu. These officers work hard and do their best under difficult circumstances. There are certainly many tactical successes, including high seas interdiction of tonnes of cocaine and inflicting damage on the organized crime groups involved in drug smuggling. However, there is little or no evidence that the investment in Security (defined as personnel and equipment) has delivered security (defined as safe and peaceful communities). On the contrary, in the two decades of pouring

---

[2] James Sheptycki (1995), 'Transnational Policing and the Makings of a Postmodern State', *British Journal of Criminology*, 35/4: 613–35.

many millions of dollars into security, the problems of serious crime—armed violence above all—have escalated to bloody civil war proportions.[3] The region now has the highest homicide rate in the world. A generous assessment of this apparent paradox is that the Caribbean has become more dangerous and disorderly *in spite of* the multi-million dollar investment in security. A more critical conclusion is that prohibition regimes and their attendant security practices are iatrogenic—*they produce more harm than they prevent.*

The reconfiguration of policing documented here has profound implications for the local and global governance of crime and for state sovereignty and accountability. Local patterns of crime are shaped by transnational forces. In a maritime neighbourhood through which well resourced organized criminal activity flows, the security of an island population of 100,000 inhabitants cannot possibly be guaranteed by a police force that it can afford. The nation state simply cannot deliver its end of the social contract. For this reason, the island political elite look to their neighbours across the region for collective security. But they find that—even when political in-fighting and division can be resolved—their capacity is insufficient for the task. So, it is to the British and Americans that the islanders must turn. But reliance on the former colonial masters and the world's sole superpower comes at a cost to national sovereignty and self-determination, for 'he who pays the piper calls the tune'. The security agenda is set by those who provide the resources and although there are mutual interests, deployment is geared firstly to the interests of the metropolitan countries rather than those in the Caribbean. The 'law enforcement pragmatists' prefer the diminution of sovereignty to 'an ally under treaty rather than to drug runners at will' but this invidious choice is resented by the 'sovereign nationalists', proud of their independent nationhood, hard fought-for after centuries of colonial rule.

The questions of sovereignty, authority, and accountability confronting the Caribbean political elite are echoed in everyday practices of security cooperation. Collaboration among regional police forces and between island police and agents from overseas blur the boundaries of accountability and control. Further

---

[3] Biko Agozino, Ben Bowling, Geofrey St. Bernard, and Elizabeth Ward (2009), 'Guns, Crime and Social Order in the West Indies', *Criminology and Criminal Justice*, Vol 19(3): 287–305.

questions arise from the collaboration between civil police (who are at least notionally accountable to the communities they serve) and military forces, Customs enforcement, and secret intelligence services whose work is explicitly secret and restricted from public scrutiny and accountability. Most frequently, these tensions are resolved amicably and pragmatically, oiled and glued together by a shared culture of control that privileges the pursuit of the 'bad guy' above all else. The more general question of how the contract between state and citizen can be re-established when the security forces are transnational and multilateral is a long way from being answered.

The conditions of contemporary world society seem set to push the police further towards transnationality. All the indications are that local communities—all of us in the villages, towns, and cities in which we live—are feeling the effects of global insecurity. Consequently, police officers will increasingly share intelligence with their overseas counterparts and the number of overseas police and intelligence officers posted abroad will increase, most of whom will be invisible to the untrained eye. This development represents an unprecedented extension of global policing power which raises important questions about how we ensure that transnational policing contributes to community safety and is legitimate, transparent, and accountable. The problem of corruption is endemic in policing and abuses of power (such as extraordinary rendition and extrajudicial execution) are far from rare, so how can we prevent this mighty power from turning back on the citizens that it is supposed to protect? How do we prevent policing from having the unintended damaging consequences of contributing to the problems that it sets out to solve? The principal question at the heart of this book, in other words, is how can we ensure that policing—within and without the boundaries of the nation state—is good enough to provide safe and peaceful communities?[4]

---

[4] Ben Bowling (2008), 'Fair and effective police methods: towards "good enough" policing', *Scandinavian Studies in Criminology and Crime Prevention*, Vol 8/S1: pp 17–23.

Acknowledgements

The idea for this project originated in discussions with numerous people who have continually refreshed my thinking about policing. The first of these is James Sheptycki who acted as my guide into the study of transnational policing, a field with which his name is almost synonymous. In the early phases, I benefited from conversations with Maureen Cain, Basil Wilson, Bill Saulsbury, Tony Bottoms, Janet Foster, Maurice Punch, Coretta Phillips, Nigel Fielding, Ivelaw Lloyd Griffith, Loraine Gelsthorpe, Leanne Weber, Robert Reiner, Tim Newburn, Dave Byrne, Graham Farrell, and Dick Bennett, many of whom have provided constant support throughout the project. In preparing for the fieldwork, a number of senior police officers—Matt Baggott, Gillian Parker, Sean Price, Paul Robb, Vincent Harvey, Mike Fuller, Frank Dwyer, and Leroy Logan—wrote letters in support of my funding applications and in so doing added new ideas into the mix. At the Police College at Bramshill, I had unstinting support throughout the research from Sue Roberts, Simon Stephenson, John Abbott, Kurt Eyre, and especially Richard Baker and Roger Gaspar who bravely sat through repeated presentations on this topic.

I am grateful to the Economic and Social Research Council which provided funding (grant number RES000220102) which, with research leave from King's College London School of Law, enabled me to undertake fieldwork. Meeting John Parker, former secretary to the Association of Caribbean Commissioners of Police provided a breakthrough into the field, and this was followed up by a hugely valuable contact with the Association through Keith Renaud, Marcia Mannings, and Shirley Flatts enabling me to make my way through the complex world of the Caribbean security sector. I would also like to thank the staff of the British High Commissions and various police, military, Customs, immigration, coastguard, and other organizations who helped me to arrange interviews and navigate my way through the sometimes labyrinthine security clearance processes.

I was well looked after by colleagues at the University of the West Indies, especially Farley Brathwaite whose interest in the project led me to the Cave Hill campus in Barbados, and to Andrew Downes, Sandra Tull, Elsie LeFrank, Don Marshall, and Jonathan Lashley. In Trinidad, at UWI St Augustine, Ramesh Deosaran and Vidya Lall provided support and in Jamaica at UWI Mona, I was well looked after by and benefited from conversation with Anthony Harriott, Bernard Headley, Stephen Vaccianne, Hilton McDavid, Ivan Alert, Suzette Haughton, Moji Anderson, and Michael Barnett. At the University of Guyana, Michael Scott, Mark Kirton, O'Neil Greaves, and Andrew Hicks provided advice and information. Journalist and lecturer Enriquo Woolford got the ball rolling at UG and helped me out with background information.

This book would have been even slower coming were it not for the generous help that I was given by many research assistants. Jasmine Chadha spent long hours checking interviews, coding data, and helping me to theorize the globalization of policing. Frances Ibekwe, James Ross, Annell Smith, Michelle Harrigan-Thangaraj, and Stacey Lauterbach all provided help at various points along the way. Cian Murphy contributed to developing the ideas and shaping them into readable prose. The bulk of the interview transcription was conducted with outstanding speed, accuracy, and efficiency by McKensie Transcription. My fieldnote audio-recordings were cheerfully transcribed by Carolina Cordero and along the way I have had more help than I deserved from King's administrative staff, Grace Alleyne, Kua Kessuwan, Lauretta Alexander, Malcolm Bishop, Steve Warburton, David Cordero, and Catherine Calder. My academic colleagues at King's have been fantastically supportive, especially Elaine Player, Mike Hough, Paul Turnbull, Alan Norrie, Mary Vogel, and John Phillips. Nic Groombridge, Tammy Ayres, Renee Olivel, and Rachel Walsh deserve special mention for helping me trim the text to a (hopefully) readable length. Thanks also to my editors at Oxford University Press—especially Peter Daniell, Lucy Alexander, and Rob Crossley—and the people who provided anonymous reports on the work for the Press.

The book has benefited from much feedback on work in progress and I'd particularly like to thank Robert Reiner, Roger Grimshaw, Paddy Rawlinson, and Nigel Fielding for their perceptive comments on my early fieldwork reports. Greg Davey, Georgina Sinclair, Elizabeth Kirley, P.A.J. Waddington, and many of those academics mentioned above also provided comments on written work, all helping me to fill gaps and preventing me from making elementary errors. I benefited immensely from the opportunity to speak about this work at various stages and I would like thank the people who organized and participated in seminars at Manchester Metropolitan University, Oxford University, the University of Cambridge, University of Leeds, Queen's University Belfast, University of Durham, University of Leicester, the Free University of Amsterdam, and the Open University Walton Hall. I'd also like to thank those who attended panel sessions at the British Criminology Conference in Leeds, London and Cardiff, the American Society of Criminology Annual Meetings in Atlanta, Nashville and Toronto, and at the three campuses of the University of the West Indies Cave Hill (Barbados), St. Augustine (Trinidad), and Mona (Jamaica). I am grateful for the comments made by the participants, many of which—no doubt—have found their way into the text.

I have given presentations on more than a dozen occasions at the police college at Bramshill including the International Commanders Programme, the International Strategic Leadership Programme, the Strategic Command Course, and the Chevening Programme. I have also spoken about the work to police audiences on the Caribbean Security Sector Command Course, Chaguaramas Conference Centre, Trinidad; Distinguished Lecture Series commemorating the 165th Anniversary of the Royal Bahamas Police Force; Gerald Bartlett Police Headquarters, Freeport, Grand Bahama; and the National Centre for the Performing Arts, Nassau; Jamaica Constabulary Force Staff College Seminar Series, Twickenham Park; Caribbean Staff Officers Course; ACCP annual conference; and at Interpol Headquarters in Lyon. On each occasion, the practical concerns of the police participants anchored my work on the 'so what' and 'now what' questions. This research was the basis for my Professorial Inaugural Lecture at King's College London—*Bobby, Bond or Babylon? transnational police cooperation in the contemporary Caribbean*—in October 2005. It also informed my teaching and I'd like to thank my postgraduate students at King's who probably heard more about Caribbean policing than they really wished to know and who asked many perceptive questions that have helped me to improve my ideas. I am grateful to the publishers who have allowed me to draw on my published work in the *Caribbean Journal of Criminology & Social Psychology, Criminal Justice, and Policing: An International Journal of Policy & Practice*.

The most important people in the research are the 160 or so people who gave their time to be interviewed for this study. I was welcomed everywhere and was provided with more information than I had any right to expect. I sat in on meetings, saw presentations, and learned how police officers worked beyond national boundaries. Interviewees often shared quite sensitive information with me and gave me an exceptionally privileged insight into their perspectives on crime and security in the region. For reasons of anonymity and confidentiality, these people must remain nameless. I hope they will feel that I have captured their perspective on the knotty problems in this field and will forgive any errors of fact and interpretation for which I alone am responsible. I hope that the insights that I absorbed, analysed, and present here, can contribute to a clearer understanding of the problems involved in transnational security cooperation.

Finally, I want to express my love and gratitude to my friends and family—especially my wife Susi and three sons Samson, Johannes, and Frederik—without you none of this would have been possible.

Ben Bowling
September 2009

Contents

Lists of Figures and Tables

Figures

Tables

List of Abbreviations

ABC	America, Britain, Canada
ACCP	Association of Caribbean Commissioners of Police
ACP	Africa, Caribbean, Pacific
ACPO	Association of Chief Police Officers
ACS	Association of Caribbean States
AGM	Annual General Meeting
AUC	Autodefensas Unidas de Columbia (United Self-Defence Forces of Columbia)
BMATT	British Military Advisory & Training Team
CARIBPOL	Caribbean Police Organisation
CARICOM	Caribbean Economic Community
CARIFTA	Caribbean Free Trade Area
CCLEC	Caribbean Customs Law Enforcement Council
CDRU	Caribbean Disasters Response Unit
CFATF	Caribbean Financial Action Task Force
CIA	Central Intelligence Agency (USA)
CID	Criminal Investigation Department
CITES	Convention on the International Trade in Endangered Species
CLO	Central Liaison Office (RSS)
CMU	Crime Management Unit (Jamaica)
CRO	Criminal Records Office
CSME	Caribbean Single Market and Economy
DEA	Drugs Enforcement Administration (USA)
DFID	Department for International Development (UK)
DHC	Deputy High Commissioner
DLO	Drugs Liaison Officer (UK)
DPP	Director of Public Prosecutions
DS	Drug Squad
EEZ	Exclusive Economic Zone
ELO	Enforcement Liaison Officer (Customs)
EPIC	El Paso Information Centre
EU	European Union
EUROPOL	European Police Office

FARC	Fuerzas Armadas Revolucionarias de Colombia (Revolutionary Armed Forces of Colombia)
FAT	Fugitive Apprehension Team (USA)
FBI	Federal Bureau of Investigation (USA)
FCO	Foreign & Commonwealth Office (UK)
FTAA	Free Trade Area of the Americas
G8	Group of Eight Industrialized Nations
G20	Group of Twenty Finance Ministers and Central Bank Governors
GCHQ	Government Communications Headquarters (UK)
GDP	Gross Domestic Product
HC	High Commissioner
HMCE	Her Majesty's Customs & Excise (UK)
IATA	International Air Transport Association
ICAO	International Civil Aviation Organization
ICC	International Criminal Court
ICITAP	International Criminal Investigative Training Programme (USA)
IGCP	Inspector General of Colonial Police (UK)
IMF	International Monetary Fund
INTERPOL	International Criminal Police Organization
IUCN	World Conservation Union
LED	Law Enforcement Detachment (or Shiprider)
MLAT	Mutual Legal Assistance Treaty
MOU	Memorandum of Understanding
NATO	North Atlantic Treaty Organization
NCB	National Central Bureaux (Interpol)
NCS	National Crime Squad (UK)
NCIS	National Criminal Intelligence Service (UK)
NGO	Non Governmental Organisation
NIM	National Intelligence Model (UK)
NJHQ	National Joint Headquarters
NYPD	New York Police Department
OAS	Organization of American States
OECS	Organisation of Eastern Caribbean States
OLO	Overseas Liaison Officer
OTRIS	Overseas Territories Regional Intelligence System
PACE	Police and Criminal Evidence Act (UK)
RAF	Royal Air Force (UK)
REDTRAC	Regional Drug Law Enforcement Training Centre
RCO	Regional Clearance System

RICO	Racketeer Influenced and Corrupt Organizations Act (USA)
RIISS	Regional Information and Intelligence Sharing System
RILO	Regional Liaison Office
ROCCISS	Regional Organised Counter Crime Information Sharing System
RSS	Regional Security System (Eastern Caribbean)
SAUTT	Special Anti-Crime Unit (Trinidad & Tobago)
SB	Special Branch
SIS	Secret Intelligence Service (MI6)
SLO	Security Liaison Officer (UK)
SOCA	Serious Organised Crime Agency (UK)
SSU	Special Services Unit (Eastern Caribbean)
SWAT	Special Weapons and Tactics Team
TREVI	TREVI group of European Interior Ministers
UNCLOS	United Nations Conference on the Law of the Sea
UNDCP	United Nations International Drug Control Programme
UNDP	United Nations Development Programme
USCIS	US Citizenship and Immigration Services
VAT	Value Added Tax
WCO	World Customs Organization
WIR	West India Regiment
WTO	World Trade Organization

1

Introduction

The Caribbean islands form a 2,500-mile arc from the tip of Florida to the coast of South America, dividing the Atlantic Ocean from the Caribbean Sea. For hundreds of years these islands have seen the traffic of goods and people moving among them, their neighbours, and the more distant shores of the Americas, Africa, and Europe. Characterized as the 'crossroads of Empire', in this post-colonial moment they are a node in the global flows of the licit and illicit transatlantic economy. This book examines this moment, focusing on how the police, Customs, immigration, military, secret intelligence, and others are responding to the problem of insecurity. It aims to provide a theoretically informed empirical account of the reconfiguration of the coercive and intrusive capacities of the state.

The islands exhibit extraordinary contrasts and puzzling ironies. Many of them have a dense tropical rainforest interior, their mountainous windward coasts plunging straight into the Atlantic. The sheltered leeward shores, with their hotels, golf clubs, and beach resorts, are the epitome of the Caribbean holiday destination: turquoise water lapping over coral reefs and white sand beaches fringed with palm trees. The mountains and the lowland plains are home to people living in sumptuous villas with luxury vehicles parked in the driveway while others live in poverty in corrugated zinc shacks with only the meanest of amenities. Plantations, lush with sugar cane, cocoa, banana, citrus, and spice are overgrown and abandoned in many places as production has become uneconomical after the collapse of farm-gate prices, aggressive competition from enormous mechanized US-owned plantations in Central America, and the end of preferential trade agreements with Europe. With the demand for agricultural labour gone and little to replace it, erstwhile workers lime idly on the block, migrate into the hills to grow ganja, or are drawn into the city to hustle. The beaches, populated mainly with European and American tourists sizzling in the sun, are serviced by the local population working in the restaurants and bars or hawking jet-skis, sun-beds, and parasols. At the beachside margins groups of young men deal weed and coke, play dominos, or just lime in the shade of a coconut palm. The region's capitals are vibrant urban centres built around their ports and at night are abuzz with tourists mingling with the local party crowd, the sounds of reggae, soca, and urban dance music thumping from massive speakers inside and outside the bars and clubs; 'jerk' pork and chicken's feet grill in homemade barbecues fashioned from oil drums all accompanied by an intensified night-time hustle.

Whether one considers the lush interior, peaceful beach scene, or the buzz of the city, scratching just a little beneath the surface reveals some very significant problems. While some islands are relatively safe, violent crime has been rising across the region since the 1980s and in some parts, the murder rate has reached startling proportions. On some islands, notably Trinidad, 'new crimes' like kidnap for ransom, have become disturbingly common. In addition to anxiety about personal safety, there are other insecurities stemming from the economic consequences of declining cash crops, a fickle tourism industry, and the local impact of global economic recession. Drugs money, flowing through business, commerce, and construction props up the economy but opens up the financial sector to charges of money laundering and corruption. Threats from other spheres are also on the radar: natural and man-made dangers such as hurricanes and toxic waste spillage, global warming and rising sea levels, unregulated migration, and anxiety about the thousands of people being deported from prisons in the USA, UK, and Canada. Following the September 11th 2001 airplane bombing of New York City's World Trade Centre, the 'War on Terror', and the attacks on Madrid, London, and Bali, the vivid, but as-yet distant, threat of a terrorist attack—targeting an American cruise liner in one of the region's harbours, for example—sits ominously at the back of security chiefs' minds.[1]

---

[1] Ivelaw Griffith (ed) (2004), *Caribbean Security in the Age of Terror: Challenge and Change*. Kingston, Jamaica: Ian Randle Publishers.

Caribbean Security

Perceptions of Caribbean security are shifting with the world-wide emergence of a 'new security agenda'.[2] At the end of the Cold War, a new security discourse emerged which emphasized the dangers posed by less institutionalized transnational threats. This blurred the boundaries between crime, migration, and war and the distinctions between criminal, migrant, and enemy.[3] James Sheptycki describes transnational criminals as the 'folk devils' of late modernity.[4] While external threats preoccupy police chiefs and their advisors, local crime and disorder—theft, burglary, robbery, bar-room fights, and domestic violence—occupies their constables' time. After all, transnational crime, like politics, is 'local at all points'.[5] Neighbourhood disorder is also a matter of concern for police and community alike. Juvenile delinquents, clustering in neighbourhood gangs or 'posses', are a source of local anxiety and it has become apparent that they have been recruited as foot soldiers in local battles for dominance in the global drugs trade.[6] 'Most wanted' are the kingpins of clandestine transnational trade networks and the businessmen with 'clean-skin' who reap the profits.

[2] Paul B. Stares (1998), *The New Security Agenda; A Global Survey*. Japan Centre for International Exchange; Barry Buzan, Ole Waever, and Jaap de Wilde (1988), *Security: A New Framework for Analysis*. London: Lynn Rienner; Joseph S. Tulchin and Ralph H. Espach (2000), *Security in the Caribbean Basin: The Challenge of Regional Cooperation*. Woodrow Wilson Center Current Studies on Latin America. Boulder Colorado: Lynn Reiner Publishers.

[3] Susanne Krassman (2007), 'The Enemy on the Border: Critique of a Programme in Favour of a Preventive State', *Punishment and Society*, 9/3: 301–18.

[4] James Sheptycki (1995), 'Transnational Policing and the Makings of a Postmodern State', *British Journal of Criminology*, 35/4: 613–35; Leanne Weber and Ben Bowling (2008), 'Valiant Beggars and Global Vagabonds: Select, Eject, Immobilize', *Theoretical Criminology*, 12/3: 355–75.

[5] Adam Edwards and Pete Gill (2002), 'The Politics Of "Transnational Organized Crime": Discourse, Reflexivity and the Narration of "Threat"', *The British Journal Of Politics And International Relations*, 4/2: 245–70.

[6] Alfredo Molano (2004), (trans James Graham), *Loyal Soldiers in the Cocaine Kingdom: Tales of Drugs, Mules and Gunmen*. New York: Columbia University Press; Darius Figuera (2004), *Cocaine and Heroin Trafficking in the Caribbean Vol 1: The Case of Trinidad and Tobago, Jamaica and Guyana*. New York: iUniverse; Darius Figuera (2006), *Cocaine and Heroin Trafficking in the Caribbean Vol 2: The Case of Haiti, the Dominican Republic and Venezuela*. New York: iUniverse.

Of course, these 'new' security threats are by no means restricted to the Caribbean. All over the world, security sector leaders have become concerned with transnational organized crime, drug trafficking, international terrorism, people smuggling, human trafficking, money laundering, and cybercrime.[7] However, the history, geography, and political economy of the Caribbean make it uniquely vulnerable to particular forms of transnational criminality.[8] The Caribbean islands sit directly on a cocaine smuggling route between the Andean producers—Columbia, Bolivia, and Peru—and North American and European consumers. The islands are easily accessible by sea and have excellent air links to the metropolitan markets in New York, Miami, Toronto, and London. Characterized as 'smuggling havens',[9] the size and the vulnerability of the islands' coastlines and accessibility to the open seas surrounding them makes protecting these countries extremely difficult, perhaps even impossible.

Because illicit drugs have a high value and must be moved clandestinely, the trade is accompanied by firearms; essential tools for market protection. This includes handguns, of course, but also battlefield weapons and those used in guerrilla warfare—AK47s, Tech 9s, and Uzis—many of which remain on the island to protect players and payload, as a means to inflict punishment, and sometimes payment to the drivers, sailors, minders, and enforcers. The money involved in the narcotic and psychotropic drugs business

[7] There is a rapidly growing literature on transnational organized crime illustrating the increasing anxiety about this phenomenon around the world. See for example, Phil Williams and Ernesto Savona (ed) (1996), *The United Nations and Transnational Organised Crime*. Frank Cass; Phil Williams and Dimitri Vlassis (eds) (2001), *Combating Transnational Crime: Concepts, Activities and Responses*. Frank Cass: London, Portland; Katja Franko Aas (2007), *Globalization and Crime*. London: Sage.

[8] West Indian Commission (1992), *Time for Action*. Black Rock, Barbados: The West Indian Commission; Ivelaw Griffith (1997), *Drugs and Security in the Caribbean*. University Park PA: Penn State University Press; CARICOM (2002), *Crime & Security: Report of the CARICOM Task Force on Crime and Security*; United Nations/World Bank (2007) *Crime, Violence, and Development: Trends, Costs, and Policy Options in the Caribbean*, A Joint Report by the United Nations Office on Drugs and Crime and the Latin America and the Caribbean Region of the World Bank Report No 37820 March 2007, *emphasis added*.

[9] 'Smokkelparadijzen in het Caraïbisch Gebied/Smuggling Havens in the Caribbean', Centre for Information and Research on Organised Crime, Amsterdam, Seminar, 17 May 2006.

is staggering—an estimated $320 billion worldwide.[10] The UN estimates that South America produces more than 1,000 metric tonnes of cocaine each year destined for US and European markets, with a US wholesale value of $24 billion and a street value of somewhere between $75 and $125 billion.[11] As a recent joint UN and World Bank report put it:

wedged between the world's source of cocaine to the south and its primary consumer markets to the north, the Caribbean is the transit point for a torrent of narcotics, *with a street value that exceeds the value of the entire legal economy.*[12]

The islands' tainted economy is reflected in widespread money laundering that compromises the banking system and legitimate businesses. It also leads to widespread corruption ranging from the junior Customs officer paid to 'look the other way' when baggage handlers are packing aircraft luggage holds with parcels of cocaine at the international airport, to the senior officials who take a cut of the cash generated on their watch. The whiff of flagitiousness rises to the high offices of government and respectable society. Politicians are thought, at best, to be unable to prevent the drug trafficking believed to make up 40 per cent of some island economies and powerless to protect society from the armed violence that accompanies this clandestine trade. At worst, government ministers and businessmen are seen as complicit, profiting personally from the organized crime that penetrates to the very heart of commercial and political life on the islands.

Transnational Policing

The problems facing the Caribbean are part and parcel of a growing concern about transnational organized crime around the world, an anxiety reflected in increasingly vocal calls for greater international law enforcement cooperation. As Robert Mueller, Director of the United States Federal Bureau of Investigation, contends:

The globalization of crime—whether terrorism, international trafficking of drugs, contraband, and people, or cyber crime—absolutely requires us

---

[10] United Nations (2007), *World Drug Report*, p 170.

[11] *Ibid*, p 175.

[12] United Nations/World Bank (2007), *Crime, Violence, and Development, op cit, emphasis added.*

to integrate law enforcement efforts around the world. And that means having our agents working directly with their counterparts overseas on cases of mutual interest—not only to solve crimes that have been committed, but to prevent crimes and acts of terror by sharing information in real time.[13]

The view that the globalization of crime *absolutely requires* transnational law enforcement to be 'integrated around the world' is a new orthodoxy among law enforcement professionals. In all regions of the world, we are seeing the emergence of new forms of policing that transcend the boundaries of the nation state.

This is an interesting development for a number of reasons, not least because, historically, policing has been based on clearly defined geographical places. Since their origins, most police forces have had responsibility for a neighbourhood, a parish, a town, a city, or a shire. In some countries, local police have been supplemented by national or federal agencies, but the traditional locus has been a locality. While there have been many examples of international cooperation among police officers since the birth of policing, these have tended to be ad hoc and reactive, rather than sustained and strategic. A growing body of research has begun to explore this development and the ways in which police officers now regularly exchange information about crimes and criminals, conduct joint surveillance of suspects, engage in coordinated crime investigations, share training facilities, and exchange information about police techniques. Most research on this subject has examined developments in the European Union[14] and North America,[15]

---

[13] FBI Website, <http://www.fbi.gov/contact/legat/legat.htm>, accessed 24 September 2009.

[14] For example, see M. Anderson, M. Den Boer, P. Cullen, W. Willmore, C. Raab, and N. Walker (1995), *Policing the European Union: Theory, Law and Practice*. Oxford: OUP; J. Benyon, L. Turnbull, A. Willis, R. Woodward, and A. Beck (1993), *Police Cooperation in Europe*. Leicester: University of Leicester CSPO; B. Hebenton and T. Thomas (1995), *Policing Europe*. London: Macmillan; P. Rawlinson, F. Gregory, and G. Brooke (2001), *Crime, Borders and Law Enforcement: A European 'Dialogue' for Improving Security*. ESRC End of award report; J. Sheptycki (1998c), 'Police co-operation in the English Channel Region, 1968–1996', *European Journal of Criminal Law and Criminal Justice*, 6/3.

[15] Ethan Nadelmann (1993), *Cops Across Borders: The Internationalization of US Law Enforcement*. University Park, Penn.: Pennsylvania State University Press.

although there are a handful of studies on the Caribbean region[16] and some that have taken a more general comparative and theoretical perspective.[17]

There are many examples of police cooperation extending across wide geographical spaces, the British colonial experience being one apposite example.[18] The literature points to the creation of *new structures* of transnational policing during the late modern era. The early work in this field described the evolution of Interpol,[19] European developments such as the Schengen agreement, TREVI, and Europol and considered its implications for the policing field.[20] In the same vein, Ethan Nadelmann described the extending reach of US law enforcement overseas through the growth of the Drugs Enforcement Administration (DEA) and international assistance programmes such as the Department of Justice International Criminal Investigative Training Programme (ICITAP).[21] Caribbean scholars have also taken an organizational approach. Ivelaw Griffith, for example, has described the complexity of national, regional, and international arrangements within the Caribbean, especially in the field of drug enforcement.[22] Griffith

[16] J. Tulchin, and R. Espach (eds) (2000), *Security in the Caribbean Basin*. London: Lynn Reinner; Ivelaw Griffith (1997), *Drugs and Security in the Caribbean: Sovereignty Under Siege*. University Park, PA: Penn State University Press.

[17] See, for example, James Sheptycki (1995), 'Transnational Policing and the Makings of a Postmodern State', *op cit*; James Sheptycki (1998a), 'Policing, Postmodernism and Transnationalisation', *British Journal of Criminology*, 38/3: 485–503; James Sheptycki (1998b), 'The Global Cops Cometh', *British Journal of Sociology*, 49/1: 57–74; James Sheptycki (ed) (2000), *Issues in Transnational Policing*. London: Routledge; James Sheptycki (2002), *In Search of Transnational Policing*. Aldershot: Avebury; Andrew Goldsmith and James Sheptycki (eds) (2007), *Crafting Transnational Policing: State-building and Police Reform Across Borders*. Oxford: Hart; Peter Andreas and Ethan Nadelmann (2007), *Policing the Globe: Criminalization and Crime Control in International Relations*. Oxford: Oxford University Press.

[18] Georgina Sinclair (2006), *At the End of the Line: Colonial Policing and the Imperial Endgame 1945–80*. Manchester: Manchester University Press.

[19] Malcolm Anderson (1989), *Policing the World*. Oxford: Clarendon Press; F. Bressler (1992), *Interpol: A History and Examination of 70 Years Crime Solving*. London: Sinclair Stephenson.

[20] James Sheptycki (1995), 'Transnational Policing and the Makings of a Postmodern State', *op cit*.

[21] Ethan Nadelmann (1993), *Cops Across Borders*, *op cit*.

[22] Ivelaw Griffith (1997), *Drugs and Security in the Caribbean*, *op cit*.

identified seven multilateral anti-drug organizations active in the region including the Association of Caribbean Commissioners of Police,[23] the UN International Drug Control Programme, and the Caribbean Ministerial Conference on Regional Law Enforcement.[24] The English speaking Caribbean countries are signatories to a Commonwealth mutual legal assistance scheme and have similar arrangements with the USA. Most countries have protocols for collaboration in maritime interdiction, such as ship boarding, shipriding, and overflight.[25]

Although much of the existing research focuses on new supranational institutional structures, the literature indicates that globalization is affecting *every aspect* of policing—from the local to the global. The typology set out in Table 1.1 is an attempt to delineate the dimensions of transnational policing at different socio-spatial levels.[26]

First, *global policing* networks are being strengthened through improved communication systems and joint training.[27] Interpol, which remains the only truly global policing entity, has grown in sophistication and capacity within the region, including a sub-regional bureau in Puerto Rico. As the Interpol website declares, because 'national boundaries are increasingly meaningless to criminals, effective international police communication has become more important than ever before'. The constabularies of the region are connected with one another and to the world's police through Interpol's global communications network headquartered in Lyon, France. The United Nations Police Division promotes global police cooperation and the UN Office of Drugs and Crime maintains an

[23] The AACP was established formally in 1987. A permanent Secretariat was set up in Barbados with the assistance of the UK Department for International Development Association of Caribbean Commissioners of Police. *United Against Crime. ACCP First Annual Magazine*, January 2001.

[24] UN International Drug Control Programme (UNDCP), *Focus on Drugs*. Caribbean Regional Office, November 2000.

[25] Ivelaw Griffith (1997), *Drugs and Security in the Caribbean, op cit.*

[26] See also Ben Bowling (2009), 'Transnational Policing: The Globalisation Thesis, a Typology and a Research Agenda', *Policing: A Journal of Policy & Practice*, 3: 149–60.

[27] One aspect of transnational policing that falls beyond the scope of this book is the work of the UN Police Division, including the UNCIVPOL missions that step in to support policing in post-conflict situations such as Kosovo. See for example, B. K. Greener (2009), *The New International Policing*. Basingstoke: Palgrave Macmillan.

Table 1.1   Transnational policing: a socio-spatial typology

Locus	Network	Examples
Global	Policing entities that have a global reach	Interpol Headquarters, UN Police Division, UN Office of Drugs and Crime (UNODC)
Regional	Regional security structures and associations	Association of Caribbean Commissioners of Police (ACCP), Regional Security System (RSS), Caribbean Customs Law Enforcement Council (CCLEC), Council of Caribbean Security Ministers, Caribbean Regional Law Enforcement Technical Committee
International	International liaison officers posted in overseas diplomatic missions	UK DLOs, Serious Organised Crime Agency (SOCA) liaison officers, FBI, DEA, US Treasury Department, US State Department Security Service, Caribbean officers posted in the UK and USA, Operation Trident (MPS) liaison officers
National	National security structures created to be able to coordinate a national response and to work with international partners	Serious Organised Crime Agency (SOCA), Caribbean National Joint Headquarters (NJHQs) linking police, Customs, immigration, and airport security
Local	Local law enforcement agencies (neighbourhood, BCU, police force) linked with overseas counterparts	Caribbean Drug Squad, Special Branch, Criminal Investigation Departments, Interpol National Central Bureaux (NCBs)

office in the Caribbean and sponsors collaboration in counter-narcotics.

Second, new *regional entities* have been created such as the Association of Caribbean Commissioners of Police (ACCP) and the Caribbean Customs Law Enforcement Council (CCLEC). The Regional Security System (RSS) of the Eastern Caribbean has the capacity to provide paramilitary police responses to civil emergencies and natural disasters across the region. The impetus for the creation of these entities includes both domestic and regional imperatives, but they are also encouraged—and funded—by the metropolitan countries.[28] Caribbean security ministers have thought long and hard about regional cooperation, and plans for a CARIBPOL conceptualized along the lines of EUROPOL are on the drawing board.[29]

Third, *overseas liaison officers* (OLOs) are posted abroad to an embassy or High Commission for extended periods with the assistance of foreign ministries. Liaison officers (including UK Customs Drugs Liaison, US special agents from the DEA, Treasury Department, State Department, and Legal Attachés from the FBI) play a key role in advice and capacity building, training and mentoring, and coordinating joint operations in the hemispheric, regional, or national domain. While the USA and the UK are the countries who have the most officers resident, Canada, France, and the Netherlands are also represented in the region.

Fourth, *national security structures* have been created that link police with military, Customs, immigration, airport security, and secret intelligence agencies. Strategically, this involves a range of systems and structures for sharing information and collaboration. Operationally, it has led to the creation of national coordinating bodies, known as National Joint Headquarters (NJHQ). These help to coordinate a national security response and provide a single point of contact for the liaison officers who help to link one island with another and also with the metropolitan countries.

Fifth, *local policing has transnationalized* in ways that create linkages with national, regional, and supranational structures. This can be referred to as 'glocal policing' where, as Maureen

[28] The term 'metropolitan country' is commonly used in both vernacular and academic language in the West Indies to describe the USA, Canada, Britain, and other Western European countries. The origins of its usage lie in an expression of the relationship between colony and 'mother country'. The *Oxford English Dictionary* defines metropolitan as 'of, relating to, or designating a mother country or parent state in relation to its colonies'. Although the relationship between most Caribbean nations and Britain can no longer be described as colonial, the continued usage of the term in the vernacular hints at the nature of contemporary 'postcolonial' relationships.

[29] Regional structures have also been created in other regions: Southeast European Cooperation Initiative (SECI), Regional Centre for Combating Trans-Border Crime (Bucharest, Romania), South East Europe Police Association (SEEPA), Association of South East Asian Nations Police Association (ASEANPOL), and Southern African Regional Police Association (SARPOL).

Cain describes it, practitioners are 'indigenous but globally aware'.[30] In many police specialisms—and in particular Criminal Investigation Departments, Interpol National Central Bureaux, Special Branch and Drug Squads—the work of local policing now involves extensive collaboration with counterparts from other islands and with those in Europe and the Americas. This local transformation is one of the least explored aspects of globalization in the policing field and speaks to its 'in here' as well as its 'out there' qualities.[31]

Questioning Securitization

A theme explored in this book is the idea that the architecture of contemporary Caribbean island policing has become plural and multilateral, comprising an assemblage of domestic and international security sector organizations working sometimes independently and sometimes cooperatively, to create a what Sheptycki refers to as a 'patchwork quilt'[32] of policing or, in Didier Bigo's terms, a security archipelago.[33] To some extent, security provision has always been diverse, but organizations like the coastguard and Customs have fallen outside our idea of policing. The focus of existing research on institutional frameworks and organizational structures also leaves a gap when it comes to describing these new forms of policing 'on the ground'. With a few notable exceptions,[34] most accounts of transnational policing *in practice*, especially in the Caribbean, are available only through press reports. For example, 'Operation Libertador', a three-week drug enforcement effort in November 2000 was launched simultaneously in 36

---

[30] Maureen Cain (2000), 'Orientalism, Occidentalism and the Sociology of Crime', *British Journal of Criminology*, 40/2: 239–60.

[31] Anthony Giddens (1998), *The Third Way: The Renewal of Social Democracy*. Cambridge: Polity Press, cited by Katja Franko Aas (2007), *Globalisation & Crime*, p 3.

[32] James Sheptycki (1995), 'Transnational Policing and the Makings of a Post-modern State', *op cit.*

[33] Didier Bigo (2005), 'Globalized –(In)security: The Field and the Ban-Opticon' in Didier Bigo and Anastassia Tsoukala (2008), *Terror, Insecurity and Liberty*. London: Routledge.

[34] Ivelaw Griffith (1997), *Drugs and Security in the Caribbean*, *op cit*; James Sheptycki (1998c), 'Police Co-Operation in the English Channel Region', *op cit.*

Caribbean-basin countries resulting in 1,000 arrests.[35] This study seeks insight into these intriguing accounts by speaking with those involved and, to the extent possible, to witness transnational policing at first hand.

The globalization of policing raises some fascinating theoretical and practical questions that this book explores in the Caribbean context with an eye on the lessons that can be applied to other places. First, there is the question of how transnational policing works in practice: is there such a thing as a 'global cop' and, if so, who are they and what do they do?[36] How are the practical matters of inter-agency communication, coordination, and cooperation organized? What are the enablers of, and barriers to, collaboration with other islands and with the metropolitan countries? Evaluative questions asked about domestic policing apply equally to emerging transnational policing practices. For example, to what extent is it effective and efficient? When things go well, what are the results of collaboration? Creating regional associations and posting officers overseas is an expensive business; to the extent that it is possible to judge, how far does transnational policing practice enhance domestic security? As a result of these collaborative efforts, can we be sure that the people who inhabit the islands of the Caribbean, or the north Atlantic region more generally, live safer and more peaceful lives?

It is also relevant to ask what happens when things go wrong. Again, we know from research on domestic policing that from time to time there are problems, such as incompetence, corruption, and the abuse of force. When wrongdoing transcends national boundaries new questions are added to the old ones. For example, where does accountability lie when criminal intelligence is shared among officers from different countries or when joint operations are mounted? Who is responsible for investigating complaints? Who will provide remedy and redress for those harmed—physically injured or wrongly arrested, for example—in transnational policing operations? Transnational policing raises questions about the relationship between state

---

[35] *Operation Libertador Concluded; Jamaica Praised.* US Embassy Kingston, Press Release. 21 November 2000. Similar operations are documented by Ivelaw Griffith (1997), *Drugs and Security in the Caribbean*, p 220–1.

[36] James Sheptycki (1998b), 'The Global Cops Cometh', *British Journal of Sociology*, 49/1: 57–74.

and citizen. If law enforcement powers migrate beyond national boundaries, what are the implications for police accountability and national sovereignty? Where does responsibility for security of the person lie if we are moving, however slowly, to a global order? This book attempts tentatively to start to answer these questions by looking at the way in which the Caribbean is policed and how networks of law enforcement stretch between neighbouring islands and link with transatlantic counterparts in Britain and the Americas.

Methodology and Fieldwork

This account of transnational policing is based on fieldwork in the Caribbean[37] and interviews with police officers from across the region during their senior officer training in England.[38] I travelled extensively through the Commonwealth Caribbean during the main stage of the fieldwork, spending time on the islands of Barbados (where I lived for the academic year 2003–4), Bermuda and the Bahamian islands of New Providence, Paradise Island, and Grand Bahama. I visited Guyana on the South American mainland, the twin island state of Trinidad and Tobago, Jamaica, Saint Vincent, and the Grenadine islands of Mustique and Bequia. I conducted 80 tape-recorded interviews and the same number again where circumstances didn't permit taping, as well as observing and interacting with security sector personnel as they went about their business at conferences, workshops, and during training and, on a few occasions, as they policed the islands' inshore waters. The interviews provide first-hand accounts of the experiences of policing the islands and collaboration in pursuit of regional and transatlantic security and these are set in the context of Caribbean history, politics, cultural, and social life.

Some readers will be disappointed to learn that this book does not offer a comparative analysis of the various locations studied. Instead, I have sought to portray the common features of the

---

[37] The bulk of this fieldwork was carried out during 2003–4 and supplemented with five additional visits (Jamaica 2001; Bermuda 2003; Bahamas 2005; Barbados 2006; Trinidad and Tobago 2006 (twice) and Jamaica (2007) to carry out further interviews and attend conferences and training courses.

[38] This included taped interviews with officers from the Bahamas, Bermuda, Saint Kitts and Nevis, Montserrat, British Virgin Islands.

patterns that I observed. There are some obvious disadvantages to this approach. For a start, travellers to the Caribbean are always struck by the differences between islands in their size and topography, economy, industry, agriculture, and architecture arising from their diverse histories. Moreover, one of my research sites—Guyana—is not even an island, but is part of continental South America! There are great social, political, and economic differences as well as wide diversity in ethnicity, dialect, and unique cultures reflected in food, music, literature, and visual arts. Moreover these differences from place to place are relevant to understanding crime and insecurity as well as the security sector responses that are the focus of the study. For example, Barbados is a prosperous small island of a quarter of a million people that has had an average of around 20 murders a year, a figure that has hardly changed in decades.[39] A thousand miles away, the much larger island of Jamaica has 2.5 million people, and had 1,620 murders in 2008, nearly double the 1997 figure and about eight times the *per capita* murder rate of Barbados.[40] Jamaica now has the unenviable position of the country with the highest murder rate in the world, recently overtaking Columbia and South Africa in the homicide league table.[41]

Describing the 'general case' precludes comparing and contrasting Caribbean territories on important dimensions. No doubt, one could learn much about the globalization of security by comparing smaller with larger, richer with poorer, the safer with the more dangerous, and the chaotic with the well governed. A related point is that of making generalizations; how can one speak of the 'general case' when there are such striking differences from place to place? It is partly *because* there is such extensive regional variation

[39]   Barbados Draft National Plan on Justice, Peace and Security (2002). Attorney General's Office, Bridgetown, Barbados. See also Chris Nuttall (undated), 'Homicide in Barbados 1979–2000'. Paper produced for the Attorney General of Barbados (unpublished). Christoper Nuttall, De Courcey Eversley, and Inga Rudder (2002), *The Barbados Crime Survey 2002: International Comparisons*. Attorney General's Office: Bridgetown Barbados.

[40]   Biko Agozino, Ben Bowling, Elizabeth Ward, and Godfrey St Bernard (2009), 'Guns, Crime and Social Order in the West Indies', *Criminology & Criminal Justice*, 9/3: 287–305.

[41]   'Sun, Sea and Murder', *The Economist*, 31 January 2008.

Country	Murder rate
Antigua and Barbuda	23
The Bahamas	25
Barbados	11
Belize	33
Columbia	36
Dominica	10
Grenada	11
Guatemala	47*
Guyana	15
Jamaica	59
Mexico	25*
St Kitts and Nevis	33
St Vincent and the Grenadines	36
Suriname	6
Trinidad and Tobago	30
Venezuela	45*

Note: Murder rate per 100,000, 2007
*2006 data

Figure 1.1 Homicide rates in the Caribbean (source (data); Economist, 2008)

and potential for comparison that I have chosen to generalize, setting out an analysis of the emerging pattern of transnational security practice within the Caribbean *region*. It is also impossible to be an expert on everywhere. If there was ever an excuse for general ignorance about the West Indies, there certainly is none today. There is extensive research in all fields, much of it carried out by scholars working in the universities of the region but also by many others based in Europe and America. I have been able to draw on this extensively, particularly in the fields of economics, political science, sociology, and international relations.[42] Even with the support of my Caribbean colleagues, it was challenge enough to gain sufficient expertise on the region in its most general sense to understand and interpret the complexities that unfolded during the fieldwork. I think it is more or less impossible to write a competent comparison of security practices in the seven territories where the bulk of the fieldwork was conducted, certainly not without far more extensive research. It is also true to say that academic criminology is underdeveloped within the region. There are studies of Caribbean security,[43] and good books covering crime[44] and policing on specific islands;[45] however, there is no basic research on patterns of crime and criminal justice country-by-country or for the region as a whole that provide a good foundation for comparative

[42] I found the following texts particularly useful to set the current research in context: The West Indian Commission (1992), *Time for Action*; Cynthia Barrow-Giles and Don Marshall (eds) (2003), *Living at the Borderlines: Issues in Caribbean Sovereignty and Development*. Kingston Jamaica: Ian Randle Publishers; Ramesh Ramsaran (ed), *Caribbean Survival and the Global Challenge*. Ian Randle Publishers; Axel Klein, Marcus Day, and Anthony Harriott (eds) (2004), *Caribbean Drugs: From Criminalisation to Harm Reduction*. Kingston, Jamaica: Ian Randle Publishers; James Ferguson (1998), *A Traveller's History of the Caribbean*. Moreton in the Marsh, Gloucs.: Windrush Press.

[43] See for example, Ivelaw Griffith (1997), *Drugs and Security in the Caribbean*, *op cit*; Ivelaw Griffith (ed) (2004), *Caribbean Security in the Age of Terror*, *op cit*; J. Tulchin. and R. Espach (eds) (2000), *Security in the Caribbean Basin*, *op cit*.

[44] For example, Bernard Headley (1994), *The Jamaican Crime Scene: A Perspective*. Mandeville, Jamaica: Eureka Press; Laurie Gunst (1995), *Born fi' Dead: A Journey Through the Jamaican Posse Underworld*. New York: Henry Holt and Company; Anthony Harriott (ed) (2005), *Understanding Crime in Jamaica*. University of West Indies Press.

[45] For example, Anthony Harriott (2000), *Police and Crime Control in Jamaica: Problems of Reforming Ex-Colonial Constabularies*. Kingston, Jamaica: University of the West Indies Press.

analysis.[46] A baseline study of this sort is an urgent priority for future research in the region.

As I analysed the mass of data that I collected, I struggled to focus the study. The project had too much qualitative data (described perceptively by Mathew Miles as an 'attractive nuisance'[47]) collected too from many places and organizations. It had competing levels of analysis (local, national, regional, transnational), various literatures (criminology, international relations, law, sociology, history, etc.) on which I could draw for the purpose of interpretation and research questions that multiplied during the course of the study. A similar problem was expressed beautifully by V.S. Naipaul in his collection of essays *Finding the Centre* when he describes how after a long period of travel, reading, looking around and starting to write, his 'narrative ran into the sands'. The problem, he explained, was that 'It had no centre. I hadn't yet found the story that would do the narrative binding' to gather together all the strands—impulses, ideas, and references—'to understand what one has lived through or where one has been'.[48] In time, I found the centre of analysis in the observation that transnational policing went well beyond the role of The Police (emphatically capitalized and traditionally defined as 'stout men in blue coats'[49]). I sought to explain the ways in which globalization is generating insecurity and how this is transforming the coercive and intrusive capacity of the state within local, national, and transnational socio-spatial networks. The centre was the exploration of the reconfigured 'security sector' as it responded to the problems created by globalization and the resulting tensions between sovereignty and security.

To encourage my interviewees to speak freely about what would inevitably involve some controversial issues, I assured them that

[46] Edited collections based on papers presented at the International Caribbean Criminology Conferences in 1999 and 2001 are the best that is on offer at the present time. Anthony Harriott (ed), *Understanding Crime in Jamaica*, op cit. University of West Indies Press; Anthony Harriott, Farley Brathwaite and Scott Wortley (eds), *Crime and Criminal Justice in the Caribbean*. Kingston, Jamaica: Arawak Publications.

[47] Matthew B. Miles, 'Qualitative Data as an Attractive Nuisance: The Problem of Analysis', *Administrative Science Quarterly*, 24/4, Qualitative Methodology (December 1979): 590–601.

[48] V.S. Naipaul (1984), *Finding the Centre*. Harmondsworth: Penguin.

[49] Robert Reiner (1988), 'British Criminology and the State' in Paul Rock (ed), *A History of British Criminology*. Oxford: Oxford University Press, cited by James Sheptycki (2000), *Issues in Transnational Policing*, op cit.

the interview would be confidential and that they would remain anonymous. However, many of them held unique positions within their organizations in relatively small societies (some with a population no larger than a small British city). Therefore, to quote the Military Chief of Staff or the Comptroller of Customs describing their work on a specific island—to which they naturally referred repeatedly—would obviously reveal their identity. This again militated against comparative analysis across geographical locations. So when you read the views and opinions of a Police Commissioner, the quotation could be from the person in that role in any one of the locations—Trinidad, Jamaica, Saint Vincent, the Bahamas, Barbados, Bermuda, or Guyana—where I carried out my fieldwork. Of course, readers *au fait* with the region can play the game of 'spot the Commissioner', but attempts to do this in other similar studies—Robert Reiner's study of Chief Constables in Britain, for example—have been futile.[50]

The account of the evolving security sector in the Caribbean Islands set out in this book draws on the case study tradition.[51] This method uses multiple sources of evidence—but primarily document analysis, interviews, and observation—to describe and explain a social phenomenon in its real-life context.[52] It involves the collection of evidence through *theoretical* rather than random sampling,[53] bearing in mind the extent to which cases are representative of policing activity and can be generalized to other contexts. The study has two distinct units of analysis. It seeks to

[50] Robert Reiner (2000), *Chief Constables*. Oxford: Oxford University Press.

[51] The case study method has yielded compelling analyses of policing, eg Roger Grimshaw and Tony Jefferson (1987), *Interpreting Policework*. London: Unwin Hyman; J. Chan (1997), *Changing Police Culture*, Cambridge: CUP, 5–8; James Sheptycki (1998), 'Police Co-Operation in the English Channel Region, 1968–1996'; Ben Bowling (1999), *Violent Racism*. Oxford: OUP.

[52] See for example, Robert K. Yin (1989), *Case Study Research*. London: Sage; B. Gillham (2000), *Case Study Research Methods*. London: Continuum; C. Ragin and S. Becker (1992), *What is a Case? Exploring the Foundations of Social Inquiry*. Cambridge: CUP; C. Robson(1993), *Real World Research*. Oxford: Blackwell.

[53] Theoretical sampling involves a deliberate selection of cases, documents, and interviewees that can ensure that relevant categories, topics, and concepts can be examined in sufficient detail. Theoretical sampling is linked closely to the formulation of research questions and involves the search for information that confirms and contradicts working hypotheses (see Robert K. Yin (1989), *Case Study Research*. London: Sage; Roger Grimshaw and Tony Jefferson (1987), *Interpreting Policework*. London: Unwin Hyman.

understand the *general case* of transnational policing, including cooperation among Caribbean countries, and between them (individually and collectively) and Britain and North America. Within this, I have examined *specific cases* of cooperation among agencies in the local, national, and transnational spheres. This is what is sometimes referred to as an 'embedded case study'[54] and the specific cases in question will include examples drawn from particular islands (where these will not compromise assurances of confidentiality and anonymity to my informants), security sector organizations, and specific operations. The study makes an explicit attempt to generalize about the experiences of the Caribbean islands; it is the task of the social scientist not simply to document and explain patterns of policing in a specific village or city but to generalize to all such rural or urban settings similar enough for the data collected in one place to provide the basis for descriptive or explanatory lessons to be drawn elsewhere.

Studying small islands provides a unique opportunity to explore the entire national security apparatus. It might be possible to gain some insight into each of the different security sector organizations in other contexts, but it is unusual to be able to access everyone from the Minister of National Security, Chief of Staff of the Military, coastguard commander, and Commissioner of Police, down to the operational officers in the Drug Squad and Special Branch. It is more unusual still to be able to supplement the security sector perspective with the views of non-governmental organizations concerned with human rights, policing, and the environment, international liaison officers and other security specialists, and representatives of regional bodies and the United Nations. Accessing such people in numerous islands allowed me to explore various perspectives on security and responses to it held by people working within very different kinds of organizations. This is therefore a comparative analysis, but rather than comparing across societies, I am comparing *across institutions*—how they construct the problem of insecurity, its causes, and consequences, how they see their roles and responsibilities, their working methods, and the opportunities for and challenges of cooperation. In order to do this, it is inevitable that I have concentrated less on the differences as I travelled from one place to the next but on *organizational differences* in the context of regional similarities.

[54] Robert K. Yin (1989), *Case Study Research*, *op cit.*

There are striking differences between Caribbean islands: to know one certainly is not to know them all. But there are also many similarities in, for example, the physical layout of the capital city where, without exception, the security infrastructure is based. Most of the region's capital cities are built around the harbour with its coastguard, port authority, Customs, and immigration departments clustered around it and the police headquarters nearby. The international airport is usually a little further out from the centre of the city but on the coast with aeroplanes landing and taking off over the sea. Ministerial offices, the British High Commission, and the American Embassy are in close proximity to one another and only a short distance from the harbour front. The island-to-island similarities go beyond the geographical and extend to the cultural and institutional to such an extent that I think it is possible to refer to *specifically Caribbean* forms of policing especially where these are overlaid with collaboration with regional and international influences.

From what is inevitably an outsider's perspective, after a while, there was a certain familiarity about the Caribbean security scene.[55] The colonial architecture of the security sector buildings has, in many places, changed little since independence. The cramped and cluttered administrative offices and anterooms, the manner of the secretaries and their interaction with their superior officers are similar from place to place. Crucially, there are regularities in the differences in perspective that I found in police, military, government, and international and non-governmental organizations. Therefore, despite the geographical and political diversity, and the variations in patterns of crime and security arrangements, there are some qualities of the region's security apparatus that are *quintessentially Caribbean*. Perhaps an analogy can be made with Caribbean cuisine. Every island has its gastronomic specialities: Ackee

---

[55] Although I am, and remain an 'outsider' from the Caribbean security scene, there were times when I felt like an 'inside outsider'. The reasons for this were various. The fact that my father was born in what was then British Guiana and I can therefore 'pass' as a West Indian of sorts was significant and sometimes led to me experiencing what can only be described as the welcome of a homecoming son of the West Indies. My paternal grandfather was a policeman, as was my great uncle, the latter being celebrated as the first to rise to the rank of County Sergeant Major of the British Guiana Police Force. This certainly added to my welcome in some places. Throughout the research, there were moments when I felt like I had blended into the police environment to the extent that I was an 'undercover civilian'.

and Saltfish is the Jamaican national dish, Trinidad is famous for its Roti, and Pepperpot is uniquely Guyanese; Barbados has 'Cou Cou and Flying Fish', the Bahamian speciality is 'Cracked Conch' and the national dish of Saint Vincent and the Grenadines is roasted Breadfruit and Jackfish. Despite island variations, however, there are ingredients and culinary styles that make food distinctively Caribbean; and there are certain dishes—like 'curry goat' with 'rice and peas'—that you will find on the menu everywhere. This book therefore sets out the 'rice and peas', so to speak, of trans-national policing and to provide the reader with a strong flavour of current security practices in the countries where the fieldwork was carried out. It aims to explain the problems and describe emerging solutions that are common across the region. On some points, the Caribbean 'average' differs markedly from the experiences in specific islands. In dealing with material that relates uniquely to one place, but not others, I have either excluded it (particularly where it risked exposing the identity of my interviewees) or dealt with it by comparison with the central tendency. I hope that, for the most part, the accounts will resonate with the reader since they are based faithfully on the experiences of the interviewees who hail from those countries. It will be for the reader to judge whether the account offered here is accurate, reliable, and compelling.

It is appropriate at this point to delineate clearly the boundaries of the case study. This book does not qualify as a full account of Caribbean policing because little is said about the work of the constable patrolling on foot or in a vehicle. It is not an Antillean account of *The Policeman in the Community*[56] or *Society and the Policeman's Role*.[57] A book documenting everyday neighbour-hood policing in the Caribbean awaits an author.[58] This is not because policing the villages and towns of the islands and main-land territories of the Caribbean region is not important or exten-sive; on the contrary, routine patrolling still represents the work of the bulk of police officers' time and consumes the lion's share of resources. Instead, its main focus is on transnational policing and

---

[56] Michael Banton (1964), *The Policeman in the Community*. London: Tavistock.

[57] Maureen Elizabeth Cain (1973), *Society and the Policeman's Role*. London: Taylor and Francis.

[58] The nearest to this is Anthony Harriott (2000), *Police and Crime Control in Jamaica, op cit.*

the emergence of policing practices that look beyond the boundaries of the nation state.

Its main concern is with policing—carried out by various agencies—up to the point of arrest. It therefore does not cover in any detail the post-arrest evidence-gathering process, prosecution, or the work of the courts. These processes are also changing under conditions of globalization as prosecutors are required to collaborate with overseas counterparts and make a choice of jurisdiction and venue for trial. The extradition process in practice could be the subject of a book in its own right as could the issues of prisoner transfer and managing deportees. This book focuses almost exclusively on public agencies even though it is becoming increasingly apparent that private police and security agencies play a significant role in such areas as airport security, employee vetting, and access control, as well as the provision of consultancy, training, equipment, and secret intelligence. As well as being blind to the work of the private sector, it is open to a similar limitation in relation to gender, race, and ethnicity.

My geographical focus is exclusively on the English-speaking Caribbean. This is partly owing to the limitations of language and fieldwork capacity, but also the legacy of a myopic view of the British West Indies that is reflected in regional institutions such as CARICOM. Thus, Cuba, Haiti, the Dominican Republic, and Puerto Rico are excluded, as are the Dutch and French speaking islands and mainland Central and South American countries with Caribbean coastlines. I am nonetheless confident that the findings of this study can be generalized to other territories within the 'cricket-playing West Indies'[59] that I did not visit. I also think that many of the lessons drawn from this study may have a broader application to locations in other regions of the world. Certainly, there are few places that are unaffected by the 'new security agenda' that has led to the reconfiguration of security arrangements in the Caribbean. Small island states are particularly vulnerable to security threats linked to drug trafficking, organized crime, and armed criminality. Those that are former colonies will be particularly fertile ground for the growth of transnational policing practices developed by metropolitan countries. However, it is increasingly clear that the

---

[59] Professor Gordon Rohlehr, cited by Stewart Brown and John Wickham (eds) (1999), *The Oxford Book of Caribbean Short Stories*. Oxford: Oxford University Press, p xiii.

reconfiguration of the 'new security sector' and the emergent transnational policing practices documented in this book are replicated in many other parts of the world.[60] Throughout history, colonial territories have been the testing ground for innovations in governance and security that have then returned for application in the metropolis. Perhaps a similar story will unfold in this insecure post-colonial moment.

Outline of the Book

Following this introduction, Chapter 2 describes the Caribbean region in more detail, to provide geographical, historical, economic, and political context for the empirical work. It reviews the existing literature on crime, insecurity, and policing in the Caribbean, focusing specifically on the regional impact of globalization, clarifying key concepts in the fields of criminology and security studies. The chapter explores the fundamental insecurity facing the region stemming from the physical and economic vulnerabilities affecting small islands in general, compounded by its location directly between the cocaine producers of South America and the cocaine consumers of Europe and North America. The chapter examines the literature on organized crime and drug trafficking and its complex and contradictory impact on the islands' economy, politics, and society.

Our journey through the islands' security apparatus begins in Chapter 3 with a visit to the police headquarters to explore the perspective of Police Commissioners. We examine the Commissioners' experiences of the islands' security problems and working with counterparts in other security sector organizations and with overseas liaison officers. This provides a unique insight into the police view of the strengths and weaknesses, opportunities, and threats to effective regional security collaboration. In this chapter, we also examine the work of the ACCP in bringing together the region's most senior police officers to discuss common policing problems, share experiences, and work on specific projects such as regional intelligence-sharing systems.

---

[60] Andrew Goldsmith and James Sheptycki (eds) (2007), *Crafting Transnational Policing, op cit*; Peter Andreas and Ethan Nadelmann (2007), *Policing the Globe, op cit.*

Moving on from police headquarters, in Chapter 4 we examine operational policing units in order to get some insight into how transnational police cooperation looks 'on the ground'. This chapter describes *reactive* investigation in which detectives from the CID and the Interpol NCBs work with their counterparts in other countries in response to crimes for which a suspect is being sought. It then looks at *proactive* investigation in which officers from the Drug Squad and Special Branch work on complex transnational criminal conspiracies. This chapter shows that a large proportion of the policing activity within key operational units involves cooperation with overseas counterparts. Based on interviews and observation, we explore the day-to-day work of collecting, analysing, packaging, and international exchange of intelligence and the benefits and frustrations of inter-agency collaboration.

Chapter 5 explores the role of military force in transnational policing. We visit the Defence Force Headquarters where we meet the Chiefs of Staff and other soldiers to explore the ways in which the role of the army has shifted from defence to take a leading role in domestic and transnational policing. The chapter examines the *policeization* of the military as well as the *militarization* of the police which takes such forms as paramilitary units created within police forces such as the Special Services Units (SSUs) on each island in the Eastern Caribbean. The SSUs undertake action coordinated by the Regional Security System, through an air-wing and technical surveillance capacity. We look in detail at 'Operation Weedeater', a marijuana eradication operation undertaken by the RSS involving a range of SSUs, with military hardware and the logistical support from the US Marines. The chapter explores the advantages and disadvantages of the growing role of the army and paramilitary policing in transnational law enforcement.

Chapter 6 takes us out to the international airport, to the Customs House, Port Authority, and Immigration Service. Through interviews with their chief officers, we explore the role of these agencies in policing the islands' borders. We compare their perspectives on regional security priorities and on collaboration with those of conventional police officers. This chapter illustrates the ways in which Customs, immigration, port, and airport security agencies are involved in extensive policing activity comparable with, and yet different from, the work of their counterparts in the police service. They are engaged, just like the police, in surveillance of suspect populations, stopping passengers to interview them briefly or detain them for extensive questioning. They conduct personal and baggage searches, make reports, collect and analyse intelligence. These agencies all have the capacity to use coercive force and some have armed support units. It is clear that the policing element of the work of these agencies is becoming central to their mandate. These newly configured border protection agencies are playing an increasingly important role in an integrated transnational security apparatus.

The key challenge for the coastguard is to provide security in a 'maritime neighbourhood' where the threats to island security come 'largely from the sea'. This might be the burglar or murderer arriving under cover of darkness by boat, the drugs and firearms traffickers, or environmental threats such as hurricanes and toxic waste spills. Chapter 7 examines the roles of the police marine section and coastguard in protecting coastal waters and collaborating with the Royal Navy and US Coastguard in policing the high seas. Policing the waters surrounding the islands is an inherently transnational task requiring extensive collaboration among various security sector organizations from many countries. The chapter examines the development of maritime security cooperation agreements (known as Shipriders) and shared training exercises that facilitate coordination among water-borne police and military assets. Through interviews with the participants, the chapter investigates maritime policing in practice from the collection and sharing of intelligence about suspect vessels, the coordination of maritime operations, and the 'end game' of interdiction involving the pursuit and interception of boats carrying drugs and other contraband. The chapter explores the relevant issues arising from maritime security cooperation such as inter-agency tensions, sovereignty, jurisdiction, and resource imbalances.

International liaison officers play a key role in transnational policing, stitching together the multi-layered 'patchwork quilt' of security sector organizations.[61] In Chapter 8, we visit the British High Commission to meet the Deputy High Commissioner who has overall responsibility for the smooth running of the mission including overseas trade, consular matters, and security cooperation. We then take a few steps down the corridor to meet the liaison officers

---

[61] James Sheptycki (1995), 'Transnational Policing and the Makings of a Postmodern State', *op cit.*

who are responsible for collecting and sharing intelligence among security forces across the region and on either side of the Atlantic. We look at their strategic and operational roles and their contribution to joint operations including assisting with local drug interdiction efforts. Often, the liaison officer provides the intelligence and infrastructural coordination to make maritime interdiction possible. We examine their use of 'special investigative techniques' such as running informers, conducting undercover operations, and 'controlled deliveries' in collaboration with trusted local officers. Based on direct observation at the airport, we explore the relationship between liaison officers and their local counterparts and explore their perspectives on regional security collaboration.

Chapter 9 explores key themes in the emerging field of transnational policing. Drawing on the concept of 'prohibition regimes', the chapter considers how security priorities are arrived at and how this shapes transnational policing.[62] Here we return to the typology of transnational policing set out above, drawing conclusions about 'glocalization' of local policing, the deployment of international liaison officers, the strengthening of national, regional, and global policing structures and the broader implications of these new developments. It considers the impact of the new security architecture on the national sovereignty and security of small island states in a post-colonial context and considers questions around the legitimacy, accountability, and integrity of forms of policing that transcend the boundaries of the nation state. It raises broader questions about the ways in which security issues are prioritized and framed, and asks whose interests are served in this post-colonial moment. This chapter also considers the new security agenda and the practices to which it has given rise from the perspective of the islands' political elite. Drawing on interviews with the security ministers and senior civil servants, representatives of supranational organizations including CARICOM and the United Nations, and representatives of non-governmental organizations in the field of human rights, drugs, and the environment, this chapter considers the broader context of 'human security'. From the perspective of this increasingly 'glocal' political class, it examines the issues arising from security cooperation, covert policing, and the growing role of international liaison officers for police accountability and national sovereignty. This chapter also

---

[62] Peter Andreas and Ethan Nadelmann, *Policing the Globe*, op cit.

considers the role of democratic institutions and civil society in the governance of crime and policing in an era of globalization.

In the final analysis, the book considers whether the development of new transnational security practices has, in fact, improved the safety and well-being of the people of the Caribbean and, more broadly, that of the countries on the shores of the north Atlantic. Despite an almost crippling effort on the part of the Caribbean security sector, and many tactical successes, regional security cooperation has yet to make a marked reduction in the availability of psychotropic drugs in the metropolitan countries or in the Caribbean. Rather than bringing cocaine trafficking to an end, prohibition has created a clandestine market controlled by powerful organized crime groups that have grown, like the Children of the Hydra's Teeth, from the very attempt to destroy them. As the War on Drugs has been fought, transnational law enforcement has displaced drug trafficking to new locations across the Atlantic rim and with it, the associated harms of money laundering, corruption, armed violence, murder, and mayhem.

2

Caribbean Security in Context

Were it not for the illegitimate character of their actions, transnational criminals could be lauded as pioneers and visionaries in the age of globalisation. They have adopted facilitative and exacting measures to remain competitive, fashioned an envious organisational culture of efficiency and accountability, and maximized the opportunities provided by globalisation. They have been able to innovate, expand and flourish in a furiously changing international scenario; and to do it while being relatively cloaked so that there is an aura of mystery and ambiguity about their operations.[1]

Security can no longer be achieved by merely building walls or forts. The very large and the very small states of this hemisphere have found that security, in an age of globalization, is rather complex. Security includes the traditional notions of yesteryear, but today, security must now be extended, in the case of the small-island state, to encompass several non-traditional aspects. Natural disasters, for example, pose a greater threat to our security than does the loss of national territory to an enemy.[2]

It would be a fundamental error on our part to limit security concerns to any one area while the scourge of HIV/AIDS, illegal arms and drug trafficking, transnational crime, ecological disasters and poverty continue to stare us in the face.[3]

---

[1] Anthony T. Bryan (2002), 'Transnational Organised Crime in the Caribbean: The International Relations Context' in Ramesh Ramsaran (ed), *Caribbean Survival and the Global Challenge*. Jamaica: Ian Randle Publishers, p 65.

[2] Statement by Minister Henderson Simon of Antigua and Barbuda to the Third Defense Ministerial, Cartagena, Colombia, November 1998.

[3] Address by the Rt. Hon. Owen Arthur, Prime Minister of Barbados on the Occasion of the Inaugural Session of the 32nd General Assembly of the Organization of American States. St. Michael, Barbados, 2 June 2002.

Introduction

The *Oxford English Dictionary* defines security as the condition of being protected from or not exposed to danger. It is synonymous with safety, exemption from hurt or injury, and the state of being free from danger. Security is one of the essential goods of society, a basic element that makes life liveable and which provide the context within which other aspects of human experience can be enjoyed.[4]

Different disciplines have conceived of danger in divergent ways. Criminologists have focused on the dangers of violent crime such as homicide, assault, rape, and robbery and crimes against property such as burglary and theft. From a traditional criminological perspective, the issue is one of interpersonal wrongdoing, conceived of as the violent or predatory actions of an individual, or small group of people, against others. Studies of organized crime have extended this analysis to explore the ways in which more sophisticated criminal collaborations are involved in large-scale or systematic property crimes, extortion, and the distribution of illicit goods and services.[5] Organized or disorganized, individual or collective, the danger posed by crime is a visceral one, a direct and vivid threat to the physical body and personal possessions. More recently, critical criminologists have highlighted the crimes of the powerful, refocusing our attention on the dangers of corporate crime and crimes committed by the state against its citizens.[6]

An alternative perspective on the twin themes of safety and danger can be found in the field of 'security studies'—a distinct branch of international relations also known as 'defence', 'war', or 'peace studies'—which has been concerned with the study of the defence of the nation state against attacks by foreign armies. In this field, scholars have centred on the processes through which military attack and invasion can be deterred by the navy, air force, and army.[7] They have therefore focused on strategic and tactical

---

[4] Ian Loader and Nigel Walker (2007), *Civilising Security*. Cambridge: Cambridge University Press.

[5] Mary Macintosh (1975), *The Organisation of Crime*. London: Macmillan.

[6] Penny Green and Tony Ward (2004), *State Crime: Governments, Violence and Corruption*. London: Pluto Press; Maurice Punch (1996), *Dirty Business: Exploring Corporate Misconduct*. London: Sage.

[7] Paul B. Stares (1998), *The New Security Agenda: A Global Survey*. Japan: Japan Centre for International Exchange, p 13; Barry Buzan, Ole Waever, and Jaap de Wilde (1998), *Security: A New Framework for Analysis*. Boulder, Colorado: Lynne Rienner Publishers, Inc.

military planning to wage war and diplomacy to pursue peace. More recently, as conventional wars fought in Western Europe have slipped into distant memory (notwithstanding the continuing involvement of European powers in wars on other continents), Cold War fears of nuclear conflagration have been replaced by the threat of asymmetric warfare and international terrorism.[8]

Until very recently, the fields of criminology and security studies were quite separate; security studies textbooks made little or no reference to crime, and criminology texts ignored war.[9] The clinical separation between crime and war now seems odd partly because they share some essential elements—such as violence, coercion, and wrongdoing—but also because the boundaries between police and military forces have blurred. In recent years, there has been extensive debate about how far the attempt to widen research agendas will affect the substantive and theoretical integrity of these linked but historically separate fields. In discussions of transnational policing, scholarship in criminology and international relations has converged at the idea of a 'new security agenda'.[10]

The new security agenda

From the perspective of criminologists whose primary concerns have been crime, justice, and community safety, the newness of the new security agenda revolves around understanding crime within a broader political economic context and linking it with problems such as terrorism that lie at the boundary between the two disciplines. Criminological work is increasingly aligned with international relations in its exploration of critical issues in international security. From the security studies perspective, the challenge has been to shift the analytical focus away from the task of defending the nation-state from military threats, to protecting the

[8] Gail Verasammy (2009), 'Toward a Reconceptualisation of Caribbean Basin Security', *In-Spire Journal of Law, Politics and Societies*, 4/1; Ivelaw Griffith (ed) (2004), *Caribbean Security in the Age of Terror*. Kingston, Jamaica: Ian Randle Publishers.

[9] A radical shift in this field is signalled in Lucia Zedner (2009), *Security (Key Ideas in Criminology)*. London: Routledge.

[10] Roy Godson and Phil Williams (2001), 'Strengthening Cooperation against Transnational Crime: A New Security Imperative' in Phil Williams and Dimitri Vlassis (ed), *Combating Transnational Crime: Concepts, Activities and Responses*. London, Portland: Frank Cass.

planet and the welfare of its citizens in its broadest sense.[11] From this perspective states become the means rather than the ends of security.[12] Paul Stares argues that the concept of 'global' or 'human security' requires a horizontal extension of the field. In addition to having a *military dimension* (eg threats from foreign armies), the new security agenda has a *social dimension* (eg population growth, uncontrolled migration, and ethnic conflict), a *political dimension* (eg terrorism), an *environmental dimension* (eg natural and man-made disasters, environmental degradation and pollution, global warming and rising sea levels, and food, water, and energy scarcities), an *economic dimension* (eg economic collapse, money laundering, and corruption), and a *criminal dimension* (eg trafficking in drugs, arms, and people). Stares argues that security studies is also undergoing a vertical extension of the objects of security policy to a level above and below the nation state. Security thus becomes a matter for local and supranational governance as well as national governments.

Understanding contemporary security requires an understanding of globalization, which has been described as a process through which worldwide social relationships have intensified, linking places around the world so that local happenings are shaped by events occurring many miles away and vice versa.[13] Global interconnectedness has been driven by rapid developments in transport and communication technologies and has economic, political, social, and experiential dimensions. The globalization thesis contends that as regional and intercontinental flows have *become faster*, global interconnectedness has become *more intensive* with a *greater impact* on specific localities.[14] Driven by technological innovation, political change and neoliberal economic policies, product, capital, and labour markets are integrating

[11] Paul Stares (1998), *The New Security Agenda, op cit*, p 15, citing the UN Development Programme (1994), 'Redefining Security: The Human Dimension', *Human Development Report 1994*. Oxford: Oxford University Press; see also Mary Kaldor (2007), *Human Security*. Cambridge: Polity.

[12] Ken Booth and Peter C.J. Vale (1995), 'Security in Southern Africa: After Apartheid, Beyond Realism', *International Affairs*. United Kingdom: Royal Institute of International Affairs, p 293, cited by Paul Stares (1998), *The New Security Agenda*.

[13] David Held and Anthony McGrew (eds) (2000), *The Global Transformations Reader: An Introduction to the Globalization Debate*. Cambridge: Polity Press.

[14] *Ibid.*

and world trade is increasing.[15] The total volume of merchandise traded around the world increased fourfold between 1995 and 2007 and the global market in commercial services increased sixfold in the same period.[16] It is impossible to estimate accurately the effect that these changes have had on security, but we need only assume that the *proportion* of world trade in illicit merchandise and services has remained constant to conclude that transnational crime has grown. On that assumption, increases in legal markets will be accompanied by global flows of illicit agricultural and manufactured products (eg counterfeit medicines and narcotic and psychotropic drugs), professional and commercial services (eg sex work and money laundering) and of the people buying and selling them. Neoliberal policies such as market deregulation seem likely to increase illicit flows in a globally connected marketplace.

The people of the world are increasingly on the move. The number of British residents travelling overseas increased from under 30 million in 1987 to over 70 million in 2007 and the number of visitor arrivals from 15 to 30 million[17] reflecting a 60 per cent growth in worldwide air travel between 1995 and 2007.[18] Increasing world travel for business and tourism and the emergence of expatriate and diaspora communities creates new issues for policing, not all of which are concerned with transnational organized crime. It is probable that the number of 'ordinary crimes' involving foreign nationals in countries around the world has grown simply because the number of foreign residents and visitors has increased and because of the growing ease, speed, and frequency of international travel. The capacity to communicate around the world has radically increased through personal mobile phones and computers. Four billion mobile phones were in use worldwide in 2008, up from 2.7 billion in 2006,[19] and the number of Internet users rose fourfold between 2000 and 2008 to 6.7 billion.[20] Global interconnectedness creates new opportunities

---

[15] World Trade Organization (2008), *World Trade Report 2008: Trade in a Globalising World*.   [16] *Ibid*, chart 13, p 102.

[17] Office of National Statistics.

[18] World Travel Monitor, IPK International.

[19] *The Wall Street Journal*, 16 February 2009, citing Informa Telecoms & Media, a London-based research company.

[20] Internet World Statistics, Usage and Population Statistics.

for illegality and facilitates criminal collaborations but also opens up new possibilities for communication and collaboration among law enforcement agencies, reducing bureaucratic drag and political control.

Globalization also denotes the processes through which sovereign states are criss-crossed and undermined by transnational actors with varying prospects of power, orientations, identities, and networks.[21] The creation of a world society has been accelerated by *globalism* or the ideology of the market,[22] leading politicians to adopt neoliberal modes of governance, deregulating economic systems and empowering corporations and other non-state financial actors.[23]

While globalization denotes a range of complex shifting processes, one way to characterize its contours is to make a distinction between globalization 'from below' and 'from above'. Globalization from below is a way to characterize the chaotic, unplanned social changes and human innovation arising from advances in transport and communication technologies and emerging opportunities for global interaction. This includes the ways in which people capitalize on new market opportunities for trade within emerging clandestine and legitimate markets and human migration away from zones of war and poverty towards more prosperous places with more plentiful employment. For Bryan, quoted at the head of this chapter, the apparent ascendancy of the transnational criminal is an apposite example of globalization from below. This phrase has also been used to describe other 'bottom up' initiatives such as the anti-capitalist movement and other global interconnections within civil society.[24]

In contrast, globalization 'from above' characterizes the attempts by governments to regulate these shifts through the creation of intergovernmental and supranational institutions. This

---

[21] Ulrich Beck (2000), 'What is Globalisation?' in David Held and Anthony McGrew, *The Globalisation Reader, op cit.*

[22] David Held and Anthony McGrew (2000), *The Globalisation Reader, op cit.*

[23] Anthony Bottoms and Paul Wiles (1997), 'Environmental Criminology' in M. Maguire, R. Morgan, and R. Reiner (eds), *The Oxford Handbook of Criminology.* Oxford: Clarendon; James Sheptycki (2002), *In Search of Transnational Policing: Towards a sociology of global policing.* Hampshire, England: Ashgate.

[24] Stuart Hall (2006), 'Cosmopolitan Promises, Multicultural Realities' in R. Scholar (ed), *Divided Cities.* Oxford: Oxford University Press, cited by Katja Franko Aas (2007), *Globalisation & Crime.* London: Sage.

'transnationalization of governance'[25] includes the emergence of economic structures (such as the World Bank, International Monetary Fund, and World Trade Organization) and political structures (such as the European Union, United Nations, G8, and G20) all of which make an increasingly significant contribution to world affairs. In the sphere of crime and justice, a fledgling international criminal justice system is emerging, with a gradual codification of international criminal law, judicial and prosecutorial cooperation, an International Criminal Court, and a proliferation of formal, informal, and ad hoc policing arrangements that transcend the nation state.[26] Understanding globalization clearly has great relevance for the changing extent of real and perceived dangers and therefore the discussion of security. This is partly because many contemporary public issues, security threats among them, are transnational in nature, passing across or through national boundaries largely unfettered by the actions of national government. As George Monbiot puts it, 'it is hard to think of any issue of national importance which now stops at the national frontier'.[27]

Commentators are divided on the question of how far these shifts signal the 'withering away' of the sovereign power of the nation state.[28] Exploring the growing power of the neoliberal world economy and discussion of the prospects for a 'new global empire' is beyond the scope of this chapter, but global connections in economic, political, social, juridical, and policing spheres are evidently reshaping the relationship between state and citizen.[29] A contention of the 'great globalization debate' is that the nation state is less relevant today than at any time since the seventeenth century in understanding and influencing political, economic, and social development. This has profound implications for policing since it implies a diminution in the role of the nation state in authorizing and providing security to its citizens. The guarantee of safety and freedom from harms threatened by fellow citizens and foreign armies lies at the very heart of the duties of the state and

[25] James Sheptycki (ed) (2000), *Issues in Transnational Policing*. London: Routledge.

[26] Katja Franko Aas (2007), *Globalisation and Crime*. London: Sage.

[27] George Monbiot (2003), *The Age of Consent: A Manifesto for a New World Order*. New York: New Press, p 82.

[28] James Sheptycki (1995), 'Transnational Policing and the Makings of a Postmodern state', *British Journal Of Criminology*, 35/4: 613–35.

[29] Katja Franko Aas (2007), *Globalisation and Crime*, *op cit*.

sits at the centre of the idea of the 'social contract'. Globalization therefore presents a serious challenge to thinking about contemporary social order.[30]

The observations set out above have not been lost on Caribbean scholars and politicians (including those quoted at the head of this chapter) who have for many years observed the shifting nature of security threats and their implications for national governments.[31] There is also reason to think that global transformations are having a greater impact on the countries of the Caribbean region than elsewhere. The legacy of imperialism and foreign involvement in domestic affairs, a complex position in contemporary geopolitics, the problems that stem from small size, fragile economies, and environmental vulnerability all contribute to shaping the traditional and non-traditional security environment in each country.[32] The multidimensional nature of Caribbean security and its real world implications requires us to pause now to explore briefly some important aspects of the region that provide the context for discussions of security and the pretext for the new transnational security practices.

A Brief Introduction to the Caribbean

The Caribbean has been described as the crossroads of Empire,[33] vortex of the Americas,[34] a bridge between North and South America and between the Old World and the New.[35] For Rex

[30] Peter Singer (2002), *One World*. London: Yale University Press; Anne-Marie Slaughter (2004), *A New World Order*. Princeton & Oxford: Princeton University Press.

[31] Report of the West Indian Commission (1992), *Time for Action*. Black Rock, Barbados: The West Indian Commission; Ivelaw Griffith (1997), *Drugs and Security in the Caribbean: Sovereignty Under Siege*. University Park, PA: Pennsylvania State University Press; Ivelaw Griffith (2004), *Caribbean Security in the Age of Terror, op cit*.

[32] Gail Verasammy (2009), 'Toward a Reconceptualisation of Caribbean Basin Security', *In-Spire Journal of Law, Politics and Societies*, 4/1; Ivelaw Griffith (2008), 'A New Conceptual Approach to Caribbean Security' in Kenneth Hall and Myrtle Chuck-A-Sang (eds) (2008), *The Caribbean Community in Transition*. Kingston, Jamaica: Ian Randle Publishing.

[33] Alan Cobley (1994), *Crossroads of Empire: The Europe-Caribbean Connection 1492–1992*. Bridgetown, Barbados: Department of History, University of West Indies, Barbados.

[34] Jose Marti, cited by Griffith (1997), *Drugs and Security in the Caribbean, op cit*, p 53.

[35] Ivelaw Griffith (1997), *Drugs and Security in the Caribbean, op cit*.

Figure 2.1 Central North Atlantic

Nettleford, it is a 'meeting place, and centre of encounters of myriad cultural elements, as well as a crucible in which new forms of human expression have been forged over the past half a millennium'.[36] The region takes its name from the Caribbean Sea, one million square miles of water contained between the 2,500 mile-long archipelago running from the Bahamas to Trinidad bounded by the Central American states of Mexico, Belize, Guatemala, Honduras, Nicaragua, Costa Rica, and Panama to the west and by the Florida straits and Gulf of Mexico to the north. Colombia, Venezuela, Guyana, Suriname, and French Guiana, neighbouring countries along the northern coastline of South America, make up the region's southern boundary. Figure 2.1 shows the North Atlantic region with the Caribbean islands at its western edge.

Caribbean history has been played out in this physical geography, squeezed between the Americas and forming a gateway—via

---

[36] Rex Nettleford (2002), 'The Caribbean: Crossroads of the Americas' in Alan Cobley, *Crossroads of Empire: The Europe-Caribbean Connection 1492–1992.* Bridgetown, Barbados: Department of History, University of West Indies, Barbados.

the Panama isthmus—between the Pacific and Atlantic Oceans and to the Old World beyond. The islands lie on well established trade routes and since the end of the fifteenth century, seafarers have used them as stopping points as they travelled between Europe, Africa, and the Americas. At first, the islands were convenient places to pause to take on fruit and fresh water on journeys to and from Europe and the larger islands of Cuba, Hispaniola, Jamaica, and mainland America. For most of their history, the economic mainstay of the islands was agriculture. Columbus' importation of sugar cane from the Canary Islands—what Eric Williams calls 'the greatest gift of the Old World to the New'—created the economic foundation for the entire region.[37] The demand for sugar expanded massively during the sixteenth century and the development of the trade was assisted by technological development and the employment of indentured labour. But as the plantation system expanded, traditional sources of labour began to dry up, and an interrelated industry developed in parallel linking Africa, Europe, and the Americas in one of the seventeenth century's largest commercial enterprises: the transatlantic slave trade.[38] Traders, speculatively at first and then on a mass scale, engaged in a triangular trade, shipping manufactured garments, chains, rope, firearms, cutlasses, and alcohol to Africa where they would buy slaves to ship across the 'middle passage' to the Americas. This 'human cargo' could, in turn, be exchanged for tropical products, above all sugar, to be shipped to European markets. Most the islands were settled. Where possible, their coastal plains were cleared for sugar plantations, the more accessible hills and valleys planted with banana, cocoa, nutmeg, and allspice, and their ports grew into busy trading centres.

The territory of the sea

The Caribbean Sea has been a space of great strategic importance.[39] With fast northwards currents and vital trade winds it was the great battleground of colonial powers during the age of sailing ships. The Spanish monopoly in the region established in the

---

[37] Eric Williams (1970), *From Columbus to Castro: The History of the Caribbean 1492–1969*. London: Andre Deutsch Limited, p 25.

[38] *Ibid*; James Walvin (2001), *Black Ivory: Slavery in the British Empire* (2nd edn). Oxford: Blackwell.

[39] Stephen J. Randall and Graham Stewart Mount (1998), *The Caribbean Basin: An International History*. London: Routledge.

sixteenth century was challenged by Portugal, Britain, France, and the Netherlands, and for the next three centuries many territories changed hands repeatedly as wars raged and they were invaded or traded for peace or land elsewhere in the Americas. In the mid-twentieth century the Caribbean was critical for control of the North West Atlantic and to protect wartime supply routes during World War II. Caribbean sea lanes remain strategically important both for the movement of military assets between the Atlantic and Pacific Oceans and for freight shipping. The Caribbean links the USA 'underbelly' states on the Gulf of Mexico—Texas, Louisiana, Alabama, Georgia, and Florida—with South America and South East Asia. With 38 per cent of containerized shipping between North East Asia and the East Coast of the USA passing through the Panama Canal—310 million tonnes in 2008—Caribbean sea lanes are of major economic significance to the USA.[40]

The sea provides almost unlimited opportunities for clandestine trade. Taking the archipelago for what it is—lands dotting an arc across a great sea—there are literally thousands of islands with shores patterned with millions of secluded bays, hidden coves, and caves where business can be conducted and goods stored and exchanged. Island coastlines are not only unprotected, but *unprotectable*. Smugglers, privateers, pirates, and slavers have plied these waters alongside legitimate traders since the sixteenth century and regional and intercontinental flows have presented challenges to the islands' security ever since. Geography is a salient feature in today's most significant clandestine trade: the massive traffic of cocaine from South America to Europe and the USA. Jamaica, for example, is 500 miles from the coast of Colombia and 600 miles from Miami. Cocaine can be brought to most Caribbean islands from continental South America by boat in a day and flown from there to the USA in a few hours. While it is more than 4,000 miles from any of the islands to London, there are numerous airlines with daily flights to choose from, so transatlantic transport is fast and efficient.

Environment and security

The Caribbean islands' tropical location provides a near perfect climate: a constant year-round temperature in the high 20s Celsius, cooled by a warm breeze and watered by regular showers. The

[40] Panama Canal Authority (2006), *Proposal for the Expansion of the Panama Canal, Third Set of Locks Project.* <http://www.pancanal.com/eng/index.html>.

extraordinary vitality of the islands is one reason for their popularity with adventurers since it held the prospect of fortunes based on sugar and spice. In theory at least, food and water security should not be a problem since rich soils and tropical climate mean that the islands could easily be self-sufficient in food. The islands are well watered with extensive rainfall and freshwater springs. Fruit and vegetables of many varieties grow easily throughout the year and agriculture has provided an economic mainstay throughout their history. There is a ready supply of food for local consumption and for export, even though a taste for foods from Europe and America and a reliance on cash crops means that in fact most food consumed in the region is imported.

Hurricanes are the main climatic threat. In 2004, Hurricane Ivan did serious damage to numerous Caribbean islands. Grenada was the most severely affected, where 33 people were killed, 95 per cent of buildings were damaged, and the devastation was valued at twice the island's GDP.[41] Other environmental hazards—floods, drought, earthquakes, and volcanoes—are a source of some concern. When La Soufrière, Montserrat's volcano, erupted in 1995 large parts of the island including the capital city and airport were destroyed and 70 per cent of the inhabitants fled the island never to return.[42] There has been no repeat of the tsunami that washed Port Royal (Jamaica's erstwhile capital) into the sea in 1692, but as the climate changes and global warming produces rising sea levels, the prospects of losing land to the sea is increasing in importance. A hint of the potential impact of rising sea temperatures can be found in the recent report from the World Conservation Union (IUCN) which found that warmer seas and more frequent hurricanes have had a devastating impact on Caribbean coral reefs.[43] As well as the obvious human cost, storms damage the coral through the physical strength of waves, muddy run-off water from the land and bleaching, caused by higher sea temperatures, which cause coral to lose essential symbiotic algae. Other forms of long-term environmental

[41] OECS (2004), 'OECS Secretariat Presents Findings of Assessment of Losses in Grenada Associated With Hurricane Ivan,' cited by Gail Verasammy (2009), 'Toward a Reconceptualisation of Caribbean Basin Security', *op cit.*

[42] Gail Verasammy (2009), 'Toward a Reconceptualisation of Caribbean Basin Security', *op cit.*

[43] Clive Wilkinson and David Souter (2008), *Status of Caribbean Coral Reefs After Bleaching and Hurricanes in 2005*. Townsville, Australia: Global Coral Reef Monitoring Network/World Conservation Union.

degradation include the depletion of natural resources such as fisheries, forests, and wetlands. There are obvious risks of man-made disasters including the risk that a tanker containing oil, chemicals, plutonium, or hazardous waste will sink or break up and spill its load in the sea and there has been a gradual build up of heavy metals and contaminants in the Eastern Caribbean.[44] There are a range of health risks from tropical diseases such as dengue fever and malaria, a rapidly rising number of people infected with HIV/ AIDS, and the long-term impact of tobacco, alcohol, and drug consumption. The main threat to health in many of the islands is armed violence to which we return later in this chapter.[45]

Island nationalism and regionalization

For much of their history, each of the research sites was subject to British colonial rule. One of the key tensions since independence stems from an inwards pull towards island nationalism and an outwards pull towards sub-regional, regional, and hemispheric institutions and towards Britain and the USA. The strength of national feeling within the countries of the region can be gauged by their independence of spirit and emphasis on national identity underscored by public holidays for the celebration of national heroes and government marketing campaigns promoting consumption of local produce. On some islands, school children start their day by reciting the national pledge and singing the national anthem. Nationalism is rooted in the long struggle for independence and the need for unity across different ethnic groups and social classes. And yet, it is clear that the size of most islands, their relatively small populations, and a sense of shared history and destiny with neighbouring islands also lends weight to the view that economic and political collaboration within a regional structure is desirable if not essential.

The first attempt at a regional structure was the West Indies Federation, formed in 1958 by the British with the intention of paving

[44] Winston Anderson (2003), 'Environmental Security Risks for Caribbean States: Legal Dimensions' in Cynthia Barrow-Giles and Don Marshall, *Living at the Borderlines: Issues in Caribbean Sovereignty and Development*. Jamaica: Ian Randle Publishers, p 304.

[45] Biko Agozino, Ben Bowling, Elizabeth Ward, and Godfrey St Bernard (2009), 'Guns, Crime and Social Order in the West Indies', *Criminology & Criminal Justice*, 9/3: 287–305.

the way towards a single independent Caribbean nation state. This collapsed dramatically in 1962 after Jamaica unilaterally declared independence, followed immediately by Trinidad and Tobago, leaving prospects for Federation in tatters. Nonetheless, regional aspirations among the newly independent Caribbean states gave impetus to the creation of the Caribbean Free Trade Area (CARIFTA) in 1968, the Caribbean Development Bank in the same year, and the Caribbean Economic Community (CARICOM) in 1973. Echoing the creation of the European Community and a shifting Caribbean-Europe political axis, the region's politicians have been pushing slowly towards a Caribbean Single Market and Economy (CSME) with free movement of goods, services, and labour. The government and people of the region are as conscious of the changing nature of global governance as those in other regions. In 1992, the West Indian Commission observed that:

The part to be played by the nation state has also radically changed. Political systems, concepts about the management of economic and social forces are still based on the nation state but supranational and transnational forces and organisations increasingly affect and lessen the ability of individual states to control events. No country can fail to take account of such a fundamental shift in how the relationship between nation states is coming to be viewed.[46]

Despite the steps towards regional integration, the West Indian Commission's principal recommendation that there should be rapid movement towards a regional economic system along the lines of the European Union has been in slow motion. The Commission reached the view that the region needed:

a market structured and functioning to a large extent as if it were within the borders of a single country. There must, therefore, be freedom of movement of goods, services, labour and capital, and supportive fiscal and monetary measures and administrative arrangements. The Single Economy must be a regional economy closely approximating a national economy.[47]

The advantages of a single Caribbean economy, the Commission believed, would be in the introduction of technology for 5.5 million people rather than the 100,000 typical of many countries in the region. It meant the development of firms capable of servicing

---

[46] Report of the West Indian Commission (1992), *Time For Action, op cit*, p 61.
[47] *Ibid*, p 104.

the whole region and pan-Caribbean franchises such as restaurants and travel agencies. The process would involve elimination of trade tariffs, harmonization of Customs laws and elimination of procedures restricting the flow of goods and services, harmonization of standards and abolition of exchange controls. The Commission envisaged that eventually there would be free movement of labour and a single currency with an independent monetary authority.

Although they understand the case for integration, most West Indians are pessimistic about the prospects for closer political union, with only about half of the population supporting developments in that direction.[48] This is complicated further by the fact that the region is scattered geographically and divided linguistically. There are also occasional border disputes and conflicts over natural resources such as oil and fishing.[49] CARICOM represents the English speaking Caribbean but not the French, Dutch, and Spanish speaking islands and thus excludes Haiti, the Dominican Republic, and Cuba, the economic giant of the region. There is competition from sub-regional organizations such as the Organisation of Eastern Caribbean States (OECS) representing the Commonwealth Windward Islands. Larger regional organizations such as the 25-member Association of Caribbean States (ACS) include mainland central and South American countries bordering the Caribbean and the Organization of American States (OAS) that represents the 35 independent states of the Americas.

Relationships with metropolitan countries

The relationship between the Caribbean islands and what are frequently referred to as the 'metropolitan countries'—the United States of America, Britain, Canada, and the countries of Western Europe—is also a complex one. The emphasis on the nation state and a pan-Caribbean outlook pulls the islands inward, and yet a degree of economic and political dependence on the rich countries

---

[48] Patsy Lewis (2003), 'Is the Goal of Regional Integration Still Relevant among Small States? The Case of the OECS and CARICOM' in Cynthia Barrow-Giles and Don Marshall, *Living at the Borderlines: Issues in Caribbean Sovereignty and Development*. Jamaica: Ian Randle Publishers, p 325.

[49] Ivelaw Griffifth (ed) (2004), *Caribbean Security in the Age of Terror*, *op cit*, (p 22–5) provides a detailed list of ongoing disputes of this nature.

pulls northwards and eastwards. For the people of the Caribbean, the legacy of British colonial rule can still be felt in the islands' society and culture. Formal indicators of more informal ties to Britain include the fact that all are members of the Commonwealth of Nations; many retain the Queen as Head of State and have 'Royal' police forces. Britain was still seen as the 'mother country' long after the end of Empire, and the islands' architecture, monuments, and sensibilities all echo their colonial history. However, British political influence, relative to that of the USA was in decline even before independence, most obviously in CIA intervention to bring down the Marxist leader, Cheddi Jagan in British Guiana while it was still under British rule during the late 1950s and early 60s.[50]

Although it does not have the same historical association with Commonwealth Caribbean countries, the USA has played a very significant role in the region for more than a century.[51] Alfred Thayer Mahan, the late nineteenth century historian and advisor to Roosevelt, characterized the Caribbean as a 'great highway' to the markets of Latin America, and—through the Panama Canal—to Asia, providing the key to global naval mobility.[52] Discussions of what US commentators frequently refer to as the Caribbean Basin (encompassing the Caribbean Sea and the Gulf of Mexico) characterize the region as an American Mediterranean with crucial strategic importance.[53] The US has invaded Caribbean countries on dozens of occasions, occupying Cuba, Haiti, and the Dominican Republic at various times and intervening more subtly throughout the region on a continuous basis during the twentieth century.

[50] The USA intervened covertly in what was then British Guiana between 1953 and 1969. During the 1960s, the Johnson administration feared that if the colony gained its independence from Britain, it would become 'a second Cuba'. CIA funding, through a programme run by a labour organisation AFL-CIO, 'fomented labour unrest, race riots and general chaos' that led to the collapse of Cheddi Jagan's People's Progressive Party and the installation of Forbes Burnham. The US 'also succeeded in overawing British officials, demonstrating to the British that they could not control British Guiana without US Cooperation'. Stephen Rabe (2005), *US Intervention in British Guiana: A Cold War Story*. Kingston, JA: Ian Randle Publishers, p 176.

[51] Today, its overseas territories include Puerto Rico, US Virgin Islands, and the Guantanamo Bay military base in Cuba.

[52] Joseph S. Tulchin and Ralph H. Espach (2000), *Security in the Caribbean Basin: The Challenge of Regional Cooperation*, Woodrow Wilson Center Current Studies on Latin America. Boulder, Colorado: Lynn Rienner Publishers, p 2.

[53] *Ibid.*

The 1823 Monroe Doctrine proclaimed that European colonial powers should no longer interfere with the affairs of the independent states of the Americas. The 1904 Roosevelt Corollary went further to proclaim that the USA would intervene in the countries of the Caribbean and Central America when required to stabilize their economies. The 1940 Act of Havana stipulated that there should be no transfer of sovereignty between colonial powers. In the aftermath of the Battle of Britain, Churchill asked Roosevelt Jnr. for naval destroyers, in return for which he gave the USA bases in the British colonies of the Bahamas, Bermuda, Saint Lucia, Trinidad, Jamaica, and British Guiana.[54] The protection of the US 'backyard' or vulnerable 'underbelly' has stimulated a range of military and economic strategies to protect political and strategic interests in the region.

US policy during the Cold War has been criticized for its 'bullying tactics and support for non-democratic, repressive, even violent regimes'.[55] The Truman Doctrine, originally articulated in the context of providing military and economic aid to Greece and Turkey to 'support free peoples who are resisting attempted subjugation by armed minorities or by outside pressures'[56] (coded language for the threat of the Soviet Union), provided the basis for measures within the Caribbean to prevent the growth of communist sympathies. The Cuban revolution of 1959 was an important historical moment establishing a communist republic within the region and creating a new front for the Cold War, which was most vividly illustrated by the 1962 Cuban missile crisis. The 1960s and 1970s were a period of tumultuous social and political change within the region as the process of decolonization unfolded. While many countries in the region remained socially and politically conservative, others—Guyana, Jamaica, and Grenada among them—leaned leftwards causing US anxiety about the prospect of a region of 'many Cubas'.

The Truman Doctrine provided the ideological justification for US-Caribbean security initiatives, drawing upon the nineteenth and early twentieth century international agreements concerning

---

[54] Stephen J. Randall and Graham Stewart Mount (1998), *The Caribbean Basin: An International History*. London: Routledge, p 70–84.

[55] Joseph S. Tulchin and Ralph H. Espach (2000), *Security in the Caribbean Basin, op cit.*

[56] President Truman, speech to Congress, 12 March 1947.

contraband alcohol trafficking. The 1924 convention between the US and UK for the Prevention of Smuggling provided a starting point for the drafters of the 1981 Exchange of Notes on Cooperation in the Suppression of the Unlawful Importation of Narcotic Drugs into the US.[57] In the mid-1990s, the US embarked on a programme to secure a series of bilateral maritime security arrangements with Caribbean countries (known as Shiprider Agreements), which permit US military assets rights to intervene in the territorial waters and airspace of the signatory nation.[58] This caused deep consternation in the region and while many of the small islands signed bilateral agreements the larger territories refused to do so. One newspaper editorial called them 'an obscene and cowardly assault' on national sovereignty.[59] Former Commonwealth Secretary-General, Sir Shridath Ramphal, denounced them as 'a proposal for recolonisation'.[60] Shiprider's advocates argued that since many countries cannot in fact defend themselves from contemporary threats, they must cede a degree of sovereignty in return for greater security. From this perspective, reliance on the USA 'may be the most sensible form of nationalism'.[61] After protracted negotiations, the inclusion of reciprocal rights for the signatories to enter US waters and airspace, preferential export tariffs, money for economic development, and financial assistance with security, the process was completed by Clinton in the 1997 Bridgetown Agreement.[62]

[57] Hilbourne Watson (2003), 'The "Ship Rider Solution" and Post-Cold War Imperialism: Beyond Ontologies of State Sovereignty in the Caribbean' in Cynthia Barrow-Giles and Don Marshall, *Living at the Borderlines*, p 226.

[58] Chapter 7 examines maritime law enforcement agreements in more detail and the ways in which they have been used in practice.

[59] *Barbados Advocate*, 15 December 1996 cited by Hilbourne Watson (2003), 'The Ship Rider Solution', p 250.

[60] Sir Shridath Ramphal, 'The West Indies in the Wider World: Compulsions of Regional Engagement', *Distinguished Lecture Series of the University of the West Indies*, 14 April 1997, Mona, Jamaica cited by Hilbourne Watson (2003), 'The Ship Rider Solution', p 251.

[61] Elliott Abrams (1996), 'The Shiprider Solution: Policing the Caribbean', *The National Interest*, p 86–92.

[62] President William Clinton, 10 May 1997, cited by Humberto Garcia-Muniz (2000), 'The United States and the Caribbean at Fin de Siècle: A Time of Transitions' in J.S. Tulchin and R.H. Espach, *op cit*, p 45; Hilbourne Watson (2003), 'The 'Ship Rider Solution', *op cit*.

The Caribbean and the global economy

Global economic integration has profoundly affected the Caribbean.[63] Production has internationalized, markets for goods and services have liberalized, and restrictions on the free flow of capital across national borders have lifted. Knowledge moves rapidly around the world facilitated by new information and communications technologies. The growth in the volume and ease of air travel, faster sea travel and containerization, and the rapid development of mobile telephony, computerization, and broadband wireless technology have all transformed modes of production and consumption. In the Caribbean region, as elsewhere, 'speed in doing things has been a significant consequence of the new technologies that have impacted on the movement of goods, services, people and money'.[64] This has contributed to open markets, expansive growth of organizations, particularly transnational corporations, and an internationalization of capital markets demanding 'greater freedom from national controls and regulation'.[65] The economic consequence is that Caribbean societies are 'marked by low capital accumulation and direct foreign investment inflows; diminishing state and institutional capacities; and threats to its security landscape in the context of global restructuring'.[66]

For most of its history, the region's economies were characterized by 'mono-crop' plantations of sugar, cocoa, and coffee which were 'foreign owned and oriented for export'.[67] The dominance of agricultural production, sustained by colonial and post-colonial relationships, continued well into the twentieth century, but there has also been a significant diversification into mixed economies, including mining, manufacturing, and service industries. For example, the economic mainstay of Trinidad and Tobago is the petrochemical industry and Jamaica is the world's second largest producer of bauxite. Nonetheless, agriculture still represents more

[63] Ramesh Ramsaran (ed) (2002), *op cit*; Cynthia Barrow-Giles and Don Marshall (2003), *op cit*.

[64] Ramesh Ramsaran (2002), 'The Caribbean and the Global Challenge in the 21st Century' in Ramesh Ramsaran (ed), *op cit*.

[65] Hilbourne Watson (2003), 'The Ship Rider Solution', *op cit*, p 255.

[66] Cynthia Barrow-Giles (2003), 'Introduction: Living at the Borderlines' in Cynthia Barrow-Giles and Don Marshall, *op cit*.

[67] Ralph R. Premdas (2002), 'Self Determination and Sovereignty in the Caribbean: Migration, Transnational Identities and Deterritorialisation of the State' in Ramesh Ramsaran, *op cit*, p 54.

than half of the region's exports with cane sugar (25 per cent), shrimp (8 per cent), and bananas (7 per cent) being the dominant products.[68] The remains of the sugar and banana economy can still be seen across the Caribbean. Agriculture, despite fragility and visible decline, is still the dominant sector in Belize, Dominica, Grenada, Guyana, Haiti, Saint Lucia, Saint Vincent and the Grenadines, and Suriname and a major employer elsewhere. During the 1980s, cash-crop economies began to falter and production reduced sharply. Based on relatively small farms in hilly terrain and reliant on manual labour, Caribbean production costs are higher than those of the Latin American banana giants—such as Chequita, Dole, and Delmonte—which dominate the world market by growing their products on huge and highly mechanized farms. In 1999, the World Trade Organization ruled that the European Union's preferential tariffs for ACP agricultural products did not comply with free trade practices and required that all quotas and tariffs be removed by 2005.[69] This ruling had an enormous impact on the economies of many Caribbean nations. For example, at its peak, banana growing in Saint Vincent accounted for approximately 60 per cent of direct employment with many indirect employed. This had had a huge impact on the rural economy since a whole range of services provided work in catering and local shops.

The overwhelming majority of Caribbean people are employed in service industries.[70] In many places tourism—developing rapidly with the advent of low-cost air travel, package holidays, and rising disposable incomes in the metropolis—has replaced agriculture as the mainstay of the economy. The Caribbean is now said to be the most tourism-dependent area in the world.[71] The region as a whole receives around 22 million tourists spending a total of US$21 billion. Tourism generates foreign exchange through visitor

[68] Caribbean Community (CARICOM) Secretariat (2007), *CARICOM's Trade in Selected Agricultural Economies 2000–2003*, September 2007.

[69] Paul Sutton (2002), 'On Small States in the Global System: Some Issues for the Caribbean with Particular Reference to Financial Flows and Aid Effectiveness' in Ramesh Ramsaran, *op cit*, p 102.

[70] For example, Bahamas (95%), Barbados (91%), Guyana (62%) Jamaica (75%), Trinidad and Tobago (82%). Ransford Palmer (2009), *The Caribbean Economy in an Age of Globalization*. New York: Macmillan Palgrave, Table 1.3, p 6.

[71] United Nations/World Bank (2007) report, *Crime, Violence, and Development: Trends, Costs, and Policy Options in the Caribbean*, World Bank Report No 37820, p 1.

taxes and employment in hotels, restaurants, travel services, retail, construction, and insurance. The disadvantages of tourism as the backbone of the economy include reliance on overseas economies, seasonality, relatively low wages, and the social tension arising from a predominantly black service staff catering for a rich white visitor population. Foreign currency is often used to buy foreign goods and in some places, the 'all inclusive' holiday dominates the tourist market with the result that money is spent in hotels owned and run by foreign corporations.

Size also matters to the history and contemporary security of the Caribbean islands and in this they share similarities with small island states around the world. Although the region punches above its weight in some spheres—such as sport and music—the Caribbean islands are vulnerable because of their geographically small size, small economies, limited natural resources (and their depletion), limited industrial product range, as well as vulnerability to natural disasters, all of which cause their security to be compromised. There is a lack of skilled workers and infrastructure is disproportionately costly. The islands depend heavily on Customs revenues and therefore have relatively high import duties. There is a tendency to rely on external financial support with resultant problems in servicing debt and balancing budgets. The region's economy is limited by the size and dependency on the US and Europe for markets, capital investment, aid, and credit. The islands export less than they import and this trade imbalance is skewed further as the prices of imported foods and manufactured goods are higher than the export value of cash crops and raw materials. As with many other countries, servicing the national debt has been an expensive drag on growth.

The shifting nature of banking and finance has had varied effects on the Caribbean economy. There has been a significant growth in foreign direct investment, trade and exchange, international credit, currency flows, and financial speculation. The islands have not been immune to the penetration of international capital nor the fallout from the global financial crisis. Structural adjustment policies forged by the Washington Consensus have had a major impact. With economic recessions in the 1980s, some governments took out extensive IMF loans that were subject to 'conditionalities' such as shifts in taxation regimes and massive cutbacks in social spending. One result is that the region has become dependent on development aid. Among the responses to this economic restructuring has been migration from the villages to the cities, to neighbouring islands, and metropolitan countries, the growth of the informal economy, and involvement in the drug trade.

Caribbean migration

Migration has been, and continues to be, an essential part of the Caribbean experience.[72] The islands were populated by people migrating first from South America then from Europe, either as settlers or as transported criminals; then by slaves, 15 million of whom were shipped from Africa; by indentured labourers from the Indian subcontinent and by merchants from all over the world; and in recent years by businesspeople and tourists. Migration is integral to the neoliberal imperative for labour to move freely to meet the demands of global capital and has flowed with shifting economic and employment opportunities. Tens of thousands of people from across the islands, mainly men, travelled to work on the Panama Canal and railway construction in Central America. They travelled to Venezuela, Aruba, Curacao, and Trinidad to work in the oil industry and to the US sugar plantations in Cuba in the early decades of the twentieth century.[73] Women migrant workers often followed. When the Guyanese economy boomed in the 1950s and 60s, people travelled there for work in their thousands, moving later to Barbados and Bermuda, as their tourist economies developed. Many manual workers still travel seasonally from Guyana to Barbados to work the cane fields and in construction.

There was a marked growth in migration to the US, Britain, and Canada after World War II. Migration to Britain began with wartime recruitment into the armed forces and munitions factories. Some people formed partnerships, married, and settled while others returned to the Caribbean to stay only a short time before returning to the better employment opportunities in the UK. British government officials travelled to the West Indies actively to recruit workers for London Transport and the new National Health Service. Between 1948 and 1962, net migration from the

[72] David Nii Addy (2003), 'Trends in Labour Migration and its Implications for the Caribbean' in Cynthia Barrow-Giles and Don Marshall, *op cit*, p 378.

[73] Elizabeth Thomas-Hope (2002), *Caribbean Migration*. Kingston, Jamaica: University of the West Indies Press, p 59.

British West Indies was around 275,000, the majority of people settling long-term. In the face of a closing door to the UK in the early 1960s, the destination of choice shifted from Britain to North America. The 1965 US Immigration and Nationality Act abolished national-origin quotas, opening up new opportunities for migration. Migrants to North America were predominantly young adults, professional, administrative, managerial, and other white-collar workers. Based on the 2002 American Community Survey, the US government estimates the population of West Indian heritage to be 2.42 million,[74] 621,000 of whom live in New York City.[75]

The Caribbean diaspora is estimated to be more than 5 million people worldwide.[76] Caribbean migration, while not as extensive as in previous periods, continues; for example, some 75,000 people migrated to the US in 1998.[77] Among the advantages of Caribbean migration and diaspora interconnectedness is the economic interest of cash remittances that make a major contribution to the Caribbean economy. People of Caribbean descent worldwide sent $8.85 billion to the Caribbean in 2006,[78] Jamaica receiving $1.92 billion in remittances (18 per cent of GDP), Trinidad and Tobago $655 million (3 per cent of GDP), Guyana $466 million (43 per cent GDP), and Barbados $292 million (9 per cent of GDP).[79] The Foreign Office estimates that British citizens of Caribbean heritage send UK£1.4 billion to the region every year.[80] The sense of being part of a transnational community can be empowering, creating economic, cultural, and political resources. Layton Henry argues that:

transnationalism is seen as a form of empowerment for individuals against the overweening strength and control of the nation-state. If people are able to function successfully in more than one state, hold more than one

---

[74] Including those of Haitian (763,000) and Dutch West Indian descent (65,000), but excluding those of Spanish speaking territories <http://www.census.gov/compendia/statab/tables/09s0051.pdf>.

[75] <http://www.nyc.gov/html/dcp/pdf/census/nyc_boros_05_06_07_ancestry.pdf>.   [76] David Nii Addy (2003), 'Trends in Labour Migration', p 380.

[77] *Ibid*, p 380.

[78] Including Guyana and the Hispanic Caribbean, but not Suriname or Belize (both CARICOM member states) <http://www.iadb.org/>. See also Olwyn Blouet (2007), *op cit*, p 95.   [79] <http://www.iadb.org/>.

[80] Jack Straw, Speech to the Caribbean Senior Command Training Course, 19 October 2005.

passport and exercise rights across national boundaries, then they may be able to control their own space and activities and to escape, to some extent, the control of national governments.[81]

One disadvantage of migration is the 'brain drain': population decline and the loss of skilled workers, especially from health and education sectors, and the resulting instability, which has long been a concern of Caribbean governments. The 'sending countries' invest in the education and training of professionals who are then lured overseas by higher wages and better working conditions. The Commonwealth Secretariat noted the disappearance of nurses, midwives, laboratory technicians, pharmacists, radiographers, and public health inspectors from across the region.[82] Jamaica, for example, lost three quarters of its doctors and nurses between 1978 and 1985.[83] Some commentators have argued that this may not simply be a problem of draining skills or permanent loss of human capital, but might instead be 'the foundation for complex transnational households capable of producing a multitude of positive socioeconomic effects in past, present and future locations'.[84] Perhaps the process should be seen as one of 'brain exchange' and as an integral, beneficial aspect of globalization rather than as a linear, one way 'brain-drain'.[85] Recent years have seen an increase in the extent of 'return migration' in various forms.[86] Many people who were born in the Caribbean are returning to their islands of birth on retirement, with as many as 16,000 Jamaican nationals returning in a recent eight-year period.[87] More problematic is the growing number of people deported following conviction of criminal offences or violation of immigration law in the metropolis. The 'deportee' issue is a political issue of considerable proportions in numerous Caribbean countries, especially Guyana, Trinidad, and Jamaica.[88] Some 33,000 people have been deported to Jamaica from the US, UK, and Canada in the past 15 years, representing more than one per cent of the adult

---

[81] Zig Layton-Henry, 'Transnational Communities, Citizenship and African-Caribbeans in Birmingham', WPTC-02-07 (<http://www.transcomm.ox.ac.uk/working%20papers/WPTC-02-07%20LaytonHenry.pdf>).

[82] David Nii Addy (2003), 'Trends in Labour Migration', p 387.

[83] *Ibid*, p 387.   [84] *Ibid*, p 388.   [85] *Ibid*, p 387.

[86] *Ibid*, p 383–5.   [87] *Ibid*, p 384.

[88] A full discussion of this issue can be found in the United Nations/World Bank (2007) report, *Crime, Violence, and Development, op cit.*

population.[89] While some people are sympathetic to their plight, deportees frequently find themselves outcast and homeless. The most powerful discourse surrounding the criminal deportee is an ironic inversion of the 'alien invasion' thesis that portrays them as particularly dangerous people tainted by the 'foreign criminality' of America or Britain. Although the research evidence suggests that most are convicted of minor drugs offences, some commentators directly blame surges in violent crime on deportees. In this light it is not surprising that the central area of policy discussion is how to control the deportees on their return. Some years ago, deportees arrived without warning on scheduled flights and simply disappeared into the void. Now there is a paper trail but little in the way of (positive) resettlement or (negative) controls on arrival. Of course, things look very different from the point of view of the deportee who may have experienced the loss of family, home, and savings with limited prospects for employment. Some will be returning to a place they left as children or young adults and of which they have little or no knowledge or structures of support. Others leave behind homes and loved ones in Britain and America. As Chan argues, 'deportation is about the desire to control difference... it is not just an administrative practice, but also a political practice, a disciplinary tactic and an instrument of population regulation'.[90] It is also an integral part of the growth of the hemispheric drugs economy and attempts to control it, to which we now turn.

Drugs Trafficking

As late as the 1980s, it was impolite to suggest that the Caribbean had a 'drug problem'.[91] The morally conservative populations of the region generally frowned upon drug use which was regarded as either a moral issue akin to sin or a pathological individual psychology. It was 'a problem of individual malevolence deserving condemnation or [a] personal tragedy deserving pity'.[92]

[89] Bernard Headley, 'Criminal Deportees: What We Know and Don't Know', *Jamaica Gleaner News*, 14 July 2004.

[90] W. Chan (2005), 'Crime, Deportation and the Regulation of Immigrants in Canada', *Crime, Law and Social Change*, 44: 153–80.

[91] Ivelaw Griffith (1997), *Drugs and Security in the Caribbean, op cit.*

[92] Anthony P. Maingot (2000), 'Changing Definitions of "Social Problems" in the Caribbean' in Tulchin and Espach, *Security in the Caribbean Basin*, p 28.

By the 1990s, however, the 'drug problem' was recognized as a major threat to regional security. The Report of the West Indian Commission (1992) set out this stark warning:

Nothing poses greater threats to civil society in CARICOM countries than the drug problem; and nothing exemplifies the powerlessness of regional Governments more. That is the magnitude of the damage that drug abuse and trafficking hold for our Community. It is a many layered danger. At base, is the human consumption implicit in drug addiction; but, implicit also, is the corruption of individuals and systems by the sheer enormity of the inducements of the illegal drug trade in relatively poor societies. On top of this lie the implications for governance itself—at the hands of both external agencies engaged in international interdiction, and the drug barons themselves—the 'dons' of the modern Caribbean—who threaten governance from within.[93]

The two most important illegal drugs for the Caribbean region are domestically grown marijuana and Andean cocaine, transhipped through the islands. Drug trafficking first came to international prominence during the 1970s when the Caribbean was a major supplier of marijuana to the USA and Europe. In the early years of the cocaine trade, the substance was shipped directly from Columbia to the USA by air or overland through Mexico. In the late 1970s, cocaine began to be trans-shipped through the Caribbean islands, and the Bahamas in particular. In 1977, Carlos Lehder, a Columbian cocaine kingpin from the Medellin cartel, based himself and a major cocaine trans-shipment operation in the Bahamian island of Norman's Cay.[94] The large amounts of cocaine and drug money available on the island caused enormous problems of corruption and, by 1979, the Bahamas was being described as 'a country for sale'.[95] Gugliotta and Leen claim that there were more than a dozen marijuana and cocaine entrepreneurs working with the full collaboration of the highest levels of the Bahamian authorities. The Bahamas has a long history as a smuggling centre, creating power through involvement in alcohol smuggling during Prohibition. The Sicilian mafioso, Meyer Lanksy, financed the

---

[93] Report of the West Indian Commission (1992), op cit, p 343.

[94] Axel Klein (2004), 'The Search for a New Drug Policy Framework: From the Barbados Plan of Action to the Ganja Commission' in Axel Klein, Marcus Day, and Anthony Harriott (eds), Caribbean Drugs: From Criminalization to Harm Reduction. London & New York: Zed Books, p 23.

[95] Guy Gugliotta and Jeff Leen (1989), Kings of Cocaine. New York: Simon and Schuster, p 61; Anthony Maingot (2000), 'Changing Definitions', p 33.

election campaign of Lynden Pindling and, preoccupied with anti-communism, maintaining the support of Pindling for US missile experimentation bases in the Bahamas, the US government turned a blind eye.[96]

The United Nations estimates that the world spends around $330 billion on illegal drugs and values the Caribbean drug trade at $60 billion. The UN reports that the South American countries of Bolivia, Columbia, and Peru have around 160,000 hectares of land used for the cultivation of coca, which produces nearly 300,000 metric tonnes of dry coca leaf and has a potential manufacture of nearly 1,000 tonnes of cocaine. Columbia remains the leading cocaine producer (estimated at 62 per cent of world supply). The number of countries reporting cocaine seizures rose from 45 in 1980 to 131 in 2005 suggesting that 'trafficking in cocaine is developing into a global phenomenon, affecting all regions'.[97] Although the Caribbean is perceived as a major trans-shipment point, in fact, the majority of seizures are made in South America (51 per cent) and North America (27 per cent) with Central America (5 per cent) and the Caribbean (2 per cent) accounting for a minority of all seizures.

The central cocaine trafficking route continues to run from the Andean region to the USA, where the market is largest. Colombia's seizures mainly take place in the ports or at sea and approximately half to two thirds travels up the Pacific coast with 37 per cent on the Atlantic coast. In 2005, there was a growth in the shipment via Venezuela and Ecuador. The main trans-shipment country is Mexico where trafficking is by land or by sea and largely destined for the USA. The US seizures show that three quarters of cocaine arrives on the South West Border, 13 per cent via the US East Coast and 13 per cent via Puerto Rico and the US Virgin Islands. These figures indicate a shift. In previous years, the USA reported that somewhere between one third and half of the cocaine entering the USA did so directly from the Caribbean. By 2006, the UN World Drug Report estimated that this has fallen to below 10 per cent, since entries are made principally by Haiti and the Dominican Republic (4 per cent), Jamaica (2 per cent), and Puerto Rico (1 per cent). The second most important destination for cocaine is Europe transiting Venezuela, Ecuador, and Brazil with the Dominican

---

[96] *Ibid*, *op cit*, p 33.
[97] United Nations (2007), *World Drug Report*, p 70.

Republic, Mexico, Argentina, and West Africa countries gaining importance as transit countries. Most cocaine bound for Europe enters via Spain.

Drug trafficking is 'the perfect example of the complexity of the new security agenda'.[98] Although many people involved in the business of cocaine trafficking describe their operations as 'organizations', there is little evidence to support the stereotypical image of hierarchically arranged multinational corporations.[99] While drug smuggling requires a high level of planning, technology, and communications, it does not exhibit the characteristics of formal organizations, such as permanence, command structure, communication between ranks, or resource management.[100] Instead, smuggling groups act like chains, formed to accomplish specific tasks linking exporters with importers and distributors. Zaitch describes the cocaine enterprises as a heterogeneous and 'mutating product of fragile agreements between people and flexible articulation between legal and illegal enterprises'.[101] Decker and Townsend Chapman show there has been a significant shift in the structure of drug organizations in the past 20 years. Up until the mid 1990s, much of the trade was dominated by the Medellin and Cali cartels which had a degree of hierarchy and central control. When these cartels collapsed under the weight of US pressure in Columbia and the execution or incarceration of the leaders, the organization split into many looser groups working through brokers.[102] For these reasons, the capacity to control the clandestine Caribbean drugs trade is severely limited and smuggling persists, in relation to white goods, fuel, and commodities, as well as the drugs trade.

Griffith observes that 'in looking at the economic security dimension, one is forced to come to terms with both positive and negative aspects' of the drugs trade.[103] On the positive side, drugs operations create employment, generate income, and enhance

[98] D. Zaitch (2007), *Trafficking Cocaine: Colombian Drug Entrepreneurs in the Netherlands*. Netherlands: Verlag Springer.

[99] Scott H. Decker and Margaret Townsend Chapman (2008), *Drug Smugglers on Drug Smuggling: Lessons from the Inside*. Philadelphia, PA: Temple University Press.

[100] Ivelaw Griffith (1997), *Drugs and Security in the Caribbean, op cit*, p 175.

[101] D. Zaitch (2007), *Trafficking Cocaine, op cit*.

[102] Scott H. Decker and Margaret Townsend Chapman (2008), *Drug Smugglers on Drug Smuggling, op cit*.

[103] Ivelaw Griffith (1997), *Drugs and Security in the Caribbean, op cit*, p 175.

revenues.[104] Griffith estimates that tens of thousands of people are employed in drugs production and distribution in the Caribbean region. Direct employment includes work for farmers, pilots, labourers, drivers, engineers, accountants, lookouts, and guards as well as workers in legitimate spheres such as police and Customs officers who earn additional income through bribes to facilitate production and export. While drugs operators do not pay income or business taxes, the profits from drugs sales are spent on property and consumer products that are taxed. Griffith argues that the drug business is crucial to some countries' economic survival.[105] The UK Foreign Office, for example, estimates that the 'drugs economy' makes up about 40 per cent of Jamaica's GDP and similar estimates have been made in other countries. The informal and formal economies are entwined: the drugs trade earns foreign currency, generates savings, and sustains local economies. There is also what Griffith calls 'Robin Hoodism': the direct economic contribution made by the 'dons'. They meet social welfare needs, including paying for education, specialist medical supplies, sports equipment, church relief, and funding for beauty pageants and festivals. They also become integral to popular understandings of crime control, emerging as rule makers and enforcers. In Jamaica, for example, more than half the population believe that the 'dons do a better job of controlling criminals than the police'.[106]

Most prominent on the negative side of the balance sheet is the violent crime with which drug trafficking is 'systemically' linked.[107] Specific aspects of drug production and distribution systems create the conditions within which criminal behaviour—especially armed violence—can flourish. The resulting injury, death, and misery are obviously problems in themselves, but this also creates an image problem for the region that impacts on tourism.[108] Fines

---

[104] *Ibid*, p 181.   [105] *Ibid*, p 183.

[106] Anthony Harriott (2008), 'Bending the Trend Line: The Developmental Challenge of Controlling Violence in Jamaica and the High Violence Societies of the Caribbean'. Professorial Inaugural Lecture, 24 April 2008. Department of Government UWI (Mona) and The Institute of Criminal Justice Security. University of the West Indies.

[107] Paul Goldstein (1985), 'The Drugs/Violence Nexus: A Tripartite Conceptual Framework', *Journal of Drug Issues*, 39: 143–74.

[108] Anthony Harriott (2007), 'Risk Perceptions and Fear of Criminal Victimization among Visitors to Jamaica: Bringing Perceptions in Line with Reality', *Journal of Ethnicity in Criminal Justice*, 5/2/3: 93–108.

are imposed on tour operators and airlines caught carrying drugs which, in turn, gives rise to countermeasures that cost money. As we shall see later in this book, an extensive and expensive infrastructure has been built to respond to the problem.[109] Numerous commentators have argued that the sovereignty of Caribbean nations has been undermined by the illicit drugs trade.[110] Sovereignty is contested 'from below' by the traffickers whose economic power gives them political influence and undermines the rule of law and 'from above' in a form of 'recolonization' by the metropolitan countries through intensive surveillance and investigation.[111]

Violent Crime and Insecurity

Violent crime is one of the most prominent issues in discussions of Caribbean security. P. J. Patterson, former Prime Minister of Jamaica, reflected the thoughts and feelings of many West Indians when he declared in his 2006 New Year's address that, 'without a doubt, the high level of violent crime remains our most troubling and pressing problem'. While other threats—such as natural disaster or disease—might in fact present greater dangers to human security, violence presents an immediate, visceral, and vivid danger. It also differs from other threats in that while its distal causes lie in a social, political, and economic context (above all the illegal drugs trade) described above, the danger comes from culpable human subjects.

The crime problem has changed radically since the 1970s and is 'now more acute and complicated than ever'.[112] For many years, crime in the region was characterized by low rates of violence and relatively high rates of property crime, but now the balance between violent and property crime has shifted markedly.[113] In Jamaica, for example, property crimes halved between the 1970s and the 1990s but violent crime increased by 50 per cent.[114] In a recent victimization survey in Jamaica, Trinidad and Tobago, and

---

[109] Ivelaw Griffith (1997), *Drugs and Security in the Caribbean, op cit*, pp 187–90.
[110] *Ibid.*
[111] Anthony Maingot (2000), 'Changing Definitions', *op cit*, p 35.
[112] Anthony Harriott (ed) (2003), *Understanding Crime in Jamaica*. Kinsgton, Jamaica: University of West Indies Press.
[113] Anthony Harriott (2004), 'Introduction' in Anthony Harriott, Farley Brathwaite, and Scot Wortley (2004), *Crime and Criminal Justice in the Caribbean*. Kingston, Jamaica: Arawak Publications, p 5.
[114] Anthony Harriott (2003), *Understanding Crime in Jamaica, op cit*, p 7.

Figure 2.2 Murder rates by regions of the world (per 100,000 population)

Source: United Nations/World Bank (2007) report Crime, Violence, and Development: Trends, Costs, and Policy Options in the Caribbean, World Bank Report No. 37820, page iv.

Barbados, Elsie Le Franc and colleagues reported 'very high levels' of interpersonal violence, domestic abuse, and sexual coercion, especially in Jamaica.[115] With a rate of 30 homicides per 100,000, the Caribbean is now the most murderous region in the world (see figure 2.2).

The rise in homicide across the region is striking. When Jamaica gained independence in 1962 it had a homicide rate of fewer than 4 per 100,000 people. This doubled to 8 in 1970, increased

[115] Elsie Le Franc, Maureen Samms-Vaughan, Ian Hambleton, Kirsten Fox, and Denise Brown (2008), 'Interpersonal Violence in Three Caribbean Countries: Barbados, Jamaica, and Trinidad and Tobago', *Rev Panam Salud Publica*, 24/6: 409–21.

fivefold to 40 in 2002 and continued to rise to 59 per 100,000 in 2007.[116] Just fewer than 80 per cent of the 1,620 murders in 2008 were committed with a gun. Jamaica now has the highest *per capita* homicide rate in the world, exceeding that of South Africa and Columbia. Trinidad and Tobago had a reputation for being safe until the 1990s but in recent years the murder rate has increased sharply. There were 119 homicides in 2000 rising to 370 in 2006 and 546 in 2008, nearly three quarters of which were due to firearms. Expressed as a rate per 100,000 the homicide rate in Trinidad and Tobago more than quadrupled from 7 to 30 between 1999 and 2005. The twin-island state has also been plagued by an escalation in kidnap-for-ransom. In Guyana, the homicide rate has fluctuated between 10 and 27 per 100,000 over the past three decades, with several sharp spikes in 1992, 2002, and 2008. Some islands have bucked the trend of increasing violence. Barbados, for example, has seen no increase in homicide over a 20-year period, although the proportion of homicides committed with guns has increased.

Not only has violent crime increased across the Caribbean, but so too has the use of firearms including 'more powerful weapons resulting in higher mortality levels'.[117] Patterns of armed violence—including the use of military weapons—are established in Jamaica, Trinidad and Tobago, and Guyana and emerging in Antigua and Barbuda, Barbados, Dominica, Grenada, Saint Kitts and Nevis, Saint Lucia, and Saint Vincent and the Grenadines.[118] A major explanation of the extent of armed violence is the clandestine drugs trade which has been most prevalent in those countries with greatest increases in homicide. Drug trafficking facilitates the availability of guns which are required to protect contraband in transit and are smuggled along with these guns.[119]

This results in a further problem of 'weaponization' of society as firearm use becomes entrenched among the gangs associated with the drugs trade and then among civilian populations. One

---

[116] Anthony Harriott (2003), *Understanding Crime in Jamaica, op cit*, p 7.
[117] UN/World Bank (2007), *Crime, Violence and Development, op cit*, p ix.
[118] *Ibid*, p ix.
[119] UN/World Bank (2007), *Crime, Violence and Development*, p ixix; Biko Agozino, Ben Bowling, Elizabeth Ward, and Godfrey St Bernard (2009), 'Guns, Crime and Social Order in the West Indies', *Criminology & Criminal Justice*, 9/3: 287–305.

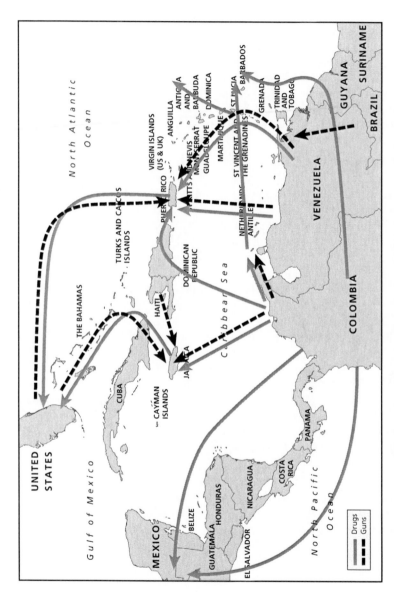

Figure 2.3 Central America and the Caribbean: major cocaine and gun import/export routes

interviewee gave a vivid example of the impact of armed violence in Guyana following a prison breakout in 2002:

the police were regularly facing machine pistols, AK47s, American military hardware, sniper rifles, hand grenades, . . . Then up to 15 men come into town in a series of vehicles, seal off the centre of town in a military style operation. Many of them are wearing helmets. Several are wearing two bullet proof vests, not one. Most of them are carrying AK47s. The Cambio is robbed. Another very wealthy store is robbed. They then tried to set the petrol station alight in the middle of town— had it gone it would have taken most of the town with it because of course, it's all wood—and then shoot the place up on their way out like it's the Wild West.

This example is also indicative of a shift in the *nature* of violent crime from *interpersonal* to *inter-group* violence. Domestic homicides in Jamaica, for example, have remained stable for two decades, while those attributed to gang rivalry have increased fivefold.[120] Violence has become more organized as inter-group conflict has become an important cause of increased levels of violence. Harriott argues that it has become an 'entrepreneurial activity', even a form of 'self-help' in dealing with social conflicts. The scale of conflict has multiplied as larger numbers of people are drawn in and more resources—including guns—are mobilized. Because members of groups suffer liability for the actions of each of their members, the pool is widened to 'soft targets'; people who may be victimized if the person who precipitated the conflict cannot be found. The process is facilitated by moral neutralization when someone kills in *the cause of the group*.[121] This breaks down constraints since social ties are not threatened when a 'soldier' kills a member of the 'enemy' group. Indeed, 'communal bonds may be strengthened, identities affirmed and the main combatants treated as heroic figures . . . [and] protectors of the group'.[122] The issue of inter-group violence reflects the fact that in many Caribbean territories armed violence is directly connected with organized crime and its complex and murky relationship with elected politicians. In Jamaica, crime has been intimately connected with politics for many decades. Sives traces the historical roots of political violence from the 1949 Hearne Commission which reported on previous years' violent conflict

---

[120] Anthony Harriott (2003), *Understanding Crime in Jamaica*, *op cit*.

[121] *Ibid*.

[122] Anthony Harriott (2003), 'Social Identities and the Escalation of Homicidal Violence in Jamaica' in Anthony Harriott, *Understanding Crime in Jamaica*, *op cit*, p 94.

between supporters of the two main political parties—the Jamaica Labour Party and People's National Party. From the 1960s onwards violent conflict flourished, especially in the 'garrison communities', the single-party political strongholds in Jamaica's urban centres.[123] The 1980 General Election was particularly bloody and, since then, electoral and inter-community criminal violence has been an ever-present danger.[124] Organized crime groups have been closely linked with politicians elsewhere in the Caribbean.

The arming of Caribbean society has unfolded in the context of inequalities of power, class discrimination, and ethnic injustice.[125] The drugs market, for example, is highly stratified with individuals from the most economically marginalized communities playing the most poorly paid and dangerous roles.[126] Obika Gray argues that in this context, the notion of 'badness honour' must be considered in understanding the problem of crime. This, he argues, is a cultural style, a repertoire of facial gestures, body poses, assertive mien, menacing or histrionic gestures, which can be found in urban ghetto cultures around the world. Gray argues that a sense of hopelessness arising from blocked aspirations has created a situation where many young men feel that they have nothing to lose and much to gain through the expression of extreme violence. Laurie Gunst, in her powerful book on the Jamaican 'posse underworld', coined the phrase born 'fi dead, to express the 'fearsome inevitability of the posses and the bitter resignation of their young soldiers to death'.[127] For Gray, that this shows not merely nihilism, lack of hope, and obsession with death but rather 'a determination that violent extremism and physical death [are] better, even redemptive options—preferable to the far worse fate of social death'.[128] The notion of group liability for the actions of individual members is connected with the idea of being at war. In this condition, members

---

[123] Amanda Sives (2003), 'The Historical Roots of Violence in Jamaica: The Hearne Report 1949' in Anthony Harriott, *Understanding Crime in Jamaica*.

[124] Mark Figueroa and Amanda Sives (2003), 'Garrison Politics and Criminality in Jamaica: Does the 1997 Election Represent a Turning Point?' in Anthony Harriott, *Understanding Crime in Jamaica*, p 85.

[125] Obika Gray (2003), 'Badness-Honour' in *Understanding Crime in Jamaica*, p 19.

[126] Vincenzo Ruggerio (2000), *Crime and Markets*. Oxford: Oxford University Press.

[127] Laurie Gunst (1995), *Born Fi Dead: A Journey Through the Jamaican Posse Underworld*. Edinburgh: Paperback Press.

[128] Obika Gray (2003), 'Badness-Honour', *op cit*, p 35.

of the group and wider communities are encouraged to protect themselves from retaliatory attacks by associating themselves with the 'dons'. Together with their lieutenants, leading combatants take charge of community life, usually enjoying an elevated status during this period of 'war'. Young men assert themselves, displaying their courage and commitment to move up in the 'ranking' or status hierarchy of the group. As the war leadership entrenches itself in community life, the perception of outsiders is hardened who associate the identity and reputation of the community with conflict which increases the potential for future 'wars'.[129] This war-like posture also increases the degree of violence. Mass-murders, sometimes involving the killing of entire families or military-style assaults on villages, and the use of methods such as beheadings, have been reported in Jamaica, Trinidad, and Guyana.[130]

The complex relationships between organized crime, politics, and corrupt elements within the police and criminal justice system also contribute to high levels of violence. Walcott, for example, argues that lack of confidence in the justice system is chiefly responsible for an embedded culture of revenge, 'The perception among most Jamaicans is that the police cannot be trusted and when people feel they will not get redress through the legally established channels, they set up their own systems'.[131] Harriott argues in the same vein that:

when the ability of the state to ensure justice breaks down, notions of self help justice or revenge become more appealing. . . . Revenge is coupled

[129] Anthony Harriott (2003), 'Social Identities and the Escalation of Homicidal Violence in Jamaica' in Anthony Harriott, *Understanding Crime in Jamaica*, *op cit*, p 99.

[130] See, for example, Anthony Harriott (2008), 'Bending the Trend Line', *op cit*. Three mass murders occurred in Guyana in 2008. In January in the village of Lusignan, 11 people, including five children, were killed during an onslaught by an armed group led by Rondell 'Fineman' Rawlins (who was himself later shot dead by police). In February, 12 people were killed when the town of Bartica came under attack in a 'military-style' operation. Under cover of darkness, an armed group arrived by boat, shooting dock workers at the wharf before attacking the police station, breaking into its armoury, stealing weapons, and shooting several police officers, robbing several businesses before leaving again by boat. In June, eight mine workers were beaten with hammers, killed, and their remains burned. Extensive reportage of these events can be found in the *Stabroek News* and *Kaiteur News*.

[131] 'Reprisal Killings Hurting Jamaica', *Jamaica Gleaner*, 1 June 2008.

with justice; it becomes the citizen reclaiming the right to do justice when faced with an ineffective state.[132]

A cycle of retaliatory violence is thus triggered in which every action incites an equal and opposite reaction: 'retaliation often spawns counter-retaliation, and progressively larger numbers of persons get sucked into retributive cycles.'[133] Police statistics support this view with 'reprisal' recorded as the most common motive for homicide in Jamaica, accounting for 30 per cent of cases.[134] Nearly nine out of ten reprisal homicides are committed with a gun.[135]

   The transnational nature of the cocaine business has implications both for Caribbean and for diaspora communities. Drug trafficking is linked into transnational organized crime networks that connect the major players from Columbia and Bolivia (who control production and export) with the players in Europe and North America (who control distribution). The development of trans-shipment through the region provided opportunities for Caribbean nationals to play a major role. Building on the ganja trade and with expanding cocaine trans-shipment, Caribbean organized crime groups—the so-called Yardies or Posses—became prominent in the USA from the mid-1980s and subsequently in Canada and the United Kingdom.[136] Gangs such as the Shower Posse, Spanglers, Renkers, and others established a power-base that extended from the garrison communities of Kingston to the cities of Bristol, Manchester, London, New York, Miami, and Toronto.[137] As in the Caribbean, high levels of armed violence in these diaspora communities have resulted from the weaponization of clandestine drugs distribution and supply systems.[138]

[132] Anthony Harriott (2008), 'Bending the Trend Line', *op cit*.

[133] R. Rosenfeld, B. Jacobs, and R. Wright, 'Snitching and the Code of the Street', *British Journal of Criminology*, 43: 291–309, p 304–5.

[134] G. Lemard and D. Hemenway (2006), 'Violence in Jamaica: An Analysis of Homicides 1998–2002', *Injury Prevention*, 12: 15–18, p 16.   [135] *Ibid*.

[136] The term 'Yardie', referring to someone from 'back a yard', or 'back home' in Jamaican patois, has become the 'official' label for Caribbean groups in organized crime taxonomies.

[137] See Laurie Gunst (1995), *Born Fi Dead*; Duane Blake (2003), *Shower Posse*. New York: Diamond Publishing.

[138] John Pitts (2008), *Reluctant Gangsters*. Cullompton: Willan. Graeme McLagan (2005), *Guns and Gangs*. London: Allison and Busby.

Summary and Conclusion

The dangers facing the people of the Caribbean are many and various. Its vulnerability, an enduring problem traceable back over the past half a millennium, stems largely from the fundamental facts of its physical and social geography and political economy. Its location at the 'crossroads of Empire', the fact of being surrounded by sea on the edge of a great ocean between the Americas and Europe, and its long and convoluted coastline, creates a unique position of vulnerability that has been manifest over the centuries. Insecurity has changed with the times, of course. The vulnerability felt by chattel slaves differs from that of freed 'apprentices' and their descendants working in the plantations of the nineteenth and twentieth century. The slow death of the sugar and banana economy heralded the end of low wage agricultural labour for the masses, but it has been replaced with extreme economic marginality with tourism, foreign remittances, and the 'red economy' holding the region's fortune together. One of the few economic alternatives is emigration. This is a risky solution for the migrant seeking his or her fortune overseas. The overwhelming majority succeed, but transgression invites deportation, the fate of many thousands of people. Emigration is also a significant loss to the islands which have invested in their upbringing, education, and training only to be deprived of their economic and social contribution and vitality. Economic collapse remains a real threat to some of the islands. So much depends upon economic stability—employment and subsistence for basic human needs, the tax base on which government depends to pay for infrastructure such as health services, education, and security, as well as hope for the future of the island's people, young and old. These serious economic threats provide a backdrop to the political threats of the corruption of government, political tribalism, ethnic conflict, gangsterism, and armed violence.

Although it would be unwise to discount it entirely, the threat of invasion by a foreign army that preoccupied Caribbean rulers and citizens alike for hundreds of years is no longer a major consideration. The significance of the old colonial powers—Britain, France, the Netherlands, and Spain—has diminished. The Cold War is over and the USA has acquired a position of absolute hegemony in the region; its awesome firepower and the rapidity of its deployment of military forces reduces the risk of a foreign army attempting an invasion. Nonetheless, many threats still come from the sea. After the Bali nightclub bombings, there is a growing anxiety about international terrorism and the vulnerability of tourist locations and cruise ships visiting the region.[139] There are environmental threats including hurricanes, earthquakes, and volcanoes, those posed by ships passing with hazardous waste, rising sea levels, and a slow death to the marine environment through pollution. By the dawn of the new millennium the political and economic future of the Caribbean region seemed uncertain. The features that shaped the relationship between the islands and the metropolis since independence—production and trade in raw materials, migration as a source of cheap labour, and post-colonial geopolitics—have undergone a seismic shift. The Cold War ended with the hollow 'triumph of capitalism' and a waning anxiety about the 'communist threat'. After September 11th 2001, US military engagement in the region became a financial albatross and political attention and economic resources shifted to underdeveloped nations to the East, commitment to military action and subsequent occupation in Afghanistan and Iraq and the so-called 'war on terror'. One view is that this geopolitical shift, the growth in air-borne transport and the fact that the Panama Canal—the Atlantic-Pacific gateway—is too shallow for a new generation of super-sized container ships may lead to a decline in its strategic importance. Others predict that the lower costs of sea freight and the expansion of the Panama Canal now in progress will maintain the region's importance in the world economy. With South American economies expanding and the interest of Russia, China, and Iran growing in the region, its geopolitical significance seems likely to continue into the future.[140]

The multi-dimensional threat of drugs trafficking features prominently in the literature on Caribbean security.[141] There are environmental issues stemming from drug cultivation and processing and health risks to users. But the greatest danger to life and limb stems from the character of clandestine markets and their intertwining with transnational organized crime and armed violence. The cocaine trade props up the economy, providing jobs and an income for many people as well as foreign earnings and indirect taxation

---

[139] Ivelaw Griffith (ed) (2004), *Caribbean Security in the Age of Terror, op cit.*

[140] Gail Verasammy (2009), 'Toward a Reconceptualisation of Caribbean Basin Security', *op cit.*

[141] Ivelaw Griffith (1997), *Drugs and Security in the Caribbean, op cit.* Ivelaw Griffith (2004), *Caribbean Security in the Age of Terror, op cit.*

badly needed by the state. But dirty money pollutes the economy and corrupts the government. However, it is violent crime, enabled by firearms flowing into the region from North and South America, which most profoundly undermines security in the region's cities, towns, and villages. While 'ordinary crime'—burglary, robbery, theft, bar fights, and domestic violence—remain problems, the upsurge of armed violence, murder, shootings, and kidnapping has created a climate of fear in the countries of the region that is of profound proportions. The threat posed by the organized and disorganized crime groups involved in drug trafficking is closely linked into the other threats to security. It threatens the economy and the banking system through money laundering, and politics through the ascendancy of the 'dons' and the corruption of public officials and in some countries—especially in the Andean region itself—the environment through the contaminants of precursor chemicals and destruction of the rainforest.

The insecurity of the Caribbean islands is the problem to which transnational policing is proposed as a solution. It comprises a multi-dimensional and complex set of dangers that requires a broad-based and thoroughgoing response. This begs the question: to what extent is the Caribbean 'security sector' prepared and equipped to meet this challenge? It raises questions about how security sector organizations understand the problems that they face, since this will inevitably be affected by the viewpoint held by each organization and will also determine the strategies that are devised to respond to it. Other critical questions concern the strategies themselves—how are the organizations responding to the complex problem of insecurity, with whom are they collaborating and with what impact? With these questions in mind, we can now make our way to the Police Commissioner's office and begin our journey through the region's security apparatus.

3

The Caribbean Police Commissioner

Policing now has no borders, it is borderless, so what impacts on me today is impacting on you again today too, simultaneous impacting, you understand? A crime is committed here today, it belongs to the UK, the US, Venezuela, whatever, you understand? Money laundering, it has its tentacles in several jurisdictions so, of necessity, you have to have those people with the skills, knowledge and expertise and the intelligence to traverse the various territories or geographical areas so as to get to the root of these problems. So policing cannot be defined in the way of strict territorial, jurisdictional sort of thing nowadays—it's borderless.[1]

What we look at is policing a global world and we can only do so with the understanding and trust and confidence in each other that the international laws, the rules and regulations governing a country, that you will respect it. We expect somehow somebody is going to step out of bounds, yes, but we hope not too frequently.[2]

The Colonial Legacy

Most Caribbean police forces were established in the early 1840s, following the abolition of slavery in 1833. They were charged with enforcing imperial law and maintaining order among the 'lower orders' and plantation labour.[3] In 1839, a Colonial Office circular

---

[1] Caribbean Police Commissioner.   [2] *Ibid.*
[3] There was a mixed economy of policing from the earliest times. Plantation owners established private estate police and the West India Regiment was available to back up the police in times of civil unrest. See Gregor Davey (2009), 'A Brief Outline of British Caribbean Policing and Intelligence Structures: 1838–1970', unpublished paper, King's College London, 18 September 2009.

despatch recommended the establishment of forces on the Metropolitan Police model.[4] In common with most of the police forces formed under British colonial rule, however, in ethos and practice Caribbean police forces tended to resemble the 'Irish model'.[5] This became particularly marked after the withdrawal of the West India Regiment in the 1880s. Members of the Royal Irish Constabulary and former soldiers were recruited to provide leadership and they instilled a strong military ethos and central government direction characteristic of forces charged with controlling native populations and distinct from the model associated with the London Metropolitan Police based on principles of minimal force and political independence.[6] The colonial approach also involved 'policing by strangers'. The Commissioner and senior officers were from the 'mother country' or from Ireland, trained at staff colleges in the United Kingdom before being posted overseas or transferring between colonial forces.[7] Constables were drawn from the local population, but often posted to different islands.[8] While there existed no uniform Caribbean policing system, each spoke of the colonial wheel connected the islands back to the metropolis. Many police forces in the region—including the Bahamas, Barbados, Bermuda, and St Vincent and the Grenadines—still retain a 'Royal' title to this day.

Until the end of Empire, most senior officers across the region were part of a colonial policing service, educated and trained in Britain.[9] This began to change in the 1950s when more local police were promoted to ranks above sergeant. In 1957, a regional

[4] Howard Johnson (1991), 'Patterns of Policing in the Post Emancipation British Caribbean 1835–95' in David Anderson and David Killingray (eds), *Policing the Empire: Government Authority and Control 1830–1940*. Manchester: Manchester University Press, pp 72–3.

[5] Mike Brogden (1987), 'The Emergence of the Police—the Colonial Dimension', *British Journal of Criminology*, 27/1 Winter; Georgina Sinclair (2006), *At the End of the Line: Colonial Policing and the Imperial Endgame 1945–80*. Manchester: Manchester University Press, esp ch 4, 'Policing the British Caribbean', pp 82–103.

[6] We return to the military character of colonial policing in Chapter 5.

[7] In the Bahamas from 1840 until independence in 1973, all commanding officers were recruited from England or were of European descent living in the Bahamas; Gabrielle Pratt and Morris A. Simmons (1990), *A History of the Royal Bahamas Police Force*. Bahamas: The Research and Planning Unit of the Royal Bahamas Police Force, p 29.

[8] For example, Bahamas police recruited from Barbados in the nineteenth century.   [9] Georgina Sinclair (2006), *At the End of the Line, op cit*.

training centre was established in Barbados to train officers drawn from across the British Caribbean.[10] To a large extent the structure and culture of the police is similar across the Commonwealth Caribbean, partly due to the common origins of the police forces, as well as the ongoing involvement of the British in the training and development of police forces during the post-colonial period up to the present day. Until independence in the 1960s and 1970s, there was extensive networking among senior officers within the Caribbean region and among a wider network of British colonial police forces. British Colonial Office policy required an 'orderly retreat' from Empire in which police forces played a paramount role. In the period of decolonization, especially during 'emergencies', the police were required to deal with public protest arising from surging anti-colonial and nationalist independence movements. As power was gradually transferred, 'so the transition of the police from agents of colonial control to an institution of the service of a newly independent civilian population became a political issue and a public reality'.[11] Across the Empire, threats to the colonial state impinged on the police who were confronted by the responsibilities for responding to ordinary crime, protest and subversion. These threats to imperial order were frequently met with quasi-military responses.[12] At a conference of Colonial Police Commissioners at the Police College at Ryton-on-Dunsmore in April 1951, the Secretary of State declared that:

the waging of the 'cold war' has inevitably increased the importance and responsibilities of Police Forces. . .they must now shoulder most of the burden for extirpating or at least of keeping under supervision and control the internal canker of communist-inspired subversion and treachery.[13]

---

[10] Training was provided at the Seawell police training centre on Barbados, opened by the British in 1957 and funded in the 1980s with about £500,000 a year. Training was provided there for the police of 11 former British colonies in the Eastern Caribbean. Nick Worrall, 'Grenada Gives up the Goose Step', *The Observer*. London, 15 January 1984. Funded and largely staffed by the British, the centre conducted courses for both Barbadian and foreign students from other Commonwealth Caribbean police forces, such as those of the Cayman Islands, Grenada, Montserrat, Saint Lucia, Saint Vincent and the Grenadines, the Turks and Caicos Islands, and the British Virgin Islands. More specialized training for officers was provided at police facilities in Britain.

[11] Georgina Sinclair (2000), 'Sir Arthur Young: The Quintessential English Policeman', Part I & II. *Proceedings of the RUC Historical Society*, Winter 1999 and Spring 2000.

[12] Georgina Sinclair (2006), *At the End of the Line*, op cit.   [13] *Ibid.*

The Inspector General of Colonial Police encouraged links between forces such as the conferences of Colonial Police Commissioners, which were held on a triennial basis in London from 1951–1960. A Caribbean regional Commissioners' conference was set up as part of a move to provide more expensive police assets, such as training colleges, on a regional basis. Special Branch heads had their own regional conference annually and also liaised directly with the US and the FBI and non-Commonwealth countries in the region.[14]

At the end of colonial rule, the Caribbean region's police forces drifted apart as the elite cadre of British police chiefs returned to the metropolis along with their counterparts working in other parts of the colonial civil service. For numerous reasons, including the political turmoil following independence, island nationalisms, limited financial resources, difficulties involved in travelling between islands, the collapse of the West Indian Federation and the process of decolonization, linkages among police forces in the islands weakened.[15] Regional training schools went out of favour and regional police leadership was fragmented and atomized.[16] Then, during the 1970s and early 80s, this process began to be reversed through initiatives leading to the creation of new structures to enable communication and coordinated action such as the Association of Caribbean Commissioners of Police,[17] the Regional

[14] Gregor Davey (2009), 'A Brief Outline of British Caribbean Policing and Intelligence Structures: 1838–1970', unpublished paper, King's College London, 18 September 2009.

[15] These political changes are charted in Chapter 2.

[16] Although the links among the newly independent Caribbean countries were underdeveloped, those between individual islands and British police, built up during the colonial period and strengthened during the 1950s, remained strong into the post-independence period. The British Colonial Office retained security liaison officers 'who travelled the Caribbean advising and passing information of interest both up and down the system' until their functions were transferred to the Foreign Office in 1966. In 1968, the Inspector General of Colonial Police also moved to the Foreign Office and was renamed Overseas Police Adviser. See Gregor Davey (2009), 'A brief outline of British Caribbean policing and intelligence', *op cit*. See also Michael Macoun (1996), *Wrong Place Right Time: Policing the End of Empire*. London: Radcliffe Press, pp 96–7, Appendix G: Responsibilities of Overseas Police Adviser/Inspector General Colonial Police, Dependent Territories Foreign and Commonwealth Office, pp 164–74, cited by Gregor Davey (2009), *op cit*.

[17] First mooted at a Caribbean regional Commissioners' conference in 1972 and established formally in 1987. We return to this later in this chapter.

Security System,[18] and the Caribbean Customs Law Enforcement Council.[19] Each of these structures was created with the assistance of Britain, the USA, or both. There was also a growth in the overseas posting of UK and US law enforcement officers in the region.[20] By the end of the 1980s, there was—once again—extensive and regular interaction among the region's police chiefs and others in the security sector.

Given this history, it is inaccurate to describe the recent development of transnational policing in the Caribbean region as new—a product of post-war globalization—which was my original, rather naïve hypothesis. On the contrary, Caribbean policing was highly interlinked during its first 130 years. There existed extensive policing links among British colonial island police forces and from the island police forces to the metropolis. During the colonial period, the British government created federal structures—including the British Leeward Islands and the British Windward Islands—each with its own system for multi-island policing.[21] Davey points out that because 'members of the Colonial Police Service were able to transfer locally between territories, moving from say Barbados to Guyana or Jamaica to Trinidad. . . there were many informal networks in operation'.[22] Thus, the two decades between the mid-1960s and the mid-1980s may be better characterized as a relatively short hiatus in a tradition of regional and transatlantic cooperation that can be traced back to the origins of policing in the region.

The existence of historically embedded policing networks across the islands means that the question becomes one of explaining transnationalization as a transformative rather than an entirely new phenomenon, raising such questions as what are the similarities and differences between transnational police cooperation in the colonial and post-colonial periods? In particular, to what extent has transnational policing shifted towards meeting the needs of the local population rather than of their former rulers in the metropolitan countries? In this chapter, we explore the role of the Commissioner of Police, the ways in which security priorities

---

[18] Established in 1983. See also Chapter 5.
[19] Established in 1977. See also Chapter 6.   [20] See Chapter 8.
[21] Georgina Sinclair (2006), *At the End of the Line*, *op cit*, p 98.
[22] Gregor Davey (2009), 'A Brief Outline of British Caribbean Policing and Intelligence Structures: 1838–1970', unpublished paper, King's College London, 18 September 2009.

are set, and how far these are influenced by the interests of the metropolitan countries. We then explore the nature of cooperation with other organizations, locally, nationally and internationally, the Commissioner's rationale for collaboration, and the strengths, weaknesses, and barriers to cooperation on the ground.

The Commissioners' Perspective on Security

The Caribbean police Commissioners that I interviewed appeared either in sharply pressed or Navy blue khaki uniform, epaulettes decorated with crown and laurels, breast decorated with brightly coloured embroidered medals or in the sharp suit befitting a senior detective. Most were in their 40s and 50s and many had more than 30 years' police service under their belts. Most chiefs had served in various operational roles during their service including periods as head of Special Branch and commander of the paramilitary Special Services Unit (SSU). Like British police officers, they started out as constables, patrolling various parishes or districts and rising through the ranks in various operational and administrative roles. Many chiefs were graduates (usually of the University of the West Indies or the University of London external programme) before joining the service. Some too were attorneys at law and had experience of prosecuting criminal cases. Most had trained in England, for example detective training at the Metropolitan Police Training School in Hendon and officer training courses at the Police Staff College at Bramshill in rural Hampshire. Most had taken the Junior Command Course on promotion to Inspector and then the Strategic Command Course along with UK senior police officers for whom the course was an essential requirement for promotion to Chief Constable. A number of Commissioners were alumni of the US international training programme at the FBI headquarters at Quantico, Virginia. Commissioners were generally intelligent, strategically-minded, relatively liberal, and progressive in their thinking about crime prevention and community policing. The Commissioners also had a tough side to their characters, an aspect that comes with the task of senior police command.

The first substantive issue was what Commissioners saw as the main crime and security threats in their jurisdiction and within the region. The Commissioners placed the 'scourge of drugs' at the top of the list, linking this with a range of other issues. They described in detail the trade routes from Colombia either directly to Jamaica or through Venezuela, Guyana, and Suriname up the island chain from Trinidad and to the islands of the Eastern Caribbean. The region as a whole, they believed, was geographically positioned in such a way that it is an 'ideal jump off point' from South America and therefore pivotal in the trans-shipment of cocaine to North America and Europe. The region's drug trafficking problem, they argued, 'spilled over' into drugs consumption within the islands and then into crime in general, including armed violence—as aggravated burglary and armed robbery. Drug dealers, they argued, often fought amongst themselves, resulting in disorder, serious bodily harm, murder, and kidnapping. When drugs are seized by the police, traffickers frequently rob and steal from others to recoup their money. The money involved, the Commissioners argued, is so huge that it outstrips many of the economies of smaller islands. This 'red economy' has a profound effect on the islands:

money is a corrupting influence and I am not one who would say that everything is well, in any part of the Caribbean. . . I believe, the vast majority of Caribbean people are good, law-abiding and would want to stay away from such activity but it is that significant few who would get involved and be tainted.

While drug trafficking was at the top of the Commissioners' list of priorities, they tended to emphasize the fact that firearms were integral to the drugs trade—'to make friends and to settle disputes', among those involved. One explained that drugs are usually protected by 'some sort of referee, some sort of mechanism for protection'. The movement of drugs, in their experience, is usually accompanied by firearms which manifests itself in all Caribbean countries in 'turf war and gun play'. Drugs and guns were closely related. One Commissioner explained that:

guns would be the greatest threat to us. But while drugs come through here, it is the drugs that fund the guns. In terms of the real physical threat guns would be number one, but it is the drugs that provide the basis, that create that wealth so that people can acquire guns, so there's that link.

The Commissioners' intelligence indicated that 60 per cent or more of the small arms that they recover originate in the United States with New York and Miami as two major ports of origin. Assault weapons—including M16s, AK47s, Tech 9s, Tech 11s—also come out of South America originating in Nicaragua, Colombia, and Honduras, and accompanying cocaine trafficking.

This was how one Assistant Commissioner described the ways in which guns come 'on a daily basis' onto the islands:

They come by ingenious means. People disassemble guns and put them into refrigerators, into all kinds of stuff. Government is in the process of acquiring some real modern and expensive X-ray equipment that should be able to help, at least those guns coming through the ports. But then we have a porous border. We are an island surrounded by sea, we do not have the capacity either by air or sea to give effective patrols to those men when they use those go-fast boats. Our shore lines are pretty open so boats can pull up almost anywhere, everywhere, offload their stuff and the problem with us or for us is that the drugs will go on, most times the guns do not and that is where our problems lie.

And this, he said, led to another problem of policing the coastlines, which was difficult because of limited resources.

One Deputy Commissioner described drug trafficking and its attendant problems as *amoebic*, shifting its shape to adapt to new circumstances including law enforcement activity:

The amoeba, it changes, responds to stimuli. And the stimuli here will be law enforcement agencies and their strategies and how they go about it. So you are in a situation, one geographical location and pressure is applied, you're going to move, you're going to adjust to that pressure, so international pressure has been so intense over the more recent 10–15 [years], two decades now, that it has forced those who are bent on gaining from the illegal drug trade and obviously firearms trafficking and so on, to adjust and adapt to the stimuli coming out from law enforcement and of course from the political directorate and so on.

In his view, drug trafficking and the attendant criminal activity surrounding it 'knows absolutely no borders and once pressures are applied in one jurisdiction, those people who are at the forefront will gravitate to other jurisdictions'. The problem—frequently referred to as the 'balloon effect'—is that when pressure is applied on drug trafficking routes in one place, the trade is displaced and new routes and trans-shipment points open up elsewhere. In the Commissioners' view, as long as demand remains strong, supplies are plentiful, and the routes are numerous, interdiction does not reduce trafficking; but simply pushes it from one place to another. As one Commissioner argued,

The drug traffickers and those bent on criminal activity in terms of the drug world will move from jurisdiction to jurisdiction and will find solace in the softer target areas and perhaps the Caribbean is seen as a soft area, well generally now we are resigned to tighten it up and toughen it and you will find perhaps in a decade or so, that they shift their focus, if they don't actually shift their focus, obviously their strategies and methodologies will change.

The Commissioners also pointed to a number of other security concerns including unemployment which 'breeds young criminals'. From an early age, those who don't attend school are exposed to criminality and drugs. Unemployment created 'a young school leaver problem and then a criminal problem flowing from that'. They were also concerned with the deportees coming back from Britain, Canada, the United States, and some of the other Caribbean countries. Some were committing offences themselves and others:

are recruiting people to commit those offences so they stay in the background, and those people they will go to go out and so we don't have anything much against them. . . . So that in itself is a threat to security.

While there are mechanisms to regulate the return of convicted offenders from overseas, there was little more that they could do than maintain the loosest form of supervision once they returned. More broadly, the Commissioners were concerned about the influence of American television programmes that were increasingly dominating the viewing habits of Caribbean young people.

Tension between local and regional priorities

As well as being concerned about the problems of transnational crimes such as drug trafficking, the Commissioners were concerned specifically about what they called 'quality of life' issues affecting people in local communities—both local residents and visitors to the island—on a day-to-day basis in a very tangible way. The police therefore could not afford to be one-dimensional in their approach to the security problems:

We deal with the local issues, and they're quite a few, those law and order problems, the tourism stakeholders, one of my major constituencies as well because as you know, the _____ economy is by and large driven by tourism and so I have to be careful that, not only that visitors to the island are not victimized, but I sense that once I have a lid on crime, once crime is reduced to tolerable levels or maintained at tolerable levels, all of the other constituencies, all the other publics in _____, will benefit.

To achieve progress locally, an approach working with local people was required.[23] Commissioners in many places said that they deliberately engaged the community in the process of urban renewal and community policing. One said that:

you have to engage the community in order to really have effective policing, because I always say, 'A police officer only has a narrow view of what kind of policing should be delivered in a community'. Because you are so close to the business you only focus on that view, but the person who stands outside of that really knows what's happening in the community and could, you know, really help you to devise the strategies that should be delivered. What a police officer may perceive to be important in a community from a policing point of view, that may not be important to the citizen, and we find that through the urban renewal process.

In their view, other government agencies were 'lackadaisical', poorly trained, and lacking discipline. The police role in providing a 24-hour emergency service meant that they could identify community priorities, from anti-social behaviour among young people on public transport to failed street lighting. Going beyond their traditional role to maintain links with communities meant that they were able to gather intelligence to solve crime. Crucially, they needed to balance regional and transnational priorities. One Commissioner said:

we have to deal with the domestic side of the house while we focus on the regional stuff. The citizen doesn't have any interest up here regionally; he wants to know that you're doing something about his problem in individual countries.

Managing the tension between local and transnational priorities required collaboration with partners from other countries within the region:

it's very dangerous to work in isolation. When you look at what's happening domestically in each other's country, I think it's in our best interests to work together. . . . I think some of the Caribbean countries . . . don't have the resources and we recognize that. In fact, some of the countries who are members of the ACCP can hardly pay their dues, but we realise that we've got to hold each other's hands in order to attempt to deal with these big international drug cultures that seem to want to take hold of the vulnerability of the citizens of these small islands.

---

[23] Community policing was the stated ethos for the ACCP.

The Priority-Setting Process

Commissioners are torn between the immediate problems of crime and disorder in local communities, security threats straddling the region's islands, and the demands of the metropolitan countries to prevent cocaine trafficking through the islands to North America and Europe. This raises questions of priorities and of how they are arrived at. The main actors in this process are the Commissioners themselves, whose priorities are shaped by the democratically elected 'political directorates', that is the Prime Ministers, ministers of national security, justice, and Attorney Generals of Caribbean countries, acting individually and sometimes together. In discussions within government, the views and opinions of the leaders of other security sector organizations—such as the Chief of Staff of the Military and the Comptroller of Customs—also play a role, along with foreign policy actors including diplomats, police, and security advisors, as well as occasional visits from government ministers from the 'ABC countries', America, Britain, and Canada. Finally, there is the role of civil society whose influence is expressed through the ballot box, in the media, and through the activity of a small number of relatively powerless non-governmental organizations. A Commissioner explained the delicate balance between the competing interests:

I try to have a participative approach to leadership and I have what is known as a Senior Command Team, I have a Deputy and I have a number of Assistant Commissioners. We meet and we try to select the priorities but of course you also have to listen to the public. We do have a number of consultative committees and you will notice that there are quite some robust call-in programmes. . . . you listen to that. I also listen to my people in the media and also I do have to listen to the policymakers in my Ministry because we get all of our funding from government and they too, the cabinet, the ministry, will also have priorities, . . . so it's a mix to satisfy government's own priorities, to satisfy the public, the various stakeholders, and also in my own deliberate judgment and the views of my Senior Command Team.

The strength of the competing interests influencing the priority-setting role of the Commissioners means that they must be careful to retain their independence. The legacy of the colonial policing system in most of the territories is that the Commissioner of Police is accountable directly to a government minister—usually to the security or home affairs minister—and may find himself directed both strategically and operationally by the political directorates. One retired Commissioner argued that the balance of forces was partly dependent on the strength of character of the Commissioner in finding his own priorities. There are, he argued, 'different kinds of Commissioners':

> They have got a Commissioner who just get the job and holding on. They get one who has been there for a long time and knows where he is and they have got one who is there at the will of the Government and hustling. Now where does this leave a Caribbean Commissioner with all of that? It depends on who is the Commissioner, how long he has been there, and how strong he is.

While the formal policy-setting process is led by the political directorate of each country, decisions are influenced by the advice that they receive from the officials in their security sector. The relationship between the Commissioner and government ministers is absolutely crucial. The Commissioner has to understand what government policy is, how it is changing, and what is required to meet the needs of the various stakeholders. A retired Commissioner argued that:

> you have got to understand what the Government policy is because the Government can't tell you all the time what has to be done. You have to understand what is the Government policy so that you could execute it without reference back.

There is also the matter of political expediency that priorities are made on the basis of what is going to play well with the electorate. As the retired Commissioner put it:

> For instance, it might be a priority to put some assistance in this depressed area because this area has a certain type of voting that I would like and if this area sees it, but at the other time if you don't have the pressure of elections you could put it in another area, do you understand. . . . I mean if you've been in the system long enough, while you travel around if you see them fixing a road you say, 'Shit, they have got elections coming up and it's obvious they need to help out these people'. That is an unfortunate truth and it happens all over the world. You pump money where you want.

The role of metropolitan policy actors in priority setting

Policy actors from the metropolitan countries influence the policy-setting process in a number of ways. First, they influence the political level, for example through the advice given to a Caribbean

Prime Minister or Commissioner of Police by a UK diplomat such as the Deputy High Commissioner or a visiting government minister.[24] At the operational level, the metropolitan countries exert an influence through, for example, the advice or training given to a Drug Squad commander by a security advisor. This amounts to a high degree of influence, especially where financial and other resources are involved, and has had the effect of skewing security priorities towards those of most importance to their own national interest. A striking example of this is the way in which the role of the regional coastguards has shifted from a 'traditional' security agenda—based on external threats, fisheries protection, environmental protection, and search and rescue—towards the 'new security agenda' of narcotics trafficking and terrorism.[25]

How far are the security interests of the islands consistent with those of the metropolitan countries? Resources—including hard cash, police officers, and coastguard vessels—now used to prevent cocaine flowing through the islands towards London, Miami, and New York could be used to protect fish stocks, encourage tourism, or spend on education. The Commissioners were concerned that the authorities were devoting a significant amount of their effort of helping the Americans and Europeans to respond to problems generated by the metropolitan countries themselves, either through the thirst of their populations for psychotropic drugs or through their foreign policy which has generated the threat of terrorism. As one Commissioner put it:

Fortunately or unfortunately, it is never a partnership between equals. It is a one-way stream most of the time. The US is only interested in stopping drugs from getting to their borders. They will help you in relation to hardening your borders so that drugs would not pass through you to get to them.

The policy skew was also obvious in relation to the tension in priority between firearms and drugs. It is clear that there is a much greater emphasis on the northwards and eastwards flow of cocaine to the USA and Europe than on the flow of firearms into the Caribbean islands. This, in one Commissioner's view, boiled down to the self-interest of the donor countries:

The threat that they perceive to their national interest is drugs and consequently the focus is on drugs. The threat that I would perceive for my own

---

[24] See Chapter 8 on Overseas Liaison Officers.
[25] See Chapter 7 on Maritime Policing.

national interest here is guns supported by funds derived from drugs. . . .
The US policies are driven purely on their own self-interests. They would
only act where there's a clear and present danger to their own interests.

The Commissioners' view was that although the main motivation
for the metropolitan countries' involvement in law enforcement
efforts was self-interest, there was still a benefit to the people of
the Caribbean. One argued, 'even as we benefit I recognize that the
thing is skewed towards a problem that is perceived to represent
some threat to themselves'. What remains a problem is that the
priorities arrived at were not those of the Caribbean people. In
particular, the exclusive focus on cocaine heading towards the US
and UK meant that too little was done to prevent the flow of firearms. One Commissioner argued:

If we were able to get the US government to do a little more, and I think
they have the resources, they have the capacity to do more, to cut the flow
of guns to this country, we could in very short order reduce homicides in
this country, very short order.

This implies that despite all the effort going into international
enforcement, a key area that could prevent crime and save lives,
this is not acted upon:

the US don't care. They will pressure you for more jobs; they will spend
any amount of resources to intercept drugs that are coming through. We
don't produce cocaine. [This country] happens, by incident of history and
geography, to be in the pathway from Colombia that leads drugs to US
and Europe. We didn't put ourselves here. It is just an accident of geography why we're here. We don't have the capacity to patrol our borders
around, but the US will spend any amount of money down here to ensure,
but they don't care. What they do is tokenism in terms of assistance with
intercepting guns. Guns are sent from the US almost daily here.

One retired Commissioner agreed and thought this was 'human
nature'. If someone only across the water is creating problems,
then:

I would attempt to put my resources into that area to try to get him to
think along the lines that I'm thinking in the interests of protecting my
own back yard and that is what I feel is happening. Also, I think that
America worldwide is interested in protecting America and in getting
their view across.

The risk that the law enforcement priorities within the Caribbean may be distorted by international law enforcement priorities

was influenced by the role of the metropolitan countries in providing financial assistance for law enforcement. In one Assistant Commissioner's opinion, the extent of the influence depended on the strength of the law enforcement leadership at a particular time:

I think the management of law enforcement agencies ought to know what are their priorities and what priorities they are influenced by. And I think the problem would arise where funding is involved because if you don't have the funds to deal with your own priorities obviously it will take second place to that for which you have been funded.

The Commissioners understood that it was important for Caribbean police forces to find ways and means to deal with the tension between the desire for independence and the reliance on foreign donors to formulate their priorities even if that does not approximate to the desires of those with the funds. Another Assistant Commissioner was outspoken, stating that law enforcement cooperation with metropolitan countries 'more or less serves other needs rather than our needs'.

Local, Regional, and Transnational Linkages

The Commissioners of Police are involved in collaboration and cooperation with a range of agencies at the local, regional, and transnational levels. The nature of the Caribbean region and its crime patterns means that communication between islands is very important, as many problems are shared. Many islands are within 100 nautical miles of one another, and in some cases, only a few miles of water separate them. Criminals thus have easy mobility by boat and by air leading to a high level of bilateral cooperation across the region:

We have a very tight working relationship with Jamaica. Our drug enforcement unit collaborates with them almost on a daily basis because most of our bad boys go to Jamaica. We've got _____ locked up in Jamaica on drug charges, we had several murders down there involving _____ it's all through the drug trade. Barbados have come, and we have put them up, we have taken them around. We had Trinidadians here, we had arrest of persons here, an _____ who committed murder in Trinidad, they came home, information was passed to us, we arrested the person, passed him over there, I think he's still serving prison time over there now.

A distinction can be made between those forms of cooperation that are reactive, occurring in response to a particular crime or event—such as a homicide investigation—and those that are proactive or strategic.[26] There are a range of ways in which reactive collaboration might come about:

Well from time to time you have detectives from England coming here in pursuit of investigation. There are protocols that they must follow, they go through the protocols and we support them. You know that in England they have this issue where they have a family liaison officer where a victim is killed. We've had requests like that where someone is killed in England, the victim or the deceased is coming out to be buried, and they send a detective in the case to attend the funeral. I recognize that the mission there is multi-purpose, much more than expressing of sympathy, it is certainly to look and to get additional information to build their case, they are supported in every regard. They track [our nationals] here who commit crimes in England and flee here, that collaboration I think is reactive. I suspect again that in terms of investigating drug cases they are active here with the support of the local police.

From the Commissioners' perspective, once you have 'international criminality crossing over territories', there is an inevitable need for closer cooperation between police forces. Organized crime groups in continental South America, including Colombia, Venezuela, Guyana, Suriname, and French Guiana are working with Caribbean counterparts and, therefore, creating a pressing need for regional collaboration in law enforcement. As one Commissioner put it, working with other countries has become a matter of 'routine, daily law enforcement cooperation'. At the strategic level, the key relationship is that among the region's Commissioners of police, interactions among whom are facilitated by a regional Association.

The Association of Caribbean Commissioners of Police

The idea for a regional chief police officers' association emerged from a conference of police leaders in Trinidad and Tobago in 1972, followed by semi-formal meetings in Saint Lucia (1981) and Guyana (1982). Then, as a later commentator put it, with 'yeoman tenacity, and a hint of nostalgia', nine Commissioners attended a five-day conference in Jamaica in 1986 where a resolution calling for the establishment of an Association of Caribbean Commissioners of Police (ACCP) was drafted, ratified, and

---

[26] This point is developed more fully in the next chapter.

adopted.[27] Eligibility for membership was based on 'similar geographical, political, social and cultural background' where CARICOM members qualify automatically. The aim was to create a policing organization for the English-speaking Commonwealth Caribbean, with funding sought from approved regional sources rather than private individuals. The inaugural ACCP AGM was held in Saint Lucia in August 1987, included the Commissioners of nine other Caribbean states,[28] and was sponsored by the US Department of Justice, International Criminal Investigative Training Assistance Programme (ICITAP).[29] The ACCP constitution set out to promote regional cooperation in the suppression of criminal activities in such areas as narcotics, terrorism, and organized crimes; exchanging information in criminal investigations; sharing common services including training, forensic analysis, and research; and the effective management of law enforcement agencies. The Commissioners requested that ICITAP provide courses in criminal investigation, firearms identification, and overview of criminal investigations for station sergeants. They also asked for arrangements enabling heads of drug enforcement units to meet in conference for mutual discussion of common problems. The US Ambassador to Saint Lucia addressed the conference, assuring that the USA would support the Association and assist Commissioners in combating crime in the Caribbean. Since then, the ACCP has met annually for a week-long general meeting held in one of the member countries, and an inter-sessional meeting usually held in Barbados—home to the ACCP secretariat.

The US State Department funded the ACCP conference, which, as a UK police advisor put it, eventually 'raised a few eyebrows with the US people because they said that's funny, that's not ICITAPs remit, and I think they did a bit of creative defining and

[27] ICITAP (1986), 'Proposals for the Establishment of an Association of Caribbean Commissioners of Police: Historical Perspective'. Unpublished.

[28] Barbados, Belize, Jamaica, Saint Lucia, Anguilla, British Virgin Islands, Cayman Islands, Turks and Caicos, Saint Kitts and Nevis.

[29] ICITAP has been running since 1986 and continues to be a leader in worldwide law enforcement development. Its website describes it as 'a law enforcement development organization whose mission is to work with foreign governments to develop effective, professional, and transparent law enforcement capacity that protects human rights, combats corruption, and reduces the threat of trans-national crime and terrorism, in support of U.S. foreign policy and national security objectives'. <http://www.usdoj.gov/criminal/icitap/about/>.

it became a training event'. This continued for several years before ICITAP moved away as its focus shifted to Eastern Europe and its creative definitions were questioned. US funding sustained the organization during its early years but it lacked political support from within the region. One observer commented that when the ACCP started, the governments of the 10 or 11 member states:

inherently felt that it was a good idea. What it didn't have was political support. Ministers were saying yes okay, we like the idea we think, and it was very difficult for them also to demonstrate what they were achieving because they actually weren't achieving very much. What they were doing was meeting and discussing, and it was very useful because on a number of bilateral bases, there were things going on that were proving to be very useful and very good, but as a regional group, they weren't producing much.

One of the first successful projects introduced under the aegis of the ACCP was the Regional Organized Counter Crime Information Sharing System (ROCCISS), built on a communication system that the British had created for the overseas territories.[30] The desire for a system enabling the exchange of information on criminal matters was on the ACCP agenda from the outset in 1987, taking nearly a decade before the system went live. An enhanced system was developed further and in May 2004, the then President of the ACCP and Jamaican Police Commissioner Francis Forbes announced that the Regional Information and Intelligence Sharing System (RIISS), would be implemented in the 24 member states of the ACCP.[31] This, he said, would be a 'model system for the world' linking into Interpol's new 1-24/7 communication and message-switching system. RIISS shared information through a 'pointer system', indicating to law enforcement officers where they could find information on individuals. In the view of one observer, 'the development of RIISS probably couldn't be driven through without the existence of something of the nature of ACCP'.

Business sessions were introduced in 2000 to focus decision-making. The ACCP has a role in policy making internally, dependent upon acceptance at a regional level by CARICOM to enable the individuals to pull together. For example, any moves towards a regional crime squad or a regional rapid response team would require legislation in each country allowing officers from another

---

[30] The Overseas Territories Regional Intelligence System (OTRIS).
[31] 'US to Fund Regional Intelligence System', *Jamaica Observer*, 11 May 2004.

country to act within their territory. The CARICOM legal affairs committee could do this, but the ACCP should contribute too, adding practicality to the legislation. What ACCP is seeking is a 'common policy and [at a] practical level, common forms of communication, [and] a common set up' such as setting up joint national headquarters in every country and common data collection standards.

The ACCP is trying to influence countries to move towards regional policy and cooperation. It is a policy-making body that can make recommendations to national governments, a network of police officers who trust one another, and a forum through which regional practices can be discussed, providing a network of contacts and relationships and exerting influence across the region. The contemporary role of the ACCP is similar to the Association of Chief Police Officers (ACPO) in England. This is how one Commissioner saw it:

it should be a leader, on law enforcement matters, very much like your ACPO . . . they speak on issues in relation to policing and law enforcement and I would dare say that their views are respected and policy makers may take their views into account . . . the ACCP does speak on matters but I think that perhaps they are, perhaps not aware of the leverage that they do have in addressing these matters . . . they need to be perhaps a bit more focussed on these matters.

. . . I think that they need to actually come out in public and engage the public on these issues, interact with the University, interact with the media, to actually get their message across because one thing that you will find in the Caribbean is that there is a quite robust debate on these matters. Normally police officers at the level of Commissioner don't treat to these debates and perhaps that is a mistake and their voices need to be heard.

Essentially a professional association, it is unlikely that the ACCP will ever have an operational role. If the comparison is taken further, however, it must be remembered that ACPO had a major role in coordinating police action in the UK against secondary picketing in the miners' strike through the creation of a National Reporting Centre.[32] There is also an important relationship between the Caribbean Commissioners collectively and the Regional Security System (RSS)

[32] Martin Kettle (1985), 'The National Reporting Centre and the 1984 Miners' Strike' in Bob Fine and Robert Millar (eds), *Policing the Miners' Strike*. London: Lawrence and Wishart; Phil Scraton (ed) (1987), *Law, Order & the Authoritarian State*. Milton Keynes: Open University Press.

since they are represented on the council of the RSS, many with previous experience as operational officers in the paramilitary SSUs. The operational manager of the RSS at the time of the study, Grantley Watson, is a former Commissioner of Police in Barbados and past President of the ACCP. Therefore, although the ACCP lacks operational capacity to direct, it has a relationship with the powers that do, namely the USA and the UK who coordinate such matters. As one UK observer put it, these structures are 'supported internationally and I think it's probably dangerous to tamper with them in the sense that they've taken a long while to build up'.

The ACCP provides connections, 'because obviously the Commissioners are all now much closer than they used to be'. But when it comes to practical cooperation, through bilateral or trilateral relationships between countries, this work is coordinated by liaison officers from the metropolitan countries rather than cooperation among the Commissioners. One informant described the nature of cooperation in this way:

So, the Drug Squad in Granada would be working with the UK DLO who would be working with the DEA rep in St Juan, Puerto Rico, or Trinidad or wherever. They say we've got a problem and we think it's coming from Antigua. Okay, I'll get the guy from Antigua to talk to his Drug Squad guy and then you can get together. So it's done through the network of international support agencies mostly.

Practical cooperation is carried out on a case-by-case basis, not dissimilar to collaboration across police force boundaries in Britain. Apart from the overarching role of the agencies—such as the Serious Organised Crime Agency—cross-border policing is carried out at the operational level, with, for example, detectives from Surrey speaking to people in the Metropolitan Police. As one police advisor put it:

If it's a big organized thing, then yes sure, and in the Caribbean what would happen I suspect would be they'd turn immediately to their international partners to try and organize it and run it because they don't have the resources or the wherewithal to do it themselves. But if it's an individual smallish type of thing, then I think they would probably just create it.

There are also concerns that since the British and the Americans fund the ACCP, the organization is another vehicle of influence for the metropolitan countries. The USA and the UK put up the money, so in relation to ACCP, 'the piper will call the tune. That is the concern of some politicians'. Part of the dynamic of cooperation revolves around the relationship between the Caribbean countries and the ACCP. As one interviewee explained:

the extent to which you can get the external influences directing the show, and I'm saying you cannot live without external influences, but we need to set up the structures for the cooperation and the collaboration where the mutual interests are served, because you are not going to get the Americans or the ABC pumping in here altruistically for your benefit and not for theirs and therefore we need to sit and recognize this.

Perhaps a measure of the effectiveness of the ACCP is if it could lead to law enforcement issues being addressed regionally and with law enforcement being supported by a single voice. On the one hand, the Commissioners are police officers who understand their individual needs. However, as one Drug Squad head explained, if they could meet as a group and say, 'hey, this is something that we see across the region', it may be more effective than having to put forward their needs individually to the relevant president or home affairs minister.

Cooperation with metropolitan countries

The Commissioners were generally strongly committed to the idea of cooperation with the US and UK. The problems arising from international drugs trafficking, the location of the islands, the fact that some of the drugs will stay on the islands, the use of human resources, and the responsibilities of the consuming countries meant that cooperation with the metropolitan countries was essential. One Deputy Commissioner argued that:

We have the law breakers and the offenders networking and establishing nice linkages and so on, the fight will only be much more difficult, so that we have to find ways to combat that networking outside there, crime, and the extent to which our technologies are affording criminals to join with each other, we have to use the same technology and really link up nicely with each other. So to me there's no other way than to have a true international linkage within law enforcement.

The Commissioners argued that the need for cooperation had existed for many years, but was much more evident today (see for example, the views expressed at the head of this chapter). In addition to the shifting nature of crime, transnational policing was essential in order to infiltrate cartels and networks to target the

senior drug players. One Commissioner explained how collaborating with the USA led him, together with six other countries on
the same day and at the same time, to arrest senior figures. Those
'big operatives that we have taken down here', he explained:

have also committed offences in those countries, particularly in the US,
because what happens, the money comes from the US to finance the operations, and the drug lords that come through _____ end up in the US. And
because of the conspiracy and the arrangement for the shipments are done
sometimes in this country and also in the US, and in Canada as well. In
one of these big operative cases we had five countries involved and the US
being the country where most of the planning and conspiracy to bring the
stuff in takes place.

Another argument in favour of cooperation was the weaknesses
of Caribbean criminal justice systems. Commentators from the
Caribbean, from the USA, and the UK have long argued that
the islands' legal systems are insufficiently robust to bring key
players in organized crime groups to justice. The region's legal
systems are open to corruption, witnesses can be bought, and
the systems are very slow and starved of resources. The USA also
has laws designed to deal effectively with criminal conspiracies—
such as RICO[33]—and that have longer prison sentences available
to judges. One Assistant Commissioner (Crime) had no doubt of
the advantages of sharing information or working transnationally to target transnational criminals.

My approach to this whole globalized investigations, globalized law
enforcement thing is that, having worked in many of these cases, I come
to the conclusion, when we investigate we are trying to procure evidence
against a drug target or a criminal family or cartel as the case might be.
If the evidence can be gotten in Canada or in the UK or in Germany for
that matter, if what I can do could lend to us procuring sufficient evidence
in any of those ports, capitals, destinations, that will satisfy the law being
enforced against that operation, I say, 'Let's do it, let's do it!'

Cooperation of this sort, one Commissioner argued, created 'a
welcome and mutually satisfying relationship':

most of the cooperation has tended to be in the area of drug interdiction because, as you know, most of the major countries would have

---

[33] Racketeer Influenced and Corrupt Organizations Act, enacted under s 901(a)
of the Organized Crime Control Act of 1970 (Pub.L. 91-452, 84 Stat. 922, enacted
15 October 1970).

drug liaison officers in the Caribbean and I think that is to be expected because of where we are located and because most of the drugs would pass through this region on to Europe and the United States and so I think that cooperation has tended to work in favour of both countries because even though drugs will be passing on to Europe and the United States, I think it's reasonable to assume that, I go beyond assuming and say that some of the drugs would remain here and as you will get to find out, drug trafficking is one of our major problems. It does, apart from the actual use of drugs, it does tend to fuel some of the acquisitive crimes like robberies and violent crimes such as burglaries and the like, and the thing too is that drug interdiction tends to be quite expensive and manpower intensive and I think that those countries, the consuming countries if I may call them that, have a moral responsibility to actually assist in the policing effort in that regard.

One Deputy Commissioner was very clear about where the responsibility lay:

we keep telling the Americans they are the ones who are encouraging the drugs because the demand is always . . . there in the United States and if they get rid of the demand then the supply will go.

Cooperation with the metropolitan countries includes training, development work, communications, procurement of equipment, and other physical resources. Caribbean Commissioners work with the region's other police chiefs and with the RSS, the US Drugs Enforcement Administration, FBI, and the military Southern Command (SouthCom), extending across the region from Florida to the southern tip of Chile, with police officers from numerous countries, including the USA, Britain, Canada, and France. They work with the British Customs and intelligence services (MI5 and MI6) and the Metropolitan Police. They also worked with US police forces including the NYPD and Miami Dade with an exchange of officers. The value of this was the 'leeway' or 'accommodation' that resulted from bringing the two police forces into contact with one another:

Police officer to Police officer who say 'I understand the situation in _____' and the _____ said to the NYPD officer 'I understand the situation in New York' therefore, they were able to informally exchange a lot of information.

One Commissioner described a 'three-pronged approach'—local training, foreign training, and interdiction at sea. Most operational work is based on bilateral relationships with Britain and the USA. He explained that:

British warships come through and they do surveillance and interdiction in our territorial waters. Well, increasingly there is joint police and military *training*, joint police and military *operations*. We have seen the necessity for it and I think for the immediate future.

The Jamaican police have two police officers (a superintendent and an inspector) based in the UK 'actively engaged in police work at operational level, and both countries benefit from this interaction.' The officers are carefully chosen on the basis of their record of performance, commitment, and training, and 'they manage themselves'. There is 'some kind of relationship' with the High Commission in London, but 'certainly not that they are supervised or managed by them but there is some kind of relationship, an informal relationship, with the High Commissioner', similar to the kind of relationship existing between the British High Commissioner and the overseas liaison officers in the Caribbean.[34] These officers have a significant role in collecting and sharing intelligence on guns and drugs and the movement of known criminals between there and the UK. They also have a specific role to monitor and supervise citizens being deported as a result of their criminal activity.

They obviously would get as much information as they possibly can on their criminal status abroad and organize and collect data on them so that that information can be sent back here on a timely basis so that it helps our law enforcement officials back here to no doubt examine the information, set up systems to track them, that kind of stuff, and aid investigations.

When known criminals escaped detection leaving an island, the police would transmit some information across to the UK and the liaison officers 'would be right there to identify persons as people who we might have an interest in' and therefore providing cooperation at the investigative and operational law enforcement levels in real time. In the view of senior officers, two officers were not really enough for the work involved, that there was room for more, but expansion was prevented because of financial constraints. The liaison officers' salaries are funded by the Jamaican government with

---

[34] This role is discussed in detail in Chapter 8.

support from the British. The Commissioner reported that this had been only positive. The essence of the initiative was to 'build relationships'. One of the Commissioners explained that:

Often times when you rely on systems to run just on autopilot, where there is no face to a name, it creates difficulty. Where people can establish relationships and establish professional contacts it smoothes the passage somewhat, so it is my view, my considered view, that it has gone very well.

Commissioners argued that there were a number of barriers to successful cooperation. There was too much bureaucracy. They were particularly concerned about procedures for formal cooperation that required them to go through their security ministries to the UK Foreign and Commonwealth Office who would then speak to the Home Office in London and from there to their relevant operational counterpart in the Metropolitan Police Service or one of the other UK police forces. The chain of paperwork creates a barrier and government policies get in the way. As a result, most frequently, police officers prefer to have direct officer-to-officer contacts with people whom they know and trust.

Building personal relationships was critical to establishing good working relationships, 'because that builds trust, it breaks down barriers, because by that personal interaction they're able to build relationships and out of the relationship comes easier access to information, greater levels of cooperation and collaboration'. Cooperation is facilitated by the sense that police officers around the world 'speak the same language' which enables them to have a shared conversation and establishes trust, mutuality, and understanding among law enforcement agencies around the world. This pointed to the idea that there is a universal cop culture, and sense of a transnational police community. Informal cooperation is valuable, and facilitated by going on training courses. As the world becomes smaller, the police services of the world have to avoid 'operating in a silo fashion':

that is why sometimes I look at all these courses that people may go on, and some of the good things that come out of that is we know that a police officer [here] can take up the phone and talk to his counterpart in the US. I have received calls here from people who have graduated from the FBI Academy, and by that police officer just taken up a directory that is issued annually and if he wants to get in touch with, he has to deal with an issue that's in _____, he will look to see who are the graduates from the FBI

Academy in _____ and he will call and we'll hear his problem, so he'll deal with an advisor and we can at that very moment activate our Interpol people and say, 'I want you to look into this for this officer', and so on.

Limited capacity was also a barrier. The Commissioners aspired to greater mobility in terms of personnel, equipment, boats, and infrastructure. There is the more general issue of making difficult decisions about whether to fund projects to reduce poverty rather than spend money on security services, but capacity building is very important. Unless Caribbean governments can build capacity, 'the question of improving and increasing the sharing of joint operations and intelligence sharing, that will to a certain extent determine how far we go'. Thus, although the will is there, the fact that the Caribbean is comprised of small island states with very open and fragile economies means that they will always need to have that international component constantly coming forward to help. As one Deputy Commissioner put it:

We just can't do it alone, so definitely there is a need for these countries who I say *would have*, countries that have to share with those that *don't have* because at the end of the day if you battle hard in your jurisdiction, the drug traffickers are going to take the soft targets and they can see the Caribbean region and they'll be looking at it as a soft target.

A Deputy Commissioner argued that lots of things were possible, but 'all of this will take money. That is what is holding us back money, money, money'.

You raised the idea of exchange officers but I told you about the difficulty of having the finance for our people to go and that's one of the reasons why we don't go to Bramshill and these places any more. We don't have the money and that is where the difficulty will come in. It is a very good idea. As I said, that the experience would be good, the interaction and everything would be good but that little [money], that is always the problem.

Regulation of Overseas Officers' Powers

One of the most controversial issues in international police cooperation is the question of where the boundary lies in what overseas police officers should be permitted to do in the islands. The Commissioners shared the view that cooperation required trust, confidence, and mutual understanding. Collaboration, they felt, needed to be based on a clear framework of international law and the confidence that all the parties would adhere to it. As the Commissioner quoted at the head of this chapter put it, they expect that officers will step out of line, but can only hope that this is not too frequent.

The Commissioners all acknowledged that foreign police officers were involved in operational matters 'behind the scenes.' Overseas officers had been working in the region for some time and had become increasingly active, although one Commissioner was keen to emphasize that they do not have powers of arrest.

Although they may be operational in a sense, they're not involved with arresting, they do not have that right to—how shall I put it—well if I just say simply to arrest other people here or to even question people. You cannot as an agent who is not protected to operate in a country carry out searches, you know, you have no powers at all. You might work alongside an officer here, meet and they'll say, 'Work alongside us' . . . but they will carry out their own investigations, particularly to have things happen on the other side, in the US, by working with us here, but their interaction with offenders here, they are very much behind the scenes in that regard because they just don't have the power to do that.

However, police officers are pragmatic, resourceful, creative people. Observing that liaison officers do not arrest people, but are doing undercover work, surveillance, running informers, and so on, Ethan Nadelmann suggests that they are similar to private detectives.[35] Like the gumshoe, lack of arrest powers doesn't prevent them from doing things that are very close to police work, such as talking quietly to witnesses or criminal suspects, and running informers. The Commissioners generally had a pragmatic view: agents understood their mission and what was required to achieve it, within an agreed framework:

he has to operate within some parameters which do not allow him to do things outside. So whatever he can do within that legal framework he feels free to do. I mean he can, and I guess they do, have informers, they're told to get information. . . . That officer who might indulge himself in gathering intelligence may tell us things which he has gathered and then we can act on it. So he, to my mind, is seeking to protect the sovereignty of the state from people who may claim to have some kind of legal right in the place but at the same time giving away the sovereignty of the state to some drug pusher up in Colombia or somewhere like that.

---

[35] Ethan Nadelmann (1993), *Cops Across Borders: The Internationalisation of US Law Enforcement*. University Park, Penn.: Pennsylvania State University Press.

One Commissioner's staff officer, who had a background in narcotics, said of overseas police officers, 'they don't actually do police work', insisting that cooperation did not extend to the overseas officers actually doing what would traditionally be recognized as policework although they exchanged information and assisted with locating persons and addresses. If the US wanted information on local people, it would be provided. The Commissioners were strongly resistant to the idea that the British or the Americans carried out policing on their soil. One Commissioner was quite offended by the suggestion:

> to say actually that they are doing policing in our country, I think that's a skewed way in presenting that type of cooperation package. . . . Because from a strictly legal point of view the only people that are mandated or that are authorized to do the law enforcement is the _____ Police Force. That doesn't say we cannot have a relationship with any other organization, whether inside of the country or whether from outside of the country in order to get information, because at the end of the day we are the implementers of whatever issues are arising from that cooperation.

> Police officers operate and they function within our constitutional set-up, within our legal set-up, there's not a direct transplantation of the policing strategy and culture in our territory. We are very keen on that and we define the lines of functioning. . . . If our laws say no, you can't do it that way, you just can't do it that way. You have to get it right. But increasingly we have to legislate and we have to make recommendations to the legislators as the nature of crime changes, so it is something that is fluid rather than static.

The Commissioners were clear that where you have US or UK or police officers from one of the other countries in the region working within a Caribbean territory, the accountability, responsibility, and leadership of any operation would lie with the local police, 'because we're accountable to our laws and to our courts for the action we take or for the action taken in our name, we are accountable for it'. This is not to say that there were not occasions when the Commissioner was concerned about overzealous British and American police officers acting within the islands. One senior officer explained that he had had experiences of people stepping over the boundaries. The senior officer explained that one of the tasks of the overseas liaison officer based in the country was to curb the enthusiasm of police officers asking to travel to the Caribbean to carry out investigations:

A liaison officer, coming out of NCIS, sits here in _____ who is so alive, so alert that a police officer in an area in London says to him 'I want to pursue a case in _____ .' He says 'No, you can't come, it's my job to do that' because he doesn't want him to come and step over bounds because I'll tell you he has difficulty with that police officer who says 'You can't do my work and if we have such an MOU working, why can't I come?' but we know if we allow that gentleman to come, he's not going to be one that we can trust to abide by the MOU that we have signed.

The issue on which this question turns is the definition of what constitutes policework. If one sticks to the specific issue of effecting an arrest, then it is possible to maintain that the British and American police officers based in the islands are there in a liaison role only and do not do anything that constitutes policework. However, the Commissioners were alive to the fact that police from overseas could in fact, carry out policework without the express approval or even perhaps the knowledge of senior police. In their view, this can happen, but in order to get away with this undetected, their work would have to be carefully concealed. Police officers from overseas who are stationed in the islands are operating like local police officers in terms of collecting evidence, and covert policing, the collection of intelligence, speaking to informers, and other forms of surveillance activity. In the view of one Commissioner intelligence officers do this all the time:

Yes, all the time! They would bring somebody here in the embassy or the High Commission, some third officer or something, and he goes about the place interviewing people. However, if they go to arrest anyone, and I don't think they would be so stupid to attempt to effect an arrest, that's where the problem will come, but they gather information all the time. The moment you start talking to somebody you know that this has got to be a law enforcement person or a person trained in intelligence gathering and you know, you pick them up early. . . . Yes, you spot them. The public may not be able to spot them easily, they might just know that this is a person from an embassy and they're talking to an embassy official and that's it for them, but there are certain things they conceal which will give you an indication as to what is their strong point.

The Commissioners argued that they would safeguard against any overzealousness by the British and Americans. One Commissioner put it:

we should not allow that to happen and we should take the proper position to ensure that it doesn't. But, if perchance it does happen, then the foreign police would be subject to prosecution.

Summary and Conclusion

Policing beyond national boundaries is well established in the Caribbean. The facts of the region's geography mean that transnational collaboration and cooperation are part and parcel of the island policing scene. Many countries are, in any case, archipelagic states and there is much inter-island communication on crime and security matters. Caribbean Police Commissioners travel from island to island to speak with their counterparts on specific issues, attend meetings and conferences, as well as communicating with each other regularly by telephone, fax, and email. Communications among the region's police forces—which can be traced back to the 1840s—has been made faster and more frequent as a result of rapid developments in transport and information communication technologies.

There is also a well established relationship between the islands and the metropolis, the roots of which lie in British colonial history and have shifted with the changing geopolitical scene. There is an unbroken line of British involvement in policing the Caribbean from the nineteenth century origins of colonial police forces to the present day. US involvement is more recent but is now much more extensive and involves a range of different agencies. In many ways each of the police forces of the region is better connected to metropolitan police forces—in London, Miami, and New York—than they are to each other. Nonetheless, there are kinship ties that cross the region and together with the creation of regional training facilities in the 1950s and the provision of training in Britain, many of the region's senior officers have personal contacts with one another. Colonial policing systems, built on similar legal and administrative systems, emphasized the need for a common approach and encouraged the exchange of personnel. Many policing linkages have been forged through the conduit of resources provided by the British and the Americans and in recent years the process of inter-island communication has improved the relationships among police and other law enforcement officers within the region. The Association of Caribbean Commissioners of Police (ACCP), created with the assistance of Britain and America, has fostered those links. Their annual conferences provide a forum in which police and security officials from the US, UK, Canada, France, the Netherlands, and others can meet the Caribbean chiefs collectively and in an informal setting.

From the Commissioners' perspective, the most pressing regional security priority, and that which dominates discussion about security cooperation, is the transnational drugs trade and its 'attendant ills'. The islands lie directly in the path of the traffic from the South American coca producers and North American cocaine consumers and are a strategically useful 'jumping off' position for routes to Europe. Although the Caribbean represents only one route among many—and in fact accounts for only a tiny proportion of cocaine traffic—the impact of the drugs trade on island life is enormous. There is a certain amount of local drug consumption, but the islands are not a major market for the drugs barons. The key issues relate to the 'spill-over' into local violent crime, and in particular armed violence, which accompanies clandestine drug markets. The economics of the drugs trade means that money laundering and corruption are also major problems for the Commissioners.

In setting security priorities, the Commissioners find themselves caught between competing pressures that reflect the political context of the islands described in the previous chapter. As in any jurisdiction, an overriding concern of the police chiefs is to ensure that the citizens of the country are safe and secure. As is the case elsewhere, however, the safety issues about which local people are most concerned often relate to what might be considered minor crimes, or even 'non-crime' issues, such as street lighting and standards of behaviour on public transport. Crime is experienced locally and local concerns have to be taken seriously. International drug trafficking is seen as a problem by the locals; but the citizens are really concerned with the *local symptoms* of the global drugs trade—for example, the internecine armed violence, homicide, and kidnapping that affect their daily lives. The Commissioners must therefore take a broader view of the problem of insecurity. They must work with regional and metropolitan counterparts to deal with drugs trafficking while keeping in mind the context of poverty and unemployment, the influence of consumerism, and American television which combine, in their view, to create an environment within which wrongdoing has become more prevalent. Part of their calculation is that people deported from the US and Europe pose a security threat because of their connections to the metropolitan countries and involvement, direct and indirect, with drugs trafficking.

At the same time, the most significant threats to the islands' security come from the sea—the island's coastlines are unprotected and physically unprotectable. Even if the capacity of the coastguard was doubled and doubled again, the Commissioners insisted, it would still be impossible to provide round the clock, island-wide protection for the beaches, coves, and caves of even the largest of the islands, much less when it comes to the numerous smaller islands. The fact of a shared physical space and a sense of shared security problems (particularly those arising from the drug trade) creates a pull towards regional cooperation in both terrestrial and marine policing.[36] This occurs at the strategic level through such bodies as the ACCP, and at the operational level through such entities as the drug commanders' conference and through day-to-day communication amongst operational officers.

The Commissioner and his top team are conscious that their security priorities are heavily influenced by the metropolitan countries and that law enforcement cooperation serves the interests of the US and UK—specifically the goal of preventing the flow of drugs to these countries. Drug trafficking is the gravest security problem for the Commissioner because of the guns, internecine violence, and corruption that come with it. It is also a priority because of the influence of the metropolitan countries. This influence stemmed partly from the diplomatic arts of British and American security advisors, but also from funding and other resources. Some of this was used in attempting to strengthen Caribbean island borders, but the focus was preventing drugs from reaching North America and Europe. That, of course, is the key reason for the posting of overseas liaison officers from the USA, Britain, Canada, France, Germany, and other metropolitan countries.[37] The Commissioner and his top team were stoical about this. They recognized that the security agenda was shaped by the metropolitan countries, but accepted that this was very much part and parcel of international relations. One Commissioner quoted Thucydides on international relations: 'large nations do what they wish, while small nations accept what they must'. This skewed security agenda was not without its frustrations. Senior officers—some more outspoken

---

[36] See Chapter 7 on Maritime Policing.
[37] See Chapter 8 on Overseas Liaison Officers.

than others—saw cocaine trafficking through their territory as a problem not of their own making, but arising from the geographical accident of their location between producer and consumer countries. Nonetheless, the police senior command felt they had no choice but to collaborate in order to protect island security. They had an interest in doing what they could to disrupt drug trafficking, but on the other hand, they saw the metropolitan countries as having a moral responsibility to contribute to their law enforcement efforts because it was the North American and European countries which were responsible for the insecure position in which they found themselves.

Because of the nature of the threat faced by the islands, the emergence of drugs trafficking as transnational criminal activity, and the sense of a shared responsibility, the Commissioners and their top team welcomed collaboration with regional and hemispheric partners which they saw as an essential component of contemporary policing. Cooperation occurred at all levels and comprised a range of activities from sharing information and intelligence, receiving of equipment and training, shared operations, and exchange of personnel. The main barriers to cooperation were incompatible legal systems and structures, a lack of resources, bureaucratic procedures that hindered the sharing of information, mistrust (some of which arose from fears about corruption), political influence, and a sense of asymmetry of power in working with foreign counterparts.

The most controversial areas of cooperation were joint operational activity and the working practices of officers stationed overseas. The Commissioners and senior command team were at pains to stress that cooperation did not mean that overseas officers were 'doing policework' within their territory. However, they were also aware of the possibility (whether through lack of trust, or over-zealousness) that sometimes those agents would act independently, pushing the boundaries of what was acceptable within a democracy. They drew a clear line around what constituted policework, insisting that no overseas police officer or agent would attempt to make an arrest in a foreign country. However, discussion of the gathering and sharing of intelligence and other forms of covert cooperation and collaboration led to much greyer and more complex areas of contemporary policing practice. It must be remembered that the Commissioners of Police are most concerned with matters of strategy and policy. They are also able politicians, keen to present as positive and independent a view of their organization as possible. To dig a little deeper and to discover what contemporary transnational policing looks like 'on the ground', we must now make our way to the operational units—the Criminal Investigation Department, Interpol National Central Bureau, Drug Squad, and Special Branch—the subjects of the next chapter.

4

Transnational Policing on the Ground: Reactive and Proactive Investigation

Introduction

> The fact that the drug trade is transnational in nature means that we in our little neck of the woods can't effectively deal with the problem because a lot of it, it doesn't even begin here and it doesn't end here. In fact, we are just a transit country and therefore if we have any real intention of stopping the problem we cannot stand here alongside the route, just taking total impact on it, we can't just stand here and do it, we have to link with all of these people.[1]

> as an officer involved in law enforcement and intelligence domestically, you never like to feel that someone else is probing without your knowledge, but as I say, it happens all the time. It happens all the time and perhaps all intelligence agencies are guilty of doing it.[2]

Detectives were among the first police to connect with their counterparts overseas. Scotland Yard's fledgling investigative branch, formed in 1842, was frequently asked by continental European police to conduct surveillance on émigrés resident in Britain.[3] When the Metropolitan Police Criminal Investigation Department (CID) was formed in 1878, one of its duties was to carry out investigations for foreign governments, regularized by the formation in 1887 of the Special Irish Branch following an upsurge in the Fenian bombing campaign and anxieties about political assassinations.[4] The end of the nineteenth century saw a step-change in collaboration among police concerned with 'international anarchist

[1] Head of Special Branch, Caribbean police force.   [2] *Ibid.*
[3] Bernard Porter (1992), *Plots and Paranoia: A History of Political Espionage in Britain 1790–1988*. London: Routledge, ch 6.
[4] Such as that of Tsar Alexander II in St Petersburg in 1881 and the plot to assassinate Queen Victoria during her golden jubilee celebrations in 1887. Bernard Porter (1992), *Plots and Paranoia, op cit*, p 102.

terrorism' and the 1898 Rome Conference established protocols on sharing information about anarchists, extradition processes, and the use of the Bertillon criminal identification system based on physical measurements.[5] Investigating human trafficking—the 'white slave' trade—across Europe and the USA in the early twentieth century stimulated the development of an international police organization that would eventually become Interpol.[6] Occasionally, criminal investigations led detectives to travel overseas, to collect evidence, interview witnesses, or return suspects for trial. Investigating criminal conspiracies spanning several countries involved collaboration through overseas travel or using new developments in information and communications technologies.

In many respects, detective work in the Caribbean is similar to that in Britain or America; but because each island is a separate sovereign state, when a suspect flees, they go by boat and to a different country rather than across a state line or the boundary between police force areas. Much investigative work is reactive, initiated by the report of crime and requiring detectives to interview suspects or witnesses, take statements, and collect physical evidence all of which is geared to bringing suspects before a court. Other forms of crime are largely invisible to both police and public, such as the criminal conspiracies involved in illegal drugs movements through the islands. This clandestine trade is extensive and requires links with business people, politicians, and law enforcement officers and it only comes to light either by accident or through using covert techniques such as intercepting telephone calls, surveillance, running informers, and undercover operations. Because these conspiracies often reach into the heart of government, investigating them is a form of 'high policing' concerned with the integrity of the state itself, not necessarily geared towards prosecution, but seeking to prevent and disrupt the organization of crime.[7]

This chapter explores transnational policing from the perspective of operational police officers 'on the ground'. It is clear that

[5] Richard Bach Jensen (2001), 'The United States, International Policing and the War against Anarchist Terrorism 1900–1914', *Terrorism and Political Violence*, 13/1: 15–46.

[6] Willem Deflem (2004), *Policing World Society: Historical Foundations of International Police Cooperation*. Oxford: Oxford University Press; Richard Bach Jensen (2001), 'The United States, International Policing', *op cit*.

[7] Jean Paul Brodeur (1983), 'High and Low Policing: Remarks about the Policing of Political Activities', *Social Problems*, 30/5: 261–74.

policing the Caribbean islands involves a great degree of col-laboration among detectives. The previous chapter showed that significant developments were occurring at a high level among sen-ior officers; our concern here is to explore transnational policing *in practice*. It is tempting to think of transnational activity as that which occurs overseas. However, one of the contentions of this study is that *local* policing is increasingly globally interconnected (see table 1.1). The chapter examines both reactive and proactive investigations carried out by four investigative units within Car-ibbean police forces based largely on interviews with the senior officers in charge of the Criminal Investigation Department (CID) and Interpol National Central Bureaux (NCB), Special Branch (SB), and the Drug Squad. It describes their work, their perspectives and priorities, interaction with other law enforcement agencies locally and transnationally, and the practical issues arising from collaboration.

Reactive Investigation: CID and Interpol NCB

Formed in 1923, Interpol was intended to be a communication net-work promoting mutual assistance between police organizations.[8] Each member country has a National Central Bureau staffed by its own police officers. NCBs cannot be forced to comply with any directive issued centrally by Interpol, remaining bound by the operational context of the policing establishment in the host country within its own legal limits.[9] Although the NCBs facilitate communications between police agencies, de facto cooperation and information sharing depends on local police priorities, reci-procity, and political cooperation between member nations.

---

[8] The 1956 Interpol constitution states that its goal is to ensure and promote the widest possible mutual assistance between all criminal police authorities within the limits of the laws existing in the different countries and in the spirit of the Universal Declaration of Human Rights and to establish and develop all institutions likely to contribute effectively to the prevention and suppression of ordinary law crimes. Interpol is forbidden to undertake any intervention/activities of a political, mili-tary, religious, or racial character. Principles and regulations that govern coopera-tion are derived from national laws, bilateral treaties, and conventions.

[9] Malcolm Anderson (1989), *Policing the World*. Oxford: OUP; James Sheptycki (2004), 'The Accountability of Transnational Policing Institutions: The Strange Case of Interpol', *The Canadian Journal of Law and Society*, 19/1: 107–34.

Interpol provides four core functions.[10] First, it provides a secure global communication system, known as I-24/7, to which Caribbean all police forces were connected by 2003, enabling police forces from 187 countries around the world to communicate. Its main role is to circulate notices concerning wanted or suspected offenders, missing persons, and unidentified bodies.[11] The basic requirement for the issue of an Interpol Red Notice—the one most commonly circulated—is whether a person is the subject of an arrest warrant in a country where a prosecutor has said they will extradite the person if found abroad. Second, it provides databases on wanted persons, lost and stolen travel documents, DNA profiles, and fingerprints. Third, Interpol offers operational support, for managing such things as major international sporting events or responses to terrorist attacks and natural disasters. This is achieved through a command and coordination centre which links the General Secretariat with NCBs and regional offices. In recent years, Interpol has provided operational assistance to murder investigations in Jamaica and credit card fraud in Trinidad and Tobago.[12] The fourth function is training police forces to develop responses to serious transnational crime and terrorism.

Interpol National Central Bureaux

Formally, the Commissioner of Police is the head of the Interpol NCB in each Caribbean country. On a day-to-day basis on most islands, however, the bureau is managed by a sergeant who answers to the head of CID who reports to an Assistant Commissioner acting with delegated authority and is therefore able to take decisions without having to ask the Commissioner. In each Caribbean

[10] Stuart Cameron Waller (2008), 'Interpol: A Global Service-Provider' in Stephen David Brown (ed), *Combating International Crime: The Longer Arm of the Law*. London: Routledge-Cavendish.

[11] In 2008, Interpol issued 3,126 Red Notices (wanted persons), 304 Blue Notices (individuals of interest in relation to a crime), 664 Green Notices (warnings and intelligence about serious criminals), 385 Yellow Notices (missing persons), 91 Black Notices (unidentified bodies), 7 Orange Notices (dangerous materials, criminal acts, or events that pose a potential threat to public safety), and 26 INTERPOL-United Nations Security Council Special Notices (individuals associated with Al Qaeda and the Taliban, as listed by the 1267 Committee of the UN Security Council). In addition 13,339 diffusions were published in 2008.

[12] Interpol, *Annual Report*, 2007.

country the NCB is an integral part of the Criminal Investigation Department which provides easy access to other detectives. [13]

NCB heads saw their work changing because the 'world has become a global village'. In the past, if a person missed their mid-day transport, they would be unable to travel until the following day, but now that night-time travel by boat is possible, criminals are island hopping by patrol crafts under cover of darkness. One detective explained that,

> because we are so close and a fishing boat will travel from _____ to _____ every day, morning and evening. So if we have a crime down here now we will inform them, they will look out for that person. Almost every month there is somebody coming into _____ who is wanted for homicide in Trinidad, Dominica, or Barbados.

Ordinary crimes, including burglary and theft, may have a trans-national element. One detective claimed that in their island, among convicted burglars, 'half of them were foreigners, people from Trinidad, Saint Lucia, Grenada, Barbados, Martinique, Saint Kitts, to name a few of those islands'. The heads of CID believed that stolen goods are moved to other islands to be sold or traded for drugs.

The role of the NCB is to receive and send information on all types of crime, particularly taking account of the capacity of criminals to travel freely. When information reaches the office, the sergeant in charge of the unit assesses it in terms of the degree of confidentiality required, and decides whether or not to communicate with others. Information will sometimes involve people that the NCB is seeking abroad or concern issues arising from foreign nationals held in their custody. Information relating to a person wanted for questioning in connection with a murder on the island would be requested either by Interpol Red Notice, by 'diffusion' to all 187 countries on the Interpol system, or through a specific message to those countries most likely to be concerned. The head of one NCB

---

[13] Criminal Investigation Departments were established across the Caribbean by the 1930s. Gregor Davey (2009), 'A Brief Outline of British Caribbean Policing and Intelligence Structures: 1838–1970', 18 September 2009. Unpublished, King's College, London. Although the arrangements for managing crime investigation differ from place to place, the investigative capacity generally includes crime scenes officers with expertise in photography and physical evidence collection, fingerprint analysis, and ballistics. In some islands, the forensic science laboratory is an integral part of the criminal investigation division, in others it is a free-standing agency.

explained that they would receive a total of about 80 diffusion messages per day and between two and ten direct requests per day, with an average of about five. The NCB would be asked to investigate whether suspects wanted for crimes overseas had fled to their island and whether they hold any information about whether they had entered illegally. The NCB checks their local databases and responds, telling the foreign detective making the request whether there is a trace of the person or not. This leads naturally to extensive worldwide contacts, but most intensively with countries in the Caribbean region, the Americas, and Europe.

Many of the messages sent out by 'diffusion' are irrelevant to the islands. Rather than being assessed by Interpol headquarters, diffusions are sent out directly from the NCB to other member countries on the off-chance that a wanted person may have travelled to their country. Red Notices, naming a specific wanted person and to which particular items of evidence are attached, are the most important as well as the most numerous. The messages remain active for one year, informing police forces that they are looking for specific persons. Most messages are filed for later reference, since it is improbable that a person wanted for murder in, say, Singapore, will turn up on a Caribbean island. At present, only those specifically wanted within the region are checked; however, if a message indicates specific information such as family background to say, 'this person might travel to the following countries', then the NCB will carry out the checks:

when we receive the message, we check to see if they actually came into the island and we check to see if they are also criminally known here. If they did come into the island we would let them know that the person did travel and where they stayed and if we can come up with any associates we will pass on that information.

A detective would be assigned to the case to work discreetly, following up contacts, going through documents, photographs, and descriptions. An NCB head described a recent case involving a request from Canada seeking information about a man who was wanted for questioning about a suspected murder. Based on information about his childhood, the Caribbean detectives had reason to believe that he might have travelled to their country. Officers from the NCB liaised with the Canadian officers leading the investigation and with the detectives on the ground doing the checking. Once the suspect was located, the NCB informed Canada, confirming that he had in fact travelled to the island:

We told them that we had reason to believe that he was here, we got his photograph, we passed that on to the police in the district, and then we informed [the Canadians] that they should make a formal request for his extradition, even though they had given us an undertaking that they would. You need something more substantial in order to get a warrant, what they call a provisional warrant here in _____, for the extradition. The individual was then arrested.

Although it was quite common for requests to come from America, Britain, Canada, or elsewhere, the bulk of the work of the Interpol section involved collaboration among the Caribbean islands inter-island:

Yes, we get a lot of them coming in from _____, like they commit crimes. Two weeks ago I sent back two chaps back to _____. They came here and they were wanted for questioning for a murder in _____ and they are back there now. The guys were here and [an informer] leaked the information and my authorities contacted me to communicate with _____ and I did so and they were actually wanted. And actually they came here legally so they had passports and so on. I sent the passport number down along with a photograph, fingerprints, and they responded by saying the passport is linked with the bearer who I sent down there for them to check out, who's wanted, so they're saying the bearers of the passports that we have here, were the person who they were actually looking for down there.

There is a good working relationship among the Interpol NCBs, with Bureau heads knowing the names of all their counterparts in the region, having met on training courses at various points during their career. This was important for the establishment of trust:

if you know the person that you're communicating with you feel more comfortable to speak with the person, but if you don't know the person you may not want to put out everything that you really want to say, so it makes it easier if you know the person personally to actually communicate.

When heads of CID wanted information they would generally work through Interpol, contacting their counterparts within the region, conducting a person-to-person phone call to the head of CID in another country only when he knew his counterpart personally:

you go on courses and you will meet people sometimes and you exchange cards and so on and if you want something done in a hurry, if you know the person on a first name basis you can call the person and he say 'Look I have a problem with so-and-so', he work for me, he work on it speedily and it will be done.

Heads of CID saw a real need for secrecy in their dealings. For example, one said,

if I call my counterpart in _____ and he is not there, you have to be careful with whom you leave the message. So this is why I tell him 'pick up a fax, the fax will be there between such and such', and that he will go right there and get it because you never know who in that department will leak out the secret.

Training Interpol officers

Interpol training normally took place at the sub-regional bureau in Puerto Rico, coming under the General Secretariat with responsibility for the Caribbean. Several NCB heads were of the view that the sub-regional bureau should be in the Commonwealth Caribbean. As one explained,

I told them to do it right there five years ago in Barbados. Puerto Rico is our sub regional bureau, right and I told them, 'yes geographically they are in the Caribbean however the traditional methods are different from ours, the people are different than ours, the culture they are different from ours and they are dependant states in the USA.

Interpol staff selection and training highlights the importance of acquiring skills and creating informal networks. Training occurred in the region, mainly related to learning how to use the I-24/7 system and how to get the best out of its facilities. Other forms of training focused on developing common standards for data entry and storage and raising awareness within the home police force of what Interpol could offer. Some training also took place at Interpol headquarters in Lyon—described by one NCB head as 'the hub'. This related to dealing with the Interpol systems and developing an understanding of the General Secretariat and what was expected from the NCB. Training together within the region—and especially at Lyon—contributed to NCB officers feeling as though they were part of a global policing network linked together through Interpol. One NCB head said that Interpol officers tended to feel 'part of the whole':

I think most Interpol officers do feel a part of an agency in a way, but you do feel some sense of belonging to something that is accomplishing a goal, it's an agency by itself, even though you're under your different forces.

NCB heads saw themselves as operational police officers and very much integral to CID. Rather than simply exchanging information, they were directly involved in conducting investigations. Interpol officers saw themselves not only as people who handled outside information, but also took the opportunity to act upon it. Heads of NCB encouraged this to keep detectives 'court sharp', maintaining their interest in cases, remaining conscious of their contribution to the investigative task. 'When you're pushing people', one sergeant explained, they feel 'a little more motivated when you know that, yes, my work is culminating in this'. One NCB head recalled, 'going to a scene to arrest a guy, and I hear a communication on the wireless, which is questioning my actions, why am I operating as both a conduit for information and an investigator as well'. The operational work of Interpol is not only reactive work, but also includes strategic, covert work:

in some cases we've actually been underground, got people to operate electronic equipment to do videotaping, covert type, for a period of time, and when we decide that something may be happening or there may be a movement of people illegally, well we have to hit the ground.

Although they were aware of the presence of US and UK liaison officers in their territory, and they might meet them from time to time, generally heads of CID and NCBs had little to do with them. (The exceptions to this were the Interpol liaison officers and training officers who travelled to the region.) Detectives in reactive units rarely travelled abroad. When they did travel, this was typically for training and very occasionally to collect suspects and escort them into their custody for questioning. The work of the NCBs creates a bridge between the global network of Interpol and local policing. Rather than being a globally mobile individual, the evidence suggests that the Interpol officer is 'loosely coupled' transnationally with access to globally situated information but with local knowledge—the epitome of the *glocal* officer. They are, in Maureen Cain's evocative phrase, 'indigenous but globally aware'.[14]

Proactive Investigation

Bringing 'high policing' into the mainstream of police research is difficult, not least because it is obscured by the terminology used

---

[14] Maureen Cain (2000), 'Orientalism, Occidentalism and the Sociology of Crime', *British Journal of Criminology*, 40/2: 239–60.

to describe it.[15] We tend to use the terms 'spy', 'secret agent', espionage officer, or intelligence officer, to conceal the policing functions of the 'security and intelligence services' and the organizations involved in the surveillance of suspect populations.[16] In setting out legislation for his 'new' London Metropolitan Police in 1829, Peel explicitly rejected the 'continental' model. [17] Earlier Metropolitan Police Bills had failed to gain political support owing to public anxiety that creating a police force would lead to development of a network of police spies along the lines of the Napoleonic *mouchards*.[18] The British constitution enabled a paradoxical situation to arise in relation to the 'spy model' in law enforcement. The use of intelligence is referred to variously as the 'lifeblood of policing' and 'as old as policing itself',[19] despite Peel's reassurance that his 'new police' would be different from their continental counterparts. And yet these 'special investigative techniques' had no legal footing until the creation of the Regulation of Investigatory Powers Act 2000. The security and intelligence services have played an increasing role in ordinary law policing in Britain and this is reflected in their work in the Caribbean. During both World Wars, MI5 were actively involved in intelligence gathering across the colonies and this continued throughout the Cold War. By 1986, MI6 was involved in developing intelligence on drug trafficking and its destabilizing impact in some of the British dependent territories in the Caribbean.[20] The end of the Cold War and the ceasefire in Northern Ireland created the danger that the security and intelligence services would run out of business.[21] This was averted by

[15] Jean Paul Brodeur (1983), 'High and Low Policing', *op cit*; James Sheptycki (ed) (2000), *Issues in Transnational Policing*, *op cit*. London: Routledge, p 9.

[16] F. Donner (1980), *The Age of Surveillance: The Aims and Methods of America's Political Intelligence System*. New York: Alfred A. Knopf, cited by James Sheptycki (2000), *Issues in Transnational Policing, op cit*.

[17] Peel himself, while arguing for his new vigorous system of police, told parliament 'God forbid that he should mean to countenance of system of espionage', *Parliamentary Debates VII, 803*, cited by Clive Emsley (1996), *The English Police: A Political and Social History*. London: Longman, p 25.

[18] Clive Emsley (1996), *The English Police, op cit.*

[19] Jack Straw in introducing the Bill.

[20] Pete Gill (2000), *Rounding Up the Usual Suspects; Developments in Contemporary Law Enforcement Intelligence*. Aldershot: Ashgate, p 88, citing G. Warner (1998), 'Transnational Organised Crime and the Secret Agencies', *International Journal of Risk, Security and Crime Prevention*, 3/2: 147–9.

[21] Pete Gill (2000), *Rounding Up the Usual Suspects, op cit.*

lobbying in Whitehall[22] leading to the Intelligence Services Act 1994 which gave the Security and Intelligence Services a remit[23] and the Security Service Act 1996 which extended the mandate of MI5 into serious crime.[24] Since that time SIS and GCHQ have been tasked to undertake this work by the cabinet-level Joint Intelligence Committee.[25] In 2006, the Serious Organised Crime Agency (SOCA) was formed from a merger of the National Criminal Intelligence Service, National Crime Squad, and the enforcement arms of the Immigration Service and Customs with leadership posts taken by former MI5 and MI6 agents.[26] This cemented the role of secret intelligence in the policing of ordinary law crime.

Intelligence-led policing in the Caribbean

Intelligence-led policing has become an orthodoxy in the development of transnational law enforcement practice in the Caribbean. It was held among law enforcement officers that the globalization of crime and its movement across national boundaries facilitated by regional integration, including the free movement of labour under the CSME, necessitated this approach. As one Customs officer explained:

I'm going regional, when one considers that narco trafficking and its related ills affects all the countries in this region because, as you are aware, we tend to be sandwiched between the drug producers and the drug consumers and there is obviously a need for better and more co-ordination and exchange of timely and quality information and intelligence.

Many front-line police officers bemoaned the sense that current policing practice was still reactive. Reflecting on how far policing is 'intelligence-led' at the moment, one NCB head replied that:

I think we are getting there. Don't forget we would have come from reactive policing you know and we don't try to get away with that where predicting what is going to happen so we are going to put something in place before it happens. And that is maybe intelligence-led policing.

[22] *Ibid*, p 88.

[23] The Intelligence Services Act 1994 (covering SIS and GCHQ) ss 1 and 3.

[24] The Security Service Act 1989 (amended 1996).

[25] Pete Gill (2000), *Rounding Up the Usual Suspects*, *op cit*.

[26] Benjamin Bowling and James Ross (2006), 'The Serious Organised Crime Agency: Should We be Afraid?', *Criminal Law Review*, December 2006, pp 1019–34.

Most believed that the globalization of the drugs trade made it necessary to have a globally-mobile intelligence process, believing that interception of communications was essential to catch the 'big fish'. A senior officer explained that:

a drug dealer or a criminal operating in the Bahamas will think that, if he goes and sets up shop in London, 'nobody is listening to me any more', so they go and they talk more freely with Jamaica because they figure they're out of its jurisdiction. And then if we follow that and we set up with them over there then . . . you see how important that is to this global situation, and necessary.

An important factor pushing the growth of intelligence-led policing is the promulgation of the model by both UK and US officers. A UK law enforcement officer explained that:

Intelligence drives most policing today, it's got to because there are capacity problems even in the larger countries. To my knowledge there isn't an intelligence model for the Caribbean at the moment. . . they need a model over there, like the National Intelligence Model in the UK. That was formed because we've got so many different police services there—we don't have a national police service—that the NIM actually was a way of pulling those services together.

Both the UK and US are pushing for legislative changes to enable the interception of communications. UK FCO representatives have a political role in trying to influence a government to pass such legislation (see Chapter 8). This touches on local sensitivities about opposition accusations of government eavesdropping. It would allow US officers to intercept mobile phone conversations locally, even if these could never be used as evidence in a criminal trial in any of the Caribbean territories.

Caribbean Special Branches

Caribbean Special Branches were set up during the late 1940s and early 1950s to monitor 'political threats' during the Cold War and to shoulder the 'responsibilities of decolonization'.[27] In

---

[27] As one official report put it, 'Having given the rider the reins, we are not absolved from responsibility for the horse'. *Report of the British Guiana Constitutional Commission* (The Robertson Commission Report), presented by the Secretary of State for the Colonies to Parliament by Command of Her Majesty, September 1954. London HMSO, Cmd 9274.

1947 the Defence Security Officers employed by MI5 to conduct counter-intelligence and to offer advice and liaison during wartime were reappointed as security liaison officers who travelled around the Caribbean islands and to London 'advising and passing information of interest both up and down the system'.[28] These officers, together with the Inspector General of Colonial Police (IGCP) encouraged the creation, equipping, and training of Special Branches in each country. These took some time to establish, to recruit informers, to develop intelligence-recording systems, and to gain the relevant skills. The first SB course run by MI5 was in 1945 for some officers of the Trinidad Constabulary.[29] Courses were held in Britain for uniformed officers as well as SB heads at Bramshill and Ryton on Dunsmore.[30] SB chiefs reported to Commissioners and directly to the Chief Secretary in the Defence Section[31] which were later formalized into special Local Intelligence Committees, including the SLO which were asked to submit intelligence reports to London on security threats.[32] In the last days of Empire, one head of SB recalled:

there was a lot of input and cooperation from the British because there was actually a Liaison Officer who used to travel to all the Special Branches in the Caribbean to share information. At that time we didn't have computers, and we hadn't telephones and all that, you know, and that person would travel from country to country in the Caribbean carrying diplomatic correspondence and so on through the countries in the Caribbean.

---

[28] J.C. Curry (1999), *The Security Service 1908–1945: The Official History*. London: PRO and CO537/4287, *Functions of Security Liaison Officers in the Colonies 1949*, both cited by Gregor Davey (2009), 'A Brief Outline of British Caribbean Policing and Intelligence', *op cit*.

[29] J.C. Curry, *ibid*, cited by Davey (2009), *op cit*.

[30] CO1035/54, *Security Service Training for Special Branch Officers from the Colonies Caribbean Area 1955*, CO1035/55, *Security Service Training courses for senior overseas police officers on intelligence and security subjects Special Branch Training 1955*, cited by Davey (2009), *op cit*.

[31] CO537/2784, *Review of Police and Security Forces in Relation to Communist Infiltration Trindad*, 1948 letter from Sir John Shaw, Governor of Trinidad to Secretary of State, 8 October 1948. Cited by Davey (2009), *op cit*.

[32] CO1035/45, *Organisation of Intelligence in the Colonies: Trinidad 1954–56*, circular letter 458/56 from Secretary of State to Colonial Governors, 28 April 1948. Cited by Davey (2009), *op cit*.

Semi-formal links were maintained by British police officers travelling the region.[33] Special Branch heads had their own regional conference annually during the 1950s which enabled intelligence sharing among island police forces.[34] At the end of the Cold War, the role of SB shifted seamlessly to gathering intelligence on drug trafficking and organized crime. As one head of SB explained:

Since it has been Special Branches, the law enforcement agencies that have been doing that intelligence all along, the shift in focus now does not create a difficulty because they have been engaged in that kind of activity over the years so the focus does not make the actual training and type of exercise that you do any different. We've been doing it all the time.

Special Branch heads saw drugs trafficking as their main priority, but were concerned about deportees and illegal firearms, the upsurge in violent crime, and all the 'criminal activities that accompany illegal drugs and guns, kidnappings, money laundering, corruption'. Drug-related activities were of greatest concern including the 'illegal firearms which can be used to commit other crimes, crimes that are committed because drug deals have gone bad and the fact that people want to get money to buy drugs'. These, one SB officer argued, are 'more threatening and more damaging than the actual passage of drugs' through the islands. Special Branch officers saw terrorism and drugs trafficking as linked threats and were more concerned about the threat of terrorism than any other officers, including the Commissioners:

While there is not a direct threat to [this island] or the countries of the Caribbean, there is the potential for terrorism to come to the region because of the presence of citizens from countries that are targeted by terrorists, namely Americans, British, Australians, and people also who were in the war in Iraq, so the mere presence of large numbers of those citizens in the Caribbean presents a target for terrorists, and while the region is physically far removed from the home base of terrorists, it is not so far

---

[33] The Metropolitan Police SB had a particular interest in West Indian migrants in the UK. SB were known to have obtained intelligence on leading figures within London's black communities such as Claudia Jones whose views were considered 'outside the parameters of acceptable political activity' (Whitfield, *Unhappy Dialogue*, p 71–4). What the precise connections were between work in the region and domestic Special Branch work is only now being documented (see, for example, Davey 2009), *op cit*.

[34] CO1035/11, *Annual Meeting Between Special Branch Representatives and the Security Liaison Officers Barbados*, 7–8 June 1956. The site of this conference moved each year. Cited by Davey (2009), *op cit*.

removed that it is not accessible and they may see the region as what we refer to as a soft target, where security is not as tight, . . . We do not have the resources that larger, developed countries have to put into protecting the island as well and therefore it's a real threat.

Heads of SB felt that the relationship with the USA skewed the security agenda, particularly through donor-beneficiary relationships. Why, they wondered, was so much effort being spent in eradicating marijuana within the Caribbean region when California produces so much of its own. The issue of US dominance was also related to issues like barriers to visas, limited entry into the USA, and 'being treated like second class citizens'. One head of SB argued that:

policy is always skewed to some extent by developed countries, based on what their threats are or where their interest lies. At the end of the day, they have to satisfy their representatives and their voters that they are spending their money on the efforts in the right direction, and although we would like to see different policies and different programmes, I think perhaps we need to try to convince them more at the policy level that that's what's needed because it is not something that they will do automatically just for your interests. Foreign policy will always be in a country's interests.

The role of the SB officer

Special Branch is one of the main intelligence-gathering units of the police force.[35] As one superintendent put it:

In some circles we are seen as the eyes and ears of the government. . . . Regardless of which government is in power, we have to inform the government as to what is really taking place in terms of national security, what is happening in [this country].

Some of what is referred to as intelligence is simply ordinary information, about smuggling trends, concealment methods, and estimates of the size of drug markets based on recent seizures. However, a distinction must be made between strategic *open source* and *secret* intelligence. As one Caribbean police officer put it, 'If you don't need to know I don't tell you because if I tell you it's not considered intelligence anymore because everybody would know, you

---

[35] SB is also tasked with the job of providing diplomatic protection for ministers and visiting VIPs. In some places it is also the head of immigration (see Chapter 6).

see.' An intelligence officer described a key aspect of their work as driving around the island looking at all the new, expensive residences, presenting a *prima facie* case for investigation, followed up by checks examining who owns the property, their source of income, whether their property development seemed affordable, and who their contacts are. 'Good social skills' were described as being at the heart of the role of the intelligence officer: 'if you are not a person who can hold a good conversation and might be able to get into someone's mind and speak to somebody so that you can get the information, you are nowhere, you know.' The essence of the job of the intelligence officer—expressed most cogently by a Customs officer—was the ability to elicit information subtly from a range of sources.[36] As one intelligence officer put it:

'If you're talking about elicitation, that is a different thing altogether. . . . that is not peculiar to this region; that operates all over the world. You could easily go to any metropolitan country and using your craft, you could elicit the information you want.

One head of SB described how they went about their work in cooperation with officers overseas:

You would have formal meetings to talk with your counterparts in the other islands to see what their threats are, what their situation is and so on, [but] you can talk to anybody in the street, you go to lunch, you can talk to anybody, you drive a car around and you're entitled to talk to anybody, and this is one of the things that intelligence officers do. You never know what you discover.

It was vitally important, he argued, for intelligence officers to blend in with the crowd, enabling 'innocent probing', used to build an intelligence picture:

you're just an ordinary person in a Caribbean country moving around. People don't really know who you are. Intelligence officers by nature probe. You may not be doing it consciously but it's one of the traits, you probe. Sometimes you discover things and sometimes you don't, but sometimes you discover very significant things just by probing innocently.

---

[36] The US government advises that 'in the spy trade, elicitation is the term applied to subtle extraction of information during an apparently normal and innocent conversation. Most intelligence operatives are well trained to take advantage of professional or social opportunities to interact with persons who have access to classified or other protected information'. <http://www.usda.gov>.

One important role for SB in some locations was to act as the contact point for visiting overseas police and intelligence officers, who would speak to the head of SB, assigning them a detective constable or station sergeant to act as their driver and minder. The head of Special Branch would then trust delegated officers to work closely with visiting officers or agents, whilst not asking for details of the operation:

even though all of us are Special Branch officers, there are some things which a Special Branch officer would not tell another Special Branch officer and you can't go away from that. Some things I wouldn't tell certain officers. [The station sergeant] is the one who has been trusted to work along with them and, you know, they can confide in her and they can talk to her about the person who they are monitoring and stuff like that.

This is an interesting, if largely overlooked aspect of transnational police cooperation. Except where they are working autonomously or are strictly desk-bound, each overseas officer must link with a local counterpart upon whom they must rely for local information, guidance, and quite possibly transport and physical protection. This represents a significant commitment of resources for the host police force. It creates bonds of trust, but also distances the accompanying police officer from their colleagues.

Regional SB networks

Special Branch officers saw sharing intelligence with their counterparts on other islands as central to their role. Officers became familiar through periodic contact by phone, fax, and computer, and meeting on training courses. Mostly they travel for training purposes rather than to carry out investigations. These are made largely through requests to officers overseas, done typically, 'officer to officer. We write a memo, send it, or a fax requesting some checks'. The frequency of contact would vary from place to place and subject to subject:

We would keep in contact but unless there is something that we are working on and that can vary so that this month you may talk for three weeks of that month but next month you may not speak at all, and then, depending on the nature of the exercise, they may speak to me or they may speak to Narcotics or they may speak to Interpol or they may speak to Financial Investigations.

A Heads of Special Branch conference is held annually involving Antigua, Saint Vincent, Dominica, Grenada, Saint Lucia, Barbados, Belize, Trinidad and Tobago, Jamaica, Guyana, British Virgin Islands, Bahamas, as well as the Netherlands Antilles and Martinique. This is held in different islands on rotation with the head of SB in the conference location acting as coordinator for that year, enabling countries to share intelligence reports among SB heads. For one head of SB it was vitally important that they 'gather together and discuss our problems with regards to national security [and] we know who we can talk to in terms of any problem that we may have in each country'. In each country, the head of SB produced and shared a threat assessment so 'everyone will have each person's report so we will actually know what is happening in each country as it relates to the security'. Liaison officers from UK Customs, the US Drugs Enforcement Administration (DEA) and sometimes MI5, MI6, CIA, and other secret service agents attended these meetings:

We have people on the ground who work along with [UK Customs Officer] and these kind of guys. We may be able to make some hits with people from the DEA and stuff like that who come in and assist us and so on from time to time but we can't capture everything.

This provided the opportunity to establish trust between counterparts, which was described as 'fundamentally important':

as much as you talk to people on the telephone and via the Internet and so on, it is so useful to be able to sit with people and get to know them and to talk about things that are affecting you because there are some little things, or things that people may perceive as not significant, even among experienced intelligence officers, which may very well be significant to another person but is not passed to somebody else because it seems so insignificant.

As in other spheres, trust is seen by these officers as highly important, both the sharing of valuable information and also to prevent it from leaking out to people who might abuse it. This is a central paradox in intelligence gathering: that there is a need to share even apparently trivial information in order to make the necessary connections, and yet there are dangers in sharing that information beyond those that 'need to know'.

The Drug Squad

The Drug Squad (DS) is the specialist unit of the police force leading law enforcement efforts against drug trafficking. Naturally, this is viewed by officers in charge as the most significant security threat to the region, along with the broader context of unemployment, poverty, and the attendant ills of armed violence and corruption:

There is within the Caribbean a lot of poverty and unemployment. What drug trafficking does is use those unemployed poor people to facilitate the trade. Drug trafficking creates or is responsible for the majority of violence that we have within [our] society and by extension the Caribbean as well. With drug trafficking comes the arms trade and it makes available firearms which we are seeing more now than years before.

The role of the head of the Drug Squad is to plan strategies to deal with the law enforcement efforts against drug trafficking and to implement those strategies. He supervises operations and investigations, covering ports, airports, and seaports, and liaises with external law enforcement bodies in the carrying out of those duties. One head of DS described his role as both strategic and operational:

I have to bridge the gap between the strategic and the operational, so, you know, in spite of the fact that the strategy is supposed to come from [the Commissioner's Office], it does come, but to a great extent I have to do strategies as well, and this is not just operational strategy, it is strategy for the direction of the organization in the future, which is what I have been doing over the last couple of years. So I straddle the strategic and the operational, I supervise the operations and the investigations and so on and see to the implementation of the strategy.

Heads of Drug Squads liaise with counterparts in other Caribbean territories, collaborating with the American FBI, DEA, Customs, and Citizenship and Immigration Services, British Customs and Metropolitan Police, and the Royal Canadian Mounted Police. Each law enforcement agency is concerned with the same issues and is often focused on the same targets. Operations like Caribe Storm, Hurricane, and Summer Storm, described by the US Embassy as involving 20 countries, 1,000 arrests and large amounts of drugs seized tended to be coordinated by the USA based on an agreement that a concerted effort would be made over a specific period of time. The USA would provide intelligence on the flow of narcotics through the region. On this basis:

each country prepares a plan that would interdict drugs throughout for a period of two weeks maybe and that plan is submitted then be linked up. . . . And there are things to target like go-fasts and that kind of stuff which can be followed through the same system. So in a way it looks like if there is 'an operation' in the sense that there's commanders there but instead of giving instructions it's just coordinating basically and each country operates with themselves within their country's plan.

In operations, the lead organization with primacy is always the host country. As one head of DS explained:

In a joint operation the host country, always has primacy and has the operational lead in joint operations, and the different agencies come together precisely [because] we need all of the diverse expertise at the table.

Heads of Drug Squad pointed out that while resources and equipment might have been donated by metropolitan countries, they are never more than supporting partners in the operation and simply give advice. The UK and the US have resources and expertise but control is not a nominal thing. 'We are in charge', one superintendent insisted:

True, it is DEA sponsored in the sense that DEA is like the common thread in all the operations in all the countries, they pull everybody together and say, 'Hey listen, we need to do this in the region', and sometimes they give us money, most of the time they give us money, and they set up a central coordinating centre where all the information is fed into, but the operation on the ground here in [this country], it belongs to us, we have sole ownership. The DEA coordinates from the perspective of, like an overlord in the whole thing, but we have ownership of our operations, we are going after our traffickers, we are prosecuting them in our courts. We sometimes benefit from the intelligence that the DEA or anybody else has, but the operation is fully owned by [us] and what they will get out of it is ours.

On the other hand, this superintendent admitted that it was not at all 'far-fetched' that overseas law enforcement officers would feel that because they are paying for the equipment, they would have a right to say how it is used.

He who pays the piper always tries to call the tune, but in [this country] we sit down at the table and we take advice, and if we think that it is not good advice then we kindly just tell them in a kind way that, 'Hey listen here, this is not . . .' and especially from time to time people will try to do things, have you do things, that are inconsistent with your laws and so on in your country. . . . The good thing though is that we always, the majority of the time we have the same goals. . . . and so it is not uncommon for us to take the kind of advice that we take from DEA, UK Customs.

Sometimes there is a problem with the method because it depends on how you go about doing certain things . . . so sometimes there are problems with the method, but generally speaking we are able to cooperate because we all share the same ideals.

One of the key advantages of working with liaison officers from the UK and US is that they bring new skills, ideas, and—above all—information to the table. This information was often obtained from sources overseas or obtained from confidential informants or from interception of communications:

they have a piece of the puzzle that we don't have. They know their operators up there and we know ours here and we are learning the links between their operators and our operators, and in forging this alliance, police on police, we are able to understand and to see the bigger picture, the bigger picture in the drug trafficking community in _____ and _____, and in Colombia. And we were not able to make the kind of inroads that we have been making in the last two or three years until we appreciated the fact that we needed to work together, and that is the main advantage, the main benefit that comes from cooperation.

The network amongst drug enforcement officers was such that they tended to be on first name terms with their counterparts in the neighbouring islands, those nearer to the South American mainland and those towards the USA. Drug Squad commanders felt a need to be in contact with their counterparts in continental South America, but despite having wide ranging contacts with regional law enforcement agencies in Colombia, Venezuela, and Panama, much of the operational work was done through liaison officers from the metropolitan countries:

a lot of the time we find that it is much easier working through intermediaries like the DEA and HM Customs and Excise. These organizations have representatives in Colombia and these reps are much closer to the Colombian people than we are . . . so these reps are able to liaise with the Colombian people and through their reps here in [this country] who will sometimes channel information to us and requests and so on, so that we are able to tie up that link between [us] and the Colombians.

All interviewees spoke of the importance of establishing personal contacts as a way of overcoming the barrier of mistrust:

I think to avoid that, from time to time our officers need to have conferences and that's why they encourage, especially the need to have the drug commanders' conference in different countries and we all attend the conference, so after a while we can tell of this one to one, so if I have something I will call the head of drugs, I wouldn't just call any person because we would have developed that relationship.

The Caribbean drug commanders' conference used to meet immediately prior to the ACCP AGM in order to be able to report directly to the Commissioners (see Chapter 3). Now the drug commanders have developed an independent network, so while reports are still produced and sent to the ACCP secretariat, the link is not so direct. One of the region's drug commanders acts as secretariat to the drug commanders' conference, seen as an important way to link up regularly to establish what he called the 'good old boys' network':

You get to see the same people over and over, you share telephone contacts, you have email addresses and so on, and if there is a problem in _____ that has its origins in _____ I can pick up my telephone here, I can look in my thing here, pick up my cell phone and dial my friend's cell phone anywhere in _____, he might be on the road, and he takes this number and he answers and he says, 'Okay, I can tell you, this is what I know' or 'I'll get back to you in a few minutes', and you have the information right on your desk in a few minutes.

In one sense, he argued, these are formal relationships based on the sharing of contact details during training courses and conferences. 'Real good friendships' are established enabling informal contacts, eradicating the need for 'formal formal' networks, like a memorandum of understanding. A UK law enforcement officer expressed a strongly opposing view on the value and significance of informal intelligence gathering in the UK. In his view, what he described as 'informal gateways' for intelligence have long been abandoned in Britain:

informal gateways for intelligence kill trials in this country. If you cannot predicate your activity on the basis of solid intelligence that is recorded, there is an audit trail, you can take it right back to the source and prove it to a judge, if you cannot do that, you wave goodbye to about £3 million-worth of job.

Informal information sharing is clearly problematic in terms of evidential value, but it has other purposes. Only once trust, rapport, and open communication has been established is it possible to exchange information and 'interact effectively'.

Issues in Intelligence-Led Transnational Policing

It was widely held among operational police officers that attempting to prevent or disrupt organized crime required the use of covert policing techniques. A head of SB argued that 'if you're really trying to control or trying to stop drug trafficking, the only way to address it is to go undercover because it is so large, so much money is involved'. Although deemed necessary, it was also seen to be difficult to work undercover in a small island context. A lack of resources including personnel, technical equipment, and money, is a major barrier, limiting the amount of work they could take on and the techniques they could use. Although they carry out covert operations, this is limited because of the nature of policing small societies.

In Britain it is a lot easier to be covert because of the size of the country and the nature of the population and the nature of the environment as well as the fact that you have much better resources to do covert work than most Caribbean countries had at one stage, you know. In developing countries it is sometimes difficult to have those resources . . . so it's a lot more difficult and therefore we used to tend to get a lot of our information from open sources, but we do do covert work as well.

Generally, there is not the funding to carry out such operations. Moreover, the likelihood for undercover officers' cover to be 'blown' is great. There is a need to ensure that undercover officers are safe, taking action if the situation becomes troubled since they do not have the equipment to transmit and receive covert information. They do small 'buy and bust' operations, but don't have the capacity for deep cover operations. One officer commented that 'we don't have the legislation that will allow a whole lot of things. A lot of times we get visits from developed countries and they ask, "how the hell do you do anything here?"'.

One of the main problems was the extent of kinship networks preventing the concealment of identity:

They seem to know who your father is, who your mum is, your sister probably went to school with someone, so a lot of relatives involved, so it's very difficult to go undercover in [this country]. I could leave [the capital] today and go to another part of the island but they know exactly who I am as soon as I get there, they know, they say, 'Oh that's him from CID' or they'll say 'him from the police', so you really cannot do any undercover work [here], so the DEA will actually do the undercover side of it so if they want to come in and join in an undercover operation you will see that from the US side.

A pragmatic response to this is to bring in officers from outside, especially the USA where undercover operations are part of law enforcement practice, lasting months or years. DEA agents would pose as pilots, boat captains, or drugs buyers, participating in, and even infiltrating smuggling organizations. Local law enforcement agents would be informed only on a 'need-to-know-basis'. If arrests were made, the undercover operatives would also be arrested with the local police simply acting as though all of the people involved were criminals. Not all agreed that working undercover was beneficial. For example, a UK Customs liaison officer believed them to be expensive and dangerous. 'It's a very personal thing', he argued, 'I've been involved in undercover work, I think it's a nightmare and I'm not always convinced of the benefits of what you get out of it.'

A controversial aspect of covert policing is the use of 'controlled delivery': the practice of observing the movement of drugs from a source or trans-shipment country to its final destination.[37] It offers the prospect of arresting importers as well as couriers and may lead to further intelligence about the 'clean skins' behind the operation through intelligence sharing. If, for example, British intelligence informs that a shipment is passing through one of the islands, local SB and Drug Squad might have information about the target's contacts then a joint operation can be planned. An obvious objection is that if drugs are passing through an island and being handled by citizens or foreign nationals, there is an imperative for the authorities to intercept. Heads of SB disagreed, arguing that this should not be a barrier to cooperation. Controlled delivery therefore requires a high degree of cooperation and an agreement about 'non-enforcement' of criminal activities. It is a high risk strategy because if there is an intelligence failure or leak, then the drugs may not be interdicted at the final destination.

The whole question of controlled deliveries, is something that requires co-ordination among several different agencies and sometimes more than one nationality . . . Although in effect an individual would not know that a controlled delivery has been made, it is something which I think needs to be kept a little bit more under the carpet, especially where jurisdictions

---

[37] Stephen David Brown (2008), 'Controlled Deliveries' in Stephen David Brown (ed), *Combating International Crime: The Longer Arm of the Law*. London: Routledge.

do not necessarily have a legal basis from which they can deal with certain aspects of this controlled delivery.

While there is some communication between NCB, DS, and SB, the proactive units rely on networks within their own specialist areas. In particular, the Interpol NCB was not seen by Special Branch as a good conduit for information:

I don't know where Interpol is in _____ or in _____, whether it's in another district or whether it's in police headquarters, whether the head of Special Branch has access to it, how difficult it is to gain access. I know it is not in his office so, you know, if you use that system, by what means are you going to reach the head of Special Branch? Can you say, 'Well okay I'll get him, I'll call back in the next ten minutes or so', so there are logistic difficulties when it comes to using those systems.

There were some exceptions: Special Branch use Interpol for carrying out security checks on persons; Interpol always inform SB of terrorism watch lists, people suspected of involvement in terrorism, known to be passing through the islands. Sometimes other officers from detective, uniformed, other branches, or other organizations will approach the NCB with information for the Interpol bureau alone. The head of CID said that the biggest problem was sharing information within his own service:

We have five or six different people doing intelligence and nobody knows what the other is doing, so I am very aware because there is two different units meet up in the same house, so we have the Assistant Commissioner for Crime he is now trying to put something together.

There were also times where communication is inadequate between island police forces:

there is not a conference for heads of CID and it is always something that I thought should happen, right, because we are just separated by a couple of miles and issues that affect one island generally affect the other. . . . Interpol has to send a fax, has to send documents, but you might want to ask them something that you don't want somebody else to hear.

One NCB sergeant spoke favourably about opening up Interpol systems to other law enforcement agencies, such as immigration and Customs, whose databases would be useful for name searches and sharing information on concealment methods (see Chapter 6). There is, however, a tendency for organizations to guard their empires, which was a major barrier to cooperation. Although access may be restricted for security reasons, one officer argued that while it is human nature to:

hold onto what is yours and guard it fiercely. . . if you are saying that we are running the forces of the Caribbean by intelligence and it is intelligence-led policing, it means that you have to open up and share.

The widespread use of informal networks raises questions about the integrity of the system and the possibilities for abuse:

if I'm sending a message from Interpol to Southern Division I'll send them what you call an official telephone message, making note of the time, the person receiving it and so on. We still practice here, for instance, at times that when a person calls from abroad we make a note. We may not have all the details but you may have official conversation . . . That protects us to some extent, to at least show that a call was received. It doesn't eliminate the possibility that somebody could be malicious. We can't eliminate the possibility but we minimize it.

One head of SB said that the 'level of communication has been a sore point for some time' between other intelligence agencies within the Caribbean and among 'friendly countries' such as the US, Britain, and Canada. Part of the reason for this is the problem of establishing trust:

It may happen that the head of Special Branch is being changed in one of the other islands, you know, sometime this year and therefore sometimes there's a difficulty in knowing who you're talking with in another country. . . . but I think more important than that is the absence of proper systems to communicate safely and those are lacking. Computer systems aren't safe unless you're going to encrypt them, so some kind of encrypted voice communication or computer communication network would suffice.

Opposition to the interception of communications relates not just to privacy, but also an anxiety that such technology would be used to spy on politicians from opposition political parties. One informant explained that the role of the SB in the 'old days' would be to spy on 'political enemies'. Special Branch would listen to what was happening in the opposition political camp and then brief the Prime Minister. One SB head noted that:

in some countries, because of the nature of their domestic political arrangements, some Special Branches are particularly close to political figures. That is not the case in [this island], has never been the case since I worked at Special Branch. I think we are very fortunate to be able to maintain an apolitical stance and have a more objective view of what's happening.

Another problem is the difficulty in distinguishing rumour and hearsay from valuable intelligence, especially when it comes to the issue of police corruption. Several detectives pointed out that Caribbean people 'love a lot of rumour mongering'. The problem is that:

everyone knows everyone. You walk down any road and they're shouting, 'Hey what's up?' And so it's not, I mean not a real friend, but because of the friendly nature of everyone here everyone gets along well and we talk to each other. Sometimes that does not necessarily mean that you are involved with someone, you have to have the evidence actually to say, 'Well, yes, there's a lot of corruption'.

What is required is a rigorous process through which intelligence is 'developed' and checked. Without this, there is a risk that inaccurate or even malicious information could be passed on. As one intelligence officer put it:

it would be embarrassing for someone if you are to make someone in authority like the Commissioner of Police, the Prime Minister, the Minister of National Security, to take some action against someone when it is not so.

The head of SB was also concerned that new legislation protecting human rights and privacy was creating a barrier to the collection and dissemination of intelligence.

Intelligence sharing with metropolitan countries

Heads of SB complained that there was an imbalance in the sharing of intelligence between Caribbean locations and the metropolitan countries:

They won't give it. But they want to work with, you know. Sometimes they want to do a study on something, they may invite you to a big conference, get all the heads together, and they do it on the computer. And they format a big document and when they are done they send you home and they've got the document for their own study. So you come back home with nothing, or you go and you just talk talk talk, you never come back with a sense of achievement. . . . Sometimes they might not even get back in touch with you weeks on end. While we need help, we need help sometimes with tangible equipment to help us in some kind of ways or the other, you know.

The head of SB saw the failure to share intelligence as 'yet another characteristic failing of intelligence agencies'. He was sanguine about problems of intelligence sharing with metropolitan countries:

I believe that all agencies normally will look at information and decide what to share with you. The amount of information that is being shared then how small that information is you should be able to take that information and work with it. You should not say, 'Well the British people only give me a small bit so I'm not going to work on it', you know, or 'the DEA give me a lot so I'm not going to look at the British'.

The key point, however, was that while access to databases was important, informal personalized systems were more effective than formal systems.

Sometimes, because of a lack of capacity, information that could be acted upon within a country is not passed on to other authorities. For example, there may be intelligence that a person is leaving an airport having swallowed drugs. It may not be possible to act on this in a timely fashion within the country so the authorities might allow the person to travel on to another Caribbean territory or to the UK or USA, informing those authorities. In recent years the exchange of information had been made easier by two interconnected factors. Firstly, the requirement to use formal vertical channels of communication has been relaxed. Secondly, the availability of mobile telephones has made the need for formal channels of communication largely redundant:

What happens with our phone because of a lack of financing, we can only make local calls from the telephones here so definitely there were no calls. As a matter of fact there was one time this entire complex had one phone that had access overseas and that's the grand chief so if you need to make a call you need to get clearance from him and use his phone to make the call.

A mobile phone allows operational officers, such as head of Drug Squad, to phone overseas, with the bill for equipment and calls picked up by the UK or USA. One Drug Squad head explained that he had a monthly budget for calls on the mobile phones provided by the US DEA, so only uses the mobile phone when absolutely necessary. Otherwise he would use email.

The view of the superintendent heading one Drug Squad was that they cannot cooperate without a shared understanding and a common culture, but also the need for funding and the provision of communications systems, as there is 'no way it is going to happen unless it's funded'. Heads of Special Branch saw their role expanding over the next five years with more human resources and equipment available. Officers in the larger territories were also of the view that there was a need for decentralization and the creation of district posts. The view is that they:

> need to have persons on the ground, a lot of sensitive areas where we can have intelligence gathered. It shouldn't be just centralized or when we want information we send a guy out onto the ground, we should have spread out so that we have everything cooperated properly.

One further reason for the growth in the intelligence-gathering role of Special Branch relates to a widening gap between police and public and a lack of trust. As one officer put it, '[g]one are the days when we would walk down the road and somebody would tell you something. It's not that the police force is that divided from the citizen, but people have their different feelings about certain police officers'. The belief that many police were corrupt and that information might be leaked back to organized crime groups was a major barrier to gathering information from civilians.

Tensions in multinational cooperation

By virtue of the Commonwealth Scheme on Mutual Legal Assistance, information can be shared with counterparts.[38] This enables police officers to travel to other Commonwealth Caribbean territories, to collect information, interview witnesses, take drug samples, then return with that evidence to prepare for prosecution. For the USA, there is a requirement to work through a Mutual Legal Assistance Treaty (MLAT). Officers must apply through the central authority, the DPP or the prosecutorial authority within the country. The central authority, even without an MLAT (in the case of Colombia, for example), can provide permission for another country to come and gather evidence.

Operational heads were aware that officers from metropolitan countries ran their own informers and sometimes worked undercover. One head of the Drug Squad argued that 'people will have

---

[38] This is not a legally binding agreement but a mutual understanding that the Commonwealth states will provide assistance. See Clive Harfield (2007), 'From Empire to Europe: Evolving British Policy in Respect of Cross-Border Crime, *The Journal of Policy History*, 19/2; David McClean (1988), 'Mutual Assistance in Criminal Matters: The Commonwealth Initiative', *The International and Comparative Law Quarterly*, 37/1: 177–90.

their sources of information', and that they 'would want to use all the skills and resources at their disposal to get information'. But, one insisted, 'that's not enforcement'. No officer from overseas could engage in enforcement activity within the territory of another state. However, defining what 'enforcement' actually means is problematic. For the operational heads, 'effecting arrests, conducting searches and what we call raids' were examples of enforcement, as was the conduct of formal suspect interviews. Running informers and collecting intelligence were not enforcement. The key point is that collecting confidential information is—by definition—secret, but it did not infringe sovereignty because no enforcement activity was occurring.

Whatever is happening between them and their confidential sources is really a man talking to another man really and true, they can produce that later on in court or whatever, but as far as enforcement is concerned, you know, you have to define enforcement strictly, as far as *enforcement* is concerned they do not have jurisdiction here.

Carrying out test purchases while posing as a buyer would go beyond what was permissible and would be illegal. One head of DS was adamant on this point:

No, no, no, no, these, no, no, no, no, no, not at all, no such thing, they can't do that. They cannot go to buy drugs and stuff like that, no way. All of that is illegal. . . . I can't say that it has never happened. They have all their cars with the diplomatic plates, they work from the embassy. If a confidential DEA informant has to come from overseas to come here he has to get clearance from here, you know. They have to inform us.

For the operational heads of unit, the issue of enforcement is a matter, firstly, of the use of coercive force. Employing force against a citizen could only ever be a matter for the police of that country and therefore only they could make lawful arrests. It did not matter where the information came from on which the arrest was based, nor that the arrest was made at the request of a third party, nor necessarily whether the requesting party was at the scene at the time (although several officers did explain that it was preferable for overseas officers to stay in their vehicles or better still in their offices). What mattered was that force was, and was seen to be, deployed by the local police. The second issue concerned the collection of evidence that would be admissible in court. One of the Drug Squad heads explained that:

anybody can go anywhere and gather evidence, you know, but it will not be admissible in court if it was not gathered in the proper way and this is the reason for all these formal treaties and agreements and arrangements.

The officers felt that the results of collaboration can be satisfactory in the sense that the capacity to keep a person in custody, secure a conviction, and sentence a person to a very long prison term was greater in the USA than in any of the Caribbean territories. One Drug Squad commander said that he was pleased with collaboration with the USA knowing that a person would be sentenced to a very long jail term, sometimes extending to life sentences. Some officers took a very pragmatic view that action was acceptable if it helped to dismantle organized crime groups and made their countries safer. But, in terms of carrying out arrests based on evidence, those coming from a metropolitan country would have to be secured by an arrest warrant issued locally.

The only ways that we would arrest someone is having information from overseas as if we find there are two types of things here. One, if there is a request for extradition then there would be a provisional warrant for arrest. We arrest and there is no liability on us. . . . On the other hand if they provide information that there may be drugs or something in a house then we get a search warrant to search. Again, we search under a warrant, we are not liable for the search.

One of the basic operating assumptions of a multilateral, multi-national intelligence-led approach to security is that overseas agents must have at least some autonomy in order for them to carry out their work.

I do believe that happens in cases where a foreign country has informants operating in country. On the other side since they have missions, foreign missions all over the place for all kinds of information and spy on countries and that is unacceptable. In this case, I think that it is not acceptable for law enforcement to do it without permission obviously but I do believe this happens. And I think that one of the things that cause that is because of lack of trust and confidence in the local authorities because if they had the trust I don't think that they would. That is, I think, with the exclusion of the US; they will do it anyhow.

It is also clear that overseas liaison officers are actively employed (see Chapter 8) and therefore the activity of overseas law enforcement raised questions about sovereignty. In the view of the head of DS, this was not a problem in collaborative multinational operations, but there are instances when officers from the metropolitan countries did act autonomously. This clearly raises some knotty issues about sovereignty and accountability.

We feel that if people are working here we should know. But intelligence agencies are like that. Based on the information they have and the sensitivity of the information, it may be a case where they feel that they cannot divulge the information to anybody else. Of course, I think that in the end, if they are working within our sphere, we will still have to be involved.

I wondered whether overseas police officers would ever work covertly in any of the islands without informing the local authorities. One SB head argued that:

No, any time that it has ever happened usually they will get in touch with our Commissioner of Police because they don't want to have a conflict of interests so that they just come into a country and just operate. It probably might have happened, we do not know because these guys can sneak in, do their work, and sneak back out.

There was, of course the possibility that people came into the country as tourists, or even as volunteers. As one officer explained:

At one time we have what we call the medical students and these are guys that people say, 'No you don't trust these guys, you don't trust the Peace Corps' because you feel that these are the guys who are intelligence agents.

Neither was it impossible for officers from neighbouring islands to come into an island, on the pretext of taking a holiday, to ask questions. The head of Special Branch did not see it as an infringement of national sovereignty, explaining that the collection of intelligence was simply expected. Nonetheless, the work of the intelligence officers sometimes made other people, particularly chief officers, rather uncomfortable (see also Chapter 3). One head of SB explained the source of discomfort:

I don't think the anxiety is about what information you may collect. The anxiety from people is just the mere fact that you are moving around probing. People just don't like you to do that because they themselves don't know what you're going to discover.

Another argued that:

as human beings we just don't like people probing on our turf. But, it is something that intelligence officers do all the time, everywhere. So even though you don't like it happening on your turf, it is probably something that you yourself have done on somebody else's turf. So it is one of those necessary evils and the thing is I think, not to let people find out that you have been probing, if you have been probing, so that people don't discover it.

Summary and Conclusion

Operational policing in the Caribbean involves extensive overseas cooperation. Most crime in the countries of the region is domestic, but a growing proportion has an international element. This could be because foreign nationals—tourists, for example—are victims or offenders. It could be because suspects have fled by plane or boat. Or because stolen goods have been shipped to neighbouring islands or further afield. In each case, detectives must make contact with their counterparts in other countries, supplying or requesting information from criminal records, fingerprints, photographs, or physical evidence. This is similar to working across constabulary boundaries in Britain or State boundaries in the USA.

The Interpol NCB, nested within the CID across the region, offers the most obvious example of routine transnational police-work. Officers spend their working lives sending and receiving messages to and from foreign countries. This could be officer-to-officer; by 'diffusion' to 187 countries; through the Regional Organized Crime Intelligence Sharing System (ROCISS) targeting Caribbean countries; or through the system of notices coordinated at Interpol headquarters in Lyon. The NCB is not merely a passive conduit for information, but an example of local operational policing acting on information received from overseas. Interpol has grown in size and scope and in the complexity of its activity, although it remains principally a mechanism for sharing information. The Interpol General Secretariat is increasingly involved in operational activity, providing analytical support, intelligence, and liaison facilities. From the evidence of this study, it seems that the work of the NCBs echoes this shift towards becoming more operationally engaged. There is a sub-regional bureau in Puerto Rico, but several NCB heads were of the view that there should be one in the Commonwealth Caribbean.

While detectives sometimes travel abroad to carry out investigations, usually there is neither the need to do so nor the resources available. Most often, they are involved in sharing information through Interpol or informal networks built up through training courses or conferences. Their work is increasingly becoming trans-national, whilst remaining resolutely island-bound. Most of this work is reactive, responding to serious crimes, sharing information on suspects, and handling Red Notices—the basis for the issue of a provisional arrest warrant. NCB detectives—who see them-selves as operational officers and part of the Interpol network—are integral to searching for fugitive offenders, the provision of mutual legal assistance, extradition, and the transfer of prisoners. In a globally mobile world, dealing with offenders who are sought in other places requires mechanisms to identify them, confirm their identities, and apprehend and hold them pending further investi-gation and extradition. The people most likely to be facilitating the transfer are police officers from within these units.

Detectives from the CID and the Interpol NCB sometimes carry out proactive investigations but this is more often the preserve of the Drug Squad, Special Branch, and—in some islands—special-ist units set up to investigate organized crime. These units also respond to reported crime, but their emphasis is on collecting, sorting, and packaging intelligence on crimes in prospect—above all, drug smuggling. This work involves 'special investigative tech-niques', such as the use of informers, undercover policing, techni-cal surveillance, monitoring telephones, and 'controlled delivery'. Because the focus of these units—drug smuggling, organized crime, and terrorism—is transnational in nature, most of this work involves overseas collaboration and sometimes daily cooperation in operations requiring sustained contact over weeks and months. As with the work of the CID, the argument for overseas coopera-tion is the simple fact that the crimes were transnational. In deal-ing with drug trafficking, officers saw law enforcement agencies from other countries as having missing 'pieces of the jigsaw puz-zle' from earlier and later in the drugs supply chain. It was vital, therefore to have links with Columbia, Panama, and Venezuela—usually through the British and Americans who had liaison officers in those countries—where boats laden with cocaine were leaving northbound on a daily basis and with other islands further north which might be the next links in the trans-shipment chain and in the drugs' final destinations in Europe and North America.

The officers heading these units shared many problems. They had insufficient resources to work effectively. Their offices were poorly equipped and in need of technical and infrastructural investment. They were often reliant on overseas assistance for the provision of mobile phones, computers, intelligence systems, and the training to operate them. Many officers felt that although there was a shared imperative to control the drugs trade, security priorities were skewed to meet the needs of the metropolitan countries. Specifically, the British and Americans wanted the resources they provided to be used to stem the flow of drugs northwards and eastwards, rather than to deal with problems on the islands. The USA came in for particular criticism for its lack of effort to prevent the southwards flow of firearms that posed the greatest risk to life and limb that was in practical terms more harmful than the drugs. Many officers were concerned that the problems of organized crime and terrorism were caused by transnational forces far beyond their control or that of their political masters.

The management of transnational cooperation on the ground required some challenging inter-agency negotiation. Operational heads were adamant that law enforcement responsibility lay squarely with them and that nothing resembling policework could be conducted on their territory. However, what constituted 'operational' policework was something of a grey area. Reactive police cooperation was relatively straightforward. Officers were able to provide assistance, search for suspects, make inquiries, and facilitate the collection of evidence, largely regulated by mutual agreements. Covert policing raised more complex problems. Although the metropolitan countries' practice of conducting intelligence gathering on their soil was not something they were particularly happy about, it had occurred worldwide 'since Noah was a lad'. Because secret criminal intelligence would be shared for the benefit of local law enforcement agencies, operational police were generally happy to turn a blind eye to those gathering it. The boundary was the use of coercive powers of arrest and formal suspect interviews. These powers, they believed, should be the exclusive preserve of the local police.

There are more general issues about the use of covert policing. Objections to the spy model that were the stuff of public debate in early nineteenth century Britain remain acute in the contemporary Caribbean. Covert policing is based on deception either through concealment of the truth or blatant lies.[39] Undercover officers must develop a 'cover story' and a false identity. Informers

---

[39] John Kleinig (1996), *The Ethics of Policing*. Cambridge: Cambridge University Press.

supplying information to the police must conceal their intentions and lie to those upon whom they are informing. Controlled deliveries must be kept secret including sometimes from the senior police officers in countries through which they are transiting. Human and technical surveillance require secrecy to deceive the person against whom it is directed. Even senior police officers and government ministers sometimes may be deceived. More often, they are not informed because they do not 'need to know' the scope of the operation or its targets. In some instances, government ministers themselves, have come under suspicion and are the targets of operations. Covert policing relies on secrecy rather than openness and betrayal rather than trust. It therefore raises difficult questions about democracy and accountability to the community. The widespread use of covert policing raises questions for the Caribbean countries about the value of cooperating with metropolitan countries in terms of what can be gained in providing safety and security as well as considering what is lost in terms of sovereignty, accountability, and control, issues to which we return in later chapters. First, we must turn to the other major security sector organizations—the military, border protection, marine police, and overseas liaison officers.

5

Armed Force, the Military, and Transnational Policing

Introduction

> To put it bluntly, in its most basic iteration, military training is aimed at killing people and breaking things. Consequently, military doctrine has forces moving on a target by fire and manoeuvre with a view towards destroying that target. Police forces, on the other hand, take an entirely different approach. They have to exercise the studied restraint that a judicial process requires; they gather evidence and arrest 'suspects'. Where the military sees 'enemies' of the United States, a police agency, properly oriented, sees 'citizens' suspected of crimes but innocent until proven guilty in a court of law. These are two different views of the world.[1]

When wars on drugs and crime are declared, it should come as no surprise that soldiers and military force are called for.[2] Being on a war footing implies that a problem is not mere criminality, but warfare in which the armed forces of the nation state are pitted against an enemy. Colonel Charles Dunlap Jnr., a Staff Judge Advocate in the US Air Force, quoted above, points out that these are two very different views of the world. Conceiving of crime as warfare changes both the ends and the means of intervention. This reflects a more general trend for talk about

[1] Charles Dunlap (2001), 'The Thick Green Line: The Growing Involvement of Military Forces in Domestic Law Enforcement' in Peter Kraska (ed) (2001), *Militarising the American Criminal Justice System: The Changing Roles of the Armed Forces and the Police*. Boston: Northeastern University Press, *op cit*, 35.

[2] President Lyndon Johnson was the first US president to call for a 'war on crime' in 1966. Nixon, Reagan, Bush Snr., Clinton, and Bush Jnr. have all contributed to a 'militarized crime control discourse'. Peter Kraska (2001), 'Crime Control as Warfare: Language Matters' in Peter Kraska (ed), *Militarising the American Criminal Justice System: The Changing Roles of the Armed Forces and the Police*. Boston: Northeastern University Press.

the enemy to move into criminal policy.[3] Susanne Krassmann argues that a new 'enemy penology' has emerged which posits that 'criminal enemies' should not merely be controlled or punished, but 'have to be combated, excluded, if not extinguished'.[4] From this perspective, 'social enemies' should be denied the legal protections granted to others because they represent a 'fundamental threat to society'. This trend is fostered by the sense, discussed in Chapter 2, that the nature of crime and security have fundamentally changed, requiring new modes of intervention. Kraska makes a useful distinction between militar*ization*—preparation for the activity of war[5]—and militar*ism*, 'a cultural pattern of beliefs and values supporting war'.[6] Both are relevant to understanding police-military linkages occurring in response to anxieties about 'new' forms of insecurity that transcend the boundaries between domestic and international affairs, crime and war, constable and soldier.

From the nineteenth century onwards, the modern nation state attempted to make a clear separation between the army and the police, described by Lucia Zedner as the 'twin engines' powering the state's monopoly on the use of violence.[7] This separation, with the military focusing on the external threats posed by foreign

---

[3] Susanne Krassman (2007), 'The Enemy on the Border: Critique of a Programme in Favour of a Preventive State', *Punishment and Society*, 9/3: 301–18, esp p 301. Krassman associates the academic development of this idea with the work of Gunther Jakobs, a German professor of criminal law.   [4] *Ibid*, p 302.

[5] Militarization: the action of making something military in character or style, transforming it to military methods or status, especially by the provision or expansion of military forces and other resources. Military (*adj*): 1. Of or relating to warfare or defence; adapted to or connected with a state of war; designed for military use. Of, relating, or belonging to armed forces or an army (now freq. opposed to *civil* or *civilian*). 2a. Of, relating to, or characteristic of a soldier or soldiers; used, performed, or brought about by soldiers; befitting a soldier. b. Of fashion, colours, etc.: resembling the clothes worn by soldiers. 3a. having the characteristics of a soldier; soldierly; attitude, bearing, or conduct: characteristic of a soldier. b. Of a person, class of people, etc.: engaged in the life of a soldier; belonging to the army. *Oxford English Dictionary*.

[6] 'An ideology that stresses aggressiveness, the use of force, and the glorification of military power, weaponry and technology as the means to solve problems'. Peter Kraska (2001), 'Playing War: Masculinity, Militarism and Their Real-World Consequences' in Kraska, *Militarising the American Criminal Justice System*, *op cit*, p 153.

[7] L. Zedner, (2006), 'Policing before and after the Police: The Historical Antecedents of Contemporary Crime Control', *British Journal of Criminology*, 46/1: 78–96.

armies and police forces concerned with the domestic issues of order maintenance, crime prevention, and investigation is in fact not so clear-cut, particularly in the colonial context. This chapter explores the complex and intertwined relationship between police and military in the Caribbean. First, it charts the role of formally constituted armies—starting with the British West India regiment—and considers the historical and contemporary role of military defence forces in domestic policing. It then looks at forms of specialist 'paramilitary' policing either within the police services or hybrid police-military 'third forces'.[8] Experiments in developing police specialized in armed conflict differ from one territory to the next, but an attempt is made to draw some general conclusions from the literature and empirical material. We look in detail at the work of the Regional Security System (RSS)—headquartered in Barbados and with components across the Eastern Caribbean— which can draw together a mobile sub-regional paramilitary force. The chapter attempts to unravel the complex relationship between police and military force to explain why it is that armed force is frequently called for in a domestic setting in dealing with ordinary law crime. It looks at the problems facing military commanders in their efforts to work together with the police forces within their own territories, military colleagues elsewhere in the region, and with overseas intelligence officers, and when military force is actually used. It considers the extent to which, and in what senses, transnational policing in the region has become militarized and the implications of this for the pursuit of democratic policing.

---

[8] The definition of 'paramilitary' policing is contested in the scholarly literature. In *The case against paramilitary policing* Tony Jefferson (1990) defines it as the 'application of quasi-military training, equipment, philosophy and organisation to. . . policing'. Alice Hills (1995), 'Militant Tendencies: "Paramilitarism" in the British Police', *British Journal of Criminology*, 35: 3 considers this too broad, defining 'paramilitary' as a role undertaken by organizations operating an essentially internal security function, and 'whose training, organization, equipment and control suggest they may be usable in support, or in lieu, of full-time active or reserve armed forces'. She adds that 'it can also be a description of a style of policing'—which is what she suggests that Jefferson does—'but, if it is, it should be made clear that the term is being used as a metaphor'. I think that the OED has it about right: '*adj* : of or relating to a group of civilians organized to function like (or in aid of) a military unit *n* : a group of civilians organized in a military fashion (especially to operate in place of or to assist regular army troops) [syn: paramilitary force, paramilitary unit, paramilitary organization]'.

Caribbean Military Forces

Today, Jamaica, Guyana, and Trinidad and Tobago have the largest military forces in the Commonwealth Caribbean, each with infantry divisions, artillery battery, and air defence. In each place, the coastguard commander answers to the Chief of Staff and their vessels are considered to be integral to the defence force's capacity. Belize, Barbados, Saint Kitts and Nevis have smaller defence forces, while the Bahamas has a military coastguard. The size of the defence force depends on the size of the territory, the strength of its economy, and the specific security challenges that it faces.[9] The other islands within the Commonwealth Caribbean don't have defence forces, but have paramilitary Special Services Units (SSUs) within the police force (to which we return later in this chapter). Wherever there are defence forces, there is also a coastguard headed by a senior military figure and answering to the defence ministry (see Chapter 7). Each of these small armies can be traced back to their roots in colonial forces including the West India Regiment and island militias.

In some islands the imperial garrison has had a defensive role that has seen no military force used against a foreign state for centuries. Barbados, for example, has been under British control since 1627 and the last time that an army was engaged in open warfare in Jamaica was in 1655 when the English ejected the Spanish. Nonetheless the garrison was an important part of colonial life. It had a community life of its own—accommodating men and women providing services to the soldiers—and had a significant impact on the governance of the colonies.[10] Eighteenth century British colonial policy in the region required a large navy and army

[9] Trinidad and Tobago, for example, being very close to Venezuela with its open coastline and proximity to a major shipping lane coming out of Maricaribo, has more involvement with Venezuela than most of its neighbours, with a specific local operation, Ventri, to coordinate between them. Guyana has border disputes with its neighbours, so is the territory with the greatest need for a military for traditional purposes of physically protecting the border from an attempt from Suriname or Venezuela (both of whom claim territory) (see Griffith (1997), *Drugs and Security in the Caribbean: Sovereignty Under Siege*. University Park, PA: Penn State University Press).

[10] Roger Buckley (1988), *The British Army in the West Indies*. Gainsville: University Press of Florida; Brian Dyde (1997), *The Empty Sleeve: The Story of the West India Regiments of the British Army*. St John's, Antigua: Hansib Caribbean.

to secure its extensive trading and commercial interests.[11] In the late 1790s, the West Indies accounted for four fifths of British overseas capital investment, one third of foreign trade, and one eighth of total net revenue to the treasury in direct tax and duties.[12] To protect these interests, 69 British infantry regiments were sent to the region between 1793 and 1800. The high death toll from fevers amongst the British soldiers unused to, and unprepared for, tropical conditions was one of the key reasons that the West India Regiment (WIR) was created in 1795 when Lieutenant General Vaughan called for 'a corps of a thousand' blacks and Mulattoes, commanded by British Officers.[13] These men, he believed, 'would render more essential service in the Country, than treble this number of Europeans who are unaccustomed to the climate'. Recruited initially from African slaves bought on arrival in the Caribbean and later from freed slaves from North America, the WIR was eventually garrisoned across all the British possessions. In its early years, the regiment was deployed in fighting over trade and island territories during the Napoleonic wars (1792–1815) when islands of the Eastern Caribbean changed hands among the colonial powers. The regiment was an integral part of the British army although it was low in the military hierarchy, and according to Buckley, over the years it had no fascination for the general public, and lacked reputation and image, more a 'phantom army lurking subliminally in British imperial history'.[14] There has been no conventional war fighting within the Caribbean region for nearly two centuries and longer in some islands. The army was of course there for the purposes of defence, in the event that a foreign enemy might attempt to invade, but its focus has been primarily, even from the earliest colonial times, on internal security first against maroon insurgencies and slave rebellions, and then the repression of the riots and rebellions of the post-emancipation period.[15] Military force has been called upon, and used on numerous occasions

---

[11] Rene Chartrand and Paul Chappell (1996), *British Forces in the West Indies 1793–1815*. Osprey Publishing.   [12] *Ibid*.

[13] Lieutenant-General Sir John Vaughan, in a letter to the Home Secretary, 22 December 1794, cited by Brian Dyde (1997), *The Empty Sleeve*, *op cit*.

[14] Roger Buckley (1988), *The British Army in the West Indies*, *op cit*.

[15] Harriott (2002), 'Mission Effectiveness, Environmental Change and the Reconfiguration of the Jamaican Security Forces', *Security and Defence Studies Review*, 2/1: 24.

across the region in response to political violence, attempted coups d'état, and civil emergencies.

The military officers that I interviewed were an impressive group.[16] They were well educated, most had university degrees and many had postgraduate qualifications. They had, without exception, been trained in the USA, or the UK, some of them having served in foreign militaries. The Chiefs of Staff saw security threats as transnational, borderless, and 'intertwined with what happens regionally and internationally'. Top of their list was the risk of a collapse of the rule of law, high internal crime levels, the illegal arms trade, organized criminal networks, and terrorism. They also tended towards a broad view of security including economic threats, loss of natural resources, and the 'social threats which stare us in the face every day'—such as poverty, disorder, a lack of proper health facilities and educational opportunities and systems, and also infectious diseases, especially HIV/Aids. The drug trade sat at the centre of the security issues, especially where drug money had become integrated into the legitimate economy. As with other occupational groups, the threat was believed to arise from the islands' position as a trans-shipment point on the route between the producers of cocaine and the users in Europe and North America. Problems arose when payment for the illicit drugs was made 'in stocks or supplies rather than cash' leading to drugs being sold on the local market and 'fallout from the drug trade', including armed violence 'to protect their turf'.

There are a number of reasons that the military defence forces are called in to deal with the problems of crime and drug trafficking. First, throughout their history, the military have had a law enforcement role in dealing with disorder or insurrection and in many senses this is thought of as the defence of the country, and therefore a matter of national security—a military duty. One Chief of Staff explained that:

when I look at the mission of the _____ Defence Force, it's very simple, it's to deter and defeat threats of organized violence against the well-being

---

[16] I undertook taped interviewed with Chiefs of Staff, infantry commanders, operations commanders, and coastguard commanders in the various countries studied. I also interviewed numerous other soldiers and two retired Chiefs of Staff. I observed the two-day Caribbean Chiefs of Staff conference in Trinidad, March 2004.

of our country and its citizens and that's how I lump the mission now, it's not to defend against an external aggressor meaning another state.

In several countries—notably Jamaica and Guyana—the army has been called upon from time to time to respond to violence or the threat of violence surrounding elections. In recent years, military forces in these countries and across the region have also been deployed to deal with armed violence connected to drug trafficking and organized crime. There are also some boundary disputes within the region and potential for conflict over matters like fishing stocks and offshore oil fields, etc.[17] However, the main threats to security within the region do not relate to the prospect of invasion or incursion by a foreign power. As one Chief of Staff put it:

the fact of the matter is, the militaries in the region especially, cannot really, in today's world, be locked into the old traditional military duties. In fact, you will have *no business* because we have no threats from any state actors, they are all non-state actors who I think are far more dangerous because you're not quite sure [of] a well defined enemy. (emphasis added)

This view was shared by the British security advisors within the region:

military forces throughout the Caribbean . . . had a defensive role in the bad old days but today largely are in support of national security, and therefore they need to be able to operate in a humanitarian way with the police forces, and it's getting that linkage between the police and the military that I think is vitally important.

The British advisors argued that the experience of the British and international militaries in peace support operations in such places as Bosnia, Kosovo, Sierra Leone, and now Afghanistan and Iraq, have led to a broadening of the skills of the military in this sphere:

anybody who goes into a peace support operation, not a peace keeping, a peace *support* operation, is now taught the same skills that we taught for Northern Ireland, and that requires the police and military to work together, and I think a lot of those skills are what are needed in the Caribbean now, because we mustn't forget that the police services in the Caribbean are not mandated quite the same as our own police service.

---

[17] Griffith (1997), *Drugs and Security in the Caribbean*, *op cit*, lists all such disputes.

They have a much wider, not paramilitary [role], but there are certain paramilitary tasks they have which are defence of the realm.

A second reason that the role of the military in the business of policing has become accepted in contemporary society is because the seriousness of the crime situation has gone beyond what the police can cope with using the means and techniques available to them. Traditional forms of reactive investigation and attempts to engage public support in the pursuit of crime control seem ineffective in controlling crime or responding adequately to armed violence, leading in some instances to a loss of public support. Additionally, the police are not always prepared, equipped, or skilled to respond professionally, in ways that protect officers from injury, keeping force to a minimum and prioritizing the preservation of life. One Chief of Staff argued while police traditionally, and quite correctly, have been recognized by various governments as being the force in the forefront for law enforcement, military force is required to deal with armed criminality because 'the state sometimes finds itself powerless to enforce law in those areas from the perspective of community policing techniques and so what you have to use is the harder arm of government which is a military.' The military is called upon, he argued, because it is 'trained at the high end of the scale and can easily step down' to cope with less severe violence 'whereas the police would have to be totally retrained in order to step up'.

Defence forces have contributed to policing on a sporadic basis in the period since decolonization. Military intervention was geared towards acute problems such as riot and public disorder where the police have had difficulty coping. The military has a more extensive role in the event that there is a state of emergency. In this instance, the Prime Minister has to invoke the relevant section of the Defence Act, signing a paper that authorizes the Defence Force to employ the troops to assist the police. As one brigadier put it, 'If there's a state of emergency, then it's all on my plate'. In Jamaica, the military were given constabulary powers between 1974 and 1994 under the Suppression of Crimes Act. This gave 'security forces'—defined as the police and military—constabulary powers. Today, ongoing chronic problems, such as handling routine armed violence, was changing the relationship between police and military. As one Chief of Staff put it, their involvement is now continuous, 'so even when you don't see soldiers on the street, we are supporting law enforcement with intelligence and we have certain specific law enforcement duties'. Bearing in mind the security threats mentioned above, Chiefs of Staff felt that although the military should not be at the forefront of the law enforcement effort, 'when your nation is confronted with something [of this] magnitude... I don't think that you have a choice'.

Thirdly, the military has had a prominent role in policing because it is seen as the only agency with the capacity to provide support for other branches of government. The military is frequently drawn upon in a wide range of different spheres, because it is a well functioning element of the state. Put simply, the army is used in crime fighting 'because it works'.[18] Soldiers are generally, more professional, better trained, organized, disciplined, resourced, and equipped. In many ways, the military has become a multi-purpose force that has been reasonably well maintained and trained, both domestically and often with British, American, and Canadian armed forces. In comparison with other state agencies, the military in the Caribbean is seen as well disciplined and in possession of a 'can do' attitude. It is therefore relatively easy for governments to call on the army to carry out a range of tasks going beyond a traditional military mandate:

the Government sees the military as a disciplined body, [and] if the government tells the military, 'Come up with a plan to do so and so', the military will go and cobble up and then implement it, so the result is the Government is calling more on the military to be involved in the youths, to be involved in assisting the police, involved in external response to disasters in the region, so there is a more greater demand on the military.

The fourth reason for a growing involvement of the military in domestic law enforcement was the problem of corruption within policing and elsewhere, calling for the intervention of an agency less tainted with collusion. Senior military staff were strongly of the view that the police service has 'become more and more corrupt every day' to the extent that is effectively 'in league' with organized crime groups. Military forces in the Caribbean region are generally viewed as being less corrupt as a consequence of the military having a smaller amount of day-to-day contact with people involved in the drugs trade, in comparison with their police counterparts.

---

[18] Dunlap (2001), 'The Thick Green Line', *op cit*, p 34.

Dealing with corruption was therefore a major headache. One Chief of Staff described corruption as his 'biggest, biggest, biggest problem':

Let me say this, no criminal worth his salt or criminal enterprise in [this country], the region or internationally, survives without corrupting law enforcement arms of the State. You cannot survive, it is impossible. . . . So the difficulties we have is ineptitude on the part of law enforcement on one hand and on the other hand, because the guy is not there with a smoking gun to pin the stuff [on him] from which he is far removed. You also have to work around your own.

Police and Customs officers' collusion with organized crime groups created a major headache for the military. It was widely suspected, although its actual extent was unknown and perhaps unknowable. One problem was that many people defined corruption very narrowly as the taking of bribes for particular acts. When people turn a 'blind eye' to others' wrongdoing, this was generally not thought of as corruption. The way to respond to this was through vetting, by creating within each agency specially vetted groupings using polygraph and background tests. Despite this possible solution, the problem of corruption has been identified by one of the Chiefs of Staff as endemic in the police organization:

It is very difficult for a man to join the Police Force as a constable, 20-odd years later he's a superintendent coming all the way up through the ranks and not being touched on his way, even by his acts or his omissions. Difficult. And so it seems to me they need to develop some leadership core from a much younger stage.

Finally, in some locations, military units seem less likely to use deadly force than their police paramilitary counterparts. The reasons for this are not well documented but include the fact that soldiers tend to have less discretion in their operations than the police, including the use of armed force. There are obviously exceptions, but soldiers tend to fire only when ordered to do so, even in combat situations when shots are being fired, whereas police have wide discretion to act. Soldiers are also better equipped with body armour and bullet protection and are trained how to respond to the experience of being under fire. Academics, NGOs, and media commentators have recommended that because of the corruption, ineffectiveness, and abuse of force among the constabularies of the region the military forces—such as the Jamaica Defence Force and Guyana Defence Force—should take over the heavy end of the police function leaving 'ordinary law policing' to an unarmed community police force.

Local Security Cooperation

The military work with local agencies including police, Customs and the coastguard. They have partnerships with the international agencies with whom they operate 'on a daily basis'. This includes those from the embassies, including HM Customs, the British Security Service, the Royal Canadian Mounted Police, the US Drugs Enforcement Administration (DEA), Defence Attachés, drug squad, police, and Special Branch. A Chief of Staff explained that the military 'kind of lead that drive because we chair the meetings' involving sharing of information and planning operations. The Military Intelligence Unit—with various desks looking at drugs, one concerned with criminals, another with internal matters—is based at the Defence Force Headquarters lying at the hub of the coordination efforts. This was less than strategically planned, but 'it's something that really just evolved by their being a vacuum with a need for some leadership and it just evolved'. At the time of the research, different models of organization were being considered, consisting essentially of a national structure to pull together the police and various agencies dealing with the intelligence to create a national intelligence bureau. The Chief of Staff saw intelligence as absolutely central to the process of developing an effective response. They were far from having either the strategic, tactical, or operational intelligence processes in place; however, they are in the process of capacity building in this sphere.

For Colonel Dunlap, the attitude of the military towards its involvement in 'ordinary law' policing is captured in the idea of soldiers as 'reluctant heroes'. [19] He argues that the increased reliance on military resources for policing is in the interest of neither the armed forces nor the public and that in the USA, the call for the armed forces to become involved in policework 'almost always arises from outside the military establishment'. [20] Caribbean military leaders were similarly reluctant. As one Caribbean Chief of Staff put it, 'we know in our limitations that we are not policemen. We don't want to be policemen. We'd have joined the Police Force

---

[19] Dunlap (2001), 'The Thick Green Line', *op cit*, p 34.   [20] *Ibid*.

if we did'. There are numerous problems with having the military routinely involved in policing activity because military and policing tasks have fundamentally different orientation. The ethos of the military, its training, and specific skills are not suited towards policework. As Colonel Dunlap puts it so eloquently at the start of this chapter, the military are experts in killing people and breaking things. Soldiering has certain kinds of rules of engagement and techniques in the use of force. It is this war-making metaphor that is unsuitable for dealing with civilians. One of the brigadiers conceded that 'on war and crime, once you say war, it puts you in a particular frame of mind. . . . So I agree that the way on the war on crime carries you down a particular way.' He went on to say that:

We don't like being involved as we are right now with the police and it's bad for the soldiers, it's bad for image. The military should be shock troops, we should come into the area, come into a situation with a limited time frame with our end state clearly in mind, achieve what we have to do on patrol, and that is how we prefer to operate. We are against situations as it is right now where soldiers are out there 24/7 patrolling with the police and that is not how it ought to be done.

Recognizing this, Chiefs of Staff must attempt to devise ways that the defence force can 'work alongside the police with the intention of bringing them up to a level where they can then mount the operations and then we can patrol'. However, there are also problems with this, because 'It never works because the police then see the soldiers as just numbers in terms of assisting them to cover a wider area'. There were some occasions involving disagreements between police and military perspectives. The Chief of Staff described working with the Police as a challenge:

sometimes there are disagreements. A soldier feels that that person should be searched, the Police says no, but the Police is in charge of the law enforcement part of things and you get those little things from time to time, but we try to keep it separate.

Clearly, working with police in a context where there is a high level of police corruption is also an important barrier. There is also a more general cultural difference between the two organizations that can be found all over the world.

The sharing of strategic and tactical intelligence is relatively unproblematic. However, a new range of issues come in to play when the military and other agencies work together in conducting joint operations. The two central principles on which they operate are that, firstly, the police have primacy and, secondly, they have to work jointly. Nonetheless, even with the principle of police primacy firmly in place, the army maintained a great deal of latitude in what it was able to do. One Chief of Staff explained that primacy did not mean that they were 'just an adjunct to the police':

I meant primacy in terms of taking that law enforcement action but in terms of developing, following through, we can do that all on our own and we do a lot of that all on our own. Let's take the case with one of the top ten fugitives recently, [John Doe]. The Police Commissioner picked up the phone and said, 'Look, you need some help, can we find [John Doe]' and it's something we worked entirely on our own, we only used the Police, we brought some policemen in when we needed to make some forays in the community to try and generate something, but we had to go with the Police to do that, but when we had it, we just then called the Police and said 'Right, troops, let's go, plan this thing, move'.

We have had situations where the _____ Defence Force almost is leading but we know very clearly that whilst we may be directing the tactics and so on in a particular set of ways, we really are not leading, we are assisting the Police, and that's what you will hear, that's the party line, you always get that, and we do this too for a very practical reason. The Police here suffer from what I term as deep psychological insecurity. They want our help but the way they would want our help is for them to say, 'Look, we need help' and I just send masses of troops for them just to do with what they wish, and I have been saying, 'We're not going to do that. Our brains have to come along and we have to be a part of the planning'. That to me is my biggest frustration now because they need the help but they still want to do it on their own, and so what I've had to do is draw a hard line. I say, 'Look, that operation is foolishness, we're not going to play. We're not going to do it. It's manpower intensive. It achieves nothing'.

The army officer concerned would undertake the identification, then pass the information on to the police. As far as possible, the army are not physically involved in the operations.

I mean my team could be there. They're observing. They're reporting. They're talking. They're bringing the Police and so on. But the fact that the thing is signed, and because we don't want to necessarily expose the people anyway, they tend not to get involved. Our teams would go out, would find them, would keep track of them, the Police teams would come and we'd just vector them and say, 'Look, he's over there' and they go and they take him. The only thing we don't do is make the arrest, okay. We have no power of arrest, not anything more than a normal citizen.

A solider could physically hold a person during an operation, but in most instances they would not. If this did occur, it would not be a formal arrest and could only be temporary until the police officers present could do the formalities: 'we don't get involved with that at all, even if we had the power, Police are better at that. We grab you, we hold you, we hand you to the Police.' In many ways, the role of the military in this circumstance is similar to the work of the international liaison officer (see Chapter 8) in that they can do quite a lot of activity as long as this falls short of 'enforcement':

We can work by ourselves, we can do anything, but you just cannot take any law enforcement action, you can't stop somebody and search them because you suspect them of carrying a gun, you can't do that. . . . Unless there's a police officer, who really is the one doing it and you're assisting him. *The fact that you do it physically doesn't matter.* (emphasis added)

This is a very interesting point and in many ways it is the one on which the whole issue of sovereignty in law enforcement revolves. How far does it matter when the police and military are working together and the police have 'primacy', that a soldier physically takes the enforcement action such as a stop and search, arrest, or conduct an interview?

Regional Defence Force Cooperation

Defence forces collaborate with other militaries within the region.[21] One Chief of Staff was strongly of the view that there was need for the security sector to get its act together locally before attempting some kind of international effort:

there is always this big thing about the region, look it's a load of crap because we're trying to get the region to work together when you're not having the thing structured in your own countries. I am a great believer in the bottom up approach, get your country sorted out, get your in-country teams, then you look at the sub-region.

He was therefore against putting effort into creating a structure for regional maritime cooperation when bilateral agreements with particular countries would be more productive. One example was the attempt to create a regional intelligence process. Part of the

---

[21] There have been two occasions when the region's defence forces have operated together as a region, first operation Urgent Fury (Grenada) and Operation Restore Democarcy, UN Mission in Haiti.

problem with this was that a lot of effort might be expended in an attempt to create a mechanism for sharing intelligence without thinking about what would actually be put in to such a system:

they're trying to come from the top down, it just doesn't work, so all this thing about regional intelligence and so on and so on, I think we're all tied up too much with trying to get the means to communicate intelligence but nobody has stopped to ask, 'what intelligence?' Do we really have an intelligence to communicate and that's part of my problem because the Police are working on a system, the military too through them are working on it and everybody wants a system. To do what?

There is a strong working relationship among the region's military chiefs. The officers frequently have trained together in Britain, Canada, or the USA. Many senior officers have travelled with Defence Ministers to discuss security matters at CARICOM level and there is also a Military chiefs' conference providing a forum for discussion and collaboration. In particular, there is a great deal of conversation among the larger military forces—Jamaica, Guyana, and Trinidad. One Chief of Staff described the military as the 'most integrated organization' in the Caribbean. Relationships have also formed with the US military Southern Command (Southcom), US Coastguard, and British, French, Dutch, and German naval vessels when they are in the region. Several countries have also had experience of working with the US Marshals Service Fugitive Apprehension Team (FAT), in an operational capacity. The FAT, who pass the information to the local police, work in conjunction with these forces to 'look for their target and make the arrest but the arrest is actually made by the _____ constable who brings the person back but is escorted overseas after the extradition process by the Americans'.

Chiefs of Staff shared the view expressed by their colleagues in other security agencies that intelligence sharing with the USA often resulted in an imbalance: 'with something American sponsored, there is always the feeling that it's something you put information in, but you get nothing out.' On the other hand, Caribbean security staff were able to work best with the countries of South America through the representatives of the metropolitan countries:

you have a common link between every country: it's the United States, it's Britain. You may find it surprising but most of what we have in the linkages with Colombia and so on are through the British, not the Americans, so that's how we have a strong leg into Colombia. If we want to get information we go to our British counterpart here because we find that they have strong legs there. Cuba, we work through the British, but I mean that's obvious, the US would have some difficulty.

The Chiefs of Staff shared the anxieties felt by officers of other organizations in the Caribbean about certain agencies who perhaps felt that they would be more efficient if they acted autonomously, in doing their own work. One Chief of Staff argued that some people are of the view that 'it needs to happen', but he didn't share that view:

I don't feel so. I feel that whatever happens has to happen within a controlled environment. What I have never advocated is having mavericks running around the place doing their own thing. . . . because in the long run what it does is alienates you, your policies, what you are working towards down the line and it creates more problems for yourself and your organization than anything else. So I think everything ought, to a certain degree, to be controlled as far as the military environment and the joint operations are concerned.

The issue was that the Chiefs of Staff would always need to 'provide the guiding influence', operate with great care, but at the same time 'allow individuals flexibility.' The crucial issue was accountability and control. It is absolutely critical to work within a framework. Thus, accountability has to remain 'strictly within the bounds of law':

The accountability lies first with the individual. We tell our soldiers, for arguments sake here, that whatever actions you carry out, at the end of the day you must be able to justify them and justify them in a court of law. We also say to them, that 'Look if you go outside there and you commit an offence, no matter what it is, you make sure you come and report it and report it truthfully. That way we will back you to the hilt whether you are wrong or right, you'll know when you are wrong and you'll go and take your blows', but we will provide the legal aid for you, when you are right, you will still get the legal aid but from the moment you come in and you start to lie, then the organization takes a different perspective and you are basically on your own, the lie having been discovered. So the whole point is you know, stick within the ambits of the law.

I was interested in the Chiefs of Staff's view of how far they were keen for the international cooperation to extend to sending criminals committing crime within their jurisdiction to the US for trial. Wherever it was possible to execute an arrest warrant, and a case could be made to prosecute crimes committed in his country, then 'we are going to proceed, there's not going to be any argument about it'.

Military Force in Caribbean Constabularies

There is wide variation among modern liberal democracies in the form and style of their system of police,[22] but most maintain police forces that are distinct and separate from the military.[23] In England, piloting the Metropolitan Police Act (1829) through a sceptical parliament, Sir Robert Peel is credited with creating the template for the 'democratic', 'consensual', or 'Westminster' model of policing. The Metropolitan Police was created as a civilian force quite *opposed* to and very much as an *alternative* to the military, especially in relation to the control of public order, where—as in the Peterloo Massacre—military intervention had earlier been so disastrous.[24] This includes the emphasis on 'policing by consent' of the policed, *visible* uniformed policing, the minimal use of force, the idea of the police officer as 'citizen in uniform', the insistence that officers should normally be armed with nothing more than the impersonal authority of the state and a wooden truncheon. However, it hardly need be pointed out that the new police uniforms,[25] hierarchical badge of rank, forms of internal discipline, and the fact that one of its first Commissioners was a former commander of

[22] David H. Bayley (1979), 'Police Function, Structure and Control in Western Europe and North America: Comparative Historical Studies' in N. Morris and M. Tonry (eds), *Crime and Justice: A Review of Research*. Chicago: University of Chicago Press; David H. Bayley (1985), *Patterns of Policing*. New Brunswick, NJ: Rutgers University Press; Rob Mawby (1990), *Comparative Policing Issues: The British and American Experience in International Perspective*. London: Routledge.

[23] P.A.J. Waddington (1999), 'Armed and Unarmed Police' in Rob Mawby (ed), *Policing Across the World: Issues for the Twenty First Century*. London: UCL Press; Marcus Dubber (2005), *The Police Power*. New York: Columbia University Press.

[24] In 1819, the cavalry charged a crowd of 60–80,000 in St Peters Fields, Manchester, leaving at least 11 dead and many hundreds wounded, many inflicted by cutlass blows.

[25] Townsend points out that Metropolitan Police uniform 'was distinctly military, in colour, cut, and accoutrement, and became gradually more so. The famous helmet. . . was directly modelled on the Prussianized headgear adopted by the army after the German victory over France in 1871', C. Townsend (1993), *Making the Peace: Public Order and Public Security in Modern Britain*. Oxford: Oxford University Press.

the Light Brigade (the other was a lawyer), all point to its military origins. Townsend argued that because of the 'unmistakably military style and, in many respects, behaviour of the new police it was naturally christened a 'force'.[26] The police force that was created by the Metropolitan Police Act had many military trappings, but it may reasonably be contrasted with a form of policing based on French *gendarmerie* or *mouchards* with their foundations, respectively, in militarism and espionage.[27] One of the primary political justifications for the introduction of the Metropolitan Police in the early nineteenth century was to quell riotous behaviour without recourse to the army. Peel made every effort to ensure that the 'new police' were as distinct as possible from soldiers or spies (see Chapter 4).[28] In the face of popular resistance to the police, which continued well into the late 1840s, government sought to make the new police less obviously an arm of the state. Resistance, captured by the cry 'no standing armies' resonated with the eighteenth century distinctions between 'continental despotism' (standing armies, police spies, *lettres de cachet*, and Bastilles) and 'English liberty' (rule of law, balanced constitution, unpaid constables, and local justices of the peace).[29] Resistance was strong in the late eighteenth and early nineteenth centuries and for a considerable period it appeared that reformers would not succeed in introducing a police force in the capital. Though a number of factors enabled Peel eventually to prevail, a crucial one was the experience of Peterloo, the shock of which 'opened many eyes to the dangers of employing armed men against crowds'.[30] Part of the solution for Peel was to be able to utilize public and political concern about the use of the military in civil disturbances and to present the new model police as being as different from the military as it was possible to be.

The model for British colonial forces in the Caribbean, in common with other countries in the Empire, was the Royal Irish

---

[26] *Ibid*, p 17.

[27] Clive Emsley (1983), *Policing and Its Context 1750–1870*. London: Macmillan.

[28] T. Critchley (1970), *The Conquest of Violence*. London: Constable; Pete Gill (1970), *Rounding Up the Usual Suspects: Developments in Contemporary Law Enforcement Intelligence*. Aldershot: Ashgate, p 196.

[29] Michael Ignatieff (1979), 'Police and People: The Birth of Mr Peel's "Blue Locusts"', *New Society*, 30 August, reprinted in Tim Newburn (ed) (2004), *Policing: Key Readings*. Cullompton: Willan, at p 26.

[30] Critchley (1970), *op cit*, at p 29.

Constabulary, interspersed with aspirations to follow the civil policing model pursued in some other places.[31] Sir Robert Peel—who gave his name to the benign unarmed British Bobby—was also creator of the Irish Constabulary in 1812, based on an explicitly militarized model of policing which assumed the *absence* of consent from native populations, if only because it was a mechanism to maintain colonial rule.[32] Policing in this model requires selective enforcement in favour of the dominant group, the criminalization of minority activities, and suppression of the right to protest or to demonstrate for political change.[33] The strategy of 'policing by strangers' requires that recruitment to the police is generally not from among locals. Where the indigenous population is employed, most officers above the rank of constable and all the senior command are from the 'metropolitan or settler group' and do not reflect the demographic characteristics of society at large.[34] The Irish model formed the basis for British colonial police forces around the world.[35] Whilst democratic, consensual policing was reserved for the settlement of disputes and investigation of crimes within the settler community, the majority of the population had no such recourse but were instead subject to colonial policing when their interests or behaviour threatened the status quo. Paul Gilroy notes that the 'history of colonial power overflows with evidence of. . . a destructive association of governance with military power and marshal law', reaching beyond the army to medicine and public administration.[36]

Following the abolition of slavery in 1833 and the Morant Bay Rebellion in 1865 the problems of the use of soldiers in policing a civil population were starkly illustrated as Peterloo

[31] John Brewer (1994), *Black and Blue*. Oxford: Oxford University Press, pp 5–10; Georgina Sinclair (2006), *At the End of the Line: Colonial Policing and the Imperial Endgame 1945–80*. Manchester: Manchester University Press.

[32] Mike Brogden (1987), 'The Emergence of the Police – the Colonial Dimension'. *British Journal of Criminology*, 27/1.

[33] Trevor Jones and Tim Newburn (1996), *Policing and Disaffected Communities: A Review of the Literature*. A Report to the Standing Advisory Committee on Human Rights. London: Policy Studies Institute, p 3–4.

[34] Trevor Jones and Tim Newburn (1996), *Policing and Disaffected Communities*, *op cit*.

[35] Mike Brogden (1987), 'The Emergence of the Police – the Colonial Dimension', *op cit*.

[36] Paul Gilroy (2004), *After Empire: Melancholia or Convivial Culture?*. London: Routledge, p 47.

had done half a century earlier in England.[37] Following rioting and the burning of a courthouse in the town of Morant Bay, the unpopular Governor Eyre placed the island under martial law and punished those he considered to have taken part in the uprising. During the further rioting that followed, the West India Regiment was actively involved in destroying houses, making arrests, and carrying out executions.[38] The Jamaica Constabulary Force was established a year later. In many islands the West India Regiment garrison was a community which underwent major transformation as the regiment prepared to leave. When the West India Regiment was withdrawn from the Bahamas (in November 1891), a new police force was recruited from Barbados. This was distinctly military in nature. Headed by a Captain Learmouth from England (formerly of the 12th Royal Lancers), staffed with 42 recruits from Barbados and a new Police Act of 1891, the force started work in 1892.[39]

The Jamaica Constabulary Force, modelled on the Royal Irish Constabulary, had control of colonial populations, was militarized, heavily armed, subjectively controlled, and practised differential enforcement rather than adhering to the Westminster ethos of minimal force and political independence.[40] After independence in 1962, there were attempts at reform of the organization, including a 'Jamaicanization' of the leadership and an attempt at civilianization. Harriott's analysis of the reform process concluded that the former succeeded, but the latter failed and the force became increasingly politicized. Harriott describes the attempts to introduce community-based policing in Jamaica.[41] He concludes that the community-police consultative committees are ineffective and therefore there is little real community input into policy

[37] John Newsinger (2006), *The Blood Never Dried: A People's History of the British Empire*. London: Pluto Press, pp 31–2; Paul Gilroy, *After Empire, op cit.*

[38] Humphrey Metzgen and John Graham (2007), *Caribbean Wars Untold: A Salute to the British West Indies*. Kingston, Jamaica: University of West Indies Press, p 78.

[39] Gabrielle Pratt and Morris A. Simmons (1990), *A History of the Royal Bahamas Police Force*. Bahamas: The Research and Planning Unit of the Royal Bahamas Police Force.

[40] Harriott (2000), *Police and Crime Control in Jamaica: Problems of Reforming Ex-Colonial Constabularies*. Kingston, Jamaica: University of the West Indies Press.   [41] In Alexanderville and Normanville.

priority setting or problem solving. Consequently there is a general deficit of police accountability to the community. The forms of police-community contact are 'emptied of their democratic and consensus-building content' while 'the typical constable becomes steeped in authoritarian practices' and therefore has 'great difficulty fitting with the style of community policing'.[42] The organizational values and culture of the organization remain resolutely military. Harriott concludes that the concept of police-community relations 'remains a public relations concept'.[43] Caribbean police forces, unable to shake off their military origins, have become ever more militarized and militaristic in recent years, and attempts at reform have tended to be more symbolic than substantive.[44] In Harriott's assessment, today's Jamaica Constabulary Force operates in ways 'consistent with the military model'.

Paramilitary Policing

The use of quasi-military armed force by police officers is an issue that is linked to, but separate from, the use of defence forces in policing. The use of military training, equipment, philosophy, and organization has a long history in policing.[45] The acquisition and use of armaments (such as firearms, gas, water cannon, and military vehicles), the use of military language and symbolism, secrecy, and the collation of intelligence on suspect populations (often demonized as 'enemies'), are all common in paramilitary police forces. In some instances, these units are under the direct control of governments and are partisan in enforcing the rule of a specific political regime. The militarization of policing is evident around the world and notably in the UK and US, the sponsors of a significant amount of police development and training in the Caribbean region.

In the English summer riots of the late 1970s, Bobbies defended themselves from the rioters' stones and bottles with dustbin-lids as improvised shields. In response to the riots, through the policing of the mid-1980s miners' strike and drawing on the experience of policing the 'troubles' in Northern Ireland, and with the assistance of advice from the Royal Hong Kong Police, the police forces of

[42] Harriott (2000), *op cit*, 117.   [43] *Ibid*, 93.   [44] *Ibid*, 125.
[45] Tony Jefferson (1990), *The Case Against Paramilitary Policing*. Milton Keynes: Open University Press.

England and Wales acquired paramilitary equipment, techniques, and training. A national reporting centre was created in 1972 that would enable the Association of Chief Police Officers to coordinate public order policing across police force boundaries.[46] While Scarman is best remembered as the re-invigorator of community policing, *The Scarman Report* also set out in a few short paragraphs, the seeds from which the militarization of British policing would grow.[47] The Law Lord bemoaned the Metropolitan Police's lack of preparedness for riot control and, while rejecting the calls for a 'third force', recommended the acquisition of paramilitary capacity within domestic police forces. There followed the acquisition of CS gas, plastic bullets, flame-proof suits, NATO helmets, long shields, extendable truncheons, armoured vehicles, and a permanent paramilitary training facility in West London known colloquially as 'riot city'. The extent of militarization has gradually become visible over the past two decades in the gradual arming of police at airports, the posting of armed police outside police headquarters and government buildings, the creation of specialist armed police units (such as the Metropolitan Police CO19) and the deployment of armed 'area cars' in most parts of the country. In the wake of the terrorist attacks on London in July 2005, the full extent of the military capacity of British policing by way of men and women in black military fatigues, bullet-proof vests, black and white checked baseball caps, and automatic weapons appeared on the streets of British cities.

The extent of paramilitary policing has also grown in the USA as forces have become professionalized. A survey in the 1990s, for example, found that 90 per cent of police departments in cities with populations in excess of 50,000 had paramilitary units, as did 70 per cent of departments in smaller cities.[48] This trend started with the creation of a Special Weapons and Tactics (SWAT) team by the FBI in 1973. By the 1990s all 56 of the FBI's field offices had their own SWAT team. The growing role of the military in law enforcement was given its greatest boost by the 'war on drugs'.

---

[46] Martin Kettle (1985), 'The National Reporting Centre and the 1984 Miners' Strike' in Bob Fine and Robert Millar (eds), *Policing the Miners' Strike*. London: Lawrence and Wishart; see also Phil Scraton (ed) (1987), *Law, Order & the Authoritarian State*. Milton Keynes: Open University Press.

[47] *Scarman Report*, paras 5.72–5.74.

[48] Peter Kraska and Victor Kappeler (1997), 'Militarizing American Police: The Rise and Normalization of Paramilitary Units', *Social Problems*, 44.

One 'fragment' of European culture that was passed to colonial America was the view that a permanent military presence was to be distrusted—indeed viewed as despotic and tyrannical.[49] The establishment of civilian control of the military became a key issue in the drafting of the constitution.[50] The 1878 Posse Comitatus Act subsequently outlawed the use of federal troops for civilian law enforcement. A century later Congress passed the Military Support for Civilian Law Enforcement Agencies Act 1981 to provide for a role for the military initially in drug interdiction and subsequently in broader domestic law enforcement efforts in the drug war,[51] though in all but exceptional circumstances members of the military are still prohibited from direct participation in 'search, seizure, arrest, or other similar activity'.[52]

Paramilitary Units in Caribbean Police Forces

In the past decades, Caribbean governments have created specialist paramilitary units that are either entirely separate hybrid police/military agencies under separate command or specialist paramilitary units nested within police forces. In each of the Caribbean territories studied, new paramilitary policing units had been created with specialist weapons, military training, equipment, and a 'crime fighting' ethos. In the Eastern Caribbean countries the Special Services Units serve this function (and fit into a regional capacity to which we return). In general, these units are deployed either in support of anti-crime initiatives such as drug interdiction, in riot control, or in fugitive apprehension. The advantage of these units is that they have power to respond to armed criminals. The logic is that the forces of law and order should be no less well equipped than the 'forces of evil' against whom they are pitted. The disadvantages are that these units seem unable to arrest suspects, much more frequently shooting them dead. Sometimes these deaths are the results of fire-fights between armed police and armed criminals. On other

---

[49] L. Hartz (1979), 'A Comparative Study of Fragment Cultures' in H.D. Graham and T.R. Gurr (eds), *Violence in America: Historical and Comparative Perspectives*. Thousand Oaks, CA: Sage.

[50] W.S. Fields and D. Hardy (1992), 'The Military and the Constitution: A Legal History', *Military Law Review*, 136: 9–13.

[51] See also Ethan Nadelman (1993), *Cops Across Borders: The Internationalization of U.S. Criminal Law Enforcement*. University Park, PA: Penn State Press.

[52] Quoted in Dunlap (2001), 'The Thick Green Line', *op cit.*

occasions the deaths have the hallmarks of executions. Moreover, it is often the case that innocent civilians are killed in the process. In Guyana and Jamaica, paramilitary police units have been closed down because of allegations of extra-judicial execution.

The best documented example is the Crime Management Unit (CMU) of the Jamaica Constabulary Force. This was created in September 2000 by former Prime Minister P.J. Patterson and the then Security Minister K.D. Knight in response to extreme levels of criminal violence. Its remit was to respond to armed criminality. CMU head Reneto Adams had a 'tough-guy image' which included black combat gear and dark glasses. The Unit found itself embroiled in controversy almost from its inception. In March 2001, the CMU killed seven young people in a house at Braeton, St Catherine and also played a major role in three days of shootings in West Kingston in July 2001 when at least 25 people, including a policeman and a soldier, were killed. It was also alleged that Mr Adams reported directly to the Security Minister, K.D. Knight, and occasionally to the Prime Minister. When K.D. Knight was asked in March 2001 whether he was pleased with the performance of the Crime Management Unit he said:

It's early days yet, and one doesn't want to make any definite assessments, but my preliminary view is that it has the capacity to make the difference, particularly if it operates within the parameters of community policing and if it operates along the intelligence driven line.[53]

By the time that it was disbanded, the CMU was involved in 40 fatal shootings in 30 months. To put that in context, the police have killed an average of 139 civilians per year since 1983.[54] In May 2003, CMU officers in pursuit of a suspect, shot dead four of his associates including his girlfriend, another woman, and two men in the village of Crawle. The ballistic and forensic evidence taken from the scene (which had been was disrupted) showed that the people had been shot at short range and were unarmed. With the assistance of a UK senior investigating officer, the scene of the shooting was examined carefully and a thorough investigation was carried out. The head of the CMU and some of his officers

---

[53] 'Security Minister under the Microscope', *Jamaica Gleaner*, 25 March 2001.

[54] Susan Goffe (2004), 'Watching the Watchdogs: A Jamaican NGO's Experience with Lobbying for Policing Oversight and Accountability'. Paper presented at the Independent Complaints Directorate Conference for Policing Oversight and Accountability, 26–29 January 2004, Johannesburg, South Africa.

faced prosecution for murder. Adams was acquitted after what was described as 'the mother of all trials' and was received as a hero outside the courtroom.

Regional Security System (RSS)

The Regional Security System for the Eastern Caribbean is a hybrid multinational paramilitary policing organization that brings together both police and military forces. It was created in 1982 to promote cooperation among the member states in:

the prevention and interdiction of traffic in illegal narcotic drugs, in national emergencies, search and rescue, immigration control, fisheries protection, customs and excise control, maritime policing duties, natural and other disasters, pollution control, combating threats to national security, the prevention of smuggling, and in the protection of off-shore installations and exclusive economic zones.[55]

It is based on a centralized, sub-regional control of specialist paramilitary policing sections, 'Special Services Units' (SSUs), which are of platoon size. This includes Antigua and Barbuda, Barbados, Dominica, Grenada, Saint Kitts and Nevis, Saint Lucia, and Saint Vincent and the Grenadines. The RSS forces are commanded by 10 security chiefs (seven Police Commissioners and three defence forces commanders). The Central Liaison Office (CLO) answers to the chairman of the RSS who is Prime Minister of one of the participating countries on a revolving basis, annually, and in alphabetical order. The Chair is advised by a council of ministers (of defence and national security) which acts as the 'supreme policymaking body'. Action is with the consent of the Prime Minister of the country concerned. The RSS treaty establishes individual and collective capacity to assist. It declares that personnel on operations in another member state, in a territorial sea, or exclusive economic zone (EEZ) shall have 'all the rights, powers, duties, privileges and immunities of the member state in which the operation is taking place'. Also, it establishes the right of hot pursuit within territorial waters and the EEZ. The requesting state has operational control while senior officers of the sending state have 'tactical control' over their service personnel's conduct and discipline. Coastguard vessels on operations or training fly the RSS flag in addition to their

---

[55] Treaty Establishing the Regional Security System (1996).

national flag. A model for the structure of an anti-drugs operation coordinated by the RSS is show in figure 5.1.

The first operation embarked upon by the newly formed RSS was in support of the US military invasion of Grenada in 1983 following the coup d'état and execution of Maurice Bishop. It then acted in Hurricane Hugo in 1989 (affecting Antigua, Saint Kitts, and Montserrat), the aftermath of an attempted coup d'état in Trinidad in 1990, a prison uprising in Saint Kitts Nevis (1994), Hurricanes Luis and Marilyn in Antigua and Saint Kitts, Hurricane George (Saint Kitts and Nevis) and Operation Weedeater (1998, 1999) in Saint Vincent. More recently, they have been deployed to assist with the transfer to a new prison in Saint Lucia (2003) and to quell a prison uprising in Barbados (2006). The system is coordinated by a Central Liaison Office based in Barbados. Here are situated the RSS coordinator, the air-wing, and a centralized training facility. This facility does maritime law enforcement training and land-based training, aiming to develop a paramilitary capacity, by exposing police officers to 'military type training'. An interviewee explained that:

this was necessary because not all of the countries have defence forces, so you had to prepare them to deal with any military threat, at least to make us take a stand initially until we get support. But we didn't only train all the Police forces, so all seven Police forces have what we call Special Service Units that are actually military type people, they are policemen but selected because of their attitude to this kind of thing.

It is therefore possible to deal with instances of public disorder or civil emergencies in the smaller territories without using the army. As Hills suggests, these units can properly be called paramilitary police units because they can act in lieu of soldiers.[56]

The funding for the RSS comes entirely from the ABC countries (America, Britain, Canada), principally the USA. The US set up the SSUs in the 1980s as part of its international policing initiative. It provided the resources to equip and train the SSUs and funded the central coordinating facility. One official explained that today:

they are our principal supporters in terms of financial support, logistical support generally and support in terms of training. They give us money or they might give us equipment or they might give us courses that they have funded themselves. For example, our Command and Staff course, which is for today's officers, is funded between Britain and the US, okay. The basic course that we do used to be funded by Britain but they

[56] Alice Hills (1995), 'Militant Tendencies', *op cit.*

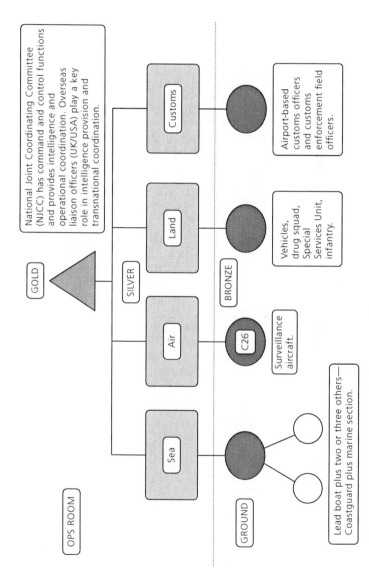

Figure 5.1 Structure of joint anti-drugs operation, RSS

shifted their focus so we had to shift to the US to get support for that. The US fully support the air-wing. The US also provides support for all the Coastguards, in terms of fuel and maintenance. Some countries they give ammunition, right, and they provide training of officers, all of them, America, Canada, Britain for training officers.

Of course that has implications for the dependency of the RSS. As one source put it, 'all the funding comes from the United States. If that funding ceases, we are in trouble, do you understand?'

Despite an enthusiasm in some quarters for the RSS to be extended beyond the Eastern Caribbean to include Guyana, Jamaica, Trinidad, and Tobago, the military personnel that I interviewed from those countries were quite hostile to the idea. They believed that there was an 'excellent working relationship' with the RSS 'in terms of military to military', but there was a lot of resistance from the Chiefs of Staff for the Regional Security System to be widened beyond the Eastern Caribbean:

We are taken up with all kinds of structures and agreements and so on and I think it's a load of time wasting. If they say the RSS is working, which they keep saying, I say leave it alone. Military and the Police is oil and water, doesn't mix. If we want to have some other kind of Treaty, then I say let the military forces have their own thing and then you have the RSS, but you need to have a trigger that brings in the wider military to an RSS issue, but Brigadier Lewis, who was the RSS co-ordinator for many years, far too long, you have to look at motives too, everybody wants to be a General, so if we could bring this thing broader, what does it do for me? We are not in that game and we're not playing that game, so this expanded RSS thing is not supported from here.

There was a very keen awareness of the sense that US funding of the RSS resulted in its agenda being largely set by the USA:

the RSS has two [surveillance aircraft] but they determine how the RSS pay for the pilot, they pay for everything, and once you do that, we look at it and say, 'Well, you know, they are running the show' and they do not take into consideration our sovereignty and our need to patrol our territorial waters, as the case may be, so in the case of [this country], we say, 'Alright, thanks mate but no thanks, we will purchase our own sur- veillance aircraft'. If we do so then we don't have anyone to tell us. If we are part of the RSS, then we are locked into a situation where we have to, they say 'who pay the piper calls the tune', and we are not prepared for somebody to keep calling the tune for us all the time.

Another Chief of Staff expressed an equally strident view. He argued that the larger territories are unhappy with the 'doorway' used by the larger metropolitan countries to access territorial areas through the RSS. What he meant by this 'doorway' is that under the RSS agreement, a vessel from any the RSS countries can go into the territorial seas of any other. The kinds of problems that the Chiefs of Staff envisaged were the question of who was going to fund it, that there were other strategic partners within the sub-region including Cuba, Haiti, and Columbia that were at least as important as others within CARICOM, and that regional agreements often require 'watering down' because of the people that need to be satisfied. There was some deep distrust between the countries that agreements reached have too many reservations. As one Chief of Staff put it, 'we are not too interested in a broader CARICOM thing because the broader you get these Agreements, the more watered down it becomes'.

Operation 'Weedeater'

Few policing operations bring the image of the 'forces of Babylon' into sharper focus than Weedeater, a series of cannabis eradication operations conducted in collaboration between Caribbean police forces and US marines. It is believed that most of the marijuana grown in Saint Vincent is for consumption within the Eastern Caribbean. Commencing in 1995, two- and three-week operations were carried out in Trinidad, Grenada, Saint Lucia, and Saint Vincent. In each case, the marijuana fields are located in regions that are difficult to access on foot and are therefore accessed by US military helicopters. In December 1998, 120 officers from the Regional Security System and 100 US marines joined with US State Department and US DEA officials in Operation Weedeater. The US Helicopter Marine Light Attack arrived with three HU-1N 'Hueye' helicopters and three CH-46 'Sea Knight' helicopters transported to the region by two massive Lockheed C-5 carrier aircraft. The US Marines air-wing was based in nearby Saint Lucia because of its better air support and maintenance facilities. The RSS troops cut and destroyed more than 1.2 million marijuana plants. One hundred and forty-two marijuana curing huts were found and burned. A police officer described the operation:

First of all we get all the people together and we do two days of training, doing rappelling and so on, movement by helicopter and different things and then we go into the fields. We destroy the drugs. We drop off at mornings, pick up at late afternoons and come back and we go all over again. If we make prisoners, we the Vincentians will do the arrests once we have prisoners. Whatever exhibit we have, we also keep them, and we destroy whatever marijuana we meet, we cut them down, we burn them, we work with our kerosene and burn them right in the field.

In December 1999, a similar operation was carried out.[57] This time, the operation burned more than 5 million marijuana plants, 7 tonnes of cured ganja, and destroyed 250 cedar wood huts. These serve a purpose equivalent to a garden shed, for shelter, storage for farm tools, and a sleeping place for the person who will watch over the crop close to harvest time. During this operation 13 farmers were arrested. On the last day of the operation, one farmer was killed by a Vincentian police officer.[58]

All of the people involved with Weedeater were agreed that the attempt to eradicate cannabis production in Saint Vincent failed. The number of marijuana fields was much higher than most people involved in planning the operation believed. One officer complained that 'there's just so much of it . . . To make a significant dent, it's something that would have to be done on a much more regular basis'.[59] A senior Vincentian officer argued that there would need to be a consistent and ongoing approach to eradication in order to 'defeat' the growers. Using the current approach, he explained, the marijuana grew back more quickly than they could eradicate it: 'I can tell you this', he said, 'when we are on one hilltop destroying . . . their guy's on the other hilltop planting'.

In the light of the obvious ineffectiveness of these operations, one might wonder what the reasons are for the operations. Certainly, it works well as a training exercise. Mark Thackson, US marines acting sergeant major for Weedeater, said that the operation had given him and his unit a unique sense of accomplishment: 'so often we train, and train, and train, and it can get routine. Operations like this remind us of who we are and what real purpose we serve'.[60] For the US, this is a valuable training exercise, providing an opportunity to work in very 'real' conditions of asymmetric warfare. In the US press releases, James Mitchell, former Prime Minister of Saint

[57] *The Los Angeles Times*, 16 January 2000; *San Jose Mercury News*, 6 February 2000.

[58] see Axel Klein (2004), 'The Ganja Industry and Alternative Development' in Axel Klein, Marcus Day, and Anthony Harriott (eds), *Caribbean Drugs: From Criminalization to Harm Reduction*. Kingston, Jamaica: Ian Randle Publishers and Zed Books, London.   [59] DEA agent cited in *Marine* magazine.

[60] Master Sgt. Mark Thackson of Hiram, Ga. Cited in *Marine Online* Magazine, January 1997.

Vincent emphasized the fact that the officers carrying out the eradication exercise were largely Vincentian police working with their
Eastern Caribbean neighbours under an RSS mandate. However,
this was not how the Vincentian ganja growers saw it. For them it
was 'the product of US aggression, the wrath of Babylon'.[61] This
sense that the 'Babylon system' had unleashed its military might
runs deep, most acutely among the ganja growers many of whom
are Rastafarians of the Nyabinghi order. Axel Klein, who spent
time interviewing the growers out in the field, found that while few
engaged in collective worship or ritual, there was a strong adherence to a moral code, the wearing of dreadlocks, and the 'copious
consumption' of ganja.[62] The theme of the oppression of Rastas
through the criminalization of ganja is a long-standing one in the
region and one that is unlikely to disappear anytime soon. In Saint
Vincent there is widespread ambivalence about marijuana use and
an acceptance that it is seen as sacred by the Rasta community. In
Jamaica, the Ganja Commission concluded that its personal use
should be decriminalized.[63]

Junior 'Spirit' Cottle—representative of the growers and also
employee of the Saint Vincent Department of Forestry[64]—argues
that marijuana growing is 'the key to our economic independence'.[65]
As Klein argues, a significant proportion of Saint Vincent's GDP is
accounted for by the trade, a significant proportion of the work-
force are engaged in its production or distribution and a high proportion of households are dependent on marijuana income.[66] The
operation helped Cottle's United Front for Progress—'an alliance
of revolutionary community groups' to recruit members and promote its pro-marijuana agenda through protests. Gonsalves recognized that widespread opposition to ganja on moral grounds
had shrunk. The attitude within the society is that marijuana 'was
not really bad'. It produces economic advantage and has elevated
the social status of some people. There is a clear economic imperative—one fifth of Saint Vincent's economy arises from its export

---

[61] Klein (2004), 231.   [62] *Ibid*, 231.
[63] National Commission on Ganja (Chair Professor Barry Chevannes) (2001),
*A Report of the National Commission on Ganja, to the Rt Hon P.J. Patterson, QC
MP, Prime Minister of Jamaica.*
[64] Appointed by Gonsalves, Cottle's job is to assist the ganja growers to work in
such a way that hillside erosion is minimized.
[65] *Los Angeles Times*, 16 January 2000, by Mark Fineman.
[66] Klein (2004), 226.

of ganja. As, Tornado, one of the growers, put it: 'If the Americans destroy all the marijuana in Saint Vincent, they'll destroy Saint Vincent. It's the backbone of the economy. It's our livelihood. And now that the Americans have killed us on bananas, we have no other choice'.[67] After Weedeater, the growers' association (claiming 800 members) demonstrated outside Parliament and wrote to President Bill Clinton claiming compensation for the lost marijuana plants. Then opposition leader Ralph Gonsalves (now Prime Minister) referred to Vincentian ganja as 'our most successful agricultural diversification project'.[68] 'He also commented that 'the ganja industry here has not been accompanied by much violence… It's simply amazing for an industry that generates so much money to have been so free of violence'. There has been no recurrence of Operation Weedeater in Saint Vincent since 1999.[69] Reasons for this are numerous. They include the election of Gonsalves as Prime Minister, the failure to pay for the previous operation, the political embarrassment that arose from the previous occasion, and the protests that resulted.

Summary and Conclusion

Colonel Dunlap of the US military believes that 'the involvement of the armed forces in what might be considered policing or law enforcement activity is posed to increase exponentially in the near future'.[70] In his view, this is because the threat of terrorism and weapons of mass destruction have the potential to overwhelm police resources. In the contemporary Caribbean, terrorism or other forms of political violence cannot be ruled out,[71] but it is

---

[67] *Los Angeles Times*, 16 January 2000.   [68] *Ibid.*

[69] 'Operation Weedeater' US airlift-assisted eradication exercises in St. Vincent and the Grenadines scheduled for autumn 2001 were postponed due to US military airlift resource constraints arising from homeland defence requirements and the war in Afghanistan. <www.state.gov/documents/organization/8697.pdf>. There has been one more recent operation in Trinidad in 2002.

[70] Charles Dunlap, *op cit*, p 32.

[71] The only major instance of politically motivated sabotage leading to loss of life is the 1976 bombing of a Cubana Airlines flight from Barbados by a Cuban dissident group with links to the CIA. In recent years, there have been a small number of 'rubbish bin' and channa bomb attacks in Trinidad. Some argue that there are linkages between armed drug traffickers and terrorist organizations—referring to 'narcoterrorism'. cf Stephen Vasciannie (2004), 'Security, Terrorism and International Law: A Skeptical Comment' in Ivelaw Griffith (ed), *Caribbean Security in the Age of Terror: Challenge and Change*. Kingston, Jamaica: Ian Randle Publishers.

the possibility of breakdown of social order and armed violence stemming from the clandestine drug trade that give police commanders and Chiefs of Staff most cause for concern. This chapter suggests that there is a complex relationship between police and military force. Police forces have, since their origins, the power to muster armed force, and soldiers have undertaken police duties. Nonetheless, it seems that the worldwide process of 'policeization' of the military is occurring simultaneously with the militarization of the police.[72] However, it should be borne in mind that in this region, police forces in general have a history of being militarized in their ethos and training. This produces a conundrum. Caribbean police are attempting to shed their military legacy, demilitarizing and democratizing, at the same moment that the forces around them—especially the UK and USA—are themselves extensively militarizing their own police forces. This leads, in the Caribbean context, to a general tendency for police and military forces to converge.

Caribbean defence forces are, in operational terms, working almost exclusively in the policing field. As a British defence advisor put it, the only real role for a military force in the region is in peace support operations, 'working in support of the police'. Military forces have taken a prominent role in the task of policing, taking numerous forms including its military role as an aid to the civil power during a declared state of emergency, in providing intelligence, logistical, and other support in response to specific threats. In each of the countries studied the primary function of the military was in support of police operations.[73] There are, of course, differences from location to location, not least because not all the islands have defence forces. The precise nature of the military involvement with domestic policing varies from place to place, but the key similarity is the shift towards routine involvement in policing activities, above all those involving drug trafficking and armed criminality. In all countries—whether or not they have a defence force—the regular police have a paramilitary policing capacity. This is in place for emergency public order policing, but is also routinely used in support of counter-drugs operations. These units are also the most mobile and therefore are frequently

[72] Peter Kraska (2001), 'Playing War: Masculinity, Militarism and Their Real-World Consequences' in Kraska (ed), p 152.

[73] 'Crime-Busters: Jamaican Forces in Front Line of Island's Violent War against Drugs and Extortion', *Soldier* Magazine of the British Army, August 2005, p 30–1.

called upon in relation to policing and law enforcement activity at borders—and in the case of the SSUs—as part of the Regional Security System (RSS) as part of a concerted transnational force. Several places have armed units within Customs, and in Trinidad and Tobago there is an entirely separate Special Anti-Crime Unit (SAUTT)—a third force—headed by a brigadier and therefore equal in rank to the military Chief of Staff and the Commissioner of Police.

The indications are that Caribbean policing has militarized in recent decades. External and internal security functions are blurred and civilians are targets. There is a new emphasis on intelligence and an ideology of militarism emphasizing the idea that military technology is essential in order maintenance. Military armaments, clothing, and equipment are being acquired and there is evident collaboration and convergence between defence and crime control industries, and the use of military language to describe social problems of crime and disorder.[74] In the Caribbean region, taking into consideration the role of the army in policing and the militarization of the police, each of these indicators points in the direction of a greater degree of militarism and militarization.

The espionage and military models of policing have eclipsed the consensual model in the contemporary Caribbean. The military model, the founding formula for colonial policing, remains the guiding philosophy for Caribbean policing and it is upon this that regional transnational policing strategies have been built. Even while the ideology of community policing is being promulgated by security ministers and chiefs of police, its democratic ethos is undermined by the spread of a transnational model based on espionage backed up with military force. Paramilitary structures created, funded, trained, and made operationally viable by Britain and the USA work to an agenda set by these metropolitan countries. The 'high policing' systems and structures introduced to supplement post-colonial diplomatic and military involvement in the Cold War against communism have now been turned to provide an adjunct to the wars currently being fought—metaphorically and literally—against organized crime, terrorism, and the drugs trade (see Chapter 4). The 'military' and 'spy' models of policing succeed because they are both inherently transnational in their

[74] *Ibid*, p 17.

historical origins and contemporary essence. The military model was designed for export to control British interests in the colonies and travels well. Its military origins lend themselves precisely to the goals of providing force against foreign nations and against the so-called 'enemy within'. The intelligence-led paradigm is similarly designed to move freely across national borders (within limits prescribed by *diplomacy* rather than democracy) to provide the knowledge required for military action to proceed. We should hardly be surprised that the military and intelligence-led paradigms of policing tend to eclipse the community-led paradigm in the transnational sphere. This is troubling because the policing paradigm that can be fully democratic is the 'community-led' model. This paradigm privileges direct communication between police and public and is based upon the principles of openness, transparency, and democratic accountability. It follows that neither the 'military-led' nor 'intelligence-led' models of policing—which I take to be two sides of the same coin—offer the prospect of democratic policing. The colonial-military paradigm in policing is anti-democratic in its origins and essence. It is explicitly authoritarian and is designed for use against non-citizens who have no basis upon which to call police-soldiers to account. The espionage paradigm (see Chapter 4), with its secrecy and lack of transparency suffers a similar lack of accountability to the wider community.

It may also be that the military and community paradigms of policing are, in fact, intertwined rather than distinct. DeMichele and Kraska,[75] noting that that military-led and community-led models of policing have emerged simultaneously, argue that the two models can be applied in an ideologically and operationally consistent manner.[76] Thus, paramilitary policing units (also known as SWAT teams) can be used to conduct saturation patrols, aggressive stop-search, and field interviews to deal with so-called 'quality of life issues' as part of a departmental emphasis on community policing.[77] Thus, the 'softer, regulatory aspects of community policing can be intertwined with the hard edge of paramilitary policing tactics',[78] creating a 'type of harmony'—like the old metaphor of the iron fist in the velvet glove—between community

---

[75] Matthew DeMichele and Peter Kraska (2001), *Community Policing in Battle Garb: A Paradox of Coherent Strategy?* in Peter Kraska (ed), *op cit*, p 82–104.
[76] *Ibid*, p 97.   [77] *Ibid*, p 95.   [78] *Ibid*, p 96.

policing (especially the 'zero tolerance' strand) and paramilitary policing. Grimshaw and Jefferson argue that community policing is hegemonic work, required to provide legitimation for the use of coercive power.[79]

Finally, there is the question of the effectiveness of military and paramilitary force in controlling crime. Views are divided about the extent to which paramilitary policing practices provoke or prevent public disorder.[80] Paramilitary policing has not proved to be particularly effective in reducing crime (except perhaps *in extremis*). In general, paramilitary police action seems able to suppress the symptoms of social disorder but at an unacceptable cost to the body politic and indeed to human life. Some paramilitary police and soldiers undertaking policing functions have executed their powers much more harshly than their regular counterparts—with extrajudicial execution being common at certain places and times. Armed units—whether they are military, quasi-military, or paramilitary—sometimes fail to arrest suspects or bring them to justice. In such conditions, the threat of extra-judicial killing becomes a threat to democracy. The increased use of the military in policing has not universally led to increased or decreased levels of deadly force, but it has in certain key instances included the shooting of armed criminals by the police—for example, in Guyana and in Jamaica. Similar experiences have also been documented in South America[81] and India.[82] In some instances, the military involvement in policing has led to severe loss of life, but the contemporary examples in Trinidad

[79] Roger Grimshaw and Tony Jefferson (1985), *Interpreting Policework*. London: Allen & Unwin.

[80] Tony Jefferson (1990), *The Case Against Paramilitary Policing*, see fn 46; P.A.J. Waddington (1993), 'The Case against Paramilitary Policing Considered', *British Journal of Criminology*, 33/3: 353–70; Tony Jefferson (1993), 'Pondering Paramilitarism: A Question of Standpoints?', *British Journal of Criminology*, 33/3: 374–81. See also Alice Hills (1995), 'Militant Tendencies: "Paramilitarism" in the British Police', *British Journal of Criminology*, 35/3: 450–8 and P.A.J. Waddington (2008), 'Policing Public Order and Political Contention' in Tim Newburn, *Handbook of Policing*. Cullompton: Willan.

[81] Mercedes Hinton (2006), *The State on the Streets: Police and Politics in Argentina and Brazil*. Boulder and London: Lynne Rienner Publishers.

[82] Jyoti Belur (2007), 'Police Use of Deadly Force: Analysing Police Encounters in Mumbai', unpublished Ph.D. thesis, London School of Economics; see also Jyoti Belur (2010), 'Why do the Police Use Deadly Force?: Explaining Police Encounters in Mumbai', *British Journal of Criminology*, 50/2: 320–41.

and Jamaica suggest that soldiers are generally more careful with the trigger than their police colleagues.

The examples discussed in this chapter point to a complex relationship between police and armed force. The possession of firearms and military training for riot-control and counter-insurgency has long been a part of the police organization. The early Metropolitan Police Commissioners wore swords, still displayed in the Commissioner's office in London's New Scotland Yard. Caribbean police forces always had access to arms. More recently, the paramilitary power of the police has been enhanced in various forms, including by powerful weapons and armour. Where defence forces exist, these are largely working in support of the police. As we shall see in the next chapters, there are numerous other organizations, including the coastguard—which answer to the Chief of Staff—and border protection agencies that also collaborate with the military. We turn in the next chapter to an exploration of the role of Customs, immigration, and airport security authorities before returning in the concluding chapter to the questions about accountability and control raised by this blurring of the boundaries between police, military, and border protection agencies.

6

Border Protection: Customs, Immigration, and Airport Security

> tourists move because they find the world within their reach irresistibly *attractive*; the vagabonds move because they find the world within their reach unbearably *inhospitable*. The tourists travel because they want to; the vagabonds because they have *no other bearable choice*. ... Globalization is geared to the tourists' dreams and desires. Its second effect—its *side*-effect—is the transformation of many others into vagabonds.[1]

> airport security is a commercial problem, it's a national problem, it's a police problem, it's an immigration problem, it's a Customs problem and it's an international problem, and it's that understanding that I think has got to be brought across.[2]

Introduction

The world is in motion.[3] People and things are moving so swiftly and extensively around the globe that contemporary theorists describe world society as being like liquid.[4] Others argue that the speed of global travel, the movement of goods, services, capital, and information is now so great that we now live in a 'space of flows' rather than a 'space of places'.[5] Every day, millions of people and hundreds of thousands of tonnes of goods move across national

---

[1] Zigmunt Baumann (1998), 'On Glocalization: Or Globalization for Some, Localisation for Some Others' in Peter Bilharz (ed) (2001), *The Bauman Reader*. London: Routledge, p 309.　　[2] British security advisor to the Caribbean.

[3] Franko Katja Aas (2007), 'Analysing a World in Motion: Global Flows Meet "Criminology of the Other"', *Theoretical Criminology*, 11/2: 283–303.

[4] Zygmunt Bauman (2000), *Liquid Modernity*. Cambridge: Polity Press.

[5] Manuel Castells (1996), *The Rise of the Network Society*. Malden, MA: Blackwell Publishers; Franko Katja Aas (2007), 'Analysing a World in Motion', *op cit.*

boundaries. Much of this human and commercial flow is through the world's seaports, airports, and other nodes in transport systems and, while on the move, it is subject to human and technical surveillance, repeatedly documented and sometimes detained for more intensive checking. Other border crossings go undocumented. Some people, fisher folk or smugglers for example, cross freely from one jurisdiction to another by customary practice or by travelling clandestinely.

These flows bring into sharp relief a paradox of globalization. On one hand, sustaining the contemporary economic order relies on the freest possible movement of goods, labour, and capital. On the other hand, the sense of insecurity requires borders to be as strong as possible to minimize the risks of harm to a nation's infrastructure and its people from the threats of organized crime, terrorism, or other 'toxic waste' of late modern society. Contemporary borders must act like a membrane, facilitating the flows while keeping unwanted 'residues' out.[6] For Wonders, the border acts like a sieve, sifting and sorting flows according to their entitlement to move.[7] Policing the flow of goods and people through national borders is a transnational activity, defined by the attempt to control movement *between nation states* as it arrives and departs, especially through transport nodes such as seaports and airports. But contemporary border policing extends far beyond physical boundaries to control movements before and after arrival.[8] Goods and people in transit are monitored, inbound flights are profiled long before they land, and people in transit, especially those defined by their extra-territoriality—such as deportees and asylum seekers—are often documented and monitored long after their arrival.[9]

Policing migration has changed over time as the balance between internal, external, and extra-territorial controls has shifted.[10] Police

[6] Katja Franko Aas (2007), 'Analysing a World in Motion', p 292, *op cit.*

[7] Nancy Wonders (2006), 'Global Flows, Semi-Permeable Borders and New Channels of Inequality' in Sharon Pickering and Leanne Weber (eds), *Borders, Mobility and Technologies of Control.* Amsterdam: Springer, pp 63–86.

[8] Leanne Weber and Ben Bowling (2004), 'Policing Migration: A Framework for Investigating the Regulation of Global Mobility', *Policing & Society* 14/3: 195–212.

[9] Leanne Weber and Ben Bowling (2008), 'Valiant Beggars and Global Vagabonds: Select, Eject, Immobilize', *Theoretical Criminology*, 12/3: 355–75; Leanne Weber and Ben Bowling (2004), 'Policing Migration', *op cit.*

[10] Leanne Weber and Ben Bowling (2004), 'Policing Migration', *op cit.*

and immigration authorities have been charged with the function of securing territory through the identification and exclusion of those deemed to be undesirable and police have also been involved in the ongoing surveillance of existing 'suspect populations'. As we saw in Chapter 2, Caribbean migration has been driven by the desire to move to richer countries for chances of a better life. Governments are keen to pick the most highly skilled migrants while excluding the undesirable. The role of migration controls, therefore, is '*not to prevent* but to *control* the transnational movement of labour'.[11] For Bauman, inequalities in mobility can be seen in terms of two 'post-modern types', the welcome tourist (including businesspeople as well as holidaymakers) and the unwelcome vagabond who he describes as 'the waste of the world which has dedicated itself to tourist services'.[12] Tourists stimulate local economies through investment or consumption, are financially independent, and have the capacity to leave. Vagabonds—construed in the contemporary Caribbean as the 'deportee' (see Chapter 2)—are perceived as a fiscal liability in that they will seek to stay and make demands on the state. As people with obvious *needs* they are out of step with the prevailing free market mentality.[13]

This chapter explores Caribbean border protection practices. We look at the border protection infrastructure: airport security, immigration, and Customs.[14] In each case we look at the agencies involved, the spaces they police, and the roles they play in the attempt to secure borders, what their personnel see as their main priorities, and how these have shifted in recent times. Our central concern is to examine agencies' policing functions and how this has grown in recent years to eclipse other roles. We then look at the ways in which border protection agencies collaborate with police and other agencies domestically, with regional partners and with metropolitan countries, exploring some of the tensions in international collaboration in border policing practices. This enables us to explore the ways in which these agencies are slowly being knitted

[11] W.I. Robinson (2006), '"Aqui estamos y no nos vamos!" Global Capital and Immigrant Rights', *Race and Class*, 48/2: 77–91, esp p 83.

[12] Zigmunt Bauman (1998), *Globalization: The Human Consequences*. Cambridge: Polity Press, p 92.

[13] Leanne Weber and Ben Bowling (2004), 'Policing Migration', *op cit*.

[14] Other transport nodes including the seaport, marinas, and the Post Office are of interest here, but have been excluded owing to space restrictions. We look in more detail at policing of maritime borders in Chapter 7.

together with police and military forces to create a national security capacity linked with regional and hemispheric counterparts as an essential component of the new security archipelago.

Airport Security

Airports are perhaps '*the* symbol of contemporary mobility'.[15] They are certainly critical to the global flow of people around the world. Aircraft carried an estimated 2.2 billion passengers worldwide in 2007 with 40 per cent of international tourists travelling by air.[16] More than 44 million tonnes of freight passed through the world's airports in the same year, amounting to 35 per cent of interregional annual exports of goods by value.[17] Although they are not always at the geographical edges of a territory, airports are—in effect—borders, 'non places'[18] constituted by the massive transient flows of people and things. As such, airports are an intense focus of contemporary security strategies. During the fieldwork, I saw Caribbean airports from a variety of different angles. I travelled extensively by air and saw them like any other traveller, but as the research progressed, I took the opportunity to interview the chiefs of airport security and to take a guided tour of each of the island's airports. Now, I saw the airport through different eyes, talking with staff of the various organizations, observing them as they went about their business and passengers as they moved through the concourses, lounges, and security checkpoints. From this perspective, the airport resembles a theatre with a sharp division between front-of-house and backstage. The extensive backstage activity, invisible to passengers, creates the illusion of seamless passenger travel. Accessed through doors, unmarked or marked 'restricted', a large 'airside' area opens up, that includes baggage-handling, Customs and administrative offices, and from there to the runways and aircraft. There is a complex array of different security agencies that work within the airport. Some are employed by the airlines themselves as well as Customs, immigration, private contractors, and the airport security service, which has overall responsibility for the safety of the public travelling through the airport.

The mission of airport security is 'to protect civil aviation against acts of unlawful interference'. This includes acts as diverse as

---

[15] Katja Franko Aas (2007), *Globalisation and Crime*. London: Sage, p 33, emphasis added.   [16] IATA, July 2009.   [17] *Ibid.*

[18] Katja Franko Aas (2007), *Globalisation and Crime, op cit*, p 33.

smuggling weapons or explosives onto planes, deliberate sabotage, preventing mentally disordered people from walking onto the runways, and maintaining the perimeter fence. Airport security is responsible for 'anything going airside', guarding entry and exits into secure areas. In some places, the person holding this responsibility is the Director of Airports and in others, there is a chief of airport security who answers to the director. Both positions are civil service roles, working on behalf of government to ensure that the airport meets International Civil Aviation Organization (ICAO) requirements.[19] The director's role encompasses the day-to-day management of airport security and maintaining a strategic overview. The security ambit also includes security supervision of baggage handlers, catering staff, cleaners, and those working to fuel and maintain aircraft. The chiefs typically have a background in law enforcement or the military and have high level security management training. Airport security is also responsible for issuing temporary and permanent airside security passes for the airlines' ground staff, cleaners, caterers, and duty-free shops staff. In this they collaborate with Special Branch who carry out the background security screening checks for all the staff at the airport; no-one is employed permanently until they have been security cleared.

Airport security services have a general policing duty akin to routine beat policing, much of which is maintaining order rather than dealing with crime. Two or three officers, including some in plain clothes, patrol the departure lounge. Staff start work at 8am with a briefing and when they finish their day's work, they complete a report on anything unusual. They have police powers, including powers of arrest, under the Police Act and can do 'anything a policeman can do when they are on duty'. The staff have a

[19] The International Civil Aviation Organization, a UN Specialized Agency, is the global forum for civil aviation. ICAO works to achieve its vision of safe, secure, and sustainable development of civil aviation through cooperation amongst its member states. To implement this vision, the Organization has the following strategic objectives (for the period 2005–2010): (A) Safety—Enhance global civil aviation safety; (B) Security—Enhance global civil aviation security; (C) Environmental Protection—Minimize the adverse effect of global civil aviation on the environment; (D) Efficiency—Enhance the efficiency of aviation operations; (E) Continuity—Maintain the continuity of aviation operations; (F) Rule of Law—Strengthen law governing international civil aviation. <http://www.icao. int/>. ICAO requirements were considerably beefed up after 11 September 2001 with the ICAO revising their Annex 17 Security requirements for international aviation, but under amendment 10 for domestic operations.

strong *esprit de corps* and while they are distinct as airport security personnel, 'when they are on duty, they are policemen under the arc of the airport'. Security officers discharge their patrol function in collaboration with the Police Force Airport Division whose responsibility encompasses the airport, approach and perimeter roads, and regulating licensed taxis. The police deal mostly with various relatively minor offences within or immediately outside the airport such as petty crimes, scuffles among passengers, shop-lifting from the duty-free shop and so on. In most locations, it is only the police who are permitted to carry firearms in the airport, so may be required to deal with more serious incidents.

Private contractors manage and run the baggage screening machines. The funding for the airport screening comes from the airline association and from the international airlines that pool their resources, buy the equipment and pay for the personnel. They screen the luggage going through the restricted zone into the departure area and operate the ion scanning machine which detects traces of explosives. The private contractors are also answerable to the chief of security who must ensure that they are meeting the standards and recommended practices and must intervene in the event that anything goes wrong. For example, the chief has to ensure that the contractors have the appropriate number of people operating the scanning machines and that the staff are duly attentive.

Airport passenger flows

The movement of passengers through an airport illustrates the sense that it is a 'space of flows'. It is like the movement of a migrating flock. Although it moves through a physical space, the flock of airline passengers also *constitutes a space*. Some staff cater for its needs at specific points while others—notably the security staff—move with the flock as it travels from the airport entrance to the aircraft. As passengers enter the terminal, an airport security officer carries out a preliminary passport check before pointing them through into the first area inside the terminal. Next, assisted by two baggage-handlers, passengers must weigh their luggage to ensure that it is under the required weight of each individual bag. Passengers with overweight bags have to decant some of their belongings—breadfruit, bottles of honey and white rum, tins of cheese—out of their bags into their hand luggage or into cardboard boxes. Bags are then stickered: 'checked under 27kg'. Approaching the check-in desks, about one in ten passengers is selected to undergo 'rummage searches' of their hold and carry-on luggage by private security staff working alongside Customs and police officers. The police explained that they searched on a random basis (on the premise that drug traffickers use people from all walks of life) while UK Customs liaison officers were trying to encourage more profiled searches. The rummage searches were extremely thorough. One officer that I observed went through every item carefully, explored every nook and cranny within the bags, turning bottles of white rum upside down.[20] In most searches, clothing was removed from the suitcases, vanity cases and wash bags were opened, jars had their lids taken off, and everything was inspected very closely. As the searches were carried out, police officers working alongside would examine passengers' travel documents asking questions about their planned journey: reasons for travel, where were they going to stay, and for how long? At this point, some passengers would be asked to undergo an ion scan check and those that had positive readings were required to take a urine test.[21]

Once at the check-in desk, boarding passes and passport were checked by a security officer employed by the airline. These officers also work closely with the police who would be alerted if any suspicions were aroused. Before entering the departure lounge, hand luggage was checked through the baggage scanning and also manually searched. Luggage, now going onto the cargo hold, has also been x-rayed. On the walk to the gate, two Drug Squad officers walked up and down looking at the departing passengers. At the gate, a police Drug Squad officer conducted clothing searches on selected passengers, while two officers from a private security company carried out a final hand luggage search of all passengers. On several occasions, I observed private security and Drug Squad officers passing through the aeroplane, feeling under the seats, taking up seat covers and liners, checking whether there was anything hidden under the seats.[22] In all, processing two outbound flights

---

[20] One Drug Squad officer explained that there had been attempts to smuggle liquid cocaine. At first glance this looks identical to white rum but because the liquid cocaine is viscous, when bottles are turned upside down the bubbles move much more slowly.

[21] This process is examined in more detail in Chapter 8.

[22] Of course a very large number of people have access to aeroplanes during the flight. For example, many flights from the US or UK land in several Caribbean locations before reaching their final destination.

involved 13 officers from a private security company (including two supervisors), four Drug Squad officers and four UK liaison officers (three Customs and one Metropolitan Police). One UK overseas liaison officer described the process as 'a bit of overkill.'

Airport security priorities

The principal objective of the airport security service is to identify weapons, dangerous articles, and dangerous goods. As an 'offshoot' of this, the officers have been involved in picking up controlled drugs, and handing suspects over to the police Drug Squad. The role of airport security in policing drugs in recent years has grown simply because of the frequency with which drugs are detected. Therefore, as one chief of security put it, 'they have given more importance to looking for drugs. Not that they are paying less attention to looking for weapons and so on but it has taken on a greater importance in their job'. Like the head of Special Branch (see Chapter 4), chiefs of airport security tended to see drugs trafficking and terrorism as part and parcel of the same threat because the drugs players have the infrastructure, logistics, and capacity to support terrorism as long as the money is right. The general view of chiefs of security was that the airports' vulnerability to terrorist attack was high but the actual risk of an attack was low:

Sabotage is not that much of a threat locally; but of course in saying that, I also have to acknowledge that security doesn't stay at home because we form part of a worldwide chain. And in that chain the weakest link is the downfall of the whole chain so we have to maintain certain standards. Although our level of threat may not be [high], of course we could be used to get at other people.

While there was very extensive screening of passengers and hand luggage, there was much less attention paid to perimeter fencing, security of car parking areas, and checking of people like baggage handlers, cleaning, and catering staff. The salaries that people are paid here are so low that that people are easily bought, so there is a perverse contrast between the close scrutiny with which cabin baggage and hold baggage is checked coming into the airport and, on the other hand, the ease with which staff come and go into the airport. In an interview with one chief of airport security, I raised the possibility that the lack of a strong perimeter fence and the fact that most Caribbean airports had sides that were open to the sea offered an opportunity for smuggling. In his view, the problem was not one of drugs being brought in through the perimeter fences which are only a way to keep out wild animals and to mark the airport perimeter:

The network is so well established that the person at the top will have to be involved and unless you have that in your mind, you'll never get it. Nobody's coming through the fence with a suitcase with half a million dollars worth of drugs, that's bull, that's fish and chips, it's bigger than that, you've got to be at the top. Let's put it this way, hypothetically, someone—say, the chief of security or chief of immigration, chief of Customs—can get anything to move and no-one would question you driving in and driving out with your vehicle or anything because you're who you are and so we have to look at the higher level to say this is where these fellows with all that money's going to be aiming.

The chief of security argued that lower level operatives are also unlikely to be the targets. In his view, the drug smugglers are aiming for a 'higher level than the red cap'. This chief of security also stressed that while the focus on the airport to prevent drugs from arriving and exiting the island was essential, it was not going to be the answer to the problem. The reality was that the islands have open shore lines. 'How many guys', he asked, 'will move twenty kilos of white stuff through the airport when they know I have scanners and dogs right here and my guys are sharp, when I have an open shore line'. The fishing fleet, he argued 'goes in and out with impunity'. So, 'if you're sensible what you do is put them under ten tonnes of fish for God's sake!'

Customs

Customs' traditional role is to collect import and export duties and other taxes and to protect this revenue by controlling the movement of goods and people through ports and airports, checking cargo and luggage for concealed items so as to ensure that all taxable goods have been declared. Two fundamental changes have occurred in this role.[23] First, the massive volume of world trade has increased, encouraged by neoliberal policies emphasizing the free flow of goods across international borders and removal of fiscal barriers to trade increasing the freedom and flexibility of the market. As markets are deregulated nation states are less extensively

---

[23] Pravin Gordan (2007), 'Customs in the 21st Century', *World Customs Journal*, 1/1: 49–54.

involved and therefore, have to find new ways of raising revenue that do not impede the free market. The role of Customs in raising revenue is therefore diminishing. Trade rules have become more complex and are accompanied by a proliferation of regional trade agreements as the number of participants in world trade increases. A shift towards manufactured goods with increasing use of shared and component parts production changes the types of transactions handled by Customs administrations. The issue of time has become crucial to world trade, with the introduction of 'just-in-time' distribution, low inventory retention, and multi-modal transport creating new ways of moving goods across borders and putting new pressures on supply chains. The blueprint for modern Customs operations is the Kyoto Convention which sets out what Customs administrations should do to facilitate legitimate trade and travel.[24] The essence of the Convention is that Customs procedures should not be a barrier to trade. A second shift, occurring simultaneously, is the extension of the role of Customs beyond revenue collection to become the 'first line of defence' in border protection.[25] This has led customs administrations to recognize that a 'fundamental

[24] International Convention on the Simplification and Harmonization of Customs Procedures (Kyoto, 18 May 1973). Entered into force: 25 September 1974.

[25] In the British tradition Customs' role in border protection, has existed for some time. While the role has focused on collecting and administering Customs and Excise duties and Value Added Tax, HM Revenue and Customs is also responsible for preventing the evasion of revenue laws including smuggling and has historically drawn them towards a policing type role on land and in coastal waters. Customs have been responsible for enforcing prohibitions and restrictions on importing particular goods including alcohol, prohibited drugs, infected goods, indecent and obscene articles, and counterfeit goods. Customs Commissioners also have a role in controlling coastal traffic, with a strong relationship with other countries due to historical links with foreign trade. Customs also have a general power to 'hold inquiries into any assigned matter in relation to HM Customs and Excise', to 'appoint ports for the purpose of customs and excise', and 'to detain ships by Order of the Admiralty Court, and to control the movement of aircraft' including the enforcement of public health regulations. It has a role in enforcing immigration controls in small ports and airports and laws relating to fisheries, and in recent years, the role of customs in law enforcement more generally has grown, so that the emergence of transnational organized crime networks is seen as a major shift requiring changes in patterns of working, due to their diversity, flexibility, low visibility, and connections among different networks. The sense that 'security threats recognise no national boundaries', and most obviously the major terrorist attacks, but also anxiety about public health and the environment—including the Convention on the International Trade in Endangered Species (CITES) and the Basel Convention on Hazardous Waste are implemented by customs.

shift' in their role has occurred.[26] Gordan argues that the strategic drivers—the globalization of goods, capital, people, and technology—have created increased complexity, range, and scope in their functions. Customs is no longer only a collector of revenues at the border, its role expanding into 'trade facilitation' and preventing unfair competition. There has also been a shift towards automation, risk management, and intelligence, requiring 'a sharper ability to identify which goods or travellers should be allowed free passage and which should be stopped and checked'.[27] This means that the emphasis is moving away from being largely concerned with import control to deal with export and transit in developing a 'total view of the supply chain'.[28]

The overall responsibility of the Comptroller of Customs is to manage the imperatives of tax collection, 'facilitating trade' and border protection. Answering to him is a Deputy Commissioner, who is head of Enforcement, Intelligence and Quality Assurance who supervises, investigates, and detains suspect imported and exported goods. Customs have responsibility for all border points as well as approved ports of entry and they conduct patrols, including of rivers and highways, to investigate smuggling. They have an investigation unit, an intelligence unit, a marine interdiction unit, and a canine unit. A Customs Intelligence Unit collects and disseminates intelligence, focusing on invoicing—'the heartbeat of customs'—in relation to import and export. Their 'main plague' is contraband. People use the islands to load goods which 'then flood the market and create an unfair trade practice for the legitimate traders, especially the local manufacturers'. Smuggled goods include beer, liquor, and appliances (such as refrigerators, televisions, and other electrical goods), petroleum, and fuel oils. Smugglers bring in the goods without paying duties—which can be as much as 70 per cent on some goods—and can therefore make a very large profit in comparison with those where duty is paid. One way that smuggling occurs is through 'under declaration' of goods, so Customs' job is to make sure the declaration is accurate. The problem with detecting smuggling is that it is practically impossible for the Customs Service to witness the loading of goods. They have to do physical checks after loading which may include the use of technology—but it is very difficult to detect

---

[26] Pravin Gordan (2007), 'Customs in the 21st Century', *op cit*, p 51.
[27] *Ibid.*   [28] *Ibid.*

cleverly concealed goods such as cocaine concealed in shipments of rice or sugar. Similarly with fuel, inbound vehicles may have tampered documents to show that the fuel was above or below a marker. They work alongside the energy authorities, who have powers to impose very large fines. Enforcement activity is also hampered by the fact that the court process is time-consuming. Customs officials tended to think that it was impossible to eradicate smuggling; all they can do is minimize it. They conduct joint examinations with other law enforcement agencies at the ports and do passenger profiling. Customs also have a role in monitoring imported chemical fertilizers and other poisons and investigate criminal activities such as firearms, ammunition, and narcotics smuggling. In this they work closely with the Drug Squad. They also have a responsibility under the Financial Action Task Force to take action against money laundering, for example interdicting cash from drug operations.

After the general task of ensuring that revenue is protected, heads of Customs now saw drugs trafficking as the region's security priority and with it the importation of illegal firearms, illegal ammunition, the movement of precursor chemicals (such as acetone), money laundering, and within recent years, the tools of terrorism such as explosives and weapons of mass destruction. Other priorities included the movement of transnational criminals, regionally or extra-regionally, including criminal deportees, child pornography, cybercrime, and commercial fraud. Since Customs historically had been about the protection of revenue, the number one security threat in the past would be damage to the economy from failing to protect tax revenues. In the view of the head of Customs, the view that it was exclusively concerned with revenue was 'regrettably, a misconceived notion as to the mission of Customs administrations':

in the metropolitan countries, Customs administrations have always been major law enforcement agencies. Revenue collection has been part of their remit but they have historically also had a wider, not a wider notional remit, but a wider *practical* remit. Within the Caribbean region a lot of emphasis was placed, in the past, on revenue collection. I think that Customs administrations in this region now can no longer be seen as merely revenue collectors. They have to be seen as integral part of the law enforcement apparatus.

Whereas revenue protection and action against smuggling was a priority, Customs' responsibility has grown distinctly wider.

Customs have 'agency duties', that do not relate to revenue violations, but for which they have a worldwide agency responsibility under the programme of the World Customs Organization
(WCO), such as the protection of endangered species. Heads of
Customs had not yet seen a reduction in the role of Customs in
revenue protection. At present, it was not a question of 'either/or',
but of 'both/and':

Customs administrations have historically been multitask and I think that
one cannot say that you are reducing emphasis in one area in order to
increase emphasis in the other. Customs administrations are at the borders, they are primary border control agencies. They provide government
with one of its greatest resources. Customs administrations clearly have a
much wider remit than any other government agency.

Looking into the future, Customs chiefs saw a time when there will
be a significant amount of imports under WTO agreements that
will not attract Customs duties. Their role in revenue collection
will diminish, but at present, they are doing border protection *in
addition* to their revenue responsibilities. In such a context,

somewhere along the line we are moving on a continuum which will
take us into full-scale border protection. If you take into consideration
that under World Trade Organization provisions probably all imports in
five years time where there wouldn't be Custom duties. Of course, you
will have a responsibility for that still, right. You become more now of a
border protection than a revenue agency.

This, one head of Customs argued, meant increasingly that they
had to work with others. The World Customs Organization has
been dealing with issues such as facilitating and expediting the
movement of legitimate trade, but also undertaking risk analysis
and encouraging a 'risk management environment'. The focus is
now much less on legitimate enterprise, travellers, and businesses;
rather it is to 'concentrate on the areas of greatest risk'. World
Customs have implemented trade facilitation bringing legitimate
businesses on board to work hand-in-hand with Customs. Law
enforcement cannot be done in a vacuum and therefore Customs
have had to engage with other law enforcement agencies to deepen
and strengthen cooperation and partnership among security agencies and with the business community, non-governmental agencies,
and partners in the supply chain to assist them in improving their
own security. The intention is that 'the more they step up their
security, the more difficult it is for transnational criminals to use

legitimate carriers to move their illegitimate goods as well as using legitimate goods now to hide their illegitimate goods'.

Given the convergence of Customs enforcement with other spheres of law enforcement, I was interested to know how far they see themselves as police. The answer was resolutely that they saw themselves as Customs officers although they conceded that the role was a *policing* one. One Customs officer argued that 'law enforcement as a whole involves policing so from that angle it also involves policing, whether it's policing the borders or whatever the case may be.' They also thought that there had been a gradual reduction in the dividing lines between organizations. One of the goals of the National Joint Headquarters (NJHQ) was to enable better communications and improve the relationship between Customs, the coastguard, and the police. Nonetheless, the tendency within the region was for Drug Squad to speak to Drug Squad, Customs to Customs and so on. This, they argued was:

just a natural thing. You know you tend to, if you pick up the phone to call, say, Customs in _____, when you think if you know somebody in that country in the Customs, that's the first thing you tend to do. Who do I know in that place? And you tend to want to talk to that person, you ask for that person first.

There was a strong sense of regional solidarity. Customs people within the region were thought of as culturally similar in terms of the types of people involved, and their career background and outlook. As one head of Customs put it, 'It is very very very similar because most of the training they have is really similar training and like you say, the culture in the Caribbean is basically the same. So, a law enforcement from _____ could go to another Caribbean country and fit in'. We return to the issue of regional integration among border protection agencies later in this chapter.

Immigration

The existence of an immigration department as a separate entity in some of the islands has a relatively short history, dating back only to the 1980s, prior to which immigration control was dealt with by the police service. That arrangement still exists in some of the smaller islands where the Commissioner of Police is the de facto Chief Immigration Officer and the work is carried out by a police officer who is combined head of immigration and Special

Branch. Immigration officers have responsibility for all issues concerning the documentation of arrivals and departures of visitors and residents, issuing passports and visas, handling applications for citizenship and naturalization, refugee protection, and deportation both 'backwards and forwards'. The Chief Immigration Officer has responsibility for the day-to-day management of the headquarters office and the immigration officers stationed at the airports and the major seaports. He is also involved in implementing and setting policy under the direction of the permanent secretary in the security ministry.

In 2003–4 with the memory of 9/11 still fresh in their minds, the heads of immigration departments saw the most serious security threat as a terrorist attack: 'Terrorism is our number one major concern and we have to be very vigilant.' As one immigration officer explained, it is not possible to 'rule out someone from the Middle East coming in and causing something like a terrorist bombing, something like Bali'. Although they had no direct experience of a post 9/11 terrorist attack, the threat didn't seem distant because the Caribbean region has a significant amount of investment from people from the UK and the USA. While none of the islands were themselves targets, terrorist activity could be targeted against the British and Americans based there. People sometimes enter the country using forged travel documents and so there had to be a heightened vigilance in order to detect and prevent people with terrorist intentions from entering the country. The main challenge was the sheer number of people that they had have coming through the region amounting to more than 22 million tourists plus 20 million cruise passengers all of whom have to be processed quickly. It was easy to make a mistake and allow someone in who should have been on a watch list. There is at present a lot of new investment into the work of immigration enforcement. On one island, a new unit is being established that will have the mandate to manage the watch list. This is linked to the passport system so that all the passports they issue can be verified to ensure that they are *bona fide*, and can be flagged if there are questions. This is funded by the US State Department and should get them beyond the problems faced by their previous reliance on paper-based systems.

The second priority for heads of immigration is the matter of criminal deportees. Some criminal deportees arrive without the authorities' knowledge, but those who arrive through normal channels present an administrative problem: that of establishing their identity and nationality. As one head of immigration explained:

Typically they deny they have a travel document that is credible because either they entered on something that was false or they strenuously attempt to resist being removed and therefore they do not provide credible information to the investigators.

People who left the Caribbean as youngsters often have few family connections. There are situations where a person born in Britain to parents of Caribbean origin assumed that they were British because they were born in Britain and have a British birth certificate.[29] Only when finding themselves subject to deportation at the end of a criminal sentence, do they then discover that they have no right to British citizenship and are deported to the country of their parents' birth despite never having lived there:

people who are born in England don't necessarily get British citizenship now. So what we are finding is that there is a whole load of _____ women and men who have children there who are effectively rendered stateless. . . . The British wouldn't issue them a travel document so they are not British subjects. So it means that they have to come back and claim the citizenship of their parents. And recently something happened where a document was being issued and the person put in it British because the person had a British birth certificate and that stimulated some adrenaline from discussion between ourselves and 'how dare we put British'?

The authorities cannot refuse entry to their nationals, so the question then becomes what to do with deportees on arrival. Immigration must manage them, to 'identify persons who are candidates for deportation elsewhere' and decide what to do with those who are to remain within the country. Even if they have committed an offence in another country, they cannot be excluded. Nor, in principle, is it possible to prevent CARICOM nationals from moving around the Caribbean region. If a person has committed a crime elsewhere in the Caribbean or in a metropolitan country where they had been punished, there would be no formal justification for restricting their freedom of movement. As one immigration officer put it, 'once a person comes here if that person does not have a record and is not of any interest to the security forces here, let's face it he's a free man here and he may choose to move around'. On the other hand, there were certainly people within the law

---

[29] The right to British citizenship to people born in Britain was abolished by the 1981 British Nationality Act.

enforcement community who felt that there should be some kind of attempt to confine them or restrict their movement. However, there are problems with this:

if you think of it practically there is a limit to any restriction of movement. You cannot keep these people forever. People speak of rehabilitation but they would prefer if these people are stigmatized because they feel that that is a deterrent. I'm not so sure that we are not fostering something that could blow up in our faces but that is my view because if you are going to have all of these people they are not free to move neither within their country or within their region. How do you expect them to live and won't you be causing something to fester?

CARICOM policies on free movement of labour would not necessarily provide the right of entry to an individual who is of security interest. This then raises the question of identifying those deportees who present a risk to the country because of their criminal histories. The authorities tend to get information of the antecedents of criminal deportees by working through Special Branch, who interview them. They aim to profile them on arrival and to monitor them afterwards. The real concern is to distinguish between people who have committed minor crimes or immigration offences and those who have committed murder or robbery or been involved in drugs importation. For one head of immigration, on the issue of criminal deportees, the concern is not numbers per se, but is to do with the size of the problems that some can cause in the context of a small island. Chief Immigration Officers were also conscious of the social needs of the deportees some of whom had physical and mental health problems. They were concerned that people without family ties would drift into homelessness and find networks among the criminal elements in their society.

The immigration officers reported no evidence of organized people smuggling; in the opinion of one immigration officer, 'we don't have snakeheads and these types'. The more pressing issue is the ability of CARICOM nationals to move freely within the region. One immigration officer described the problem as being 'similar to when West Indians went to the UK' in the 1960s when:

people like Enoch Powell, whipped up anxiety about people considered to be foreign. Now there is a similar debate within the Caribbean about the numbers of immigrants coming in from other Caribbean islands, people who are perceived to look a little bit different, have a different accent, be a different kind of people.

That discussion, evident in the newspapers in some Caribbean countries, he argued 'is a reflection of anxiety about the arrival of people from other countries'. A related issue is undocumented arrivals. Because the islands' coastlines are largely unguarded, people can enter through the beaches or harbours instead of legitimate ports of entry. The only time that undocumented arrivals are picked up is when they leave by air, as their passports are checked, discovering that there is no arrival stamp and indicating that this person has entered illegally.

Inter-Agency Collaboration

There is extensive collaboration among the numerous organizations responsible for border protection. The organizations have established working relationships at the national level with mechanisms to coordinate port and airport security; they have also established regional networks with their counterparts on other islands and collaborative arrangements at the hemispheric level with their counterparts from the metropolitan countries. We examine each of these forms of collaboration in turn.

National security integration

One of the key transformations in policing, identified in table 1.1, is the reconfiguration of the national security apparatus. Increasingly conscious of unconventional security threats and the region's vulnerability because of lack of capacity and gaps in service provision, the region's governments, with the assistance of the metropolitan countries, have sought to build a strong national security infrastructure. This is most clearly illustrated by considering security collaboration at the airport. As the quotation at the head of this chapter indicates, the organizations mentioned in this chapter—police, Customs, immigration, the airlines, private sector security contractors, airport authorities, and international liaison officers—all have an interest in airport security. In order to coordinate security activity across the piece, at the highest level, is a national security committee, which is chaired by the Permanent Secretary in the Prime Minister's Office, and includes all the security chiefs and chiefs of immigration and sets out matters of policy, for example, for port and airport security.

In terms of day-to-day working, the various agencies responsible for airport security are coordinated by a 'law enforcement committee' chaired by the chief of airport security involving Customs, police, Special Branch, and Securicor to 'thrash out areas of concern'. These meetings are important, because the organizations are, as one chief of security put it, 'very insular, everyone wants to hold his little place' and these meetings 'dilute that attitude a bit'. Any issues that need to be taken from there to a more senior level go up to an airport security meeting that is mandated by ICAO to occur once every six months as a controlling mechanism for the airport. This meeting is chaired by the airport manager and includes 'the big Chiefs'—Police Commissioner, Defence Force Chief of Staff—and receives the minutes from the local law enforcement committee. This reports to the cabinet level meeting discussed above. Other operational activity would be coordinated by the National Joint Headquarters (NJHQ), located within the police department which might, for example, task the immigration department to carry out background checks. If there was an operation it would either be done on a day-to day-basis or initiated through the NJHQ. This could be initiated by either Customs or the coastguard. The intention is for all operations to be 'intelligence-driven'. As one Comptroller of Customs put it, 'Once we have the intelligence to justify the operation, then we will act. That intelligence need not be only Customs intelligence. It could be intelligence from the Coast Guard or it could be intelligence from the Police'.

Interviewees from all of the agencies identified a need to improve communication and collaboration within particular territories. One interviewee described cooperation as 'functional but. . . not as developed as it should be'. This had to do with 'territorial sovereignty' between agencies so 'while we might intellectually understand that there should be that kind of dovetailing it is not an active arrangement'. Gaps in service provision remained because:

people see themselves in boxes. One person might say 'I am a police person and unless the issue is specifically brought to my attention I am not going to interfere. Let them deal with it.' . . . So there are times when we have seen a kind of—hands off, 'let them do it' attitude—and in the process somebody escapes.

In one location, a gap between police service and the immigration department was a legacy from creation of an immigration department separate from the police service. This decision was made after a management audit showed that this was a function traditionally undertaken by police but which could, in fact, be undertaken by

trained civilians. There was no need for a 'law enforcement cultur-
alization' hitherto seen as invested exclusively in a police officer.
So, a new service was created by recruiting ordinary people to be
immigration officers. Unfortunately the police officers who had
previously undertaken this duty—who had previously seen themselves as 'an elitist core' because 'they didn't wear the regular uniform' and had certain other kinds of privileges—felt that they were
being ousted and were resisting the change. This partly explained
the operational stand-off between police and immigration.

Another gap is evident between Customs and other colleagues
within the airports. In each of the airports I visited, airport security, despite being responsible for the entire airport, have no jurisdiction in the baggage hall, which is known as 'Customs territory'.
As one chief of airport security put it, 'it's Customs the world
over, Customs says anything twelve miles out, twelve miles down
belongs to them'. Chief Immigration Officers also commented on
this sharp demarcation line across the Customs hall that prevented
entry to immigration officers. One said:

customs is almost sacrosanct. Immigration is landlocked if you will. They
don't have an independent entrance so they either move through customs
or move through the other areas while customs has its own exit point.
And typically you can go into the immigration hall let's say to meet someone but you certainly won't be allowed into the customs hall.

The dominance and independence of Customs was attributed to
'the strength of their organization over the years and the fact that
there is money involved'. Customs are a major generator of revenue and therefore have a higher status.

Regional collaboration

There are numerous mechanisms for cooperation and collaboration among the various organizations at the regional level. The
most extensive regional cooperation is within the 'Customs fraternity' through the Caribbean Customs Law Enforcement Council
(CCLEC). This was established in the early 1970s as an informal
association of Customs administrators to exchange information on
smuggling and to help smaller administrations 'adjust to the new
threat of organized drug trafficking'.[30] With a growing membership and an increasing diversification into other areas of Customs

---

[30] <http://www.cclec.net/>.

business, the Council established itself more formally. In 1989, its 21 member states (now 36 countries) formalized the exchange of information through the adoption of a memorandum of under-standing (MOU) on 'mutual assistance and cooperation for the prevention and repression of Customs offences in the Caribbean zone'. CCLEC's mission is to assist its member administrations to fulfil their mandate to collect and protect revenue, to interdict illicit drugs and other prohibited goods, and to facilitate legitimate trade and international travel through the use of modern business systems.[31] Each Customs agency in the region has an enforcement liaison office (ELO), so that each country has a contact and regular communication among them. CCLEC headquarters used to be in San Juan (Puerto Rico) but subsequently moved to Saint Lucia. This regional liaison office (RILO) collects and shares information on Customs offences which is loaded onto a bulletin board at the WCO headquarters in Brussels and is a worldwide system avail-able on a regional basis (Europe, Caribbean South America, Asia, etc) that members can access to inform themselves.

CCLEC developed a system to monitor the movement of yachts and small pleasure craft, passengers and crew. This regional clear-ance system (RCS) aimed to improve vessel tracking, suspicious craft profiling, and improve communications to enhance the effi-ciency of Customs activities and interdiction efforts. Unfortunately, owing to problems with updating, interviewees felt that it was unreliable. As with the other operational organizations, informal communication and networking is often created through training courses. As one Customs officer explained:

when you know people and we have been able to meet a lot of people on a one-on-one basis, have personal contacts with them, and that works fine because when you call somebody you know who you are talking to and they are more likely to respond.

[31] *Ibid.* In support of its mission, CCLEC has established the following *six* strategic objectives which guide its actions and plans: (1) enhance customs law enforcement cooperation and sharing information; (2) improve human resource management and development within customs; (3) modernize customs legislation and customs procedures; (4) implement measures to fight corruption and enhance integrity; (5) contribute to trade facilitation including preparation of member administrations for the implementation of the Free Trade Area of the Americas (FTAA); (6) increase awareness of CCLEC within the region to bring about a greater level of support and commitment from governments and enhance relations with the other international organizations.

Nonetheless, as in other areas, a common lament was that the 'structure for communication' needed development. There has been a discussion about creating an Association of Caribbean Airport Security Chiefs, modelled on the Association of Caribbean Commissioners of Police (ACCP), with the assistance of the British government. There are informal networks, but creating an association would formalize it and gain national and regional government support. Some airport security chiefs attend the Special Branch conference (see Chapter 4). Similarly, there is regional communication among immigration officers, partly as some heads of immigration are also senior police officers so meet as a matter of course. There is a proposal for an Association of Chiefs of Immigration within the Caribbean region.

North Atlantic collaboration: relationships with metropolitan countries

International law enforcement cooperation echoes throughout the airports in the proliferation of tiepins and the bright blue or red ribbons that hold local security passes with USCIS woven into it, a gift from a visiting US immigration officer.[32] One security officer was wearing a tiepin from Canadian Immigration Services Enforcement and another wore a gold US federal special agent tiepin. This reflects the fact that within the airports, much of the communication was between the airlines and people from the metropolitan countries—UK Customs, US Homeland Security staff—working out of their embassies and High Commissions. As one interviewee explained, the Canadians, British, and the US are particularly active in the airports:

They have links with the major airlines and they are called upon from time to time to deal with issues right there even before it gets to us. So that in a sense they have their own networking that doesn't necessarily have to include us.

Overseas liaison officers also frequently coordinate inter-agency training for Customs officers, police, coastguard, immigration, air, and seaport security personnel.

Interviewees often complained that they were 'between a rock and a hard place'. The training and provision of other resources were geared to the national interests of the donors, sometimes in

---

[32] US Citizenship and Immigration Services.

ways that undermined efforts to protect their economies. A Customs officer explained that:

the focus of the Americans and the donor agencies with regard to training might be narcotics, our focus might be revenue, so they would tab the courses geared towards narcotics. They would give the funding geared towards narcotics and our country might be left with what I'd call the things that we see as necessary for us for survival.

Nonetheless, local border security officers felt compelled to bow to these pressures, for fear that they will lose their funding for training and equipment. Officers complained that assistance from the metropolitan countries required something in return. For example, the Customs service had to provide documentation and accountability for how resources are used, providing evidence, for example, that vehicles are properly maintained and used for the purposes for which they have been provided. They must show that it is used for 'enforcement-related' rather than 'revenue-related' activities, and produce regular administrative returns demonstrating 'improvements in performance' or productivity. However, the head of the Enforcement Unit said he had no problems with this as it was a matter of transparent and efficient organization that was subject to audit.

Officers also noted a policy skew more generally towards the foreign policy objectives of metropolitan governments. For example, the region was facing major problems with its export markets in relation to sugar or bananas without assistance from the WTO or the US:

but at the same time they expect us to spend all of our revenue fighting drugs. That is not really of value to us because you would realise you are either a source country or transit country. I don't think in my estimation, that drugs is really a big problem in terms of usage.

Customs Enforcement people were aware that the law enforcement agencies were drawn into a US agenda making drugs the overriding issue, and confusing the US agenda with their own national interest to become dependent on the US for overseas trips and technological equipment. As one Customs enforcement agent explained:

definitely for law enforcement agencies it must be drugs, but Customs are picking at this now because remember our so-called main function is revenue collection, and we have protecting our borders and keeping out undesirable drugs and people and so on, but at the forefront is revenue collection. I'm sure my boss is concerned that [assets] could have been better used [for] revenue recovery but instead we have to be here and work on other things like drugs.

This has happened because of the wish to 'satisfy the desires of outside forces and our treaty obligations and so on'. Clearly, there must be some place for fighting drugs because 'indirectly there going to be some kind of negative effect on the country', but policy makers do not see it as being primarily in their interests.

Customs–Interpol collaboration

In 1998, the World Customs Organization and Interpol signed a memorandum of understanding premised on cooperation between police and Customs 'in the fight against transnational crime'.[33] Its starting point was the Interpol mandate to promote the 'widest possible mutual assistance' between police authorities and to develop all institutions likely to contribute effectively to the prevention of crimes, and the WCO's mission to enhance compliance with trade regulation and protection of society. The MOU emphasized their shared competence in combating, 'inter alia, illicit drug trafficking, money laundering, illicit diversion of precursors and essential chemicals, counterfeiting, traffic in human beings, intellectual property fraud, firearms trafficking and smuggling, and environmental crime' and stressed the need to avoid the duplication of effort. The MOU agreed that they should consult, exchange information on developments in their fields, and exchange 'information relevant to transnational crime'. It noted the need for ensuring the accuracy and validity of information, the need to safeguard confidential information, and to observe restrictions in communicating information. It agreed that there should be reciprocal arrangements at meetings, to make arrangements for implementing joint projects on matters of common interests. To support this, a German Customs officer was appointed as a full-time attaché at Interpol headquarters in Lyon to set up all the protocols, memoranda, and letters of agreement between Customs and Interpol. This attaché also worked with Customs officers within the Caribbean region to work towards a memorandum of understanding between CCLEC and INTERPOL, taking about two years and reaching its

---

[33] Memorandum of understanding between the World Customs Organization and the International Criminal Police Organization, signed in Lyon, 9 November 1998.

conclusion at the time of the fieldwork.[34] The agreement is substantially identical to the one signed with the WCO, except that the provisions relating to information sharing are more explicit.[35]

This MOU paved the way for providing Caribbean Customs organizations direct access to the Interpol communications systems. The motivation for CCLEC reaching this agreement was based on the lack of communication between intelligence agencies following 9/11. The aim was to address this through reciprocity between police, Customs, immigration, and military intelligence, with the intention to move beyond the need for individual CCLEC members to agree to exchange information. As a Customs official put it, the 'sharing of intelligence is always a touchy thing because nobody gives everything that they have and sometimes they give only to where it is their advantage'. There were also concerns that the flow of intelligence tended to be from the Caribbean to the USA and the UK with not enough information shared in return. A head of Customs explained that, 'the exchange of information is not even and the flow tends to be one way more than the other'. This created frustration owing to insufficient international flows of information. It was particularly frustrating to hear about enforcement activity through news media or on the street, rather than through intelligence communications channels:

I think we need to have an increase in the level of communication internationally, it is too few and far between. . . . A lot of the time you hear [that one of our nationals] gets caught in one of the other countries and you either hear it on the news, you hear somebody on the street saying that. I'm saying stuff like that, we should get the information right away and be asked to do some background check.

Chiefs of airport security consult with international agencies in a number of ways. Threats are assessed by the US Federal Aviation Administration, so chiefs of security draw on these threat

---

[34] CCLEC took the final decision to go ahead at their executive committee meeting in Anguilla, July 2004.

[35] Article 2(2) in the CCLEC agreement has an additional provision which reads: Practical arrangements concerning the exchange of information, in particular concerning direct access by one organization to the other's telecommunications network and databases, shall be specified in an exchange of letters between both organizations. Where information is made available through direct access to a database, such access shall be governed by the specific rules and conditions applicable to the operation of that database. Cooperation agreement between the International Criminal Police Organization–Interpol and the Caribbean Customs Law Enforcement Council, 22 October 2004.

assessments as well as on information provided by the US Embassy, British High Commission, and their counterparts from other European countries. They may call on international agencies because of their greater capacity and access to information and databases, such as information on the tailplane of an aircraft or about aircraft operations, accessed through international organizations. For example:

if an aircraft is coming in here . . . and I say that I am suspicious about the cargo coming in, they give me an idea of the concern here, aircraft tail numbers, X amount, they can come and tell me who owns it, where it's coming from, what it's carrying perhaps, and then we look aboard and if the manifest is something else, then we can make a move.

Discussions with military advisors are important to establish the infrastructure. Military advisors would ask tough questions about the airport's readiness for disaster and emergency planning and evacuation. This involves a close formal relationship, but also a more informal relationship:

I had my meeting with my guy yesterday but I got something further, we can come back this afternoon, so he can call my house and come there, and we go by his and we have a drink and chat, so it works. . . . You know, when I say to you, if it works, it's important, you know, some people feel that if your mouth is open, something will come out, so if you're eating and chatting and relaxing, it serves a purpose, and anything informal is very good, because I promote that even amongst my security officers, I tell them at break time we should go and, during–army term–'gnashing break', you go off to your thing and sit down round the table and have a coffee, that's where you get the information.

There was a strong view among border protection agencies that the exchange of timely and quality information and intelligence needed to be enhanced and developed on a regional scale to respond to drug trafficking affecting the whole region. All were agreed that there was room for improvement and a need for funding to deploy equipment and personnel. This required more effort in paying for the collection of intelligence and processes to test its reliability. One head of Customs saw information sharing as a potential barrier to their work, in case it got into the wrong hands. However, he was confident that they could move beyond that:

Well of course you know that one has to be careful with whom one shares information and/or intelligence and again a closer working together on a number of occasions would sort of minimise that feeling because once you get to know an individual in a working environment, then it makes it a lot better for the sharing of that information, so one of the things that is suggested is to have more and continual operations so that you build that kind of confidence in the other party and of course you have an idea as to how far you can go with an individual or with of course the information or intelligence which you have.

One airport security chief was concerned that information is not always shared, partly due to corruption, resulting in a tendency for organizations to keep information to themselves:

we seem to have a problem with wanting to hold everything to ourselves you know. Like knowledge is power . . . We find that some organizations especially those that are accustomed to dealing with secrecy and they tend to find it very difficult to release information to other persons. . . . Without the sharing of information I think you lose quite a lot of your effectiveness and sometimes you miss quite a lot if you don't share.

One airport security chief said that there were mixed attitudes within society about intelligence gathering. Some people thought of it as malicious snooping, considering it 'anti-social':

In the Caribbean that's a no-no, you know, that's for the standpipe, most people when they use that term, it's there, the pub talk and malicious gossip, they don't see it as intelligence, right, so you have to inculcate into them the importance because it's about safety here, come on, and what I do is, I use the time frame, you know, if I say from London 3,800/600 miles back here, hey, I can get back here hours before I can get to Saint Lucia on a crowded day, I am back here, so don't talk about barriers, they don't exist any more, so the man who wants to do something here, let him do it and bugger off, there's no barrier in distances, so you let them know what's happened here, can happen there tomorrow if the interest is such, so let's start preparing for this, and so I do a lot of that, I do a lot of talking and showing them the relevance.

This, he argued, was vital to bring people up to speed with the nature of the threats, particularly in relation to terrorism. It is not expected and they have had no experience of it so are not sensitized to the problems that have been faced 'miles away' in Europe and North America. 'If you shout "Bomb" in London, people know what to do. If you shout "Bomb" here, people ask you where and want to have a look at it.' Thus, developing an intelligence capacity was absolutely vital. As one chief of airport security put it:

If we look at the airport security service as some place where it is vital to the security of the country, absolutely vital, it's the number one key point, then I feel you should get the support commensurate with that.

One common complaint was that the implementation of the international port security code has cost the Caribbean governments a large amount of money even though the benefits are largely in the interests of US homeland security. Caribbean islands pay the price, particularly since additional security is required because the US has made the world more unstable through its foreign policies and because the US is a major consumer of illegal drugs. It seemed unfair to many interviewees that the Caribbean should pay for improvements in security for the benefit of the metropolitan countries. The purchase of the security upgrading, particularly electronic equipment, scanning equipment, vehicles, technicians who run the equipment, maintenance of the equipment, and the training of the people involved impacts on the balance of payments as these are almost all American products. A person from the port authority commented that:

There are ports in the States that have not met the codes but yet you are hearing a lot of talk about the ports in the developing countries not being able to meet the codes. If you are setting the standards, then you ought to be leading by example and that again is just another example of what I'm talking about. The other thing of course is that if you are imposing these lofty standards which are not bad in and of themselves, but they also have enormous resource implications, you ought to be providing some assistance to the countries which need that assistance in order to meet the standards that you have set.

There was a strong view that there was a responsibility on the part of the metropolitan countries to provide resources to meet security needs that were largely for their benefit. Many officers argued that the enforcement activity, especially in relation to drug trafficking is 'to the benefit of the metropolitan countries' and therefore 'their support and assistance in these areas, is also vital'. Officers believed that the measures were contributing to protecting their countries, but 'the bulk of the illegal drugs that come through here end up in the metropolitan countries' and in the areas of technical assistance and acquisition of equipment they felt that they were shouldering much of the burden themselves. For example, the purchase of millions of dollars worth of scanning equipment and training to use it. As one argued, 'I think we need to see a lot more of that, not just within the Customs but within the other law enforcement agencies'.

Overseas liaison officers and operational activity

Heads of Customs enforcement saw the overseas liaison officers (OLOs) as working with them to develop 'very special operational intelligence'. They were 'not visibly operational', but played a role of providing intelligence. One head of Customs enforcement expressed it like this: 'They give the information to me so I can go and put handcuffs on somebody.' The strategic intelligence that they develop involves both the OLOs and Operations Intelligence Office in London, which has a group of officers with specific geographical responsibilities. The Customs officers see this as having great benefit:

I'm very patriotic and I don't want anybody who is not [a citizen] to come and take over [this country] but criminals don't recognise borders. Criminals operate anywhere . . . and the fact that we have law enforcement officers who are here, who are willing to provide us with information in our country, about people operating in our country, you know, we are happy for that. It is not a case where, you know, they will go and arrest one of our citizens without passing on the information so that we can go and arrest but at least they are working, they will provide us with information about that criminal.

The advice that they received from the metropolitan countries was always treated with circumspection and was checked and considered in terms of local priorities. In essence, they treated the information coming from the Americans and British as advisory. Operational information comes into the organization perhaps with a recommendation as to what could or should be done. This is then evaluated and, on the basis of the local officers' knowledge and experience, appropriate action is taken. If for any reason, there is some doubt about the information, operational officers would seek further advice. It was vital to be circumspect about what they are being told by the USA. One officer explained that he would not simply 'jump up and do it because when the shit hits the fan, it's only going to hit you, you know what I mean?'. Border protection officers argued that accountability always lies with the national agency because, 'at the end of the day . . . it is your responsibility to your country for whatever you do, if it goes bad and there are going to be some, say, international or regional or whatever kind of implications or even as it relates to an organization, I mean you are going to be responsible'.

The absolute boundary lay in attempting to make an arrest. One Customs officer argued that in the same way that Shiprider Agreements prevented foreign vessels operating:

in any of the territorial waters of this region without the authority and in most instances the presence of a local law enforcement representative on board the vessel . . . the issue of sovereignty internally also would have to follow along the same principles.

Noting that there was a time when the US courts authorized US law enforcement agencies to go into other jurisdictions to make arrests, he noted that:

that created a hue and a cry. I think they've backed away from that now. . . . What the courts had purported to do was to allow, let's say drug enforcement agents, to go into countries to effect arrests and that is patently not proper.

Heads of Customs felt that any foreign law enforcement personnel should, if they're doing an investigation, be accompanied by local counterparts and before you get even to that stage, you will have had to have gone through the channels. If they work outside of this, pushing the boundaries of what is formally legal, then they should be prepared to accept the consequences. In one location, the head of Customs enforcement insisted that the role of officers from overseas was now restricted to communicating by telephone and fax rather than being present during operations. In this location, there had previously been problems with a US Customs officer who had become directly involved in operations and as a consequence had inadvertently undermined their efforts. This officer had previously worked in the Gulf of Mexico border areas and had a lot of experience with the use of scanning equipment and so 'he would go out on the raids'. This raised questions about what he did there. As one head of Customs enforcement put it, 'it may be that on one or two occasions he got a little more involved than he should have':

it was pointed on by the then legal advisor that it was not the wisest thing to do, to have him there. You see they act as technical advisors. They would organise technical training, they assist us in providing the canine, the vessels, and they should assist us in, let us say, technical training. So the advice would be greatly appreciated but they should not actually be involved in the operation as such.

The basis of reciprocity specified in the memorandum of under-standing was limited to providing technical knowledge and 'for them to be here to do enforcement they would have to be part of our team', which they were not. This raised the question of what counts as providing technical advice. If the person is mentoring or providing advice, this is acceptable, but 'if he is involved in the arrest or touching the item that is being challenged so to speak we call that being involved'. One crucial issue was that the US Customs officer concerned had effectively started to pass himself off as a local officer. As the Customs officer explained, 'One of the objections raised and one of the things that was happening is that we have a crest of seal, a badge, and he used to sport one'. This had clearly been a step too far and had led to cases in which this officer was involved being seen as compromised in a court of law.

Conducting a formal interview went beyond the boundaries of acceptability and even speaking to a suspect during an operation could be construed as crossing the line. The line between conduct-ing an interview and attempting to draw information out from a casual conversation was a thin one, but a highly important one nonetheless:

if you are going to do an interview and dependent on the nature of that interview, you would have to identify yourself and you'd have to give the person being interviewed some idea as to what it is you want to talk to them about and any individual who comes out of the blue and says "I am drug enforcement" or whatever, the person being interviewed is quite within their rights to tell them to go and fly a kite, they have no authority, provided that is how they want to go about it. If you're talking about elicitation, that is a different thing altogether.[36]

Customs officers accepted and expected that some officers from overseas would use their craft to collect intelligence, but this was not specific to the Caribbean region and could be used in met-ropolitan countries. On the covert side, attempting to specify a boundary was problematic and again, the head of Customs argued that this was not something that was specific to the region. As one put it, 'that is true of every country, that is why, for example, you have diplomats being summoned to Foreign Ministries and being declared *persona non grata* and being invited to leave the country'.

[36] See Chapter 4.

Summary and Conclusion

The context within which border protection officers operate has fundamentally changed in recent decades. The number of people travelling and the quantity of goods imported and exported has increased dramatically and therefore the routine administrative workload of Customs, airport and port security, and immigration officers has also grown. At the same time, anxiety about security has increased. If we were to assume there had been no change in the danger posed by each individual travelling passenger or tonne of goods shipped, then the extent of that danger will have increased proportionately. But the working assumption amongst the officers that I interviewed is that that the risks have grown even more rapidly than the flows of goods and people. Not only are there more people and things on the move, but the business of drugs, weapons, and other forms of trafficking have expanded massively and so has the number of people engaged in armed violence. In this context the policing role of Customs, immigration, port, and airport security has become increasingly important undertaking myriad tasks concerned with protecting the borders, especially at key transport nodes such as ports and airports. It is hardly surprising that many of the officers interviewed felt stressed by the way in which their traditional workload had grown alongside the expectation that they would become expert in a range of new tasks.

Central to the role of border protection is the task of speeding the flow of welcome tourists while managing, and wherever possible excluding, unwanted vagabonds. In the Caribbean, the vagabond is personified in a very powerful 'folk devil': the deported drug smuggler, for it is he (or she) who is most prominent in public debates about the 'waste products' of late modern capitalism (rather than the asylum seeker, prominent in so many narratives in the global north).[37] A moral panic has grown around the deportee in the Caribbean, who has become the repository for public fears about crime and disorder. Deportees are seen as triply polluting since they are an exported waste product washed up on home shores, contaminated by the hyper-consumerist society within which he has been nurtured, and are actively involved

---

[37] Sharon Pickering and Leanne Weber (eds) (2006), *Borders, Mobility and Technologies of Control*. Dordrecht: Springer; Elspeth Guild (2009), *Security and Migration in the 21st Century*. Oxford: Polity.

in the clandestine drugs trade, itself armed and dangerous. While border protection officers are on the lookout for other dangerous people—terrorists among them—it is the deportees who are the focus of official attention.

The role of Customs and airport security in managing the flows of goods is less prominent in public debate, but no less important in contemporary border protection practices. Customs must 'facilitate trade' by ensuring the hassle-free passage of agricultural and manufactured goods through ports and airports while contributing to security by controlling the flow of dangerous products. The old regime of Customs, based largely around the collection of import and export taxes, is starting to disappear with the gradual abolition of tariffs encouraged by the WTO. In its stead Customs is becoming a border protection agency responsible for investigating and interdicting in the flow of illicit goods—especially drugs—in collaboration with other security organizations. Airport security plays a major role and in some places was well integrated into the broader security sector networks. National security coordination is often informal but also draws on a variety of formal meetings and—in terms of operations—through the NJHQ. This also links with the military forces on land[38] and the coastguard at sea,[39] suggesting an increased militarization of the borders.[40]

Contemporary police research has begun to explore the role of agencies other than 'blue uniformed police' in the extended police family. Most of this new exploration has focused on developments in the local sphere, but it has also started to look at the role of national and transnational policing actors. To some extent, the use of the idea of 'policing' in this context is novel. It could be argued that the role of the organizations examined in this chapter is primarily about something other than policing, and that its role in policing is an *ancillary* function, at some distance from its 'core business'. Thus, Customs exists to collect tax revenue, while the Immigration Service exists mainly to issue passports, visas, and residence permits and to check identity documents as people pass through ports and airports. This is a valid point, but there are certain aspects of the work of these organizations that can only be described as policing, analogous to the role of beat police officers. The everyday work of the airport security officer and, to some

---

[38] See Chapter 6.   [39] See Chapter 7.
[40] Franko Katja Aas (2007), *Globalisation and Crime, op cit.*

extent, that of the Customs and immigration officers within Caribbean airports is policework, little different from how it is traditionally defined. These officers are policing in a narrowly defined space with a correspondingly narrow set of duties. All are engaged in surveillance of general and suspect populations, stopping individuals to conduct brief interviews or detaining them for extensive questioning, conducting searches of their bags and personal possessions, making reports, and maintaining databases. Just like the police.

There are numerous reasons that the work of the 'border protection' officer has fallen outside our definition of policing. First, there is the sense—alluded to above—that they are primarily doing other things. Second, the discipline of police research has been preoccupied with street policing and, in our neglect of other kinds of policing agencies through lack of interest or lack of access, the boundaries of the field have been narrowly drawn. Third, the work of the agencies discussed in this chapter has changed over recent years in ways that increasingly bring their policing role to the foreground. To some extent, this has developed through shifts in the core business of some of these agencies. For example, revenue collection has diminished in comparison with border protection for the Customs agencies as trade tariffs have reduced and threats to the integrity of borders have increased. It could be argued that the more general phenomenon of 'securitization' has impacted on the role of border protection agencies in ways that have increasingly emphasized their role in security and law enforcement. It is also clear that the new security agenda has led to a reconfiguration of the coercive and intrusive capacities of the state with a general expansion of power and a tightening of the networks within and between agencies. The creation of Joint Intelligence Committees and NJHQs that bring together all the agencies within the security sector and tie them closely to the work of the police, military, and secret intelligence agencies have also played a key role in emphasizing the security aspects of the border protection agencies described in this chapter.

The changing relationship between domestic police, border protection agencies, the military, and other security sector institutions has profound implications for the way in which security is provided within a nation state. Boundaries between the domestic and the transnational, between institutions of criminal justice and regulatory agencies, between civil and military are blurring.

New hybrid organizations have been created such as Customs drugs enforcement units which are regulatory, yet possess extensive criminal law enforcement powers and military firepower. As these organizational boundaries are reconfigured and as domestic agencies become meshed more closely with one another, but also with transnational entities, fascinating and troubling questions are posed concerning legitimacy, accountability, effectiveness, and control. We consider these questions in the conclusion, but first we must consider the role of maritime policing and the overseas liaison officer who make up other important constituents of the new security sector.

7

Maritime Policing

You have a lack of synergy and inter-dependence among
countries of the region, hemispherically and within the
Caribbean Sea. [We should] invest in a hemispheric approach
or in a Caribbean approach. I mean why on earth can't we,
in the Caribbean, look at a grouping which brings together
Barbados, Trinidad and Tobago, perhaps Grenada, Guyana,
Venezuela, and Suriname, to deal with the southern Caribbean
Sea, and Bahamas, Jamaica and so on to deal with the northern
approach, so that the coastguards' investments and the air,
the fixed wing and helicopter, is a shared responsibility and
not that, 'Okay, my territorial waters end here, yours begin
there, therefore you must have a coastguard, I must have a
coastguard, even though I can't sustain it'. It doesn't make
sense.[1]

Introduction

Approaching the Caribbean by air, you get a panoramic view of
the island chain, clearly visible as the peaks of a submerged moun-
tain range, clothed in tropical vegetation and ringed with white
sand and electric blue water. As the Atlantic Ocean meets the Caribbean Sea, the gradual change in hue from indigo to aquamarine
and then turquoise reveals the water's depth, the islands' underwa-
ter topography, and the extent of the reef. The shoreline, with its
seaport, marinas, and beaches is a hive of activity: tourists bathe,
surf, and dive in waters alive with jet-skis, sailing yachts, pleasure cruisers, and fishing boats. Container ships and cruise liners
glide slowly in and out of the ports, whilst hidden in the vessels
and among the goods are drugs, guns, money, and people, being

[1] Retired Military Chief of Staff, Caribbean.

smuggled from one place to the next. Open waters provide almost unlimited space for illegality and the island shorelines, punctuated with myriad coves and caves, have for centuries offered a perfect setting for clandestine activity. The islands, said one coastguard captain, are 'a drug runner's cheesecake with icing on the top'.

The recent upsurge in piracy off the coast of Somalia and the water-borne launch of a terrorist attack on Mumbai has brought maritime security to the forefront of public attention.[2] The scope of ocean affairs has rapidly expanded in recent years and maritime security and safety have become prominent in such forums as the United Nations Conference on the Law of the Sea (UNCLOS).[3] The most obvious area of interest to the criminologist is 'crime at sea', including piracy and armed robbery, illicit traffic in drugs, guns and ammunition, and weapons of mass destruction.[4] Broader security issues, falling under the rubric of the 'safety of navigation', include oil tanker safety, the transport of dangerous goods by sea, the provision of places of refuge for ships in need of assistance and for persons rescued at sea, and the balance between maritime security and the freedom of movement of seafarers. A still broader set of maritime security issues—boundary disputes, claims on the seabed, conservation of the marine environment, maritime military conflict, territorial integrity, sovereignty, and political independence—merge into the field of international relations and the maintenance of peace and security.

This chapter examines how Caribbean maritime spaces are policed, first considering the proposition that the sea needs policing and exploring the specific security issues that attach to shorelines, coastal, and open waters. It then looks at the development of maritime security agreements that enable cooperation between small island states and the marine forces of the metropolitan countries. Drawing on interviews with officers from coastguard and police marine sections, and observation of inshore patrols, the

---

[2] Martin Murphy (2009), *Small Boats, Weak States, Dirty Money: Piracy and Maritime Terrorism in the Modern World*. London: Hirst & Co; John S Barnett (2002), *Dangerous Waters: Modern Piracy and Terror on the High Seas*. London: Plume/Penguin; William Langewiesche (2007), *The Outlaw Sea: Chaos and Crime on the World's Oceans*. London: Granta.

[3] United Nations General Assembly (2003), *Oceans and the Law of the Sea*, Report of the Secretary General, Addendum, Fifty-eighth session, A/58/65/Add.1 29 August 2003, para 1.   [4] *Ibid*, paras 31–59.

chapter describes the form and function of maritime policing and the commanding officers' perspective on regional security. We then look at the various forms of coordination and cooperation occurring locally and regionally, and explore some of the issues arising from operational practice, and conclude with a discussion of the broader implications of maritime law enforcement for the emergence of transnational policing practice.

Policing Maritime Spaces and Places

Maritime security can be delineated according to jurisdictions relating to the physical boundaries of the nation state. Security, from this perspective, can be seen in several layers, zones, tiers, or concentric circles: (i) inshore waters (up to three miles); (ii) territorial waters (up to 12 miles); (iii) the Exclusive Economic Zone (up to 200 miles); and (iv) the high seas. Some of the occurrences requiring 'policing' intervention are similar between zones—people or vessel facing difficulties in the water or posing a danger, crimes occurring as they might on land, and the pursuit of people attempting to smuggle household goods, alcohol, drugs, and guns. Other problems relate to specific zones due to the physical and social context of different spaces of water. For example, policing ports, harbours, and beaches involves a very different set of tasks, boats, equipment, training, and transnational cooperation compared with that required to carry out drug interdiction on the high seas.

Inshore waters are marine spaces that directly adjoin dry land such as shorelines, ports, and harbours, with which we can include *internal waters* such as rivers, estuaries, and bays, and are usually the responsibility of specialist harbour and marine police agencies around the world.[5] Inshore waters such as harbours and beaches clearly 'belong' to the nation state and therefore lie within *territorial waters*: the area of sea adjacent to a nation's coastline, which is under its full control.[6] The question of what counts as 'adjacent' was contentious for centuries and is now resolved to be 12 nautical

---

[5] The Thames River Police, formed in 1798 (later to become the Marine Division of the Metropolitan Police), is reputed to be England's first 'preventive' police force.

[6] I.C.B. Dear and Peter Kemp (2006), *Oxford Companion to Ships and the Sea* (2nd edn). Oxford: Oxford University Press.

miles from shore.[7] In the islands, the marine section of the police service patrols the inshore waters using small boats. They regularly patrol the waters directly adjacent to the shoreline including beaches and around marinas, ports, and harbours dealing with myriad 'police-relevant' matters. During these patrols, they look out for suspicious activity among the fishing boats and pleasure craft, try to prevent unauthorized entrance to restricted areas of the harbours, and ensure that inshore water sports are undertaken safely. The marine section of the police is, in theory, responsible for the full extent of the territorial waters, but the limited capacity of their vessels prevents this from becoming regular practice.

The *Exclusive Economic Zone* (EEZ), a product of the 1994 Hague Convention, constitutes the third concentric zone. This established jurisdictional right allows nation states to exploit resources in the water and on and beneath the seabed in a zone extending 200 miles from its shore. With the right to exploit the oil and fishing reserves comes the responsibility to manage fish stocks and to control pollution and environmental degradation. In the case of archipelagic states, the EEZ extends 200 miles beyond the most distant island, and for islands that are very close to one another, territorial limits are contiguous and drawn at the median between the two nations. Patrolling the EEZ tends to be beyond the scope of the marine sections of domestic police and therefore a specialist agency is called for. Although a ship may travel through territorial waters and the EEZ on 'innocent passage', they are subject to the enforcement powers of maritime law enforcement agencies, which differ markedly around the world.[8]

---

[7] It was resolved in the 1703 Hague Convention that a nation should be sovereign over only those seas to the extent that it could defend them from the shore, a distance specified as the range of a cannon, which was then three miles; waters outside this limit should be considered 'open' to all ships without hindrance. This position was radically revised when in 1945 President Harry Truman declared that the US had the right to the offshore oil and gas resources on its continental shelf. Other countries, such as Iceland, followed in 1958 with claims to fisheries within a 12-mile radius, which was extended to 200 miles in 1976, sparking 'cod wars' with Britain. The 1994 UNCLOS codified territorial waters as the 12 nautical miles over which the state has full sovereign rights. *Oxford Companion to Ships and the Sea, op cit.*

[8] In Britain, Her Majesty's Coastguard is a civil force, concerned largely with search and rescue both at sea and on the coastline with the help of emergency services and other life-saving organizations backed up with military helicopters. It is part of The Maritime and Coastguard Agency, an executive agency of the

Most countries in the Caribbean have a coastguard in addition to, or instead of, a marine section of the constabulary, undertaking the same range of tasks as their counterparts in Britain and America. However, the form that it takes varies from place to place reflecting the complexity of their histories. Where there are defence forces—for example in Jamaica, Barbados, Guyana, and Trinidad & Tobago—the coastguard is seen as part of the military with the commander answering to the Chief of Staff and ultimately to the Minister of Defence (see Chapter 5). There are separate police marine divisions for specific inshore work and there is by necessity some collaboration, as well as conflict, between the coastguard and constables from the marine division. In some of the smaller islands, the coastguard answers to the Commissioner of Police. Whatever the precise form of the maritime law enforcement capacity, there was much in common among the officers working in this field. The marine police are sailors, trained in the islands as well as the US, UK, and Canada. Their work takes place, largely, on water and therefore involves the training, skills, knowledge, and equipment required to work at sea. Much of the work relates to sailing and other water-borne activities, handling boats and their physical maintenance, and seafaring tasks such as weather watching, understanding tides, currents, shipping lanes, navigation, communications, and dealing with maritime safety matters.

Beyond the 200 mile EEZ lie the *high seas* where vessels have 'flag state' jurisdiction. The High Seas Convention requires that ships must sail under the flag of one state only and, apart from exceptional cases, are subject to its exclusive jurisdiction on the high seas.[9] Coastguards generally have the authority to undertake general law enforcement within the 12-mile limit and carry out fisheries protection and environmental patrols within the 200-mile EEZ. On the high seas, the coastguard may hail, stop, board, and search only those vessels flying its flag. No one country can claim

UK Department of Transport that manages emergency response and has responsibility for maritime law enforcement in relation to pollution for shipping, 'port state control' inspections, and inspection of UK vessels. The US Coastguard, by contrast, answers to the US Navy and is very much focused on enforcing US maritime laws and suppressing piracy. During the inter-war years, its principal task was enforcement of US Prohibition Laws (1920–33) and today it is a major player in operations to counter drug trafficking.

[9] Article 6(1).

jurisdiction in the high seas, but 'universal jurisdiction' can be claimed by all nations in specific circumstances. Article 110 of UNCLOS stipulates that a ship may be forcibly boarded on the high seas if it is reasonably suspected of engaging in piracy or the slave trade, is broadcasting in an unauthorized manner or lacks a flag. If the vessel is registered in the state and flying its national flag,[10] state authorities may board and search vessels on the high seas and can grant permission to others to do so for the purposes of fisheries protection and where the vessel is suspected of drug smuggling.[11] Typically, the granting of permission is facilitated through assigned duty officers, especially where bilateral security agreements exist. The issue of 'weapons of mass destruction' is re-engaging the debate about flag-state consent.[12]

The existence of the right for maritime law enforcement officers to stop and search vessels on the high seas is a moot point for the majority of Caribbean coastguards. For the most part, the vessels available to the islands are designed for coastal waters and even those that can work in open seas do not have the capacity for operations involving several days and nights at sea that are required. This space of ocean is not unpoliced, but it is only the ships of the US Coastguard and the naval forces of Britain, USA, France, Germany, and Holland and other industrialized nations, that have

---

[10] Michael Byers (2004), 'Policing the High Seas: The Proliferation Security Initiative', *American Journal of International Law*, 98/3: 526–45.

[11] *Ibid.*

[12] Byers detects, on the horizon, an extension of the 'right to preemptive self defence' in maritime law enforcement to be asserted by the USA in the context of the threat from global terrorism and WMD. The Proliferation Security Initiative (PSI), designed to respond to WMD, is an attempt to develop a global regime in this area but has not abandoned the requirement of flag-state consent. Byers, 'Policing the High Seas', *op cit*, but see also Douglas Guilfoyle (2007), 'Interdicting Vessels to Enforce the Common Interest: Maritime Countermeasures and the Use of Force', *International Comparative Law Quarterly*, 56/1: 69–82; Chester Brown (2003), '"Reasonableness" in the Law of the Sea: The Prompt Release of the Volga', *Leiden Journal of International Law*, 16: 621–30. The USA has been willing to declare that it would nonetheless act in the instance that a non-consenting state were suspect of transporting WMD or missile technology on the high seas. John Bolton, architect of the PSI, declared that 'We are prepared to undertake interdictions right now and, if that opportunity arises, if we had action-able intelligence and it was appropriate, we would do it now'. (Byers, 'Policing the High Seas', p 545.)

the capacity to undertake extensive maritime law enforcement on the high seas.

The maritime law enforcement cooperation agreements negotiated with Caribbean islands during the 1980s and 90s draw on the traditions of bilateral arrangements in transatlantic policing on issues such as slavery, piracy, and alcohol prohibition.[13] The creation of bilateral agreements in the field of counter-drugs operations can be traced back to the late 1970s. After the increase in maritime traffic in psychotropic drugs through the Western Caribbean, considerable policy-making effort was expended, leading to the 1981 US-UK Exchange of Notes concerning cooperation in the suppression of the unlawful importation of narcotic drugs into the United States,[14] similar to the 1924 bilateral convention on alcohol smuggling.[15] This 'Exchange of Notes' permits US authorities to board private British vessels in search of drugs in an area comprising the Gulf of Mexico, the Caribbean Sea, the Atlantic Ocean West of longitude 55° West and South of latitude 30° North, and everywhere within 150 miles of the Atlantic coast of the USA. When drugs are discovered, vessels are seized and liable to forfeiture to the US authorities where the crew can face criminal trial. As Siddle puts it, 'the agreement represents a significant departure from the customary rule that on the high seas jurisdiction follows the flag'.[16] Siddle points out that:

[t]here is no *quid pro quo* for the new agreement, beyond the satisfaction for the British Government that it is protecting the good name of the British flag and cooperating in the suppression of a trade which is part of a universal problem.[17]

---

[13] It drew, for example, on the Convention between the United Kingdom and the United States respecting the Regulation of the Liquor Traffic, concluded in Washington on 23 January 1924 (UK Treaty Series 22 (1924); Cmnd. 2199); cited by John Siddle (1982), 'Anglo-American Cooperation in the Suppression of Drug Smuggling', *International and Comparative Law Quarterly*, 31: 726–47.

[14] The Government of the United Kingdom and the Government of the United States Exchange of Notes concerning cooperation in the suppression of the unlawful importation of narcotic drugs into the United States, 13 November 1981, see Appendix I, Siddle (1982), 'Anglo-American Cooperation'.   [15] See n 13.

[16] John Siddle (1982), 'Anglo-American Cooperation', p 726.

[17] John Siddle (1982), 'Anglo-American Cooperation'.

The 'Shiprider Solution'

Under the Model Shiprider Agreements,[18] which were negotiated bilaterally with individual Caribbean countries, the US was given the right to designate officials—the Law Enforcement Detachment (LED) known as Shipriders—to embark on the vessels of that country, advising and assisting in boarding suspect vessels to enforce the country's laws, and enforce US law outside their territorial waters. The Caribbean state also designates its own Shiprider to travel on US ships with the power to authorize US ships to pursue suspect vessels and aircraft fleeing into the country's waters and to conduct counterdrug patrols in the country's territorial sea. It also gives the right for a US ship to enter the country's territorial seas to investigate or board and search any suspect vessel, confers a right of overflight for US aircraft to order suspect aircraft to land, and provides diplomatic immunity for US law enforcement officials involved in Shiprider. It has been argued that this, in effect, 'gives the US primary jurisdiction on the high seas and contingent jurisdiction in a country's territorial waters'.[19]

This initiative raises questions about national sovereignty conceived conventionally as territorial exclusivity and seen as a core ingredient of the nation state system. The 1933 Montevideo Treaty articulates the basic elements of the idea of sovereignty, such as the definition of a permanent population within a defined territory with a government that has the capacity to enter into relationships with other states. In late modern society, however, 'like capital, sovereignty is becoming increasingly unglued from its traditional moorings in nation states'.[20] There is a sharp division in views about national sovereignty between those that see it as the *sine qua non* of nationhood, of independence in a post-colonial world and those who appeal to sovereignty as an expression of 'outmoded protectionism', a hindrance to efforts at international assistance

[18] The US signed a Shiprider Agreement with China in 1993. Commander John Davis, Chief, Fisheries Enforcement Division, US Coastguard, '*How International Enforcement Cooperation Deters Illegal Fishing in the North Pacific*'. US State Department Journal.

[19] Hilbourne Watson (2003), 'The "Ship Rider Solution" and Post-Cold War Imperialism: Beyond Ontologies of State Sovereignty in the Caribbean' in Cynthia Barrow-Giles and Don Marshall, *Living at the Borderlines: Issues in Caribbean Sovereignty and Development*. Jamaica: Ian Randle Publishers, p 232.

[20] *Ibid*, p 265.

and detrimental to national welfare and security.[21] The debate over the Shiprider Agreements brought these issues to a head.

Although many countries within the region had signed Shiprider Agreements by the end of 1995, Barbados, Jamaica, and Trinidad and Tobago had strong reservations against the proposals and refused to sign. An editorial in the *Barbados Advocate* described Shiprider as an 'obscene and cowardly assault' on the integrity of Caribbean nations in pursuit of US national interests 'disguised as a generous and unselfish offer of assistance to states unable to help themselves'.[22] Distinguished statesman and former Commonwealth Secretary-General, Sir Shridath Ramphal, said that the US proposed to 'turn back the clock of history and remove from West Indian hands the right to determine the nature of our engagement with the wider world'.[23] It was, he declared, 'a proposal for recolonisation'.[24] Describing the Shiprider Agreement as 'one of the latest US strategies for dominating the Caribbean',[25] Watson argued that it challenged 'the most basic principle of international law. . . that a foreign sovereign has no enforcement jurisdiction' in the territory of another state.[26]

The advocates of the 'Shiprider Solution' acknowledged that giving up any measure of sovereignty would cause anxiety among those whose self-determination, independence, and control over their resources are at stake. This, they concede is especially acute in the context of a region whose history has been defined by struggles against foreign powers, with a legacy of inequalities of power among the countries of the region and with respect to its northern neighbours.[27] Advocates of Shiprider argue that nonetheless, diminution of sovereignty is inevitable:

The idea of relinquishing one's control over police or military forces can be extremely discomfiting. The increasing magnitude and transnational

[21] Joseph S. Tulchin and Ralph H. Espach (2000), *Security in the Caribbean Basin: The Challenge of Regional Cooperation*, Woodrow Wilson Center Current Studies on Latin America. Boulder, Colorado: Lynn Rienner Publishers, *op cit*, p 10.

[22] *Barbados Advocate*, 15 December 1996, cited by Watson, *op cit*, p 250.

[23] Sir Shridath Ramphal, 'The West Indies in the Wider World: Compulsions of Regional Engagement', *Distinguished Lecture Series of the University of the West Indies*, 14 April 1997, Mona, Jamaica cited by Hilbourne Watson (2003), 'The 'Ship Rider Solution', p 251.

[24] Ramphal 1997, *ibid*.   [25] Watson, *op cit*, p 226.

[26] Watson, *op cit*, p 238.   [27] Tuchin and Espach, *op cit*, p 10.

nature of today's security threats. . . require *a revision of the traditional concept of national sovereignty*. Today most countries find it difficult to defend themselves from threats such as large-scale migration flows, natural disasters or drug-related corruption and violence. In times of crisis, a rigid defence of traditional sovereignty can hinder efforts towards international assistance and prove detrimental to national welfare and security.[28]

The argument, crudely put, is that countries that cannot defend themselves from these new security threats must cede a degree of sovereignty in return for the security offered through collaboration with regional partners including the USA. Abrams, for example, contends that reliance on the USA 'for security and prosperity may be the most sensible form of nationalism'.[29] Caribbean states, he suggests, face a choice between 'having sovereignty invaded by Americans under treaty' or 'by drug runners at will'.[30] In redefining the notion of national sovereignty, Tulchin and Espach argue that mutually agreed cooperative participation in international activities 'should not be viewed as diminishing autonomy, but as a means of improving security and stability for the region as a whole as well as for each individual nation'.[31]

The Shiprider controversy was resolved in 1997 when President Bill Clinton met with Caribbean leaders in Bridgetown, Barbados.[32] The resulting Plan of Action (known as the Bridgetown Declaration) was a wide ranging document on trade and the environment, justice, and security.[33] Declaring that this was 'not a meeting between Caribbean nations and the United States, but rather a meeting among Caribbean nations, including the United States',[34] Clinton re-established preferential treatment on exports and his security chief first acknowledged a shared responsibility on drug trafficking, offering financial and infrastructural support. The Shiprider Agreements were redrafted to offer more reciprocal arrangements—to include the right for the Caribbean nations to

---

[28] Tulchin & Espach, *op cit*, p 10, *emphasis added*.

[29] Elliott Abrams (1996), 'The Shiprider Solution: Policing the Caribbean', *The National Interest*, p 86–92.   [30] *Ibid.*   [31] Tulchin & Espach, p 10.

[32] Caribbean/United States Summit Partnership For Prosperity And Security In The Caribbean. Bridgetown, Barbados, 10 May 1997.   [33] *Ibid.*

[34] President William Clinton, 10 May 1997, cited by Humberto Garcia-Muniz (2000), 'The United States and the Caribbean at Fin de Siècle: A Time of Transitions' in Tulchin and Espach, *Security in the Caribbean Basin*, p 45.

have the rights to enter and fly over US territory. With this move, Clinton finessed opposition to Shiprider, persuading reluctant Barbados and Jamaica to enter treaties.[35] The government of the United Kingdom and the United States of America signed a Shiprider Agreement relating to the waters of the Caribbean and Bermuda on behalf of the United Kingdom Overseas Territories (UKOTS) the following year.[36] The Caribbean Regional Maritime Counter-drug Agreement (CRA) has been agreed by numerous countries but has yet to come into force.[37]

The Coastguard

The authorities responsible for maritime law enforcement have as bewilderingly wide and complex role as their counterparts who police dry land. The physical environment is obviously different and the coastguard must contend with the unique challenges of policing on water, but the myriad routine tasks involved in policing the sea is not very different from those involved in terrestrial law enforcement. Coastguard officers have the powers of a constable at sea for fisheries enforcement, and a more general

[35] Humberto Garcia-Muniz (2000), 'The United States and the Caribbean at Fin de Siècle', p 45.

[36] Agreement Between the Government of the United Kingdom of Great Britain and Northern Ireland and the Government of the United States of America Concerning Maritime and Aerial Operations to Suppress Illicit Trafficking By Sea in Waters of the Caribbean and Bermuda, Vol 2169, I-38031, done at Washington, 13 July 1998.

[37] The US *International Narcotics Control Strategy Report* states that 'There are now 26 bilateral maritime counternarcotics agreements in place between the U.S. and our Central, South American and Caribbean partner nations, moving toward our goal of eliminating safe havens for drug smugglers. Most recently, the USCG signed a set of operational procedures with the Bureau of Coastal Navy & Merchant Affairs of Ecuador, which facilitate cooperation in cases involving Ecuadorian flagged vessels suspected of engaging in maritime drug smuggling activities. Discussions for a similar agreement with Peru are in progress. In addition, the United States, Belize, and France have signed and taken the necessary steps to bring the Caribbean Regional Maritime Counterdrug Agreement (CRA) into force; however, two more countries need to take action for the CRA to come into effect', United States Department of State Bureau for International Narcotics and Law Enforcement Affairs, *International Narcotics Control Strategy Report*, Vol I, Drug and Chemical, Control, March 2008. It is interesting to note that the report on this area of activity is largely unchanged from 2007. <http://www.state.gov/documents/organization/81446.pdf>.

responsibility for maritime law enforcement including crimes at sea and the protection of the maritime environment.

Like the border protection agencies and the military described in earlier chapters, the role of coastguard has shifted in recent years. One coastguard commander explained that 15 or 20 years earlier, their primary law enforcement focus was on illegal contraband such as cigarette and alcohol smuggling together with their responsibility for search and rescue. That, he said, 'used to be our focus but now it is counter-drug operations and since 9/11, counter-terrorism'. This, the commander agreed, was traditionally territory for the constabulary because they have jurisdiction on both land and at sea, but the coastguard were playing an increasingly important role in maritime law enforcement. The coastguard were 'moving away from traditional roles such as search and rescue and fisheries protection to a more direct involvement in terms of actual law enforcement'. Search and rescue, was still a priority for the coastguard but 'not at the top of the list' because it had been displaced by their role as a law enforcement agency:

we will stop pretty much everything for search and rescue that's first priority call on our time. But in the absence of a search and rescue case it's going to be narcotics first, fisheries protection second, and the other things like marine environmental protection and so on cascading down the line. But the first order of business in terms of law enforcement is anti-narcotics.

In common with other security sector organizations, the commanders of coastguard had strong views about the dangers of the drugs trade. In their view, the most obvious threat is from the:

drug trade and the spin-offs from that threat, money laundering, corruption of government officials and institutions, the threat to democracy that will arise from that. And potential worst case scenario of a government being bought and owned.

There are also direct linkages between the drug trade and firearms coming in that protect the trade and as part of the payment to locals involved in the trade. In the context of this level of threat from narcotics, the captains did not question the necessity of the coastguard focusing on drugs interdiction. They must maintain a search and rescue capacity to deal with marine emergencies and environmental protection and collaborate with the police on the protection of tourists on the beaches, but to this substantial core mandate has been the addition of routine drugs enforcement and contributions to coordinated drugs interdiction exercises with other law enforcement agencies. Thus, much of their 'underway time' (time at sea) is spent patrolling for the prevention of narcotics, maintaining a deterrent presence, and acting on specific intelligence. Again, this highlights parallels with the policing of dry land.

There are also concerns about terrorism related to the Caribbean as a soft target:

we don't consider [this country] to be high on the agenda of any potential terrorists, [but] she can be considered a soft target in that we don't have the kind of security arrangements as let's say, the United States or the United Kingdom or Israel or European countries for that matter, so we have started to look very seriously at counter-terrorism [because] we are a soft target and looking at the possibility of a terrorist incident happening [here], the kind of effect that that could have on our society . . . and economy that is primarily based on tourism. One small incident could basically shut down our country so within recent times we have started to look at . . . the financial resources [needed] to be able to mount some kind of response to any possible threat.

The demand in relation to terrorism was such that the coastguard commanders were of the view that they were 'not equipped to deal with any kind of terrorist threat'. They would need to redirect and develop their human and physical resources, upgrade their ships, acquire equipment to detect explosive ordinance aboard ships, and develop their diving capabilities.

The broadening of the mandate of the coastguard has come with only modest increases in resources. To some extent, this has been achieved by adjustments in the way in which they direct their forces. For example, in relation to drugs operations, they have focused on smaller vessels capable of high speed in order to tackle the 'go fast' boats and pirogues that are running drugs northwards and onto the islands for onward trans-shipment by air. However, it is inevitable that there will be tension between the law enforcement and the search and rescue roles, especially when coastguard vessels are engaged in a joint operation:

That's always a problem because whenever a coastguard vessel [participates] in a joint operation with other assets from other countries, a search and rescue issue comes up, and we find ourselves at times shifting focus to do search and rescue. So yes, it is a concern and it is a role that is just as important as the other roles, but that's a challenge that we face I think, you can never have enough assets to really take care of all of these roles.

The threat of drugs and its 'attendant ills' has displaced the traditional focus of the coastguard from revenue protection, environmental protection, search and rescue and, in the commander's view, those areas suffered as a consequence. The issues are interlinked and need to be seen in a wider security framework including economics and other broader issues, requiring a much stronger emphasis on maritime security within the Caribbean region. The region's security threats need to be understood in a regional context of multiple jurisdiction and the geographical reality of the Caribbean location as a drug transit zone, with the key issue of building on the counter-drug agreement, to create better collaboration—along the lines of the Association of Caribbean Commissioners of Police (ACCP)—for the Chiefs of Defence Forces. 'Historically', the commander argued, 'we have focused on security from a terrestrial perspective, geography will again inform that we need to have a different focus now . . . because the threat is largely from the sea'.

Security in a Maritime Neighbourhood

Local coordination

Policing the sea's edges inevitably involves collaboration between land and water-based forces. The marine division and coastguard work together on a day-to-day basis, but these agencies also coordinate with defence forces (see Chapter 5) and border protection agencies—port authorities, Customs, and immigration (Chapter 6). They enforce the laws relating to any department of state. Most were agreed that local agencies should be able to work better with one another with better training and development. The use of the National Joint Headquarters (NJHQ) to emphasize maritime law enforcement and development of trust were all needed and would 'come over time'. In the opinion of one Inspector heading the marine division of the police, there was a strong bond between his crew and the coastguard arising from their joint training, for example at the British Military Advisor Training Team (BMATT) training centre in Antigua and at the coastguard commanders' conference where they meet with the heads of police marine sections. This created support, fraternity, and consequently, a good working relationship:

as people working in the sea, you know, there's that bond, you're doing the same job and so on. 'I look out for you, you look out for me', because when you're out there you can't really call for help, so you've got to depend on your brother that is out there, so the relationship is good. I have never heard about any wranglings between the islands because the coastguard and the marine police, we work together, you know.

The marine police must also work closely with the coastguard since the latter do not have authority to bring prosecutions nor do they have any cells to hold arrested prisoners. Therefore, if the coastguard make an arrest at sea, the suspect is handed over to the police to take statements, lay charges and, if necessary, hold the person awaiting a court appearance. The coastguard and marine police frequently train together, and offer mutual assistance, but there are issues of trust and tensions that arise since their work covers the same territory.

Regional cooperation

There are extensive inter-island links among the region's coastguard and marine sections because individuals from different places get to know one another through training courses and conferences. In terms of operations and activities, there is less collaborative working among the Caribbean islands than there is between the metropolitan countries and the Caribbean islands individually and collectively. This is a function of distance in some instances. For example, it is over 1,000 miles from Guyana to Jamaica, and even the two or three hundred mile round trip between neighbouring islands would be beyond the range of most countries which only maintain a small number of ocean-going vessels and in many cases only one. It would therefore be a risk to sail far beyond their territorial waters leaving the island vulnerable and the vessel at a risk of mechanical breakdown. Despite this, there is cooperation in search and rescue with neighbouring islands, and with the Regional Security System (RSS). There are Rescue Coordination Centres in Trinidad, Martinique, and Puerto Rico, the latter involved in counter-drug operations. However, one of the problems that comes with smallness is 'diseconomy of scale', where there is a duplication of services.

The annual 'Tradewinds' exercise, now in its twenty-third year of operation, enables coastguard and marine section officers to work with each other.[38] It is in a given country each year and

---

[38] Tradewinds 2007, Closing Ceremony at Price Barracks, Ladyville, Belize, 16 May 2007. The Canadian Navy also has a note on Tradewinds, 'The TRADEWINDS Exercise is a Light Urban Search & Rescue Exercise which is an annual event, held

focuses on a particular form of security threat, which could be terrorism, counter-narcotics, or environmental disaster such as a hurricane relief operation. Through this, countries exchange information and spend time together so as to provide readiness in case they are called upon to deploy within a short period of time in an emergency. It provides the opportunity also for training and cooperation at the regional level 'for troops to work together'. Tradewinds dealt with four components: internal security, coastguard, civil defence, and some exercises as a climax. At the time of the research there was a discussion about the possibility of deploying in Haiti. In the commander's view, the training conducted during Tradewinds could be 'a stepping stone for the CARICOM battalion that would have worked together during exercise surveillance to deploy to Haiti'. Out of this there is CDRU; the disaster response team made up from the soldiers and sailors from the various territories, who are on call to respond to any area that is threatened.

Cooperation with metropolitan countries: Shiprider in practice

Since the 1980s, there have been extensive operations with codenames such as Operation 'Libertador', a three-week drug enforcement effort in November 2000, launched simultaneously in 36 Caribbean-basin countries and resulting in 1,000 arrests.[39] Since then, regular operations such as Caribe Storm and Caribe Venture have been undertaken. In these operations, the infrastructure and logistics are coordinated by the USA, which has an overview of the entire operation, and coordinates all the elements, with each country coordinating its assets through the National Joint Headquarters. These operations tend to be Caribbean-wide operations where the US makes a 'big thrust for a period time'. The US provides an 'over the horizon picture' from the centre:

in various locations throughout the globe. This past year, it was held in Barbados. In conjunction with the fire and police representatives, our PNCT Troop sends trained personnel to share their knowledge and expertise with the other participants'.

[39] *Operation Libertador Concluded; Jamaica Praised*, US Embassy Kingston Press Release, 21 November 2000. Similar operations during 1996 are documented by Ivelaw Griffith (1997), *Drugs and Security in the Caribbean*, pp 220–1.

so if they are concentrating on, let's say Saint Vincent, Barbados, Saint Lucia, they would be flying the aircraft, doing patrols and feeding the information back into our ops room so if there's a boat coming out of Saint Vincent for instance, they would be able to track that and provide an adequate response to provide a successful endgame.

The aim is to use the C26 surveillance aircraft to allow a 'kind of blanketing or shutting down' of as wide an area as possible. Such extensive coordinated operations occur no more than once a year in most places, with more regular but ad hoc cooperation year round. The role of the coastguard would be to provide local intelligence, small boat coverage, and they would 'up [their] operations so that the guys can't move from some other place and find safe wreckage here'.

Most cooperation at sea is with the US coastguard and British navy vessels and occasionally the French and Dutch. The coastguard have a number of operations involving the US, under the bilateral Shiprider Agreements. These involve US assets being sent to the region:

we find ourselves working quite a lot with our American counterparts, coastguard in particular, more than our partners within the region, and it's probably because of the lack of capital assets to exercise or operate in a particular area. The Americans have the assets, they come down here, we have Shipriders on board, we have certain agreements, and we conduct quite a lot of law enforcement exercises.

Whenever there are ships in the region, the island authorities might be involved under the Shiprider Agreement. One commander explained that whenever there is a US or UK ship in the region a local coastguard officer will embark, which 'gives legitimacy to the whole exercise'. In addition to coordinated operations, there is routine information sharing, so that if information about, for example, a drugs boat moving through their territorial waters or EEZ, is passed to them by the USA, they would feel compelled to act. While on a day-to-day basis they are operating independently, they are quite frequently requested or tasked to undertake activity in support of a multinational operation and will do so:

if something happens in our area of responsibility and we don't have that information but it's had by the Americans, they would task us or request from us that we deal with a particular situation because it just falls in this area. Even in areas out of our jurisdiction, if they require a surveillance for something, if we have the asset they would task us for it, and it's that understanding that has been taking place over the years.

Thus, the majority of cooperation is not along the lines of a joint or integrated team, but a set of agencies working together, deploying assets within their areas of jurisdiction, coordinated by intelligence from the metropolitan countries. As the commander described it, with operations like Caribe Storm, 'you are more or less left with your own assets' and are on standby to conduct patrols or provide air surveillance.

One commander argued that the colloquial term—Shiprider—does not quite describe the full scope of maritime cooperation agreements. Other aspects, such as enabling overflight and communicating observations about suspect vessels, are more common. So, for example, a US aircraft observing a suspect vessel or an aircraft entering an island's airspace or in their waters can inform the authorities, and can get permission to enter to continue observation of that aircraft or vessel. Once an identified vessel is heading towards an island, the US can be granted permission to continue observation and if local officials are not in a position to do the interception themselves, they give permission to hold the vessel and carry out law enforcement activity until they can hand it over or decide to dispose of it by agreement.

One commander commented that in the early days of the agreement, there was a reaction to fishing boats which were being stopped on a daily basis. The agreement in practice is that permission has to be sought to enter territorial waters on every occasion, but there would have to be extremely strong reasons not to give that permission. There is an understanding among the duty officers, who will make the decision or the first call before reaching the coastguard commander that:

at no point in time we are going to stop the pursuit of a suspect vessel, based on some issue of sovereignty or any of those things at that point in time. We'll work out afterwards what should have happened or what may have been. The aim is to get the bad guy.

This sense that 'everyone understands very clearly the issue is to get the bad guys', ensures a 'kind of pragmatic approach' to capture the suspect instead of allowing sovereignty to disrupt an operation. Nonetheless, failures do sometimes occur if a ship's captain is not sufficiently au fait with the terms of the agreement, or if there is a lack of trust between the groups hindering communications. Nonetheless, granting permission is compulsory since this establishes responsibility and provides protection for local people:

It also provided a system in place where I mean if a local felt that he had been disadvantaged if we don't have something here in the law to protect that person you could have a foreign vessel come in, do something and get out afterwards. . . . Because permission has to be given, the government of _____ now assumes . . . the liability to protect the _____ citizen. Then if government of _____ needs to take her course against its own partners, or whether it does it by arbitration . . . the citizen is protected.

The key point is that the island authorities must give their agreement for all law enforcement activity, and thus are held accountable in the event that something goes wrong—a mistaken arrest, or in the event that somebody was injured or killed during an operation. This was absolutely essential, the commander argued, since if there were free entry and a foreign ship were to come within the waters and take action, the citizen would have no recourse. An injured party might not know which vessel was responsible, from which country, and who was on the vessel. Therefore:

If we have a system in place where permission has to be sought, the coastguard and his duty officer has given permission, it is logged, he knows which vessel was there, he knows what action. There is a trail. There is an accountability so that citizen can say, 'well, who gave permission to do this?'

So far, legal action has been avoided because 'both parties have been quite careful and the procedures have been followed fairly scrupulously'. Sometimes fishermen have called the media to say that a ship had come so close as to interfere with their fishing, but according to the head of coastguard 'by the time we investigate and answer the questions it is clarified and people understand it'.

The aim, wherever possible, is to get a team on board at the outset and to have operations carefully planned. In any case, the coastguard officers have trained and worked alongside the US and other coastguards for many years, long before the most recent maritime law enforcement agreements, and generally:

we have a good healthy working relationship with the US Coastguard and we find that they treat things and people with respect. And even when it's a big grey ship that is out there, it's usually the small coastguard attachment on board that calls the shots in terms of the operationalization of this agreement.

Intelligence for the operation comes through the military intelligence unit, acting as a filter and working closely with Special Branch, the Drug Squad, and with the international partners. Sometimes, the Drug Squad contacts the coastguard directly if the situation is immediate, but normally the local, regional, and international intelligence resources would come through their intelligence unit. They would have no contact with the other intelligence agencies, or their sources, themselves, 'We prefer it that way', the coastguard commander said. There would be some meetings to discuss cases, but all 'actionable intelligence that requires our deployment. . . comes through the intelligence unit'. When that intelligence comes in it is accepted as 'good intelligence' assessed only in terms of the commander's knowledge of the sea:

I take that as good intelligence. I may ask certain questions if with my knowledge of the marine environment some of the time/distance things seem to be totally out I might ask questions. You're saying these people are here but they are landing there in two hours? Impossible! Recheck your sources or recalculate but I am going to assume that, yes, somebody is coming in, somebody is landing somewhere so I need to deploy. What I am trying to narrow down now is where do I deploy, you know.

The coastguard try to coordinate an intercept on land, usually a beach. The coastguard will start the pursuit together with the air-wing and 'try as much as possible to funnel them into an area' where the air-wing—ie helicopter—has a team of people, narcotics agents, intelligence people, and sometimes troops to hold an area until he can get others in there and bring the operation to a conclusion. One coastguard commander explained that, in general, 'we prefer to have the end game on the beach'. This practical solution creates its own logistical problems, and also security concerns. On one occasion, a group of drug smugglers landed on the beach on one island where US coastguard boats and helicopter had pursued them,

The air-wing landed a team of our people and we are trying to surround the area and catch three guys who had made off onto the bushes and also to secure the drugs and the vessel. And the local community came down, I expect maybe wanted to give some help to the guys who were escaping and to get to the drugs. So they started throwing stones at our people but we were able to get the situation under control fairly quickly though. . . . We didn't have to shoot anybody but we had to bring in more troops and hold the area.

In most instances, US ships had pursued suspect vessels into Caribbean territorial waters, then collaborating with the coastguard and local police, were instructed to go to a particular area, perhaps a marina or a beachhead. They might give instructions to the vessel to 'follow no further'. From the commander's experience, the US coastguard was reluctant to land, perhaps because they do not wish to give 'any sign of infringing sovereignty', or are concerned about security 'that if I land on this beach what will they do to me?' It might, he said, 'be borne out of the two, but I find that they are very reluctant to go beyond the water's edge'.

At the other edge of the Caribbean area of maritime jurisdictional interest, at the outer limit of their territorial waters, the authorities are largely content to leave law enforcement to those with an ocean-going capacity. Since the US coastguard can stop and search all Caribbean flagged vessels suspected of drug trafficking, outside their territorial waters, much of the communication between the two countries is on that basis:

it could be the US calling and saying they are in no known passage, they see a vessel flying the _____ flag, they have reason to believe it has contraband on board can you give me permission to board. And we'll say yes, if we are satisfied it is a _____ vessel and they have a good basis, reasonable basis for their suspicion, we will say go ahead.

Resources, demand, and donor–beneficiary relationships

The typical Caribbean island coastguard may have two ocean-going vessels (only one of which may be serviceable at any time), four 45 foot medium-sized boats, and four small speedboats—which can only patrol the inshore regions and the shoreline itself. The problem is the miles of open coastline, inlets, and rivers with 'cricks', allowing a lot of room for drug smugglers with fast boats. The coastguard have few crafts, no night capability such as night vision, infra-red cameras, or binoculars, and no flares. In order to prevent drug smuggling they would need more extensive equipment with speedboats deployed all the way around the island fully equipped for coordinated night-time operations. Without this they do not have the capacity to respond.

The risk in the shifting focus was that the national needs are not met as well as those of the region and the security interests of the metropolitan countries. One coastguard commander explained that,

The risks, in my view, are twofold. One is that the interests of the larger parties—UK, US, the French—while they do have Caribbean interests—because they have a greater capacity, . . . and because they are working off a national strategy which will perhaps provide for funding or support but with specific conditions geared towards their interests and rightly so. If those become predominant in the Caribbean reality, without getting the national and regional views of the Caribbean states partnering on an equal footing it would be problematic. . . . You might then end up with a situation where the parties then do not perform, the parties that feel that they are disadvantaged do not perform as they ought because the question is, 'What is in it for me?' And then, on the other side you will have discontent by the parties who are saying, well look we are putting resources into it and what is happening. . . . we would never get the best out of the relationship unless that can be well and properly addressed and agreed upon.

In this commander's view, there was a sense that that relationship was not in perfect balance, requiring a review of the current situation, to ensure within the participating states that 'there is the capacity to address their needs and then have some additional capacity to focus on the kind of coordination that's needed externally'. There was also a very strong concern that the vessels provided by the USA were unsuitable, even when they were serviceable, as the Caribbean was receiving old, used vessels: 'So therefore, it's all well and good accepting gifts from people but the gifts that people give must be able to be effective and I don't believe that they are effective enough.'

Coastguard commanders felt they needed a much greater maritime capacity. On their own assessment, they argued that in order to provide a proper response to terrorism, drugs, and all the other roles and responsibilities which they had been given, the coastguard would have to double its human capacity. This itself was problematic as they had limited availability of qualified staff, and because the larger states, including Britain, sometimes recruit from within the Caribbean coastguard. The coastguard in one island had undertaken an internal assessment of what equipment they required. They concluded that 'serious capital investment' was needed to meet the 'layered security' responsibility:

we would have to have vessels capable of offshore patrolling, vessels for the medium area of territory from 12 miles in and then vessels from

3 miles in, and in addition then you still have to consider environmental, you know, all that comes into _____ on a regular basis. What would happen if there's an oil spill? If the oil reaches the beaches, that impacts on tourism so it is . . . if you look at it, it's like a wheel, everything kind of feeds into each other.

Donors sometimes raised questions about the uses to which assets were being put because recipient countries have specific requirements of their own for such resources. In some instances an asset 'may be dedicated solely to a particular role and function'. A coastguard commander explained that:

Recently the question came up as to what are the details and terms of these memorandum of understanding for the C26 [spotter plane] for us here, because we have been doing other things other than drug interdiction; fisheries protection, for example; surveillance out at EEZ. . . . we were to look at the details of the memorandum of understanding to find out exactly what that asset is there for, whether or not it was specifically for that, and this was something that was discussed between the Chief of Defence Staff, the Minister of National Security, and the Ambassador.

Sometimes, according to one coastguard captain, there was misconnect between the interests of the donor nations and those of the recipients. He said:

national interests for the United States may not be national interests for a Caribbean state or territory and that's clear. I think what we as Caribbean nations have got to do is be fairly firm in what we want and what we don't want and we have to stick together and make a decision.

The coastguard generally felt that the region should have some kind of independent response that was not dependent on the metropolitan countries. Donors would inevitably have their own priorities:

wherever you get that assistance from, they're going to have a specific focus which is going to come over to you as assisting you . . . for example if it is the UK Customs, they're stopping drugs from going into UK and Europe. If it is DEA, they're predominantly looking at stopping drugs from going into the US.

The commander explained that the regional coastguards were reliant on the metropolitan countries for human and technical intelligence. I wondered how far it was possible for the island authorities to verify intelligence before acting on it. The commander replied that it is impossible to verify the quality of intelligence and therefore they had to take that intelligence on trust. There was, he said, 'no checks, no balances'. It was impossible to verify their intelligence; 'who would we go to?' he asked:

We don't take security very seriously, I don't think so, in the region . . . It doesn't matter to me who's in charge but we need one central facility. If SB is in charge, fine. If coastguard is in charge or I happen to be in charge, fine, it doesn't matter to me who's in charge. What matters is the mechanism to be put in place to establish those relationships and to do what you just said, checks and balances because the Americans are listening, the Brits are listening, the Dutch are listening and we need to be able to build our own picture based on their inputs. Once we can do that, then we make the decision that, that boat is out there and is likely to be running drugs, then a decision is taken, . . . these are the people who need to know, the coastguard because they are responsible for the maritime law enforcement, the Drug Squad just in case it gets ashore. If the Drug Squad and coastguard then want to co-opt additional assistance from the Task Force or from the [Defence Force], then they do that. The operation is planned, executed and brought to conclusion and information is then fed back to the people who can close the file. That is how the mechanism should work.

An issue for the coastguard, as for other agencies, was concern about the integrity of coastguard officers. They had undertaken an approach based on UK and US integrity testing, including vetting and polygraph testing. Coastguard officers have to undergo their analysis and to clear these tests in order to stay in the unit. One commander explained that, 'If they don't come up with a clean slate, they have to move. You can't get away from integrity failure. I think you have to be very conscious of it and get somebody to guard the guards'. The coastguard did not find people reluctant to work with them because of allegations of corruption but there were people within local agencies and they were 'not sure how much information we can share and give'. They work at the senior level with the basic assumption that within their midst, they must have people who are compromised, or are working in the pocket of the drugs runners. They try to minimize their ability to compromise the system by randomly rostering people for duty, keeping a close eye on lifestyles, and watching for changes in patterns. At sea, they take a range of steps to communications with the shore:

We try to restrict cellular phones being carried on operations at sea, and within certain sensitive areas of our system. We also operate on a fairly strict 'need to know basis' and tight timelines for operations where we might tell the guys get a vessel ready for sea for 24 hours and have it at half an hour standby to move. But no more information than that, so we try to control the information. You are not going to be able to save it all but we try as much as we can to minimize. I know people understand say, 'look at least if you didn't know, nobody can point a finger at you when information is leaked.'

One commander felt it was necessary to have some kind of international inspection, with testing on an annual or 18 month basis to 'make sure that you're not sleeping with the enemy'. The captain was happy for this to take place, and for himself and his senior people to be vetted. However, they were uncomfortable with the US or UK retaining records on their staff. This, in their view, was their responsibility:

You can vet me because you're forging a relationship with me or let's say, three people, myself as the Commanding Officer, my number two, my Executive Officer, my Operations Officer. Those are the three people that you will relate to. I don't have a fundamental difficulty. You want the ordinary seaman that I just brought in. I need to be comfortable with him. If I'm not comfortable with him, then I re-assign him or say 'Well look Skipper, I'm not comfortable with you based on your polygraph, your analysis, you're like you're sleeping with the enemy, you've got to go or I'm going to put you in an area that is non-sensitive'.

Reciprocity

From the commanders' point of view, the key issue at the heart of the Shiprider debate is the question of reciprocity. Once a reciprocal arrangement had been agreed, then this made the relationship equitable.

I firmly believe in reciprocity. I believe, although you may not have the capacity or the desire or need to sail up to the US, the facility should be there. There is no big nation/small nation if you're talking globalization, if you're talking a one world and a nation state being equal to another nation state.

If every nation was independent, and each had a vote at the United Nations, then it should not be possible for one state to sail into the waters of another without offering a reciprocal relationship.

We thought, if we are going to have this agreement we want full reciprocity whether we are in a position physically to exercise fuller reciprocity, or not. We are going to be negotiating on the basis of equal partners.

So that was maybe the single biggest bone of contention for the US to give us reciprocity.

With this in place, Caribbean coastguard vessels may enter any part of US territory, 'including Guam' joked one commander.[40] The theme of reciprocity was also echoed by one the Military Chiefs of Staff (see Chapter 5):

The fact that we are not able to go into your space to reciprocate the thing is unimportant. . . . What really is useful is the optics, how it looks [to] everybody, yes, how it looks, and I believe it's a fundamental thing to say, 'Right, let's do this or let's do it this way' and I think we have scored a great victory, the principle with our Agreement. I think the biggest obstacle in the sovereignty is the American attitude and abrasiveness. I think that is the biggest problem with it. I personally have great difficulty in that I only want you to do something in my space, only if it is absolutely necessary. I don't want you to parade the conditions which almost make it necessary. Let us work together, and that's my own view of sovereignty.

Reciprocity was also undermined to some extent with the uses of either conditions or 'sweeteners' attached to the offer of assistance. One coastguard commander said that Shiprider:

had some sweets tied on to it . . . Whenever there is something to be signed, there will be something attached to it, there is a little carrot dangling up ahead that, you know, if you take this then maybe you'll get this and that is always, always.

Commanders reject these inducements on principle: 'if you can give me something, give me something, don't come bearing gifts just to sign something.' Even more to the point, one said, that what was being offered as an inducement was not particularly helpful, rejecting the offer of additional vessels firstly on principle and secondly because they were not serviceable. One commander was very frustrated by this:

I curse it! A lot of bullshit that they bring in was old vessels, 30 year old vessels. You've managed to get them, sail home, then there are no spare parts, [they] have long since stopped making those engines. It's ridiculous! If you can give us something, give us something that can be useful.

---

[40] Guam is an island in the Western Pacific and is an unincorporated US territory.

In some negotiations, in addition to 'sweeteners', there was also the use of punitive measures for states not compliant with US wishes. In pursuing its opt-out of the International Criminal Court, the US expended time and effort encouraging countries within the region to sign 'Article 98' in which states agree not to send Americans to the ICC. Those that did not faced US Congress-approved sanctions including the withdrawal of US international military education and assistance training in a range of fields including engineering, electrics, and electronics and ironically, anti-drug operations:

Has that impacted upon us? The short answer is yes. We now have to look at ways and means of developing other areas of training, some of it I would suggest has been discussed also, it's self-help throughout the region where, let's say Barbados, takes on the responsibility for running a particular series of courses and Jamaica does likewise, Trinidad does likewise, Guyana does likewise, but now has to be agreed to at a much higher level, the political level in the first instance. I think at the military level, we would jump at it and cost it and so on but at the political level, there has got to be buy-in for it to be executed.

Sovereignty

For the coastguard, the question of national sovereignty was always at issue in bilateral or multilateral engagements. Sovereignty can be demonstrated in the right and ability of the state to enter into agreements, but having entered into an agreement, a nation is not sovereign unless it has the capacity to implement it. One coastguard commander was outspoken about his views on American imperialism and the problems that arose because of US global hegemonic power stating that despite being the most powerful country in the world and considering themselves as the 'world police' this didn't place them above the law. Accountability and reciprocity are still required, in a globalized era:

I would prefer to view the relationship as a shared responsibility in respect to how we deal with security and that's why any language that is used in correspondence in agreements or so on has got to come across and this may be simple but it's got to come across as a shared responsibility, and again I go back to the issue of reciprocity, it's got to come across as that. Perhaps if you view it as somebody giving you something and tying something to it, they can come across as colonialism but I prefer not to view it that way. I prefer not to.

There was scope for work in the field of maritime security, but it was woefully under resourced. One commander explained that:

in terms of cooperation, there's a lot more we can do on the national front, on the regional front, on the international front, so I think we have to look at how much emphasis we want to place on security and don't pay lip service to it.

One of the difficulties with investing in security is that it does not offer a financial return. Unlike the Customs service that brings in millions of dollars in revenue, security does not. Rather, it is 'more like an insurance policy' that 'you may not be able to measure in dollar signs', but provides the stable environment necessary to facilitate other areas for the society and the economy to be funded. What is required, in the commander's view, is a political decision that has to be taken to decide on the emphasis. This is not merely a matter of 'capital investment in one year and then not the requisite human resource development' with training to enable maritime law enforcement agents to provide an adequate security response to whatever threats face them.

Summary and Conclusion

Policing shorelines and the sea-borne traffic flowing among the Caribbean islands is an inherently transnational activity. It is concerned with law enforcement, order maintenance, crime prevention, and the surveillance of fishing boats, yachts and pleasure craft 'island hopping', and commercial vessels moving goods between continents or from one island to another. The main focus for marine law enforcement is the smugglers attempting to move goods in much the same way as their counterparts in the legitimate economy and using the same flotilla of large and small vessels. Many security risks facing these islands emanate from island life, but as a coastguard commander put it, the threat is 'largely from the sea'. Interdependence among the islands' maritime law enforcers stems from the sense that the people of the region inhabit a shared expanse of water; the goal of maritime policing therefore is to 'provide security in a maritime neighbourhood'.

The attempt to provide security in terrestrial neighbourhoods has been well documented in criminology and the related disciplines of policing and criminal justice studies. The present research shows that policing a maritime space is closely linked to policing neighbourhoods on land. The agenda of these relatively neglected members of the 'extended police family' is concerned with order maintenance, the enforcement of minor and serious offences, as well as the more general issue of maritime environmental protection and the maritime safety role of police work. The exact nature of policing activity depends on its proximity to the shoreline, with a big difference between inshore policing and law enforcement in open waters. The most significant division of labour is between the police marine division who do inshore patrols focusing on beaches, ports, and harbours, and the coastguard who patrol the territorial waters and the EEZ. Responsibility for policing this zone—whether it relates to maritime safety, pollution, or crimes at sea—falls to the nation state which has a mandate as custodian of the marine environment. Of course, this is limited by that nation's capacity in terms of boats, crew, and equipment, and it is relevant that many trafficking routes pass through the waters of numerous countries and through the contiguous zone.

The capacity of Caribbean nations to patrol their EEZ is severely limited and, for most, non-existent when it comes to the high seas. Most islands do possess ocean-going vessels, but often only one of these is serviceable at any one time. It would be a serious risk to island security—particularly for search and rescue—if that vessel were away for too long. Only in extreme circumstances, such as a major environmental disaster on a neighbouring island would an exception be made to undertake a lengthy operation. Outside the 12-mile boundary of their territorial waters, the role of the marine police is largely restricted to being placed as a 'Law Enforcement Detachment'—commonly known as a Shiprider—on a US or UK vessel. Roles traditionally undertaken by the coastguard, for example search and rescue, shoreline policing, and fisheries protection remain 'priorities', but most 'underway time' involves drug interdiction and deterrent patrols. In common with their colleagues in border protection and the military, maritime policing has become increasingly oriented towards law enforcement. The range of problems in which it is expected to intervene has grown wider, the severity of those problems has grown (for example armed criminality), and there is pressure to expand the geographical scope of their interdiction efforts in order to cover their areas of responsibility.

Patrolling the high seas is the quintessence of transnational policing. Police-relevant incidents happen there including 'ordinary crimes' such as theft and robbery, clandestine trade, smuggling, breaches of maritime law and safety codes, as well as accidents and emergencies requiring authoritative intervention. No national authority is responsible for policing the high seas. No state has jurisdiction here except over vessels flying their national flag, effectively rendering the high seas no man's land in which 'universal jurisdiction' exists only for laws against slavery and piracy. The overarching legal framework within which maritime policing occurs is formed from a complex intersection between the international Law of the Sea and bilateral maritime security agreements. This results not only in legal harmonization, through national implementing legislation, but also in standard operating practices, shared training skills and knowledge with collaborative metropolitan countries, sharing the context for regional integration.

International law and bilateral agreements facilitate 'visitation' (the maritime equivalent of stop and search) of vessels reasonably suspected of involvement in drug trafficking. This could, in theory, be enforced by any or all nations. In practice, however, maritime law enforcement on the high seas is the preserve of countries with an ocean-going naval capacity. Those forces with interests in the region include the USA, UK, Cuba, France, and the Netherlands and further to the south of the region, Venezuela and Columbia. The main strategic priority for the US Coastguard and the British Navy is to interdict in drug smuggling as boats leave the northern shores of continental South America, making their way up the island chain and from there to North America and Europe. Maritime law enforcement collaboration between Caribbean and metropolitan countries therefore includes ad hoc intelligence sharing about suspect vessels, bilateral coordination using Caribbean Shipriders embarked on US vessels, and multilateral joint operations. Training exercises such as Tradewinds, funded by the US and UK, involving all of the region's coastguard flagships have been held annually for a quarter of a century. However, there are inevitably some tensions between local, regional, and hemispheric priorities, requiring coordination with other authorities locally, regionally, and transnationally.

While there is independent discussion of security issues among CARICOM justice and security ministers, the capacity for regional communication, shared training, exercises, and day-to-day operational coordination are enabled through funding from the metropolitan countries. Links are made through other structures such as the ACCP, military commanders' conference, coastguard commanders' conference, and shared training and exercises, and these create a strong sense of a regional fraternity among the maritime law enforcers of the Commonwealth Caribbean. Operational cooperation is limited by the distances between islands and by limited resources in terms of vessels and personnel. Most cooperation therefore mainly relates to bilateral sharing of information and intelligence.

It is well documented that organizations have to stretch to cooperate with counterparts undertaking similar activity.[41] It is often problems of coordination *within organizations* and at the *local level* that are the most difficult to solve. Local coordination involves, first and most obviously, partnership between the marine police and coastguard, with land-based military and police divisions including Drug Squads and the Special Branches, and also with port security, environmental protection, and other civilian agencies. The kinds of problems well documented in repeated attempts to engender better coordination among agencies, are evident here too with organizational pathologies such as data hoarding and linkage blindness.

Collaboration between the Caribbean maritime law enforcement agencies and those from metropolitan countries raises issues about maritime security priorities, tensions between donor and beneficiary countries, and vexed questions around national sovereignty. Marine law enforcers tend to agree about regional security priorities: drug smuggling and its 'attendant ills'—gun crime, money laundering, corruption, and collapse of the rule of law. Despite this sense of shared priorities, the heads of coastguard and police marine divisions identified diverging interests. For example, local problems persist at the water's edge in ports, harbours, and beaches. An effective search and rescue capacity is required as are robust mechanisms for fisheries and environmental protection on which the domestic economy depends. These are all important island priorities that are not shared with the British or Americans, creating tensions between the metropolitan countries and the islands over resource deployment, particularly as maritime law

---

[41] Martin Rein (1983), *From Policy to Practice*. Armonk, N.Y.: M.E. Sharpe, esp. Chapter 6, 'The Plea for Coordination of Services'.

enforcement assets are frequently provided by the metropolitan countries which, understandably, want these assets to be used to pursue their interests.

Finally, there is a range of questions about the consequences of this extensive maritime policing activity. Like their dry-land counterparts doing everyday coppering, marine policing is almost impossible to evaluate because of its wide omnibus mandate which extends from law enforcement to peacekeeping. Since the 1980s, Caribbean maritime policing has become increasingly transnational; thus, while local matters remain 'a priority', there is an expectation that marine law enforcers should make a contribution to the regional security of their north Atlantic neighbours. There is no question that the seafaring police, coastguard, and navy are interdicting and seizing a significant amount of cocaine and marijuana, but this relates to 'outturns' rather than results, leaving further questions to be asked about reducing the flow of drugs and containing its negative impacts. We return in Chapter 9 to the larger question of how far this maritime law enforcement activity—as part of a multinational inter-agency strategy—has contributed to maintaining security and reducing harm. But first, we turn to the overseas liaison officers and the role that they play in regional security cooperation.

8

Overseas Liaison Officers

A new specialist has emerged in policing organisations in Europe, *viz:* the liaison officer. We might stop to consider why the emergence of this new role should concern us. There are relatively few of them and they are marginal to the central mission of their respective police institutions; but the creation of this specialism is symptomatic of profound changes in our vision of crime and insecurity and of our view of the police agents who seek to control such social disorder.[1]

Introduction

The overseas liaison officer has been described as a 'relative newcomer' to the policing scene.[2] Of all the transformations in policing set out in table 1.1, the work of the liaison officer raises the most interesting questions about new forms of policing that transcend the nation state.[3] While military and trade attachés have been a feature of diplomatic life for more than a century, the

[1] Didier Bigo (2000), 'Liaison Officers in Europe' in James Sheptycki (ed), *Issues in Transnational Policing*. London: Routledge, p 67.

[2] Andrew Goldsmith and James Sheptycki (eds), *Crafting Transnational Policing: State-Building and Police Reform Across Borders* (2007). Oxford: Hart, p 11.

[3] There are a small number of empirical studies of liaison officers, for example, Neil Bailey (2007), 'Overseas Liaison Officers' in Steven David Brown, *Combating International Crime: The Longer Arm of the Law*. London: Routledge; James Sheptycki (1998), 'Police Co-Operation in the English Channel Region, 1968–1996', *European Journal of Criminal Law and Criminal Justice*, 6/3; Didier Bigo (2000), 'Liaison Officers in Europe', *op cit*. Studies that cover the more general issues of transnational policing can be found in James Sheptycki (2002), *In Search of Transnational Policing*. Aldershot: Avebury; Andrew Goldsmith and James Sheptycki (eds) (2007), *Crafting Transnational Policing, op cit*; Peter Andreas and Ethan Nadelmann (2007), *Policing the Globe: Criminalization and Crime Control in International Relations*. Oxford University Press.

conventional view is that a permanent presence of a police officer in a foreign embassy is a relatively recent phenomenon. In many parts of the world, the interchange between police officials from around the world was restricted to conferences, exchange visits, and occasional overseas travel to escort suspects arrested abroad back to face trial. This picture is made more complex, however, by the long history of British colonial policing which was built from officers recruited from the metropolis or elsewhere in the empire. These officers were often trained together in Britain and met frequently at conferences both in the region and in the metropolis. Eventually, this was consolidated into a Colonial Police Service which recruited to the various country forces. The Inspector General of Colonial Police (IGCP), whose role it was to advise on the structure and efficient functioning of police forces in the colonies, stayed with the Colonial Office until 1966. In 1968 this role moved to the Foreign and Commonwealth Office and was renamed the Overseas Police Advisor. Recruitment passed to the Department of Overseas Development and then its successors. The IGCP regularly visited the Caribbean throughout the 1960s, both dependent and independent states, and liaised with Interpol, the FBI, the DEA, US Customs, Foreign and Commonwealth police forces, and the UN Narcotics division.[4] At the time of the fieldwork, there were two FCO police advisors, one for the Overseas Territories (who was based in Miami) and one who travelled among the islands and mainland territories of the independent Caribbean. Like the security liaison officers (see Chapter 4), the FCO police advisors have no authority over the overseas liaison officers posted to the islands, but they are a key point of contact.

The overseas liaison officer, posted overseas for four or more years a time, is the first point of contact for any visiting police officers, in requests for information from the host country or from the metropolis. The heart of the job is the investigation of transnational criminal collaborations based on intelligence gathered from various sources and communicated between local policing agencies around the world. Didier Bigo describes them as marginal to

<hr />

[4] Michael J Macoun (1996), *Wrong Place Right Time: Policing the End of Empire*. London; New York: Radcliffe Press, esp pp 96–7 and 164–74, cited by Gregor Davey (2006), 'Adviser, Director or Defender of a Faith? The Role of the Inspector General of Colonial Police, 1948–1966' (unpublished masters thesis, Open University).

their respective police organizations and yet integral to a profound change in the global security architecture. The people working in this field play a key role in the management of information and are initiating new policing practices across a web of local, national, and transnational security institutions. In this chapter, we explore the world of the overseas liaison officers living and working the Caribbean. Our focus is on the Customs drugs liaison officers (DLOs)[5] who are based in the offices of the British High Commission, when they are not out-and-about meeting the Commissioner of Police or head of Customs or the Military Chief of Staff or others described in earlier chapters. Here, we explore the working life of these officers largely from their own point of view, but also from others, above all the British Deputy High Commissioner under whose diplomatic umbrella they work. We also examine the working life of these officers based on direct observation of their work at Caribbean airports. Reflecting on the views of the liaison officer, seen from the perspective of the local law enforcement agencies (described in Chapters 3–7), this chapter also explores some of the issues that emerge from the everyday practice of transnational policing. It considers the practical problems involved in 'law enforcement' work overseas, the relationships with local officers, and how these are negotiated. It also considers the questions of to whom do overseas liaison officers account and to what extent they push the boundaries of sovereignty.

Drugs Liaison Officers in the Caribbean

Until the creation of the Serious Organised Crime Agency (SOCA) in 2006, HM Customs & Excise was the lead in UK international law enforcement.[6] The UK posted its first drugs liaison officer (DLO) overseas in 1984 in Karachi. By 1998, this had grown to a force of 40 DLOs in 29 locations in 22 countries and by 2000 to 61 DLOs in 41 transit regions. Reporting to the Home Affairs

---

[5] At the time of the study, the drug liaison officer (DLO) network was part of HM Customs & Excise. Following the creation of the Serious Organized Crime Agency (SOCA) in 2004, the DLO network was moved to the new agency where the role is referred to as SOCA liaison officers.

[6] After HMCE's law enforcement division was merged with NCS and NCIS in creating SOCA, the remaining divisions moved to a new agency called HM Revenue and Customs, combining domestic tax collection with import and export duties and Value Added Tax hitherto collected by Customs.

Committee recently, the Chairman of SOCA said that there were now 140 SOCA liaison officers in 40 countries.[7] A senior National Crime Squad Officer based in London but with many years experience as a liaison officer explained the essence of their role as 'a business-driven relationship from a law enforcement perspective'. Largely bilateral and 'driven by the Foreign Office', 'it recognises that a lot of intelligence flow is very informal and that by having somebody actually on the spot assisting with that process is far more efficient than relying on people telephoning each other':

Liaison officers are placed as a result of a business requirement, which is articulated through, and by the Foreign Office to the foreign government. And there are benefits for the foreign government in this too because it enhances training, it enhances the exchange of technology, to help them become more effective. But all it does is actually displace the problem.

Liaison officers had access to technical surveillance, informants, and a range of intelligence networks. They had access to their own extensive UK-based Customs international intelligence department and NCIS strategic intelligence as well as local law enforcement information. Acting within and between police organizations, like 'station-masters', liaison officers shunt and direct information as quickly as possible to where it is needed.[8] An account of the work of the DLOs is provided in a piece by investigative journalist Tom Mangold with excellent access to the key players, including representatives of MI5, MI6, HMCE, and GCHQ.[9] This article claims that British Intelligence is behind up to 90 per cent of cocaine seizures in the Caribbean. It describes how these officers locate, meet, and educate 'incorruptible' members of the local Customs and police and bring them into the intelligence network. An RAF

---

[7] In oral evidence to the House Of Commons Home Affairs Committee on Tuesday 29 January 2008, Mr Bill Hughes stated that, 'We inherited from the precursor agencies some liaison officers from three of the agencies around the world and we have restructured and put that together so that we now have about 140 plus officers operating in some 40 countries around the world. These are SOCA liaison officers and they are there to deal with all aspects of organized crime. In many instances they are embedded in the foreign law enforcement agencies so it is a faster and dynamic turnaround in terms of sharing intelligence and joint operations. In parts of the world we do engage in joint operations with foreign law enforcement'. <http://www.publications.parliament.uk/pa/cm200708/cmselect/cmhaff/296/8012901.htm> accessed 14 February 2009.

[8] Bigo (2008), 'Liaison Officers in Europe', *op cit*, p 77.

[9] Tom Mangold (2002), 'Britain's Secret War on Drugs', *Reader's Digest*, October 2002.

Nimrod maritime reconnaissance plane, based in the region, has the capacity to follow suspect vessels for long periods and to witness the 'coopering' of cocaine at sea—the loading and unloading of drugs between a large 'mother ship' and smaller vessels. British Special Forces also play a role, fitting transmitters on vessels that can 'bleep their way across the Atlantic' allowing them to be tracked by ship or plane. According to Mangold's sources, there is an even smaller and more secret group of Customs spies—based in Britain and overseas, they live undercover, assuming false identities, and infiltrating drug cartels.[10]

The British High Commission

Overseas liaison officers were based in an office at the British High Commission. In several islands, the High Commission was a formidable grey steel and glass edifice, surrounded by palm trees. In others it was a Colonial-style administrative building. In the case of the more modern office, the experience on entering the building was like stepping into the foyer of a ministerial office on Whitehall, even down to the functional civil service furniture comprising upholstered armchairs, a two-seater sofa, and veneered coffee table. Hanging on the wall of one foyer was a David Gentleman print of the Foreign and Commonwealth Offices in London overlooking the Horseguards parade ground. The opposite wall was graced by a photograph of Queen Elizabeth II, a business-like Head of State with pen in hand and ministerial red box behind her. The banner at the entrance to the inner door proclaimed 'UK Trade and Investment: Delivering business opportunities throughout our global network'. Everything about the place seemed to say, 'this is British sovereign territory', quietly, politely, and firmly.

The first responsibility of a diplomatic mission is to provide for the welfare of its nationals. In the event of an emergency, war, internal conflict, or natural disaster, the High Commission is there to protect British citizens—residents, and holiday makers—and if necessary to repatriate them during the most extreme of crises. To that end the Foreign Office also publishes travel advisory notices to British people to warn them of particular kinds of risks or indeed to recommend against travel in extreme circumstances. The High Commission also acts as a point of reference for British interests

[10] *Ibid.*

abroad and includes links into other government departments and state-sponsored agencies including the British Council and the Department for International Development. The High Commission is first port of call for a visiting diplomat and others with diplomatic status such as police, Customs, or immigration liaison officers.

The mission deals with international relations such as treaties, protocols, and resolving a wide range of issues over trade and investment. There is also the issue of post-colonial responsibility stemming from the historical relationship between Britain and its former colonies in responding to the structural re-adjustment occurring in the Caribbean, and the demise of the region's agricultural base in bananas and sugar (see Chapter 2). The European Union, with Britain, focuses on economic diversification, for example into other forms of agriculture, but also service industries, above all tourism. As a result, large grants were given out by the European Union specifically to fund projects that would develop the capacity of local institutions. For example, police organizational reform, restructuring of the security sector by making the military much more engaged in everyday internal security issues, and introducing a more community focus to the local constabularies were all ongoing at the time of the study. Other projects sought to modernize, train, and equip defence forces and coastguards, to improve communication systems, and strengthen institutions at the regional level. The prevailing view was that security is a prerequisite to successful investment in trade and economic development.

The Deputy High Commissioner

The Deputy High Commissioners were typically affable men in their 50s, sharply dressed and with the interpersonal style that one would associate with the British diplomat. Several had had career postings in Africa—including experience in the world's most troubled locations—as well as numerous European postings. One had worked at the British Embassy in Washington DC, the Foreign Office's busiest mission. The role of the DHC is very varied and includes deputizing for the High Commissioner. On a day-to-day basis, he has overall responsibility for the mission so that the HC can go out-and-about and do his 'more roving high profile role'. The DHC heads the diplomatic and consular departments, aids in capacity building, and plays a role in commercial and 'public diplomacy'. He greets official visitors, assists in operational briefings, and assists with legislative drafting. In essence, the job is to ensure the 'free flow of activity within the mission'.

From the Foreign Office perspective, the most pressing security issue for the Caribbean was the threat posed by drug trafficking coupled with the islands' lack of resources to intervene, particularly in the maritime sphere. One DHC said, 'It's the threat of drugs together with their lack of resources; that is the main threat to the country.' In his view, the problem did not revolve primarily around the local *consumption* of drugs which was minimal and confined more to the smoking of weed rather than cocaine, crack cocaine, ecstasy, or even heroin use. None thought that the local production of marijuana was a huge priority either for the UK or the Caribbean, certainly not in comparison to the trans-shipment of cocaine. One also commented that there was a disproportionate focus on drug couriers at the expense of other methods such as parcel and freight trafficking and the use of yachts coming up through the islands.

From the DHCs' point of view, the major threat to security stemming from the drugs trade was the gang warfare, the internecine warfare, which they believed to be spreading. The problem is that success against drug trafficking in one place leads to displacement to other geographical areas (see also Chapters 3 and 9). Because the gangs are underpinned by drugs money, the more success that security agencies have in one place, the more it moves to other islands and to other routes. The authorities have had success in working with the community, getting a 'tremendous response' through building community centres and arranging sports facilities. Formerly stressed communities are now playing football, netball, and athletics against each other, and the gangs have moved out. Nonetheless, the DHCs felt the problems were becoming entrenched elsewhere:

The command and control of the drugs that come through is probably an area where people should have most concern because eventually you're going to have that command and control run by Colombians and the paramilitaries, the FARC and the AUC and so on, and if once they get their hands on these organized, well funded gangs, then the consequences are such that the criminals are going to have a business plan, they're going to have a financial director, they're going to have amounts of money probably more than the GDP of the Caribbean never mind this island, and you're not going to be able to cope with that threat, so I would say that that's the greatest threat to security in the [Caribbean].

The key issue is the drugs economy and the amount of money invested in it. It was therefore, a matter of 'criminal economics', a problem that is multinational and needs a multinational approach. Somebody has to coordinate that multinational approach. One DHC explained that, 'It's the drugs economy, yes, it's a business. We know it's a business, five hundred billion pounds a year, you know, I mean how many countries can support that? Not many, not even the United States of America'. What was required was assistance to the countries of the Caribbean. One DHC also argued the need to 'have a debate about whether you should legalise it or not and use the revenue from that' like alcohol at the end of the prohibition era in the 1930s. This was a priority in his view, and he also found that there was a considerable level of support expressed privately about debating the legalization of drugs. This was, for the DHC, a matter of great urgency:

> I can understand why politicians are reluctant to do it, but I think that the more you delay that, the more the business of drugs proceeds and crystallizes and almost becomes legitimate in many ways, because there's many legitimate businessmen behind the drugs. So that if you don't start that debate now with a view to knocking back these businessmen, these businessmen are not only going to be members, key members, of the economic hierarchy, but they are going to be sitting in positions of power, in Parliament, and they are going to be dictating, so you're going to end up with a country that's actually run by the very thing you're trying to get away without.

In his view, this process was already evident. There were extensive networks between those involved in the drugs business and legitimate business people. There was a sense that local security agencies knew who the people were, but were too afraid or otherwise unable to take action against them.

> You know these people with these big houses, no obvious source of income and so on. There is one notorious name here which my driver mentioned this morning actually, you know, 'That's drug money building that little café there', you know, 'that old so and so again he's doing that.' And the police Commissioner said to me about this particular fella, who walks around the town and smiles at him. And everyone knows he's a drug lord but they just can't, they nearly got him a while ago but he got off. He got off. In this small society, I suppose it's inevitable that they know the people, they know who they are. It's a matter of getting them whilst they are involved in doing something I suppose.

The DHCs saw their 'political role' as helping to 'shape policy' in certain respects. They tended to have a good relationship with the Prime Minister, various cabinet ministers, civil servants, and ministerial staff which opened up opportunities to lobby the government to pass legislation on specific topics. An example on one island was putative interception of communications legislation to take action against criminal targets. This was a very sensitive issue because the government (and equally the opposition) were anxious about the role of government in eavesdropping. For many years there was only one telecoms provider and historical relationships between that company and the police meant that wire-tapping happened from time to time and just went on as a matter of course—but was not often mentioned. Once the telecoms industry started to be liberalized, there was a need for a legislative framework to compel the various companies involved to cooperate and also to provide legal safeguards. To this end, a UK legal draftsman was brought in to prepare an interception bill and also to develop a strategy that would increase the likelihood of public acceptance, by emphasizing the Caribbean-wide adoption of the legislation. The DHC explained that the government could then say, 'Our brothers in Antigua, Saint Lucia, Grenada are going to bring this bill to parliament as well'. In whose interest, I wondered, was this strategy being pursued?

Well it is really in both countries' interests because it helps to interdict hard drugs. Either coming into the island, spilling over a bit locally, I mean obviously there is a large amount of UK interest because everything that they do is intelligence led, intelligence led, intelligence led, intelligence led and part of their intelligence gathering is listening to these dodgy characters and their telephone calls. So yes there is a large amount of UK interest but also for the islands as well.

In this influencing role, the DHCs have very few policy levers. Their approach was simply to use their 'diplomatic arts' to appeal to the Prime Minister's good judgment about 'what is right'. This is different from other donors—such as the USA or Taiwan—in which funding and coercion were key foreign policy levers. This is not to say that the UK did not use either coercion or financial inducements, but the DHCs emphasized that they used a more subtle approach.

The Foreign Office were aware that the degree of resource required to stem the flow of drugs to the Caribbean far exceeds what is available. One DHC suggested that if the team of liaison officers and other security sector personnel was doubled or even quadrupled, they would still have more than enough business. Seizure figures for the whole of the Caribbean amounts to about 200 tonnes, or about two per cent of the estimated product of Columbia. Resource allocation for drugs in the Foreign Office is graded in terms of scale by setting out four priority groups that dictate access to funds. In one location, when the DHC arrived, the island was box 4, the lowest. At the time of the interview it was box 2, and as a priority island with evidence of trans-shipment and international links. As a result, he said, 'we do get money and projects and attention'. There is a rationale for increasing enforcement, but if the UK government is not prepared to make more resources available, then the FCO has to target those places where the biggest consignments are going. This is not to say that the DHC is passive on this point; one said, 'I argue the case for [this country] on a regular basis' and the answer he gets is, 'The government has said this is the resources available and we have to work within it'. At a time when there was a significant focus on Afghanistan—as well as Columbia itself and Turkey—and when decisions were being taken looking at drug flow to the UK as a world problem, it is inevitable that those presenting a smaller problem will be allocated fewer resources. As one High Commission staff officer put it, 'If it doesn't touch Class A drugs appearing on the streets in the UK then forget it'.

The Foreign Office view of liaison officers

The DHC saw as part of his role to attempt to contribute to a sense of 'joined up government' amongst the UK agencies that have an interest. Their view tended to be that there was too much of a blinkered attitude amongst the UK agencies, and there was a need to 'think a bit more widely, laterally, strategically', to say:

this is not a Customs and Excise or an NCIS or a Home Office or a DFID or a Met Police problem, it's a UK problem, and there's no reason why we can't have a Caribbean strategy which covers all Whitehall, there's no reason why we can't pull in the resources from all of these different entities, put them in a pot. . .and have them at hand so that if you do have a strategy and you do have out-turns and outputs to time lines and measurements and all that, you put it back to them, they all agree it, and you just move forward and you say, 'This is how we need to do it, these are the resources that we have, and that's the time that we have to do it'. So let's move forward as UK PLC.

The Deputy High Commissioners saw the UK liaison officers as acting in an advisory capacity. Their role was to advise, carry out a briefing before any particular operation is undertaken, and debrief at the end. However, all operational activity was undertaken by local police and military forces. Although this model of operation was broadly successful, the problem was that:

you can train people as much as you like, but until they've actually carried out the operation themselves they don't understand the technicalities, so, you know, really I think our guys are there to watch and to advise and to flag up various problems and to bring that to the attention and command and control situations.

To develop operational capacity, the international liaison officers were involved in mentoring, and 'working with' local authorities. This was because:

We don't want to be over ambitious with the _____ and, you know, put too much on them at one time, but secondly we find that you can train people as much as you like but until they've got a hands-on experience it's very difficult for them to put that training into action. So our philosophy now is that we'd rather bring people out and mentor, ie *work with* the local police.

In many situations the British officers would work alongside local officers, training them in the use of equipment, but also watching, mentoring, and demonstrating particular tasks. This close working relationship inevitably means that some officers are actually doing work that resembles law enforcement or policing activity. The DHCs felt that it was critical this work is coordinated through the liaison officer. This is for political and operational reasons and above all to avoid flooding the forces with requests:

They simply haven't got the capacity to undergo all the research that we demand of them, so because of that police officers do come across here and they do work with a liaison officer from the [police force] and they do do some research, but it's definitely seen to be a cooperative approach rather than a unilateral approach, and it's very important that we are seen to do that.

The DHCs were aware of the broad scope of the work of the law enforcement officers in the islands for which they had responsibility, their role in intelligence gathering in relation to organized crime and ongoing criminal conspiracies. They understood the process of collecting, collating, packaging, and sharing information and the operational aspects of the role. Where, I wondered, did the accountability for UK liaison officers lie? One Deputy High Commissioner was very clear on this point—that it is done 'within the confines of the management structure' of the police force in the Caribbean territory concerned through regular meetings with senior management. 'Everything that's done is done with the cooperation' of the Commissioner of Police and, where relevant, the Military Chief of Staff, and therefore:

We're not autonomous in going out and creating situations where information is gathered, we do it as a joint venture with the _____ authorities here and there's two good things that come out of that. One is that we can extract the information that both of us, both governments require and can use, but at the same time we use it as a training tool so that the _____ will have the sustainability to do it on their own once the problem is solved, whenever that will be. So I mean the emphasis is it's not autonomous.

I asked whether there was ever a case for UK police officers acting autonomously within the islands, for example in conditions where their overseas police officers found the local law enforcement agencies or government to be untrustworthy. One DHC replied that in contexts where the problems of corruption were particularly deep, where there are doubts about people at the very top of the security forces and government, those circumstances might 'force a more autonomous type of action', but 'on most islands there is more cooperation than real autonomy':

I don't think the agencies' operation on the island would be as effective without the cooperation because you need the local people to help you. I've seen it in action, more by accident than design, but you know they need the local people's knowledge. They know the drug people on this island. It's just catching those people. They know the people and on an island like _____, even more so. Everybody knows everybody. They know everything about them too. Their politics and what they get up to and so on. So I don't think there is a strong case for just an autonomous operation at all. . . . in Guyana, in those sorts of circumstances maybe they are forced to sideline people and something but as a principle I don't think it's a good idea. At all.

This Deputy High Commissioner conceded that the boundaries of what was permissible within that working relationship sometimes caused controversy among the officers involved in cooperating on the ground. So, while formal accountability remains with the authorities, there is nonetheless an anomaly. Police officers can be suspicious, pragmatic, action-oriented, creative, and sometimes 'lawfully audacious' in their operational practice. Sometimes mistakes are made. Occasionally, officers are too zealous. For these reasons, the boundaries may well often be crossed. However, in some instances, when teams of investigators travelled from the UK, there were organizational and legal problems that needed to be sorted out using the DHC's diplomatic skills. At all times, these officers would be accompanied by island police officers because:

at the end of the day we've got no jurisdiction here, this is sovereign territory. [The local] police have powers to bring people in, to question and so on, but we don't. We can put questions but only with their agreement.

Nonetheless, this is clearly a jurisdictional grey area since the officers concerned have no authority and no law enforcement powers. However, existing research shows that police officers are pragmatic people, who are able to use 'the ways and means act' to achieve certain law enforcement goals. An interesting idea now entering military doctrine is that of 'leadership beyond authority' which might be a pertinent idea about how law enforcement operates overseas in the sense that they are leading, directing, going about doing things in ways that are very similar to what they might be doing as sergeants or superintendents in a domestic setting. The only difference being that they have no formal jurisdiction. One DHC cut to the heart of the matter:

the jurisdiction and powers as such come from the accompanying _____ officers. I suppose at the end of the day what you could do is say, 'And would you ask him. . .please tell him', and then when the _____ officer does it, you know, the system is short circuited because the British officer stands beside the _____ one and puts those questions direct. I suppose if you want to be technical about it, yes, then what he does is, 'Please ask him', and 'Does he think that', and you put it all through the _____ and you get, yes. I mean probably strictly in legal terms that's probably the way it should be done but we've all got to be pragmatic and realistic about these things.

The UK had a very clear media strategy that meant that they never speak on or off the record to journalists. The DHC explained that:

our policy here is—and always will be—that we have a duty of care for our people and we will always maintain that duty of care to the extent that we don't talk to the media, virtually ever. So if there's an operation that is successful that the _____ have undertaken, we're not involved in it. . . . both in methodology and in the public diplomacy strategy that we have. We like to look after our guys, we like them to leave here after a posting having enjoyed the posting, satisfied they've done a good job and they've gone home safely.

This media strategy meant that, publicly, the DLOs don't exist. The DLOs themselves are quite happy to be behind the scenes. As one liaison officer explained, 'we're very careful about who we declare ourselves to'. The person who takes all the credit for successful operations is the local Drug Squad commander. If something went wrong, it would be the local police who would be accountable and would 'carry the can'. From the DHC's point of view the work of the law enforcement officers was based on trust and 'an arms' length' working relationship:

We have regular monthly law enforcement meetings and in those meet-ings they have an opportunity to brief me on certain issues. Now I take those briefings and those issues and translate them into a policy and I will report back if they want me to report back in terms of let ministers know exactly what's going on. But they also have a duty to report back through their own channels and I can refer to that in my reporting, so it's sort of squared the circle as it were. So they work semi autonomously based on instructions from their headquarters, but they also link in to what the Foreign Office is trying to do here, both bilaterally, developmentally and in distinct policy methodology.

The approach was very much to be involved behind the scenes and to take a very English civil service approach to public relations in this sphere and essentially deny knowledge of the details of what UK policing is doing on the island. One DHC put it this way:

A number of people have said to me on the circuit, 'We don't hear very much about what the UK is doing'. I just say, 'Well, probably because we're not doing very much', and they say, 'Oh but we know that you are'. I say, 'Well, therefore you know that we are and I don't'.

This diplomatic vocabulary could be a line straight from Sir Humphrey Appleby, the permanent secretary in the satirical tel-evision comedy *Yes, Minister*;[11] the DHC seems to be saying some-thing akin to Francis Urquhart's, 'you may very well think that;

---

[11] Sir Humphrey once said: 'If there had been investigations, which there haven't, or not necessarily, or I'm not at liberty to say whether there have, there would have been a project team which, had it existed, on which I cannot com-ment, which would now have been disbanded, if it had existed, and the members returned to their original departments, if indeed there had been any such members.' *Yes, Minister*, episode 'Big Brother'.

I couldn't possibly comment'.[12] I wondered whether his arms-length role in relation to oversight of the work of the overseas liaison officers placed the DHC in an uncomfortable position:

Well yes and no. It's not uncomfortable for me because I deliberately keep out of the operational side of it, you know, my job is to maintain a free flow of activity within the Mission. . . . I have quite enough to take care of in terms of managing the Mission than managing the operational side of it.

Operationally, therefore, the DHC does not know the details of what the DLOs are doing because he does not need to know. However, if the liaison officers do step out of line by doing something that brings their activity to the attention of the authorities or to the local media, then the High Commissioner will be forced to take action that could range from offering words of advice to expulsion. In London, a senior officer from the National Crime Squad explained what happened when your behaviour was judged unacceptable:

when you're out there you're attached to a High Commission, you have diplomatic status, but you are responsible to the High Commissioner for everything that you do, even where you park your car, and I have yet to find a High Commissioner that is anything other than a pain when it comes to your appropriate behaviour. And when you don't behave appropriately, it's a fairly unpleasant experience and it generally means you get expelled. It doesn't happen very often, you know, there's a lot of faith placed in people, the selection processes are fairly robust. So in terms of ethical activity on the ground, I would generally say standards are high and the accountability, you cannot do anything without the High Commissioner knowing, you know, you cannot go sleuthing around the place trying to be a detective in [the Caribbean] because that's a mug's game. That will get you shot or in trouble or both.

In terms of their operational activity, on a day-to-day basis, the DLOs are accountable to their bosses and management in London, who will give authorizations for their operations and deal with issues of financial management and audit. As the NCS officer described it:

budgets are supplied by home agency, they are monitored so there's a management unit both in Customs and NCIS, so if you're talking about the Caribbean it is Customs. There's a management unit there, they have a line management programme, they will get regular visits, regular audits,

[12] *House of Cards* by Michael Dobbs, book and later BBC TV series.

you know, the books will be gone through, the cheque book will be gone through, you know, they will check on the use of a business vehicle, whatever.

Formally, accountability for anything resembling law enforcement on the ground lies with the local security authorities. Therefore, any operational actions arising from the provision of intelligence from the overseas liaison officers lies with the island's police, military, or Customs undertaking arrests or other enforcement activity. If the UK officers were responsible for some error—mistaken intelligence, for example—the liaison officer would say that they were simply working on the basis of the best intelligence that they had available to them and ultimately it is the responsibility of the police and military to act on that intelligence. That is a decision taken by the Caribbean authorities, not by UK Customs. The local officers can choose whether or not to act on that intelligence and, obviously, one liaison officer pointed out, it would do nothing for their credibility and reputation if they frequently made errors. If they were to plan a drug bust and their shipment didn't come in, they would lose credibility, so they only communicate intelligence that is properly verified and checked.

Intelligence passed from the UK to the local police was often not recorded, so the fact that intelligence had originated in the UK or from local intelligence gathered by the overseas liaison officer would not be a matter of public record. It would simply be that the police or military had received intelligence from an unknown or unnamed source and that they had acted on that intelligence. The intelligence would be recorded on the DLO's own intelligence systems, but the names and details of the sources would not be passed over, so the police would simply say that they had intelligence which had been communicated to them verbally. The nature of the intelligence would of course affect the nature of the operation. For example, if there were information that a criminal team was armed, then this would affect the police preparation for an armed operation.

The Drugs Liaison Officer: Background, Role, and Identity

The UK drugs liaison officers that I interviewed were generally energetic men in their 40s. One had started out working in a regional VAT office, then moved to 'working the channels' rummaging through the luggage of passengers arriving at UK airports. Another had begun his career in 'freight rummage' at one of the ports and then moved to a mobile team. All of the DLOs had previous experience in Customs investigative work. One had carried out specialized work in an inter-agency cocaine team and on the strength of this experience had been offered the opportunity to serve overseas as a liaison officer. Each DLO was based on one of the islands for a three-year stint, which could be extended for another year before returning to the UK. This is how one DLO described himself:

Well I'm employed by UK Customs . . . My main remit is to liaise between the law enforcement agencies in the UK and those in the islands that I cover, but also to act as a liaison point between the other international agencies in the region, so with the Americans, the Germans, the Canadians and obviously our own network of UK DLOs, and that is basically the gathering and sharing of intelligence and targeting major narcotic traffickers, with focus on drugs that are targeted on the UK and Europe. Obviously we don't ignore stuff that may be going up to the US and obviously that's where the liaison comes in with the other agencies, but the main focus is narcotics targeted on the streets of the UK.

The job itself is extremely varied. The main set of tasks, as the job title suggests, is to liaise with conventional law enforcement across the islands and beyond and to gather intelligence, particularly about the flow of drugs through the Caribbean to the UK, Europe, or elsewhere. The buzzword for this year, one DLO explained, is 'UK impact'. In other words, the main goal is to reduce the impact of cocaine supply to the United Kingdom. The basis of the relationship with the authorities, he maintained, is one of partnership where no one person or partner should be more dominant than the other. This threaded through everything from the selection of priorities to working practices. The job also, as the name implies, involved a liaison function, handling letters of request from the UK and operating at the 'diplomatic gateway'.

Although the DLOs had spent their entire careers in the Customs service, they generally saw themselves primarily as 'law enforcement' with an identity and *raison d'être* very similar to that of the domestic police officer. When I asked one DLO whether he was a civil servant, a cop, or a hybrid, he replied:

very much a detective, I guess, because that's basically what we do. At the end of the day what we're here to do is seize drugs and arrest bad guys, you know, and that's what I did when I was back home, you know, I went out and arrested people.

Experience of working with US Customs enforcement officers both in the USA and within the islands, and having contact with other similar agencies from the wider police family also helped to shape the DLO's identity:

> if you met Customs guys in the States, they'd never say 'I'm Customs' they'd just say 'I'm a cop' because what we are doing is policing and I think certainly in the Caribbean, if I say I'm Customs, I would never go out and say 'I'm a Customs officer'. I say, 'I'm the Drugs Liaison Officer here. I'm representing UK policing', because they think Customs out here is not a law enforcement body.

This convergence of the roles and identities among various actors across the security sector is an interesting phenomenon to which we return in Chapter 9.

Operational priorities

As the DHC made clear, the mission's operational priorities are set by the FCO to reduce the supply of cocaine to the UK, and these priorities are firmly in the DLO's mind. His targets include the couriers—strappers, stuffers, and swallowers—travelling through the airport, but much more significant, in terms of volume, is the parcel and freight traffic with individual consignments of up to half a tonne. For the DLO, a 'good job' would be to interdict a major load of cocaine either on arrival in a pirogue (a small fishing vessel fitted with powerful engines) or during warehousing and packaging among other export goods (such as frozen foods or other agricultural products) in the process of being prepared for its onward journey to North America or Europe. A seizure might comprise a container load which would result in dozens of arrests of warehouse staff from which further intelligence might lead to the people operating higher up the organization. The ultimate target is the 'clean skins', the people who appear to be legitimate businessmen with no prior records. Often, once you have identified someone at that level, you find links across the region with the capacity and contacts to be involved in regular 500 kilo shipments.

In some instances, the DLO and his team would be aware of shipments that would not be interdicted in the islands but instead left to run to their destination. On one occasion, a DLO had intelligence of a major shipment from Guyana to Wales involving criminals from the UK and Jamaica. When the Jamaican target arrived in Guyana the UK Customs sent an officer for a few weeks to 'monitor what this guy was doing' keeping the local Drug Squad and the High Commission informed. The shipment then left and was detected in the UK. The advantage of these 'controlled deliveries' is that it may be possible to identify those involved at both ends of the trans-shipment process and to make arrests in the UK. This clearly has a greater likelihood of identifying those involved in importation and distribution in the UK and potentially those profiting from the trade. Among the disadvantages of using controlled deliveries is that it reduces the likelihood of making arrests of those involved on the island during the packaging and export stages and therefore requires delicate collaboration with the local authorities. If the opportunity to interdict in transit is not taken, there is also the risk that the drugs are surreptitiously unloaded whilst at sea or before deployment of law enforcement in the destination country (we return to this issue in Chapter 9).

When demands are made locally to assist with things that are not within the DLO's priorities—dealing with the arrival of marijuana from neighbouring islands, for example—they would deal with it even though it was not a UK priority. This was the DLO's approach to the partnership agreement and because they believed there was a significant overlap between those involved in the marijuana business and those involved with cocaine and other forms of criminality. As one DLO put it:

because of the people we're depending on gathering intelligence and working with, you know, if they get intelligence on somebody's smuggling cannabis, I'm not going to walk away with it, am I? I'm a cop, you know, I always say that, and at the end of the day, if I'm faced with criminality of any shape or form, then it's my duty to deal with it.

The DLOs were very conscious of the 'bubble effect' referred to by the DHC where focus on Colombia and routes in the far western edge of the Caribbean in the late 1990s had had the effect of pushing the trans-shipment routes outwards towards the Eastern Caribbean. The key routes on which the DLOs were focusing were those using fishing boats leaving from Columbia directly, or through Venezuela, travelling along the South American coastline and up through the islands. Venezuelan and Colombian shippers would be travelling with something between 50 kilos up to half a tonne of cocaine. This could either be directly to Jamaica or one of the islands in the centre of the chain, or either along the coast of Guyana or passing Trinidad, and on to one of the smaller islands in the Eastern Caribbean. From the islands, intermediaries would use air links into Europe. Airport smuggling included cargo (packaged up along with other products) and bags that get 'ripped' onto the aircraft by corrupt baggage handlers, and then 'ripped' off again at the other side. One very important link was identified by one DLO:

you know, in this area at the moment every airport is wide open and it is dead easy if you're a drug organization to get a bag full of cocaine on an aircraft to be ripped off at the other side, therefore you've then got your airport security which then has the wider ramifications if somebody was to do a terrorist attack on here because these guys who are putting bags on do not ask what is in that bag, all they want is the lucre from putting the bag on and it's the same at the other end.

A British warship, engaged in the 'war on drugs' spends a significant amount of its time in the Western Caribbean where pickings are richer; although interdiction has also been reported in the Eastern Caribbean off Barbados. When the British Navy warship interdicts large loads in the Western Caribbean—in the areas around Jamaica or the Cayman Islands—it is much more likely that shipments are bound for the USA than for the UK. Another key route is the yacht traffic from the Caribbean to Spain and Portugal and into the UK where it is known for loads of over one tonne to be detected. Interdicting yacht traffic takes time and resources because once one has been identified it is a long, waiting game because the organizations might do just one yacht a year.

Enforcement demand and resources

The UK has invested money and equipment, knowledge, experience, and skills to help the authorities set up more sophisticated intelligence procedures to assist their response to drug trafficking. From the FCO perspective, this helps provide a strategic investment that is more effective than sending officers in a reactive capacity each time an operation is planned. When officers are sent from the UK on an ad hoc basis, an officer from the local police has to be deployed to work alongside them, and this creates an unrealistic demand on the operations people. The DLOs agreed with the DHC that with more resources they would become more effective, but they put the point even more forcefully. The amount of intelligence which is coming to the DLO is so great that his team could act on only about one tenth of it. In order to act on all the intelligence about shipments that they are aware of, he would need a team of 25 or 30 DLOs and even then, they might still have more than enough work. By necessity, they devolve that intelligence to the local security authorities. If they had the additional capacity it might mean that they would end up doing the operational work themselves, but this, they thought, might not be a bad thing. In a moment of frustration about working with local infrastructure and personnel, one DLO complained that, 'you've got very good intelligence product, but quite bluntly, a shit delivery of law enforcement'. In one DLO's view, the marine police, defence force, and coastguard vessels were practically useless for maritime interdiction and the helicopters added little. If the UK were to provide six frigates and a fleet of helicopters, then they would be able to interdict much more but as it is, they have one UK naval vessel to cover the whole of the Caribbean.

Operational practice

The overseas liaison officer differs from his counterparts in 'conventional law enforcement'. He is in a unique position, sociopolitically. He is an officer of the British state, line-managed at a great distance from an office in London, loosely supervised by the diplomatic corps of the British Foreign Service, and accountable to the local police commander in respect of his operational practice. Clearly, a range of issues arise from this—what is the boundary between direction and advice, leadership, and operation? The job, in the main, involves collecting 'operational intelligence'. That means:

proactively going out looking for the intelligence but obviously mindful of the fact that there is that borderline which you can't step over but you know, if it comes down to doing anything, you've got to do it with your host agencies and the cooperation in the region is great.

They gather information using human and technical intelligence sources in much the same way that it is done in the UK and trying to teach that methodology to local law enforcement, 'but at the end of the day, intelligence is only as good as what you can turn into evidence to then effect a seizure but more importantly, it's to effect the arrest and prosecutions'. One of the points that the DLOs stressed most forcefully was because they have no law enforcement powers, they are entirely dependent upon the local police if they wish to 'do anything'.

There's no law enforcement action we can take. We're all accredited diplomats so again you're never in an evidential situation so if we're having to gather evidence, we're dependent on the local cops to do that which would then maybe result in a prosecution in the UK where they've got to go up and give evidence.

A distinction can be made between proactive and reactive work. Some reactive work involved servicing investigations arising from British investigations such as a murder that has a link to suspects or witnesses in an island. To carry out an investigation of that sort the UK force would compile a *Commission Rogatoire* (or letter of request), setting out the scope of the inquiry and the evidence sought. This would then be delivered to the Foreign Ministry and passed, through the Attorney General's officer, to the police. British officers would then travel out to the island, and make their enquiries accompanied by a local detective. In that instance, it would be the UK officers who would undertake the interview under conditions similar to those used domestically (with a PACE caution, taped and transcribed interview etc) and therefore the evidence would be admissible in a UK court of law.

Another example of their reactive role would be that if Customs discovers some drugs at the airport through their enforcement team, they would contact the DLO and report their discovery. The DLO and his team would then become involved and work alongside Customs to investigate. The working relationship between the DLOs and the security sector organizations when they work together on the ground is probably the most controversial aspect of this work. The general case is that they are working alongside Caribbean officers who are receptive to being able to share the DLO's expertise, knowledge, and equipment. Every day the DLO will spend three or four hours working alongside the intelligence units of the police and military or with the police Drug Squad. The DLO described the role as involving, 'mentoring them, looking over their shoulder, contributing to the development of their work. It's a bit like training, but isn't just an exercise, you are actually doing on-the-job training, advising, encouraging, and actively directing'.

This raised for the DLOs, what they described as 'the problem of the old colonial days'. In some instances, they needed actually to do the work themselves and very frequently they directed the operational practice of local officers. It requires diplomatic skills to encourage, suggest, persuade, and direct in subtle ways. The local officers themselves are generally very receptive. However, what the DLO and his team found was that it is only while the DLOs are looking over the shoulders of the local law enforcement officers saying 'why don't you do this, do that'—that is actually directing them—that local staff actually sustain the operation in a way that is most effective in relation to intelligence gathering and storing it using sophisticated equipment. If you leave them to their own devices, the DLOs believed, within six months working practices will have reverted to where they were previously. The problem here is that you have UK law enforcement officers with 20 years' experience of working with sophisticated techniques and technology and the local officers are expected to learn these techniques and make organizational cultural change within a few months.

The proactive role involved using intelligence coming in from various sources to set up an operation targeted on a particular aspect of a trafficking organization. They would build up an intelligence picture and then work with the various agencies in developing and implementing the operation. The DLOs use a full range of intelligence gathering techniques, both human and technical. Although the majority of the work was conducted in direct collaboration with the island authority's liaison officers, the DLOs do undertake their own intelligence gathering in some instances. Like their colleagues in the local Special Branch (described in Chapter 3), the liaison officers are inquisitive people and oriented towards action. Their intelligence gathering activities are largely restricted to telephone and email contact with their home agencies, and with local police and law enforcement agencies, but they do sometimes carry out their own direct surveillance and collection of information from local organizations and other informants. One DLO explained that:

Operationally we're not supposed to get involved but, you know, I'm not going to lie to you, yes, now and again we go out and take photographs and look for people at hotels and that sort of stuff, but we try to encourage the locals to do that on our behalf because then obviously it's easier to get that in evidence rather than, you know, they don't want a DLO tied up with court time in the UK. . . . Sometimes I go out on my own and just take some photographs or just try and get some information on something or other, but I find here that, certainly through the [specialist agency], they can do most things for me because they've got the links into the hotels, into the yacht marinas, all that sort of stuff. I do a little bit of investigation work through security at _____ airlines, you know, I've got very good contacts in there, so if I need information on passengers I just go to them, they send it to me on an email.

The DLOs also carried out undercover operations, but always with the knowledge of the Commissioner:

There are undercover operations that have been run here on each island. Every one of them is done with the knowledge and cognisance of the Commissioner. I can, with my hand on my heart, say that I certainly have never been party to conducting an operation where I've not had the safety of knowing that I've told somebody in authority and quite often the attitude will be 'You've told me, thanks very much, now get on and do it and if it goes wrong, I don't want to know about it' which is fine, you can live with that.

In discussion with numerous overseas liaison officers, based in the islands, opinion was divided about the value of undercover work, especially its use in infiltration of criminal networks. One officer commented that they are 'expensive, dangerous [can be] a nightmare and I'm not always convinced of the benefits of what you get out of it'.

Observing Law Enforcement Cooperation in Practice

Interviews with the overseas liaison officers and with those who supervise their work provide insight into their working life and illustrate some of the tensions and dilemmas that they face on a day-to-day basis. The earlier chapters of this book also provide some insight into this role from the perspective of the local officers with whom they work—including the Police Commissioners (Chapter 3), operational police officers (Chapter 4), the military (Chapter 5), border protection (Chapter 6), and the coastguard (Chapter 7)— each occupational group seeing the liaison officer from a unique angle. During the fieldwork, I also had the opportunity to carry out observational work at several international airports, an overview of which is provided in Chapter 5. This last substantive section of this chapter describes the work undertaken collaboratively between the overseas liaison officers and the Drug Squad in 'Operation Carib Bridge', seeking to detect drugs couriers at the airport.

I arrived at the airport shortly after 4pm and went straight to the airport security desk on the first floor above the concourse. After phoning the head of security, the desk officer filled out the relevant form, gave me my pass and told me to go down and join my UK colleagues in the public concourse. I went down the stairs into the entrance to the airport showing my security pass to the security guard standing at the entrance to the airport. I passed the desk used by airport security to carry out their rummaging searches of baggage going into the airport and met the police officer from the UK stationed at the airport. From the entrance to the airport it is immediately clear that there were a number British officers standing immediately behind the security desk next to some technical equipment. I talked briefly to these officers and to the local Drug Squad officers and to their counterparts in Customs. I was told that there were two flights going out that evening—a British Airways flight and one from one of the Caribbean carriers. This flight was flying to another island airport from where it would then fly on to Gatwick. The British Airways flight was a direct flight to Gatwick.

Passenger checks and searches

Searches were conducted at random on all passengers by airport security. While watching the rummaging process (see Chapter 6). I spoke with two of the UK liaison officers as they watched passengers going through check-in. We talked about the impact that this process was having on the supply of drugs into the UK. One liaison officer said that despite the very thorough process that was undertaken here a significant amount of drugs was still making it into the UK. Some bags that had gone through (or at least should have gone through) the search process still made it through to the other end. This included cocaine, sealed inside the linings of bags or in the false bottoms of bags. One of the reasons for the searches being so thorough was that previously cocaine had been detected at Gatwick in compartments of suitcases that they had not noticed. This was a matter of extremely skilled concealment methods, that they were unfamiliar with and both UK Customs and the Drug Squad agreed that the secretion of cocaine in the linings of bags was very sophisticated and they did not know how it was being done.

The UK Customs officers also questioned whether there wasn't some collusion amongst the private security officers who had either specifically not searched somebody that they knew to be carrying drugs or searched the bags in such a way that the concealment did not come to light. In any case, there were some relatively small shipments, up to perhaps a kilo or two at a time going through that were undetected. More significantly from Gatwick were the large shipments of herbal cannabis where whole suitcases had been detected at Gatwick. It was extremely implausible that these could have got through this screening process without being detected.

The UK Customs officer thought that the most likely answer was that bags were put on the airplane without having gone through screening. He noted that airport staff of all kinds, including cleaners, porters, airport security, baggage handlers, and check-in staff for the airlines all went into the airport without being subject to any checks. While it was possible that they could be checked, they tended not to be. So people would come in with their change of clothes or a lunch box and all the staff at the airport would walk in and out without being checked. Therefore, there were ample opportunities for the staff of the airport to put some substances or packages into the hand luggage of a travelling passenger who had already had his or her bags checked in the thorough way that I had observed.

Detecting swallowers

Those passengers whose passports didn't look quite right and whose reasons for visiting the UK didn't seem quite right, were frequently brought to the liaison officers' attention by the airline ground staff during the check-in process. Throughout the check-in process the UK liaison officers and Drug Squad, walked up and down the queues of check-in passengers, watching and listening to the airline staff doing the check-in, looking out for people who presented some grounds for suspicion. These included people who, for example, were supposed to have lived in England for many years, possibly all their lives and yet were unable to identify key landmarks or name places of interests in Britain. All of those people were searched more intensively.

The work of Operation Carib Bridge involved coordination between three different law enforcement agencies—the Drug Squad, UK Customs DLOs, and the National Criminal Intelligence Service. Customs officers are those who have the greatest part of responsibility for drugs law enforcement and have a longer history and tradition of conducting searches of the sort that occurred in

Carib Bridge. They are trained to carry out the searches and have skills and experience in dealing with ion scan machines and urine testing—identical machines are used by Customs in the UK for detecting drug smuggling into UK airports.

An ion scan machine is about the size of a fax machine and consists of a screen sitting on top of an electronic testing device. To conduct a drug test, the officer takes a swab—an arrow-shaped specialized piece of material about 6 cm long and 1.5 cm wide—to wipe the hands of the person being tested. Once a sample has been taken, this sheet of material is threaded through a slot into the ion scan machine which then conducts the test. The ion scan is very sensitive and will show a reading on the screen. A police officer demonstrated how it worked. He said it is very sensitive because he had been handling baggage all day, it was likely to show a small but positive result after slotting his hand, wiping his hand on the strip of material. He set the material into the machine—a testing strip—and it came up with a value of something like 0.52, which shows a positive result albeit a very small one. The Drug Squad officer explained that if on conducting a test with an ion scan something more positive came out, then the detained person would be asked to give a urine sample. Those people who tested positive for cocaine in their urine would then be taken to the hospital where they would be subjected to x-ray to examine whether or not they had swallowed packets of cocaine. It is largely for this purpose that this equipment has been introduced. The officer was very enthusiastic about the equipment.

The officer in charge of the narcotics squad, approached the UK Carib Bridge team and said that he had a identified a person who he felt was suspicious because of his passport. He explained what he meant by working through what was suspicious about the passport. The man had flown to the UK most recently in the third week of November. He stayed just 11 or 12 days and had returned to the capital. The flight immediately before that was some three or four months earlier, again a trip of just less than two weeks, then again there was a trip in the middle of Spring, again for 11 or 12 days. The Drug Squad officer suggested that this was an unusual pattern of behaviour. The man claimed simply to be going to stay with friends. It was curious that he was not going for an extended period. If you are going to stay with friends in the UK, then usually someone will want to stay for a few months at a time. This seemed to the officer to be an unusual pattern of behaviour, especially since the person was a security guard with a low income. The tickets had been bought in _____ and yet the person wanted to fly out from _____. It seemed suspicious that somebody living in _____, working there, and buying the tickets there, would then travel to _____ before getting his flight to the UK. Why not simply get the direct flight to the UK? In short, the grounds for suspicion were that a man on a low income had, during an 18-month period, travelled every few months to the UK for a stay of less than two weeks for which he had no proper explanation. On this occasion, even more inexplicably, he had taken an expensive option to travel.

The man was duly swabbed and tested using the ion scan machine. The device showed traces of cocaine, but there was a degree of uncertainty from that result, so he was taken to the Carib Bridge 'office' comprising two tiny rooms converted from their original use as a cleaners' cupboard. The officers conducted the urine test. The suspected swallower was one of about eight or so people who were searched and subject to urine testing that evening. The urine analysis showed a high enough reading for him to be detained by the police at the airport. He was then taken to the hospital to have a stomach x-ray to identify whether or not he has cocaine in his body. The suspected man seemed relatively stoical as he sat in the tiny anteroom.

Inter-agency tension

While the Customs officers were involved in the drug testing and checking, a liaison officer from the National Criminal Intelligence Service (NCIS) was taking down details of each person who was detained or questioned. The details of each passport checked by UK law enforcement officers were recorded on a sheet of paper. Those details were then written up onto a laptop computer and a telephone call was made to the NCIS in London. There an NCIS officer took the telephone call and accessed their intelligence database, including the Criminal Records Office (CRO). Whether NCIS headquarters report 'no trace' or if the person's name appears on the NCIS intelligence database or on the CRO records, then the NCIS officer will make a record of whatever information they have.

Back at the airline check-in desk, both the Drug Squad and UK liaison officers took notice of a rotund man, about 5′6″ tall, wearing a light blue baseball shirt and cap. As the airline ground staff went through the usual check-in procedure, they noticed his brand new British passport, broad Caribbean accent, and distinctive facial scar, what the police officer described as a 'telephone scar', better known in England as the 'Chelsea smile'—a slash from the corner of the mouth towards the ear. The Drug Squad officer, standing alongside the check-in staff asked a few additional questions: 'How long are you going for?' 'Have you got a return ticket?' 'Have you travelled before?' 'Where exactly are you travelling to?' This left them dissatisfied with some of the answers that the man gave as he was checking in. Describing this as 'profiling', he later said that he had a check-list in his mind about what kind of person would be a swallower. A number of things would 'put a tick in the box', for example a brand new UK passport, a visit to the UK destined to last only a few days, and travelling to London in March for less than two weeks; London is not really an appropriate holiday destination at this point of the year. If somebody is making the effort and going to the expense of travelling to the UK in March to see family, then why not stay for a couple of months? To stay for ten days if you are going to see family is a little suspicious. Flights booked within a short period from departure would be another tick in the box. If somebody was going to travel to see family it is likely that they would have saved up the money, planned in advance, and would have booked the ticket some time in advance to avoid the expense of buying a ticket to fly close to the date of departure. This means that the flight is much more expensive, another tick in the box.

As he stood at the check-in desk, one of the UK liaison officers also asked a few additional questions to see if he could flush out any further information. The liaison officer asked how he was going to be collected from the airport. The passenger replied that a family member was going to pick him up. The liaison officer then asked, 'so if you weren't being picked up, how would you get from the airport?' The passenger replied, 'I go to Clapham Junction'. When pressed for more detail, the man could say nothing more about the route he would take from there. He seemed to know nothing about the area that he was going to or how he might be able to get around London. This, the liaison officers later explained, suggested that this man who was supposed to be a British citizen who had lived all his life in London, probably was not the person who was actually carrying the passport.

As suspicions mounted, the liaison officers were passed his passport to check against the UK criminal records. After a few moments, the NCIS officer reported that the man named in the passport had a criminal record and there was a description. The passport holder was described as a man of 5′ 10″ who was born and had lived his life in London and had a scar on his nose. Armed with this information, as the man left the check-in desk, one of the liaison officers walked alongside him and asked, 'have you ever been in trouble with the law?' The man said no, he hadn't.

At this point, the Drug Squad officer, who had moved on to check other passports in the queue, returned to this encounter and intervened. He asked the man to stop and put his bag down. The sergeant then took the UK liaison officer to one side and there was a heated conversation about what had just occurred. The Drug Squad officer was speaking to the liaison officer and seeking to clarify who should be asking the questions and what sort of questions should be asked. The UK officers insisted that they hadn't really asked too many questions, they simply were trying to help. The sergeant insisted that he should be the one asking the questions and that it was inappropriate for the UK officers to have continued to question this person independently of him.

By the end of the process, including drug testing, all of the officers, but particularly the British, were in something of a conundrum. The Drug Squad officer decided that although there was a discrepancy, there was nothing further that he was able to do. The person hadn't tested positive for drugs in either ion scan or urine tests and therefore was not a drugs suspect. Despite the discrepancy between the descriptions in the criminal record check, he was allowed to continue the flight to London. Now there was a different viewpoint from the UK liaison officers who felt that even though he wasn't testing positive for drugs, he was somebody who should not have been travelling. They felt that he should have at least been referred to the Immigration Service, so as to have a look at the passport and investigate further. The Drug Squad officer also mentioned that recent raids made during the course of investigations had located numbers of blank British passports. It seemed to them highly likely that this person was travelling on a very high quality doctored passport.

This account of collaboration in practice illustrates some of the tensions in the close working relationship between liaison officer and local police, and raises questions about who is actually in control. The mentor-mentee relationship is not very different from the relationship between supervising and operational officer in the policing context. This raises the question of how far the work of the overseas liaison officer differs from that of a middle-manager—such as an inspector or superintendent—working in the domestic context. Supervision within policing tends to be fairly distant, such that it is rare for officers above the rank of sergeant to be carrying out arrests or other enforcement action. The corollary of this is that most police officers are used to working unsupervised and enjoy an unusually wide degree of discretion in how they go about their daily work. To some extent, the liaison officer is akin to a superintending officer supplying strategic direction in ways similar to operational work in a domestic context. This also raises questions about what constitutes policing power. Most obviously, police power comprises the power to coerce, but one also needs to consider intrusive powers to stop and question suspects, to conduct interviews and to collect and share intelligence. While island and UK law enforcement officers are working side-by-side, it was certainly the view of the UK officers that they were managing the operations and in some cases physically doing the job. The DLOs are out there in the field doing the job but this is clearly a difficult and controversial task. In the DLOs' view, it would be simpler just to actually do the work themselves, but they actually can't do that. They are operating in sovereign territory and they have to consider the sensitivities of the local officers, who clearly need to feel as though they are in the driving seat and need to be seen that way publicly.

Summary and Conclusion

The Caribbean islands are home to a small force of overseas liaison officers. A team of UK liaison officers, previously with Customs enforcement and NCIS, now with the Serious Organised Crime Agency (SOCA), are a significant presence in the region's British High Commissions, at any one time. Although the existence of an overseas policing network is in some ways novel, there is also a very strong continuity with the British colonial policing model which included a network of MI5 security liaison officers and FCO police inspectors and advisors. Today, a core team of liaison officers reside permanently in Jamaica, Trinidad, and Barbados,[13]

[13] The number depends on the size of the island and its area of geographical responsibility. The number ranges from one OLO with responsibility for a group of small islands to places where there was one OLO for an island, up to as many as six resident OLOs (see Apendix II).

with additional teams coming on shorter rotation to provide additional support at airports as well as ad hoc visits from UK police officers travelling to work on specific inquiries. In addition, two FCO police advisors visit the region on a frequent basis. Although they have offices in the High Commission, the liaison officers' job is mainly on the ground working with local officers. To the UK liaison officers who have been the focus of this chapter, we can add the US Drug Enforcement Administration, Treasury Department, and State Department Diplomatic Security Service, the Royal Canadian Mounted Police, as well as regular visits or residencies from the Metropolitan Police, New York Police Department, Miami Dade, and the US Bureau of Alcohol Tobacco and Firearms. Less frequent visitors would include the French, Germans, Dutch, Brazilians, and Columbians. As Chapters 3–7 in this book make clear, the overseas liaison officer plays an important role in the lives of the people who work in the local security sector. While the everyday constable on the street would be unlikely to meet the British liaison officer, the Commissioner of Police is of course well acquainted with him, as are the heads of Special Branch, Drug Squad, and the Interpol National Central Bureau. Outside the island's police force, the liaison officer works alongside the head of Customs and the Military Chief of Staff. In his everyday life, his role is more likely to be on the phone or email communicating on island, between islands, and with the metropolis. In key operational moments, the liaison officer sits in the room with the 'gold group' of the joint agency task force, helping to coordinate both the intelligence and command and control functions tasking police, Customs, and other land forces, with the air-wing and maritime operations (see figure 5.1).

Liaison officers exist at the margins of all law enforcement agencies, including their own (from which they are very far away geographically) and inhabit a multilateral and transnational space in the interstices between organizations. Liaison officers are the human interface between policing organzations,[14] as Didier Bigo describes them, they are 'agents through whom confidential information passes without recourse to a paper trail'.[15] They put people in touch with one another as 'privileged intermediaries between . . . home and host countries'.[16] The liaison officers' role in information

---

[14] Bigo, 'Liaison Officers in Europe', *op cit*, p 74.   [15] *Ibid*, p 75.
[16] *Ibid*, p 78.

sharing is uniquely important to understanding transnational governance. It is rare for police officers from another jurisdiction to be granted direct access to intelligence files belonging to another country. However, this runs contrary to the belief that intelligence and the speed at which this can be shared is the key to modern policing. The liaison officer is therefore a crucial development here, as he 'becomes the human interface for data interconnection'.[17] Often working on specific cases and, *strictly speaking* non-operational, as Didier Bigo found in his work on European liaison officers, they do become involved in investigations.[18] Sheptycki aptly describes the liaison officer as the person who stitches together the patchwork quilt of transnational policing.[19] In the present study, it is clear that the security quilt is comprised of organizations of various size and thickness with intersecting and overlapping jurisdictions. Furthermore, the patchwork of agencies that notionally covers its land and territorial waters is itself only a piece of a more complex security blanket with regional and hemispheric layers. Whether it is helping to coordinate the work of the Regional Security System that covers the islands of the Eastern Caribbean, the Association of Caribbean Commissioners of Police, or Caribbean Customs Law Enforcement Council, the international liaison officer plays a part. The role of the liaison officer is inherently multilateral and plural in the sense that his daily task is comprised of working extensively with other organizations. It is inherently transnational in that it is largely concerned with linking together organizations from different countries. This role, lying at the edges of numerous different organizations in different parts of the world, places the overseas liaison officer in a curious place in terms of jurisdiction, sovereignty, and accountability. Liaison officers are funded partly by the British Foreign Office and partly by their home agency. They are accountable to the head of mission for their diplomatic conduct. Managerially, they account to their headquarters in London. Operational accountability rests—formally at least—with the local law enforcement agencies, although in everyday practice, the boundary lines are blurred.

The work of the liaison officer raises a number of new and challenging questions. Where does the accountability for their

---

[17] *Ibid*, p 79.   [18] *Ibid*, p 75.

[19] James Sheptycki (1995), 'Transnational Policing and the Makings of a Post-Modern State', *British Journal of Criminology*, 35/4: 613–35.

operations lie and to what extent does their work constitute an infringement of the national sovereignty of the hosting country? When a liaison officer collects intelligence from local informers, uses his contacts at an airline to check passenger lists, or takes photographs of people he suspects of being involved in cocaine trafficking, does this constitute an infringement of sovereignty? When a liaison officer monitors the movement of a suspect believed to be trafficking cocaine into and then out of the islands, informing only an officer of inspector level within the local police, does this constitute an infringement of national sovereignty? What about when a liaison officer stops and questions a passenger at the international airport and checks his details against UK criminal records and intelligence databases? In each of these instances, it seems certain that *individual* autonomy or sovereignty has been infringed and that this infringement is carried out by British rather than local police officers. A view based on an absolutist conception of national sovereignty might be that many of the actions of the liaison officers intruded into the private lives of Caribbean citizens in ways that could only ever be acceptable if undertaken by agents of the sovereign state. To which the reply might be that in order to protect the state and its citizens from serious organized crime and drug trafficking, a realistic and pragmatic approach is required to enable effective transnational inter-agency policing. We return to the tension between sovereigntism and pragmatism in the conclusion. One criterion for judgment is the extent to which these hybrid, plural, and transnational security practices are providing greater security. In the next chapter we consider the impact of the new security practices together with the broader issues of sovereignty and accountability of policing in the transnational 'realm.

9

Transforming Caribbean Security

The international orientation of policing priorities and international extension of policing practices have reached unprecedented levels. Though still far from forming a globe-trotting international police force with sovereign authority, states now agree and collaborate on more cross-border policing matters than ever before. Substantially driven by the interest and moralizing impulses of major Western powers, a loosely institutionalised and coordinated international crime control system based on the homogenization of criminal law norms and regularization of law enforcement relations is emerging and promises to be an increasingly prominent dimension of global governance in the twenty-first century.[1]

Introduction

In this chapter we stand back from the detail of transnational policing practice to explore four general themes on the changing Caribbean security architecture. First, we look at the driving force behind the reconfiguration of security, namely the 'war on drugs', and consider what effects this has had on the Caribbean security landscape. Second, we examine the changes within Caribbean security sector organizations, which links to our third theme: the emergence of a hybrid 'culture of security' that belongs neither to a specific place nor to a specific organization, but is united by common values of control. Finally, we explore the complex issues of sovereignty, accountability, and security in the new global order, drawing on interviews with Caribbean security ministers, law officers, and others with an overview of regional policing practice.

[1] Peter Andreas and Ethan Nadelmann (2007), *Policing the Globe: Criminalization and Crime Control in International Relations*. Oxford: Oxford University Press, p 250.

Prohibition Regimes

The globalization of crime control cannot be explained merely as a functional response to the globalization of crime.[2] Rather, the underlying impetus for transnational law enforcement is best understood in the context of the initial fact of criminalization and the emergence of prohibition regimes.[3] The history of policing shows that crime problems have always been used to justify the creation of police organizations, but the specific problems upon which they have focused have shifted dramatically. Goods and services that were once freely traded across national boundaries are criminalized and subject to impressive and expensive enforcement regimes. Some fall from the agenda as they are decriminalized, legalized or disappear entirely.[4] Relatively few criminal law norms evolve into global prohibition regimes. Those that do, tend to reflect the criminal laws of the most powerful countries and involve cross-border movement stimulating dominant nations to enjoin other governments, often supported by transnational moral entrepreneurs, to participate in enforcement efforts.[5] Andreas and Nadelmann argue that global prohibition regimes evolve in four or five common stages. At first, the activity is entirely legitimate and subject to minimal control. In the second stage, the activity becomes defined as evil or immoral and must therefore be destroyed entirely rather than merely regulated or controlled. Prohibition regimes against undesirable transnational activities seek not only to deter, but also to express the state's moral resolve.[6] In the third stage, proponents agitate for criminalization and suppression of the activity by all countries. In the fourth (and often final) stage, criminal law and

---

[2] James Sheptycki (ed) (2000), *Issues in Transnational Policing.* London: Routledge, pp 93–4; Andreas and Nadelmann, *Policing the Globe, op cit,* pp 224–5.

[3] Andreas and Nadelmann, *Policing the Globe, op cit,* p 225.

[4] Some of the swings between prohibition and legalization are ironic. For example, extensive US law enforcement during the eighteenth century in pursuit of fugitive slaves fleeing across the border to Mexico and Canada gave way to efforts to enforce the laws against the slave trade in the nineteenth century. Similarly, the drugs wars prosecuted by the British during the nineteenth century enforced the traffic in opium from British Imperial India to meet the demand in China. A little over a century later, Britain was playing a significant role in the global attempt to eradicate opium production, distribution, and consumption. This history explains the Customs & Excise role in drug law enforcement: it was originally employed to collect taxes on the opium import-export trade.

[5] Andreas and Nadelmann, *Policing the Globe, op cit,* p 228.

[6] *Ibid,* p 247.

police action throughout the world become focused on control. The incidence of the criminalized act may, in a fifth stage, reduce to become an insignificant and isolated activity, success depending on its susceptibility to enforcement. Punitive approaches are particularly *ineffective* in suppressing activities that have substantial and resilient consumer demand, require few resources, little expertise, and are easily concealed. Andreas and Nadelmann argue that for these reasons, the control of narcotic and psychotropic drugs is unlikely ever to achieve the successes seen in campaigns against piracy and the slave trade.[7]

In his 1971 book *The Drug Takers*, Jock Young wrote that drug prohibition would achieve the opposite of its intended effects: it would, he predicted, entrench and possibly foster the popularity, availability, and use of drugs.[8] Young argued that psychotropic and narcotic drugs are commodities. If prohibition fails to deter or incapacitate suppliers and the demand for drugs remains, their illegality means that the only possible means of supply for those who choose to use them is through illicit sources. In other words, prohibition creates a clandestine market. This observation is crucial to understanding the Caribbean security landscape. By an 'accident of geography' the region lies on the clandestine drug trafficking route between the Andean producers of cocaine and the consumers in Europe and America. The islands have porous borders meaning that drugs flow in easily from the sea, and with limited resources to secure ports and airports they can flow outwards easily by air or sea. Most interviewees thought that the drugs problem was caused by the demand for cocaine within the metropolitan countries without which the Caribbean would be irrelevant as a trans-shipment point. This 'spilled over' to create a problem of local use, but in the larger economic picture, a market of five and a half million island inhabitants was insignificant in understanding the drug global trade.

Young argued that imposing penalties for the possession or supply of drugs means that only the most organized sellers in the market can survive the risks.[9] So-called 'social supply', gives way to 'commercial supply' and a highly organized segmented market

---

[7] *Ibid*, p 22.
[8] Jock Young (1971a), *The Drug Takers*. London: MacGibbon & Kee; Jock Young (1971b), 'The Role of the Police as Amplifiers of Deviance, Negotiators of Reality and Translators of Fantasy' in Stan Cohen (ed), *Images of Deviance*. Harmondsworth: Penguin.
[9] Young (1971b), 'The Role of the Police as Amplifiers of Deviance', p 57.

is created. The capital required for trans-shipment becomes very large and linked with other forms of organized crimes. Because the market is clandestine, profits made from psychoactive drugs are much larger than normal commodities. This attracts previously disinterested members of society from all social classes to become involved in the trade. The money involved is so huge that it has the effect of skewing the entire economy so that people from all walks of life become embroiled. Smuggling requires relationships with law enforcement agents, therefore police, Customs, and airport security become corrupt. The heart of the 'drugs problem' is economic: those profiting from drugs penetrate systems of law enforcement and ultimately into government ministries and right into the heart of the state. The problem is embedded in the lack of economic alternatives and absence of sustainable equitable economic growth that would provide the foundation for gainful employment, commerce, and industry. It stems from economic restructuring, the end of agricultural trade arrangements, and bad debt resulting from an inequitable global economy. The drugs trade provides not only alternative employment, but also an alternative source of loyalty, where the leaders of organized crime groups become seen as 'godfathers' providing economic and social protection.

The war on drugs, described by the *Economist* as an 'unlucky campaign',[10] seems capable of winning battles only with extensive collateral damage. This is not to dismiss tactical successes. These have certainly been impressive, producing very large seizures of cocaine. The British Royal Navy's 2007 Caribbean Campaign alone led to the seizure of over £1 billion worth of illegal drugs in 15 months.[11] Interdiction in the Caribbean region has also had the effect of stemming certain trafficking routes. The number of drug couriers, and in particular cocaine 'stuffers' and 'swallowers' travelling from the Caribbean to the UK by air declined markedly as a consequence of a range of initiatives including Operation Carib Bridge (see Chapter 8) supported by such public education campaigns as *Eva Goes to Foreign*. However, drug import-export routes are so diverse, extensive, and complex that a particular route, a single player, and even a drug cartel or trafficking network can be replaced. Following tactical successes, new routes and

---

[10] *The Economist*, 13 December 2007.

[11] MOD Press release, 'Ocean thwarts drug smugglers in the Caribbean', 26 June 2007.

methods of supply overtake established ones. The conventional measure of drug availability is the retail price. Between 1999 and 2004, the street price of cocaine in the UK dropped from £63 to £51 per gram and fell again to £45 per gram in 2008.[12] Given that cocaine usage has been increasingly steadily, the drop in price suggests that cocaine remains freely available. The obvious conclusion is that despite these tactical successes, the strategy to 'stifle supply' has failed to achieve its goal.

The UK drugs strategy has evidently not fulfilled its promise to reduce the availability of cocaine in Britain but, more troublingly, there is a strong case that in the Caribbean drug prohibition has caused the problem that it set out to cure. If coca leaf and its derivatives were legally traded commodities like coffee or bananas, the most efficient route to consumer markets in North America and Europe would be by direct plane or boat or through containerized shipping. Trans-shipment through the Caribbean—with complex sea and air connections, numerous intermediaries, and many other risks and inefficiencies—is only worth the added expense and increased risks because the market is illicit. Interdiction has the effect of displacing trade routes rather than actually preventing supply. The drugs traffic was first displaced from direct routes from Colombia to overland routes through Central America. It was then displaced to the Caribbean starting with Jamaica, the Bahamas, and Puerto Rico and then through Venezuela, the Guyanas, Trinidad, and the islands of the Eastern Caribbean. Most recently, new trafficking routes have emerged in West Africa. This phenomenon is what many interviewees described as the 'balloon effect' because it is like stepping on a balloon: when you step on one place, it bulges elsewhere. Simply put, cocaine travels through the Caribbean islands and other trans-shipment points as a direct consequence of prohibition.

The greatest threat to security in the Caribbean is not the consumption of drugs, but the armed violence and corruption that are endemic to illicit markets. The clandestine nature of the market means that it is impossible to access formal systems of regulation. Therefore, systems of social control based on armed violence have emerged, facilitated by firearms flowing into the region from the USA and from Central and South America. Arming of street level

---

[12] *Hansard*, Written answers, 1 March 2005: Column 1103W. Royal Navy Press Release, 'Iron Duke Strikes a Blow to Cocaine Smugglers', 2 July 2008.

operatives within the drugs trade has the effect of arming society more generally. Armed enforcers begin to identify themselves as soldiers who are prepared to kill for money and are also prepared to meet their own deaths.[13] In numerous locations, armed groups have formed symbiotic relationships to business and political elites, gaining access to side arms and battlefield weapons, ammunition, vehicles, military clothing, and equipment. The arming of Caribbean society has resulted in a high level of casualties, with firearm murder rates running at record levels in many countries across the region. In many places, political violence, firearms trafficking, and lethal violence are having a severe impact on the ordinary citizen.[14]

Tactical law enforcement successes have some unintended and undesirable consequences. The seizure of drugs removes profits which must be recouped by more business activity and that causes debts which spark violent conflict. Arresting low level operatives has the perverse result of their replacement with hitherto law-abiding individuals. Post-arrest intelligence gathering and cultivation of informers creates distrust within organizations and can lead to violent conflicts. Arrest of mid- and upper-level operatives destabilizes markets and triggers internecine conflict. In spite of the best efforts of law enforcement, prohibition is one of the causes of the problems of armed violence, corruption, and money laundering in the Caribbean while failing to achieve the original purpose of repressing availability and reducing local consumption. Despite the severity of the current security situation, the full range of policy options is not being considered. Some senior officials believe that there should be a debate about drug legalization, and regimes of taxation and regulation, which is only prevented by political timidity. In their view, the longer this is delayed, the more the business of drugs trafficking becomes linked into the legitimate economy as businessmen and politicians become financially dependent on the drugs trade (Chapter 8, pp 251–2). There is an urgent need for a rational debate about how psychoactive drug supply can be

---

[13] Laurie Gunst (1995), *Born Fi' Dead: A Journey Through the Jamaican Posse Underworld*. New York: Henry Holt and Company.

[14] Biko Agozino, Ben Bowling, Geoffrey St. Bernard, and Elizabeth Ward (2009), 'Guns, Crime and Social Order in the West Indies', *Criminology and Criminal Justice*, 9/3: 287–305.

taken out of the hands of organized crime groups, disentangled from the criminal economy and the state, and its armed militias dismantled.

Transforming Policing: From the Global to the Local

The war on drugs provides both context and pretext for the reconfiguration of Caribbean policing described in this book. Security sector organizations are changing radically in terms of their objectives, form, and function. This is evident in a number of different socio-spatial spheres.

First, there is a growing prominence of policing entities with a global reach. Interpol has grown in size and in the scope and complexity of its operations and now provides intelligence, analysis, liaison facilities, and other similar activities to support domestic policing. Although Interpol remains principally a mechanism for sharing information—its I-24/7 communication system links the Caribbean islands with the rest of the world—it is increasingly involved in operational activity, including investigative support. In recent years, Interpol has provided operational assistance to the investigation of murder in Jamaica and credit card fraud in Trinidad and Tobago.[15] Moreover, the Interpol National Central Bureaux (NCBs), nested within criminal investigation departments of domestic police forces, actively undertake enforcement and identify with Interpol's global policing mission (see Chapter 4).

The second major shift is the emergence of *regional policing* which is gradually moving forward in the Caribbean. Security problems often require extensive inter-island cooperation on a day-to-day basis. There are numerous bilateral and regional agreements and regional bodies which establish familiarity, communication, confidence, and trust amongst the various security sector officers within the region, creating an environment where it is possible to have lines of communication between the various organizations within and between other islands. The 2007 Cricket World Cup provided the impetus for regional security cooperation with mechanisms put in place to manage a massive temporary increase in flows of tourists and the sharing of intelligence. In anticipation

---

[15] Interpol (2007), *Annual Report*.

of this, the CARICOM Treaty on Security Assistance, signed by 14 countries of the region in 2006, creates a mechanism to provide assistance in the event of a breakdown in law and order, armed insurrection, terrorist incidents, man-made or natural environmental disasters. Within CARICOM, there is an active discussion about creating a regional policing entity—CARIPOL—and a treaty establishing a pan-Caribbean arrest warrant was signed in 2008.

The third shift is the growing practice for police agencies, particularly in developed countries, to post *liaison officers* in their embassies or high commissions especially in places of key strategic interest relating to transnational organized crime. Caribbean police forces have not posted officers overseas to any great extent. Exchanges are not very common and the extensive travel that does occur within the region is restricted to conferences and training courses. Officers occasionally travel to conduct interviews or to accompany an extradited offender. So far, only Jamaica has posted officers in the UK and the Bahamas has an exchange programme with Miami. The obvious reason for this is that in common with other states with limited financial resources, international law enforcement is viewed as a luxury in the Caribbean. On the other hand, the metropolitan countries have an extensive transnational policing capacity.[16] It is the liaison officers who come closest to the idea of 'global cop'—a person with global mobility, police powers and resources, and the capacity to achieve law enforcement outcomes beyond the boundaries of the nation state. The job varies from place to place and from agency to agency. For some liaison officers, it is a desk job, while others are actively involved in operational policing. In most places liaison officers assist, develop, train, and mentor local police officers. On a day-to-day basis, they act semi-autonomously. They answer to their headquarters in the metropolis, are loosely supervised by their overseas embassy or mission, and are operationally accountable to local security chiefs. It is where liaison officers *work with* local security sector officers in operational practice (eg at international airports) that

---

[16] The FBI has around 340 employees assigned to permanent overseas positions and aspires to have an office in every country of the world and the US DEA has 78 offices in 58 countries. The Royal Canadian Mounted Police has 35 liaison officers in 25 countries and the Australian Federal Police has 80 liaison officers in 27 countries. The UK Serious Organised Crime Agency (SOCA) has a small force of 140 overseas liaison officers.

questions of sovereignty and accountability are most controversial (see Chapter 8). Generally, liaison officers work behind the scenes, collaborating quietly with their local counterparts. This activity, which largely involves sharing information for others to act upon, does not invoke law enforcement powers. It could be argued that this does not infringe sovereignty, but it certainly raises questions in this regard. When liaison officers stop and question passengers travelling through airports, check passports against metropolitan databases, or take hand swabs and urine samples for cocaine testing, the question of who has the power to act, where, and accounting to whom, becomes highly contentious (see Chapter 8).

A fourth major shift is the *strengthening and integration of policing capacity at the national level*. In order to create the new national security architecture, conventional police officers increasingly work with other organizations—defence forces, border protection agencies, coastguard, post office, private security agencies, and secret intelligence organizations—which were, until very recently, largely separate with a divergence of mandates and working practices. The main role of this 'new security sector' in the Caribbean is to police serious organized crime in general and drug trafficking in particular. This is being created at the national level through a process of *securitization* in which the law enforcement and policing functions of an organization are emphasized in addition to, or to the exclusion of, other roles. For example, the coastguards have become less concerned with search and rescue and Customs focus less on revenue protection. Agencies that make up the 'new security sector' are increasingly emphasizing their role in security and surveillance facilitated by the acquisition of new information and communications technologies. This new security sector is also joined closely at the centre through national joint intelligence and enforcement headquarters, joint task forces that aim to strengthen, build, and integrate national capacity. Through these headquarters 'gold groups' comprising, at a minimum, the operational heads from police and military (but frequently involving airport security, Customs, and immigration), national action is coordinated in relation to a multinational operation. Building the capacity of national institutions is a crucial aspect of the work of the overseas liaison officer. As a British Deputy High Commissioner explained, their role is to 'develop the local infrastructure so that it becomes more capable when we need to work together. That is simple strategy'.

The fifth transformation is the *globalization of local policing*. This study cannot claim that globalization has touched all spheres of policing, but it certainly has affected those units studied in detail. Many officers spend a significant proportion of their time working on transnational issues and local policing is increasingly linked into transnational networks. Even though most Caribbean police officers rarely leave their island homes, their work can be described as transnational since it involves the exchange of information with other policing organizations, sharing databases, and engaging in multinational operations. As in other parts of the world, local police commanders are required to deliver 'community safety' to their neighbourhoods whilst, *at the same time*, remaining conscious of the local impact of global forces. Commissioners and their officers must think not only about the nature of drugs markets in their jurisdictions, but also how these link with transnational supply and distribution networks. This is an example of 'interactive globalization', where people act in ways that are 'indigenous-yet-globally-aware'.[17]

As Andreas and Nadelmann correctly point out, policing matters are a 'pivotal dimension of rich-poor relations'.[18] Caribbean law enforcement agencies, like those elsewhere, find themselves under pressure to embrace law enforcement priorities and transnational policing campaigns of wealthier states. The development of transnational policing is impeded by limited resources, with a clear budgetary tension between domestic and international policing. Financial arrangements are often based on donor/beneficiary arrangements. Even for the relatively well funded British police service, national and international issues take second place to immediate local priorities. Senior British police officers are reluctant to dedicate resources to the investigation of criminals who operate largely outside their police area and so it is difficult to see how poorly resourced police services (such as those in the Caribbean region) will meet the requirements to implement 'global' strategies. The emerging 'international crime control industrial complex' means rising costs for developing countries as they struggle to comply with increasingly stringent expectations of law enforcement and the demands of wealthy states.[19]

---

[17] Maureen Cain (2000), 'Orientalism, Occidentalism and the Sociology of crime', *British Journal of Criminology*, 40/2: 239–60.

[18] Andreas and Nadelmann, *Policing the Globe, op cit*, p 241.

[19] *Ibid*, p 251.

The Transnational Culture of Policing

Understanding the practice of policing requires an examination of police culture because wide 'police discretion' means that individual police officers, guided by their norms, values, and recipes for action, determine what actually happens on the ground.[20] Comparative police research has found that, in many respects, the occupational culture of policing is similar throughout the world. Certain experiences, expectations, values, and behaviours can be found among police officers living and working in very different societies. As Andreas and Nadelmann put it, 'a cop is a cop no matter whose badge is worn, and a criminal a criminal regardless of citizenship or where the crime was committed'.[21] A *transnational value system*—formed in response to specific occupational exigencies—can override political differences and formal procedures. Handling situations that have no good outcome and dealing with human beings at their worst moments shape police outlook, expectations, and values. Expecting people to lie, being suspicious about people's motives, and the unpredictable outcomes of police intervention shape pessimistic and cynical views about the value of their work. Similarly, cultural attributes such as loyalty, insularity, authority, conservatism, and instrumentality arise from the nature of the job. For Andreas and Nadelmann, shared expertise and understandings among police officers around the world provides the 'oil and glue' of law enforcement.[22] Nadelmann argues that law enforcement officers share a 'transnational subculture based on common functions and objectives. What making a profit is to businessmen regardless of their nationality, so catching the criminal is to cops all over the world'.[23]

The culture of transnational policing

Research has documented cultural variations *within* police forces. Reuss-Iaani, for example, illustrated distinct variations in values between 'management cops' and 'street cops'.[24] Similarly,

---

[20] Robert Reiner (2000), *The Politics of the Police*. Oxford: OUP; Janet Chan (1997), *Changing Police Culture*. Cambridge: Cambridge University Press.

[21] Andreas and Nadelmann, *Policing the Globe*, op cit, p 232.

[22] Ethan Nadelmann (1993), *Cops Across Borders: The Internationalization of U.S. Criminal Law Enforcement*. Pennsylvania: Pennsylvania State University Press, p 468.   [23] *Ibid*, p 110.

[24] Elizabeth Reuss-Ianni (1983), *Two Cultures of Policing: Street Cops and Management Cops*. New Brunswick: Transaction Book.

career detectives' craft skills, knowledge, and values differ from their uniformed colleagues. Special Branch, traffic cops, mounted branch, and dog handlers each have distinct cultures. As transnational policing has emerged as a specialist role, it seems this too has a specific culture of its own arising from its specific occupational exigencies.[25] As Andreas and Nadelmann put it, a transnational 'police community' has emerged with a culture based upon common tasks and the common objective of 'immobilizing' the criminal.[26] Transnational police—overseas liaison officers especially, but also their counterparts in CID, Special Branch, Interpol, and Drug Squads—have learned specific skills such as the ability to work with people from other nationalities and within contrasting and sometimes conflicting legal systems. They have skills in diplomacy, leadership, influencing people beyond their formal authority and in creative problem solving. They are international in outlook, with a solid understanding of more than one legal system and of international law, treaties, conventions, and memoranda of understanding. They have unique skills in 'getting things done', including marshalling intrusive techniques and coercive force, without possessing formal law enforcement powers. They often have a background in intelligence and need to understand issues surrounding the use of informers, surveillance, undercover operations, and controlled delivery. Finally, they are skilled in elicitation and good judgment about whom to trust and whom not to trust, and how to use this knowledge to good effect. They are, to coin a phrase, police diplomats.

A hybrid transnational security culture

The current research indicates that elements of this culture are shared more widely than among the police and extend to officers in other security agencies. UK DLOs who have worked for HM Customs for the whole of their careers identify themselves as 'cops', 'detectives', or the generic designation of 'law enforcement' commonly used in the USA (see Chapter 8). Some of the Caribbean Customs officers interviewed in this study stressed their policing role and saw themselves as 'cops', and more were happy to identify themselves as 'law enforcement officers'. They argued

---

[25] James Sheptycki (2002), *In Search of Transnational Policing*. Aldershot: Avebury.   [26] Andreas and Nadelmann, *Policing the Globe*.

that Customs administrations can no longer be seen as merely revenue collectors, but are 'an integral part of the law enforcement apparatus'. When I asked a coastguard commander whether he saw himself as a cop, a sailor, or a military man, he replied, 'all of the above'. Airport security officers see themselves as a unique discipline, but as one airport security chief put it, they are 'policemen under the arc of the airport'. Contemporary military forces, one senior officer argued, 'cannot . . . be locked into the old traditional military duties', or else 'you will have *no business*'. A UK security advisor explained that 'the only real role for a military force out here today is probably in peace support operations where they'll be working in support of the police'.

A hybrid culture is forming within the new security archipelago based on shared working arrangements, solidarity, and the binding motive of control.[27] This 'new security culture' is formed through the engagement in *policing* that unites the various professions described in this book. Although many of the agencies described would have some difficulty with the idea of themselves as 'police officers', their daily work constitutes policing, usefully defined by Robert Reiner as:

organized forms of order maintenance, peacekeeping, rule or law enforcement, crime investigation and prevention and other forms of investigation and associated information-brokering—which may involve a conscious exercise of coercive power—undertaken by individuals or organizations, where such activities are viewed by them and/or others as a central or key defining part of their purpose.[28]

Sheptycki argues that the nascent subculture of transnational policing requires a new 'constabulary ethic' or internal moral compass.[29] This idea, first coined as a way to guide the military when engaging in policing activity, arises because of the fragmented nature of the 'institution'. The 'constabulary ethic' is an internalized set of norms providing moral direction where the law does not.

[27] Didier Bigo (2000), 'Liaison Officers in Europe' in James Sheptycki (ed), *Issues in Transnational Policing*. London: Routledge, p 73.

[28] Robert Reiner (1997), 'Policing and the Police' in Robert Reiner, Mike Maguire, and Rod Morgan (eds), *The Oxford Handbook of Policing* (3rd edn). Oxford: OUP.

[29] James Sheptycki (2007), 'The *Constabulary Ethic* and the Transnational Condition' in Andrew Goldsmith and James Sheptycki (eds), *Crafting Transnational Policing, op cit.*

Sheptycki argues that relations between police of politically hostile governments are not always successful but when they are, 'it is a reflection of the strength of the transnational police subculture—the sense among policemen that they are united by a common task that has nothing to do with politics'.[30] In the same way that police culture provides the lubrication for cohesive domestic policing, a transnational security culture helps the new multilateral and transnational security sector to function smoothly. This seems set to become increasingly common as the new transnational security officials spend progressively more time overseas, training together, and moving between organizations. This development, valuable from a pragmatic point of view, raises challenging questions about national sovereignty, accountability, and legitimacy.

Transnational Policing, Sovereignty, and Accountability

Policing, in theory, is an expression of national sovereignty. It is often said that the first responsibility of government is the provision of security to its citizens and, vice versa, that the provision of security is first and foremost a governmental responsibility. Anderson *et al* argue that 'policing is the heart of the sovereignty of democratic states and will be one of the last powers given up to supranational organisations'. Therefore,

the fundamental 'problem' of international law enforcement is the sovereign—that is, exclusive—power of governments within their own borders and virtually nowhere else . . . The sovereign power of states generally forecloses unilateral police action by one state in the territory of another. It requires that most international law enforcement efforts be in some sense bilateral, cooperative ventures. And it means that the popular image of the Interpol agent as a police officer with international arrest powers is entirely fictional.[31]

Practical problems arise from differences in political structures, legal traditions, and value systems among cooperating police officers, which in turn give rise to divergent expectations about the outcomes of international cooperation. A lack of confidence in the reliability and quality of police services, slow response

---

[30] Ethan Nadelmann (1993), *Cops Across Borders, op cit*, p 468.
[31] Nadelmann (1993), *Cops Across Borders, op cit*, p 5.

to international requests, and different degrees of importance attached to the case by the parties concerned, make effective cooperation fractious. Prost argues that:

Criminals depend heavily upon the barriers of sovereignty to shield themselves and evidence of their crimes from detection . . . by structuring their organisations to span borders, they are better able to protect their interests and organisations. They are positioned to take advantage of the differences between legal systems, the clash of bureaucracies, the protection of sovereignty, and, at many times, the complete incapacity of nations to work to overcome their differences . . . The criminals are far more skilled in using national borders to protect themselves and the evidence and profits of their crime from detection than law enforcement is in overcoming the barriers of sovereignty, in pursuing them.[32]

Understanding the extent to which national sovereignty is being infringed by transnational policing practices requires a re-examination of the exercise of powers described in this book. It is crucial to understand that the police power is the greatest and least circumscribed powers of government.[33] The most obvious power of the police is coercive force. In his classic book, *Functions of Police in Modern Society*, Egon Bittner argued that rather than defining police in terms of its ends—such as law enforcement or crime control—it is much more satisfactory to define it in terms of its *means*. The police, he said, 'are nothing else than a mechanism for the distribution of situationally justified force in society'.[34] This is consistent with Max Weber's definition of the state as 'a human community that (successfully) claims the *monopoly of the legitimate use of physical force* within a given territory'.[35] While policing *always* requires coercion (without which the duty to protect cannot be met), policing does not *only* mean coercion.[36] This is just one capacity of the police to which we should add intrusive,

[32] Kimberley Prost (1998), 'Breaking Down the Barriers: International Cooperation in Combating Transnational Crime', *Information Exchange Network for Mutual Assistance in Criminal Matters and Extradition*. <www.oas.org>.

[33] Markus Dirk Dubber (2005), *The Police Power: Patriarchy and the Foundations of American Government*. New York: Columbia University Press, p xi.

[34] Egon Bittner (1980), *The Functions of the Police in Modern Society*. Cambridge, MA: Oelgeschlager, p 39.

[35] Max Weber, *Politics as a Vocation*, Lecture to Munich University, January 1919.

[36] Dubber (2005), *The Police Power, op cit*, p 73.

surveillant, investigative, and other powers that circumscribe human autonomy.[37]

Coercive powers

The use of coercive force beyond national boundaries is rare but is not beyond the capacity of foreign police. Some interviewees cited examples of where overseas police officers effected (or attempted to effect) an autonomous arrest within their territory. One Attorney General described an incident in which a US agent made an informal request to pick up a suspect on arriving by plane from a neighbouring island. The Attorney General requested legal documents authorized by their Mutual Legal Assistance Treaty (MLAT) or extradition treaty, but the agent wanted to act expeditiously. The agent then approached the Chief Immigration Officer and the Commissioner of Police and eventually the Prime Minister. On each occasion the agent was told that without the appropriate paperwork the answer was 'no'. Eventually extradition papers were produced. The suspect did not turn up as expected and a request was faxed to the neighbouring island on an open line and the suspect fled the territory. The Attorney General commented 'they were not even ashamed to come and ask the chief legal advisor to government to participate in a kidnapping. Now fortunately things have come a long way since then and the relationship is on a far more even keel'.[38] This is similar to a publicly reported incident in 2000 when US federal agents lured a suspected drug dealer to one of the beaches in Saint Kitts on the pretext of travelling to a nearby

[37]   Ben Bowling, Amber Marks, and Cian Murphy (2008), 'Crime control technologies' in Roger Brownsword and Karen Yeung (eds), *Regulating Technologies*. Oxford: Hart, pp 51–78.

[38]   US policy was influenced by Supreme Court judgment in the *Alvarez-Machain* case. In 1990, Dr Alvarez-Machain, a Mexican dentist, was kidnapped under the direction of the DEA. He was taken from Mexico to the US by Mexican nationals in order to stand trial for his alleged role in the death of a DEA agent. In 1992, the US Supreme Court decided by a 6–3 majority that kidnapping did not prohibit Dr Alvarez from being tried in a US court. Writing for the majority, Chief Justice William H. Rehnquist cited an 1886 Supreme Court decision that the authority of a court is not weakened if a defendant is brought before it as a result of 'forcible abduction' [*Ker v Illinois*, 119 U.S. 436 (1886)]. Rehnquist held that the US extradition treaty with Mexico was irrelevant because it 'says nothing about the obligations of the United States and Mexico to refrain from forcible abductions' [*United States v Humberto Alvarez-Machain*, 112 S.Ct. 2188 (1992)].

island to receive payment for 11 pounds of cocaine. Once the boat had left Saint Kitts' 12-mile territorial limit, US undercover agents handcuffed the suspect, took him to Antigua and from there to the USA where he was charged with trafficking.[39]

As well as such blatant examples, more subtle examples of coercion were mentioned much more often. Liaison officers do not have formal arrest powers, but they are able to achieve coercive outcomes through action that could be described as remote control or 'governing at a distance'. Through lawful routes, they can use available information and other resources to enable local police officers to undertake arrests on their behalf. Overseas liaison officers are experienced senior officers within their own organizations who are perceived as senior relative to their Caribbean counterparts. Much of the formal relationship between the liaison officer and the local security authorities is at the Commissioner level and their operational work is working with an Assistant Commissioner or senior superintendent. Such 'remote control' could be carried out on behalf of an officer physically based overseas through an Interpol red notice, for example. This would allow an officer to produce a provisional warrant that would enable local officers to arrest at first sight of a suspect (see Chapter 3). With liaison officers based on the island, the closeness of the working relationship permits more direct collaboration. In some instances, US Drug Enforcement Administration (DEA) or Customs Officers have been present at the scene of an arrest and were occasionally audacious enough to wear a Caribbean Customs ID badge (see Chapter 5).

Although liaison officers are dependent on the local police for 'law enforcement', they may be there either physically present at the scene or supervising operations from the purview of a joint headquarters. One British liaison officer described himself as the coordinator of a maritime interdiction operation, although his formal role was to 'look over the shoulder' of the local 'gold commander'. A DEA agent described how they provided equipment and resources and that mentoring enabled them to instruct local officers. Mentoring was like a training exercise, except that it was a live operation. The agent explained that in a coordinated operation, while the local cops are the first through the door, he would be 'close behind' to debrief prisoners. Essentially, the DEA operate by 'steering' operations. The

---

[39] 'Arrest in a U.S. drug sting shocks Caribbean officials: Federal agents lured trafficker suspect off the island of Saint Kitts', *Associated Press*, 13 June 2000.

agent explained that they might even have to say, 'hey, you missed one over here' or, 'you dropped a ball over here'. 'We tell them what to do', he explained, 'like we're doing it ourselves'.

Investigative and surveillant powers

Transnational cooperation such as the investigation of specific crimes is regulated formally by Mutual Legal Assistance Treaties (MLATs). In most instances, evidence collection is a cooperative venture. Conducting interviews is formally carried out by local officers using questions devised by overseas investigating officers. In practice, however, the overseas investigating officer may actually ask the questions. This is on the grounds of pragmatism since it is often the overseas investigator who has the full facts of the case and can ask supplementary questions. Investigative collaboration is only as good as what can be turned into evidence and therefore requires great cooperation. The blurring of the distinction between 'high' policing and 'low' policing is accompanied by a shift in the police function of securing territory and the surveillance of suspect populations as a result of the 'deterritorialization of crime'.[40] The operating range of transnational policing has been enhanced by new information communications technologies especially the development of computers. Contemporary intelligence-led policing involves collecting, storing, and sharing information gathered secretly. The work of Special Branch and the Drug Squad involves extensive covert policing activity (see Chapter 4). This strategic and operational intelligence work is, above all, where the connection is made with the overseas liaison officer. While arrest is the obvious focus for discussion of police power, intelligence gathering and interviewing all constitute the power of the state to intrude into an individual's private life.

The examples set out above suggest that in the contemporary Caribbean, the police do not have the monopoly of intrusive and coercive force within their boundaries. While the nation state may claim primacy in law enforcement, transnational actors play an important role in the provision of domestic security. In practice,

[40] James Sheptycki (2000), *Issues in Transnational Policing*. London: Routledge; James Sheptycki (2002), 'Accountability across the Policing Field: Towards a General Cartography of Accountability for Post-Modern Policing', *Policing and Society*, 12/4: 323–38.

sovereignty—the supreme authority to use the power to coerce or intrude into the privacy of the individual—is often diffused among national and transnational agents. To put the point starkly, some of what liaison officers do in the Caribbean, at least occasionally, would be unlawful were it carried out by foreign police in the UK.[41] In light of the realities of contemporary transnational police cooperation, those involved in security in the Caribbean Islands are divided on the question of national sovereignty and whether it matters that overseas officers are involved in intrusive covert activity in their territories. There are two 'ideal type' responses to this that we could call 'law enforcement pragmatism' and 'sovereign nationalism'.

Law enforcement pragmatists

Most transnational police work is undertaken with the explicit knowledge and permission of local law enforcement officials. On the whole, Caribbean police officers were stoical about the presence and role of overseas intelligence officers and some were very pragmatic (see Chapters 3 and 4). For many interviewees, the liaison officers gathering information and working with other law enforcement present no threat to sovereignty because, as one officer put it, 'they have in fact come with our permission and they are located here and they work with our law enforcement with our permission'. Some security ministers, similarly, were pleased to have liaison officers present on their island. From this point of view the issue of sovereignty was overstated:

I think we make much ado about nothing. . . . if you are asleep in your bedroom, your neighbour looks through the window and sees an intruder coming into your house and he comes into your yard to follow that intruder in and grabs him in your bedroom when he was rifling through your things, will you be grateful to your neighbour or will you be angry [with him] for violating your privacy?

---

[41] The Regulation of Investigatory Powers Act (RIPA) requires that any intrusion into privacy must be authorized by a Chief Constable. Taking photographs of suspects, cultivating informers, requesting information from intelligence records, or airline passenger records would require a Chief Officer's authorization. The Crime (International Cooperation) Act 2003, s 83 allows a foreign officer to undertake surveillance in the UK only if the surveillance started overseas, if he immediately informs the UK, and requests a RIPA authorization. Once authorized, surveillance can only continue for a period of five hours.

Similarly, a senior civil servant was keen to emphasize the need to be realistic:

Well let's look at it this way. We have a country to protect. We don't have the resources, especially in terms of maritime assets and aeronautical assets to effectively police our coastal waters, and then of course we no longer have the original traditional threat of ideology, all that type of stuff. The threat is now drug trafficking and organized crime. We certainly don't want to sell ourselves or to give away our sovereignty, but we have to look pragmatically at what we have, what capabilities we have, and as far as possible work with our former colonial masters and their allies, the industrialized countries, to protect ourselves.

Does this mean that there is no threat to national sovereignty? Or is this a pragmatic response that concedes that there is in fact a violation of sovereignty, but not as great a threat as that posed by organized crime groups or drug traffickers? One security minister explained that he doesn't 'feel the pinch' of any violation of sovereignty:

the major threat that I face now is from criminals. I don't go to sleep at night figuring that well some guy is interfering in my sovereignty. I don't feel the pinch in the sense that there is nothing that I want to do that I cannot do because they are here. There is nothing that they are doing which prevents me or any one of the citizens lawfully going about their business, doing what they ought to do.

The view that a covert policing model had become inevitable and necessary in order to combat transnational organized crime was widely shared. It was also accepted that covert policing required the involvement of outside policing agencies due to the clandestine, hidden, and highly secretive nature of the problem, involving conspiracy at the highest levels among 'clean skins' in the world of business and commerce. As an Assistant DPP put it, the very nature of drugs trafficking means that the 'very big boys are not players'. Even the most senior traffickers that they arrest are not at the highest level of the business. The drugs industry is so closely linked with legitimate business that wider society is implicated, along with police, Customs, and government shielding people at the highest levels. Therefore, covert policing is required in order to get past corruption. In principle, collaboration in intelligence gathering and dissemination is a two-way process between overseas liaison officers and local police. There is an obvious need for professionalism and accountability but even so it is highly problematic.

Covert transnational policing within the region is rarely recognized officially and is certainly not something that is widely discussed in public. British officials in particular said as little as possible about it and never spoke to the press (see Chapter 8). It is not stated anywhere that overseas intelligence agencies may undertake covert operations within other states and this led some Caribbean Commissioners to deny its occurrence (see Chapter 3). On the other hand, its existence is widely acknowledged and accepted among security specialists:

nobody has ever said officially to us, to me, that they want this right to operate covertly and certainly I haven't come across any evidence that such a situation is widespread or a basic policy position of any one of our partners. But equally you know that there is law enforcement in intelligence gathering. And so, by its very nature, there are some things that will be done covertly, you know. So I guess you understand that that is part of the risk. I wouldn't rule it out doing it myself in other places where I might need to know things that I need to know.

Security ministers understood that the application of an espionage model, developed in response to the 'communist threat', was now being applied to new targets in the field of organized crime. Ultimately, for the ministers, how far this extends is going to depend on the 'comfort level that you have around a particular issue and so deepening cooperation will build the comfort level and the sharing of information'. This means passing on information on a 'need to know' basis. Generally, security ministers argued, you need to know the ambit of the operation, but not the details. One minister was pragmatic on this point:

Well a basic principle of intelligence, and that is how intelligence is, is operating on a need to know. Some people will need to know, some won't. In general policy terms I don't think it is good [for ministers to know the details], 'cause if it is a strict intelligence operation, you need to know the ambit of it, the scope, but I don't think you need always to know the particular individuals or the particular targets. That can end up compromising operations, even unwittingly.

One of the difficulties for the law enforcement pragmatists—borne out in earlier chapters—is to manage the problem of accountability. Security ministers are those with whom the buck stops and yet, if overseas police officers are involved on the ground in ways of which ministers have no details, they might be called to account for things about which they have no knowledge. Ministers' views on this were very diplomatic and echo those made by the British Deputy High Commissioner (cited in Chapter 8). One Caribbean security minister said, 'you need to know; and you need to put yourself in a position to know *what you are not told* as best you can.'

Security ministers were at pains to point out the cooperative nature of collaboration and suggested that it was possible to 'end up defining a problem when none exists'. One suggested a typical scenario in which two officers were working on a case involving collaboration between two Caribbean islands and the UK and in which the individual has managed to compromise some layers or elements in law enforcement and the financial sector:

You're working on them out of _____ or out of the UK. So we go up. We send somebody up to the UK. We're in, they are doing it. They might make contact with the head of a unit which they trust. They may meet. They may say that two police officers are in. Nobody else might need to know. As I say, crime is transnational, so they have to cross borders to undertake the investigations. They might share information and you might do it. There may be an occasion, I would never tell you that an officer may not decide just to come and see what happens, which is not the same thing as putting someone under deep cover as a secret agent for purposes of espionage or whatever.

The question then becomes, how far is the conduct of an investigation intruding into the sovereign affairs of another state. One government minister pondered on this: 'You can conduct an investigation. Does that represent the spear tip of the state? I don't know.'

Sovereign nationalists

Not all officials expressed a pragmatic view. In relation to setting the security agenda, deciding on priorities, and deciding how those priorities are to be pursued, some officials insisted on the 'right to an independent perspective' even while acknowledging that there was a need for a hemispheric or regional approach with shared priorities. Others argued that acceptable objectives, or even results, do not make covert policing acceptable. Some interviewees, particularly law officers concerned with the legal regulation of investigatory powers, took great exception to the role of overseas intelligence officers. A crucial point made by one Attorney General is that the impact of things going wrong had a greater impact on small islands than in the metropolis.

The 'sovereign nationalists' were well aware that the law enforcement officers on the ground are more pragmatic than their political masters and the lawyers who advise them. The reaction of one politician to the idea that local police officers simply accept the need for covert operations responded that operational police officers were unable to see the problem in a broader perspective:

you are dealing with men who when in the trees are not seeing the woods. There are people in the heat of what they are doing and the excitement of what they are doing want to get the job done. But there is a reason for a constitution. There is a reason for a framework because the mortality of human beings means that somebody is going to be prone to excesses at some point. And in small societies you do not have the institutional capacity to bounce back in as short a period of time as you do in a large country. Okay? And therefore the damage both to the society, the institution and the moral fabric is capable of blasting into a generation. Okay? If you have a group of people in the Kent Police force who are corrupt, the whole of England is not affected. Scotland isn't affected. Wales, okay? Customs isn't affected. If I have the same ten people in [our] police force brought down on a sting, it's going to take at least ten years to restore faith. So the rules are more important because the capacity for deleterious consequences is worse.

From this point of view, covert activities offend against the 'strong cultural underbelly' of even the smallest of Caribbean islands. It disrespects the rule of law, the authority of government, and the right to independence. This is particularly important in societies where imperial rule and discriminatory practices have characterized most of their history. To allow unfettered covert policing would be to pose a very high risk. One senior politician argued that they were content to cooperate and live up to their duties, but within limits:

it will not be a case that could lead to the atrocities of Abu Graib. And that's what happens when you disrespect the rule of law and when you disrespect structures: anything can occur. If you have law enforcement officers who feel that 'we can do whatever we do 'cause we are helping them', at the end of the day, at some point there is going to be an abuse of process. . . . So it may seem to be pedantic to some, but it is rooted in the belief that the small countries and small people only survive if the framework for the rule of law is respected and if there is transparency and accountability.

Some security sector officials were highly resistant to the use of covert techniques. Firstly, for some, the use of wire-tap, interception of communication, informers, and infiltration offends the traditional Caribbean constitutionalist viewpoint. The shift to covert methods, typically seen as something imposed by the USA and the UK, suggests an invasion of privacy and risks undermining trust Which would be difficult to rebuild if a breakdown occurs. Second, a shift to the covert model would require major constitutional and legal change—the passing of interception of communications legislation is just one example. Third, it raises questions of accountability and sovereignty, to which we return below. Fourthly, there is the practical difficulty in undertaking covert policing in small societies where everyone knows everyone else and which, therefore, needs overseas law enforcement officers to be involved. The view of one senior government lawyer was that this was extremely dangerous work for police officers. If they had to travel to neighbouring islands to infiltrate gangs, 'you might find policemen being killed because in order to play the part they probably have to go into areas where marijuana is grown and that sort of thing, and they might end up dead'. Some interviewees saw it as a high risk strategy that can result in serious problems in the event that people from local communities become identified as informers, potentially leading to retaliatory action. In many instances, communities lacked confidence in giving information to the police, because they were concerned about the possibilities of reprisal. An Assistant DPP argued that 'if the word comes out that these people talked to the police, you might find very soon that a whole village is wiped out'. Such practices, he argued, put innocent persons at risk. Supporting this view, the director of a Human Rights NGO described retaliation against a family who had informed on a criminal group:

the information was then circulated back to the criminals. It was a house and a business, a quite well established family, one of the old families in the village. One night they torched the house, tried to keep all the family inside and were firing at them and they tried to jump out of the windows or escape. They slit the throats of all their horses and cattle, individually, every horse and cow, their throats were cut, and they totally sort of destroyed the family and their lifestyle and they traumatized the village, but there were other lesser dramatic instances as well. It was very clear you couldn't trust the police.

Generally, the NGO community were supportive of the role of overseas officers working within the Caribbean but were also concerned about the risk of human rights violations. A spokesperson from a Human Rights NGO mentioned instances where Mutual Legal Assistance Treaties had been used to permit the searching of a lawyer's office and the removal of documents, representing 'a serious invasion of privacy in the professional relationship between lawyer and client'. The work of overseas police, therefore, required careful monitoring:

I think that we don't know the half of the involvement and that again is part of the problem that as a society we don't in fact know how far and how much is being done by overseas officers. There have again been in the past instances of DEA, I think it is, coming and being part of actual removal of persons from the island. So I mean that you have to be very aware of the possibility for abuse in those circumstances. Obviously there is a benefit to being able to have to work with overseas law enforcement on particular cases that cut across regions. I mean the very nature of the international drug trade would lend itself to that kind of involvement internally within the region. And with both the producer countries and the recipient countries but the concern would have to be how is that monitored, how does the _____ citizen have the assurance that the involvement is not going to violate the constitutional rights of _____ citizens. And unfortunately our government has not shown itself to be very vigilant in protecting those rights.

The crucial point is the need for local accountability and clear protocols ensuring that overseas police were working with local police in ways that are locally accountable:

Who would be monitoring it? That for me is the question. You cannot have law enforcement operating within a country where there is no accountability within the country. In other words I would be opposed to having that happening here where the accountability is solely to an external agency. I mean I recognise the problem of where you have got the corruption in the police force. And you have got it in the political directorate. How do you get by that? But I believe that it is dangerous to have law enforcement going on within a country and there is no accountability within the country.

Accountability

Police investigations can be conducted across international boundaries on the basis of criminal intelligence alone, exchanged through informal communication, thereby circumventing any overarching bureaucratic framework. Police officers are more enthusiastic about informal and pragmatic 'horizontal cooperation' than about

formal, programmed 'vertical cooperation'.[42] Since vertical cooperation is usually centrally directed and involves politicians, police
officers feel marginalized at their lack of direct political influence,
expressing this in their distrust towards supranational policing initiatives, potentially starving vertical cooperation structures from
their practical input. Unhindered by politics, 'horizontal', informal cooperation tends to be highly dynamic and police officers
remain motivated because it is case-oriented. This trend raises several important questions about accountability and consent which
provides the bedrock of human rights based policing.

Previous research indicates that investigators generally see
accountability and control measures as an obstruction to efficient
information exchange and try to avoid official channels. Police
officers prefer informal procedures and personal contacts to what
they see as complicated, time-consuming, and ineffective formal
cooperation agreements. A deeply impregnated work culture and
considerable discretional latitude makes formalizing practices labo-
rious with police officers never actually disclosing their informal
contact networks. Marc Alain identifies this as one of the central
obstacles facing the implementation of democratic international
police cooperation. Cooperative initiatives tend to focus on how
police officers should modify their daily practices in accordance
with new rules and procedures with very little attention paid to
how these rules may, or indeed may not, fit into existing structures.
Alain concludes that police resistance undermines formal cooperation mechanisms and information exchange systems.[43]

The disparate nature of transnational policing makes accountability difficult. Sheptycki argues that this arises from the polycen-
tricity of police power and the need for democratic accountability
in which governance must eventually be traced back to the social
contract and the voluntary consent of the governed.[44] For John

---

[42] Monica Den Boer (1999), 'Internationalisation: A Challenge to Police
Organisations in Europe' in Rob Mawby, *Policing Across the World: Issues for the
Twenty-First Century*. London: UCL Press.

[43] Marc Alain (2001), 'Transnational Police Cooperation in Europe and in North
America: Revisiting the Traditional Border between Internal and External Security
Matters, or How Policing is Being Globalised', *European Journal of Crime, Crimi-
nal Law and Criminal Justice*, 9: 113–29.

[44] James Sheptycki (2002), 'Postmodern Power and Transnational Policing:
Democracy, the Constabulary Ethic and the Response to Global (In)security',
Geneva Centre for the Democratic Control of Armed Forces (DCAF) Working
Paper Series—No 19.

Stead accountability mechanisms can be fragmented (local and diffuse), combined (where a balance exists between local and central government), or in the form of national centralized systems through ministerial responsibility to parliament or an assembly. Transnational policing initiatives do not have conventional accountability frameworks such as citizen review boards (considered by some to be a *sine qua non* of democratic policing) or parliamentary oversight or other such mechanisms relying on the purview of sovereign states. Policies and practices emanating from 'above' the nation state are shaping transnational policing. Together with the rise of private policing, this is undermining the role of the state as the sole apparatus for the governance of policing.[45] The idea of transgovernmental relations advanced by Keohane and Nye refers to direct interaction among sub-units of national governments that are outside the control or close guidance of the political directorate of those governments.[46] For Sheptycki, a distinctive feature of the transnational system is that 'State *qua* state is no longer the structural key stone'. The world system is polycentric, so that 'non-state, supra-state, and sub-state actors all play roles in the governance of security that are equal to, and perhaps even more central than, the roles played by state actors'.[47]

Although accountability arrangements are seen by some as a prerequisite to effective police cooperation the transnational policing enterprise generally lacks any framework for political accountability.[48] Anderson *et al* argue that effective police cooperation requires 'a commitment to a robust supranational system of accountability' to ensure long-term popular legitimacy of police systems and thus public support and willingness to supply information.[49] Given that transnational policing is virtually all 'knowledge work' rather than involving the use of coercive power, the importance of maintaining

[45] James Sheptycki (2002a), 'Accountability across the Policing Field: Towards a General Cartography of Accountability for Post-Modern Policing', *Policing and Society*, 12/4: 323–38.

[46] See Robert Keohane and Joseph Nye Jnr. (1974), 'Transgovernmental Relations and International Organisations', *World Politics*, 27: 43.

[47] James Sheptycki (2008), 'Policing, Intelligence Theory and the New Human Security Paradigm: Some Lessons from the Field' in Peter Gill, Stephen Marrin, Mark Phythian (eds), *Intelligence Theory: Key Questions and Debates*. London: Routledge.

[48] Malcolm Anderson, Monica den Boer, P. Cullen, W. Gilmore, C. Raab, and Neil Walker (1995), *Policing the European Union*. Oxford: Oxford University Press.

[49] *Ibid*, 287–9.

popular support cannot be overstated. The legal framework and systems for holding police commanders to account are underdeveloped, and contain few due process safeguards.[50] As Hebenton and Thomas argue, 'While it is hindered by bureaucratic tape, or perhaps because it is, transnational policing strives for results rather than propriety; in the language of criminal jurisprudence, for crime control rather than due process'.[51] Together with a lack of transparency, we are forced to trust the expertise, efficiency, and effectiveness of transnational policing operations and their legality, integrity, and proportionality.

Trust is relevant to the citizen's view of their own nation state and of friendly foreign states and is required to enable human cooperation. Criminal investigators are 'information hoarders'. They often hold unverified and confidential information which they do not communicate even to close colleagues.[52] This stems from a general distrust of outsiders, but also from corruption and dishonesty which frequently afflict policing. Other problems include limited information, transparency, public voice and participation, and a deficit in legal and democratic accountability. For Anderson, 'without these elements, the necessary institutional underpinning of trust in police cooperation is lacking' and it is difficult to see how these can be introduced without a genuine federal element.[53] Certainly, for one Attorney General, there was no prospect of much progress in a discussion about the creation of a regional police force in the Caribbean without the creation of a single political state:

A police force is a primary symbol of sovereignty. And therefore you can't have a regional police force unless you have a regional political state, a single political state. And I want to make that clear because all kinds of international agencies and others are trying to push things like that that blur the lines of sovereignty. And that is my objection to the ACCP, as you know, because a police force is one of the primary symbols of sovereignty.

    [50] B. Hebenton and T. Thomas (1995), *Policing Europe: Cooperation, Conflict and Control*. Basingstoke: Macmillan.
    [51] D.J. Koenig and D.K. Das (2001), *International Police Cooperation: A World Perspective*. Oxford: Lexington Books.
    [52] Malcolm Anderson (2002), 'Trust and Police Cooperation' in Malcolm Anderson and Joanna Apap (eds), *Police and Justice Cooperation and the New European Borders*. The Hague: Kluwer Law International, p 41.
    [53] *Ibid*, p 46.

Anderson is critical of a central state model based on a strict adherence to the principle of national sovereignty in its purest form. The absolutist conception of state sovereignty, he argues, is anachronistic in the policing field because the speed of communication makes it impossible for states to maintain a monopoly of information.[54] Where policing resources are fragmented, national authorities cannot dominate all external relations and small and poor states in particular have difficulties exercising sovereignty. The polar alternative to the absolutist conception of sovereignty is the 'decentralized state' model. Here, police officers in different countries may communicate directly with one another and informal contacts across frontiers are allowed to become standard practice. This, Anderson predicted, would create a 'free market' in police information, resulting in a reduction of nation state authority over the activities of police forces, allowing the police some autonomy of action in the international domain. In Anderson's view, writing in 1989, this 'represents an erosion of sovereignty and control, unacceptable to virtually all the advanced industrialized democracies'.[55] The decentralized model would have the virtue of ending clandestine or informal contacts, recognizing that 'modern technology makes direct communication easy and that it is difficult to control and discipline communications flows by an authoritative set of rules'.[56]

Anderson posed two intermediate models. In a model of *qualified centralization*, national offices are normally in control but in exceptional circumstances, such as urgency or geographical proximity, pragmatic horizontal cooperation is permitted, encouraging ad hoc bilateral agreements. *Qualified decentralization* allows direct communication, but requires reporting of this to national offices. Anderson foresaw a point at which police forces would:

become accustomed to direct communication with their counterparts in other states, effective intervention by the national offices could become more and more difficult, thus raising fears about erosion of state authority.[57]

In the contemporary Caribbean policing scene, the nation state does not hold a monopoly of information. Even in the most restricted

---

[54] Malcolm Anderson (1989), *Policing the World: Interpol and the Politics of International Police Co-Operation*. Oxford: OUP.
[55] *Ibid.*   [56] *Ibid.*   [57] *Ibid*, p 178.

of circumstances, the flow of information through mobile phone networks and email is extensively decentralized. Officers speak regularly to their regional counterparts and colleagues from the metropolitan countries, and in many cases, there is no requirement to report this to senior command. It is merely assumed that 'horizontal communication' will stay at that officer-to-officer level to avoid compromising operations.

As Paul Gilroy argues, we are encountering 'revised conceptions of sovereignty, invented to accommodate the dreams of the new imperial order'.[58] Williams and Savona, for example, argue that relinquishing the 'formalities of sovereignty' is a means to restore the rule of law and 'nullify the advantages that criminals derive from operating across borders and to reduce, circumvent or transcend the frictions that hamper international law enforcement'. Bigo points to the creation of 'security archipelagos' that have become increasingly independent of the requirements of national sovereignty.[59] When control agents work together they break down the 'myth of national sovereignty',[60] challenging the Weberian view of the state as a monopoly holder of the capacity to use force in the pursuit of order within a bounded territory. Globalization challenges the power of the state to claim sovereignty within its territory 'from below' by the actions of non-state transnational actors such as organized crime groups and 'from above' by the actions of transnational actors whose first allegiance is to a foreign state.

Summary and Conclusion

The Caribbean is on the frontline of the 'war on drugs'. Lying on a trade route between the producers of cocaine—one of the world's most profitable commodities—and the millions of people in North America and Europe who crave its mood-altering effects, the region has been severely damaged by the armed violence that accompanies drug trafficking. Many of the people who have been killed, injured, or harmed in other ways have been entirely innocent civilians. Others, of course, have been active participants in the drug trade, lured by the possibility of a livelihood at a time when other

---

[58] Paul Gilroy (2004: 4), *After Empire: Multiculture or Postcolonial Melancholia*. London: Routledge.

[59] Didier Bigo (2000), 'Liaison Officers in Europe: New Officers in the European Security Field' in James Sheptycki (ed), *Issues in Transnational Policing*. London: Routledge, p 85.   [60] *Ibid*, p 85.

economic possibilities are limited. Among the occupational groups most severely affected by the dramatic upsurge of armed violence and insecurity are those who work in the police and other security sector organizations. Their lives have clearly become much more difficult and dangerous in recent decades. They are often poorly paid, carrying out difficult jobs with meagre resources in unpleasant working conditions. These officers are caught between a rock and a hard place: by dint of their vocation they have little choice but to continue to deal with the violent fallout of security policies initiated and promoted by the metropolitan countries.

The transformation of security in the Caribbean region has been deep and wide and this book has sought to delineate the changes occurring in all spheres from the global down to the local. Security sector institutions—police, military, Customs, immigration, coastguard, airport security, secret intelligence services—have all undergone significant change and have become more closely integrated with one another. The boundaries between them have become fuzzy, much as the distinctions between criminal, enemy, migrant, state agent, and citizen have also blurred. The integration of the security sector is a process which is a long way from being complete, but there is clear evidence of the securitization of civil organizations, the militarization of the police, and policeization of the military. As this hybridization of security has occurred, a process of cultural change has begun, one product of which is the emergence of a hybrid culture of security held together by the binding motives of control. In this process of institutional and cultural change, driven by a region-wide crisis of public safety, questions of national sovereignty and accountability have become highly problematic. While some strive to hold on to the principles of independence and local accountability for policing practice, the dominant view is a pragmatic one that sees the best prospect for domestic security as being provided by hybrid transnational security practices for which no mechanism or model of accountability or oversight yet exists. Ironically, it is the economic restructuring and the prohibition regime promoted by the USA and Europe that is at the root of the insecurity that faces the region today. In the concluding chapter, we turn to the question of how to create safe and peaceful communities when both sources of insecurity and forces of law and order originate beyond national boundaries.

10

Conclusion

The 'war on drugs' prosecuted in the Caribbean has transformed the region's security apparatus without making its people any safer. In fact, with only a few exceptions, life in the countries of the region has become far more dangerous than ever before. Moreover, public debate about security has been diverted from some of the most pressing economic, political, and environmental dangers that face the region and threaten to do great harm to its people. The clandestine trade in narcotic and psychotropic drugs and the armed violence that spring from it are, of course, major security threats. But these are not problems of the region's own making; they are the collateral damage of a failing war on drugs. Even with the help of the metropolitan countries—which were slow to acknowledge their responsibility in this sphere—the effort to contribute to regional and hemispheric security has been at a great cost to the region's government and economy. Whatever its genesis, however, intercontinental criminality is a contemporary reality that cannot simply be wished away. We must therefore engage with the questions of how to promote good policing and community safety in the face of the globalization of crime and the accountability deficit created by new plural transnational security practices.

The police were among the last building blocks of the modern state[1] and the same is true of global governance.[2] The political sphere has become globally integrated with supranational governance structures such as the G8, G20, and United Nations playing

---

[1] Egon Bittner (1974), 'Florence Nightingale in Pursuit of Willie Sutton: A Theory of the Police' in Tim Newburn (2005), *Policing: Key Readings*. Cullompton: Willan.

[2] James Sheptycki (1995), 'Transnational Policing and the Makings of a Post-modern State', *British Journal of Criminology*, 35/4: 613–35.

a major role in world affairs.[3] In the economic sphere, manufacturing, agriculture, banking, commerce, and trade are subject to supranational regulatory regimes by such organizations as the World Bank, International Monetary Fund and the World Trade Organization. Public international law is being consolidated and principles of international criminal law and criminal justice practice are now well established. The International Criminal Court—for which Caribbean nations campaigned in the 1980s to deal with transnational drug trafficking—is now a functioning entity (albeit restricted to war crimes, genocide, and crimes against humanity). The emerging transnational criminal justice system lacks a police force even though the building blocks, deeply problematic as they are, are in place.[4] This study shows that while they may be elusive, 'global cops' do in fact exist.[5] In various spheres, transformations in policing provide examples of 'globally aware' police officers who are quite capable of acting beyond national boundaries. The question of how community safety can be provided in a world in which both sources of insecurity and forces of 'law and order' originate beyond the boundaries of the nation state is one of the most pressing issues of our time.

Theories of global governance may provide some answers. Paul Gilroy calls for planetary humanism, 'capable of comprehending the universality of our elemental vulnerability to the wrongs we visit upon each other' and providing an ethos to respond to them.[6] In future, he argues, we must learn to become cosmopolitan citizens, 'capable of mediating between national traditions, communities of fate and alternative styles of life'.[7] In the field of policing, a cosmopolitan approach requires the development of a

---

[3] Peter Singer (2004), *One World: The Ethics of Globalisation*. Yale University Press.

[4] Ben Bowling and Cian Murphy (February 2009), 'Global Policing: Transnational Criminal Law Enforcement in Theory and Practice'. Paper presented to the University of London Institute of Advanced Legal Studies. London.

[5] James Sheptycki (1998), 'The Global Cops Cometh', *British Journal of Sociology*, 49/1: 57–74; James Sheptycki (2002), *In Search of Transnational Policing*. Aldershot: Avebury.

[6] Paul Gilroy (2004), *After Empire: Melancholia or Convivial Culture?*. London: Routledge, p 4.

[7] David Held (2003), 'Cosmopolitanism: Taming Globalisation' in David Held and Anthony McGrew (eds), *The Global Transformations Reader*. Cambridge: Polity, p 425.

supranational system to regulate *from above* the coercive and intrusive powers of the state within and beyond its own borders. Some form of supranational regulation is an essential requirement for transnational policing. Exactly what form this should take remains an open question, but it must surely be rooted in a system of global governance.[8] The development of global policing also requires a strengthening of the democratic ethos, or what James Sheptycki calls the 'constabulary ethic' to guide policing agencies 'armed with the capacity to muster coercive force in the maintenance of social order towards socially good ends of peace, order and good governance'.[9] This would include such principles as responsiveness and accountability to the community, adherence to internationally recognized human rights standards, and internal democracy to ensure that police organizations reflect the communities that they serve.[10]

A cosmopolitan approach to transnational policing also requires the development of an active global civil society willing to engage with police accountability *from below*. To make this a reality, a new politics and practice of police accountability is required, built on networks of interconnectedness and solidarity that can resonate across borders and everyday cultural and economic obstacles.[11] Globalization has facilitated the development of intercontinental organized crime and transnational policing. But the same processes have enabled the development of 'transnational communities' and movements for international human rights and global justice. To some extent this role is developing within international non-governmental organizations such as Amnesty International and Human Rights Watch and those working on the ground such as

---

[8] See, for example, Paul Gilroy (2004), *After Empire*. London: Routledge; George Monbiot (2004), *The Age of Consent: A Manifesto for a New World Order*. London: Harper Perennial; Philippe Sands (2005), *Lawless World*. Harmondsworth: Penguin; Anne-Marie Slaughter (2004), *A New World Order*. Princeton University Press; Peter Singer (2004), *One World: The Ethics of Globalisation*. Yale University Press.

[9] James Sheptycki (2007), 'The *Constabulary Ethic* and the Transnational Condition' in Andrew Goldsmith and James Sheptycki (eds), *Crafting Transnational Policing*. Oxford: Hart.

[10] Ben Bowling, Coretta Phillips, Alexandra Campbell, and Maria Docking (2004), *Human Rights and Policing: Eliminating Racism, Discrimination and Xenophobia from Policework*. United Nations Institute for Social Research and Development. [11] Paul Gilroy (2004), *After Empire*, p 5.

The Monitoring Group and Liberty in the UK and Caribbean NGOs such as Jamaicans for Justice, Families Against State Terrorism, and the Guyana Human Rights Association.[12] To make transnational police accountability a reality, we might ask ourselves what the exhortations to 'think global *act local*' and 'think local *act global*' mean in this field. The former includes applying universal principles to the policing of specific local communities. The latter implies that the private problems experienced in local neighbourhoods can be transformed into global public policy issues to which solutions can be developed in supranational fora. Both suggest that we must re-invent the notion of 'community' to allow it to stretch beyond geographical borders and the narrow concerns of communities of interest. At present, secret policing practices that extend beyond national boundaries are visible only to an international security elite, violating the principles of openness, transparency, and accountability upon which democratic policing is built. In future, such activities should be accountable to local communities *and* subject to a robust and transparent system of supranational oversight.

Working to achieve 'good enough' policing in local, national, regional, and transnational spheres is important but it is only part of the answer to the problem of armed violence and unsafe local communities. The tasks involved in creating safer neighbourhoods and accountable policing must be rooted in, and routed through, community organizations. In the same way that organized crime groups and the state are connecting globally, future work in this sphere can be developed by transnational civil society. Organizations representing specific communities of interest seeking to bring about cultural and normative change within both police and community can benefit from engaging with one another transnationally. Reducing violent crime requires social and economic issues to be addressed: providing economic opportunities, reducing poverty, and offering hope for the future is an essential first step. Without this, people who feel themselves to be at the economic margins will continue to find a local role in the global drugs trade. By dealing with crime problems in accordance with the law, with respect for human rights and with a professionalism that can restore legitimacy

---

[12] Such organizations have already started to forge strategic alliances with organizations elsewhere in the world in collaboration with more formal accountability mechanisms, such as the Northern Ireland Ombudsman's Office.

and public confidence, people will be motivated to act within the law. This requires doing things that are culturally appropriate and which respect the dignity of indigenous people. Community problem solving and peace building require perceptive analysis and forward-looking, imaginative responses. This could include taking organized crime out of the supply of psychotropic drugs, disarming and reintegrating former combatants, decommissioning weapons, vocational training, rehabilitation, and psychosocial therapy for young people affected by violence. An approach emphasizing community-based problem solving would aim to reduce crime by investing in local crime prevention, public housing, environmental improvements, youth work, education, and mechanisms to promote civic engagement between police and public. The human and financial resources used to provide armaments, paramilitary equipment, communication systems, information technology, and regional mobility for transnational security agents could be put to better use. The resource invested in the new transnational security apparatus has the potential to provide engineering support for depressed communities. This capacity could be used to transfer skills and technology to ordinary people and help build schools, medical centres, sports and recreational facilities where young people can socialize and utilize their energy in positive ways. We should seek a human approach to safety rather than a technological one that offers only precarious protection. Transnational security cooperation must be harnessed more closely to the needs of local neighbourhoods if it is to become part of the solution to community insecurity rather than being part of the problem. We should admit that the 'war on drugs' has been ineffective in its own terms and counterproductive in the pursuit of human security. It is now time to redirect our resources to building a lasting peace.

Appendix 1
Interviewees

Organization	Sub-unit
Police	Commissioner
	Deputy Commissioner
	Deputy or Assistant Commissioner (Crime)
	Deputy or Assistant Commissioner (Operations)
	Deputy or Assistant Commissioner (Admin and Training)
	Head of Drug Squad
	Head of Special Branch
	Head of Organized Crime
	Head of Criminal Investigation Department
	Head of Marine Section
	Head of Interpol (HQ and National Central Bureaux)
	Head of Anti-Crime Unit
	Retired Commissioner
	Commissioner's Staff Officer
	Narcotics Intelligence
	Special Agents
	Senior Investigating Officer
Customs	Commissioner/Comptroller
	Contraband Intelligence
	Head of Information Technology
	Drugs Liaison Officer
Immigration	Chief Immigration Officer
	Head of investigation

Organization	Sub-unit
Military	Chief of Staff
	Infantry Commander
	Operations Commander
	Coastguard Commander
Airport authorities	Director Airports
	Airport security chief
	Airport security officer
Home Affairs, Justice, and Security ministries	Minister
	Narcotics Intelligence
	Special advisor
	Director of Public Prosecutions
	Attorney General
Non-governmental organizations	Human Rights
	Conservation
	Drugs
Post Office	Postmaster general
	Head of investigation
United Nations	UN Development Programme
Foreign and Overseas Development Ministries	Resident Commissioner
	Deputy High Commissioner
	Police advisor
	Defence advisor
	Governance advisor
Regional coordinating bodies (eg CARICOM, RSS, ACCP)	Coordinator/Secretariat

Appendix 2
Details of Transnational Policing in the Caribbean Region

1. National Police Agencies Working Abroad

1.1 National Police Agencies Working Abroad: UK

Organizations	Locations	Functions
Drugs Liaison Officers (DLOs) (UK Revenue and Customs)	Barbados (4, responsible for the Eastern Caribbean), Jamaica (3, responsible for Jamaica and the Western Caribbean), Trinidad (1 for Trinidad and Tobago and Guyana)	Officers resident overseas engaged in 'bilateral' and 'multilateral' information exchange, mutual assistance
Crime Liaison Officers (CLOs) (National Crime Intelligence Service)	2, based in Jamaica	Intelligence gathering and sharing. Liaison with counterparts in Jamaica and UK (esp. Trident)
Foreign and Commonwealth Office Police Advisors	1, based in London (for Independent Caribbean), 1, based in Miami (Overseas Territories—OTRIS)	Provides advice on developing information systems, training, and development
MI6, MI5	Based in the region	Intelligence collection and analysis. Cooperation with local intelligence agencies
UK Immigration Officers	Jamaica	Processing visa applications
UK Defence Advisor	2, based in Barbados	One naval officer seconded to FCO and one to Regional Security System (RSS)
British Military (BMATT)	Antigua	Provision of support and training to Caribbean military and naval officers
Operation Carib Bridge (multi-agency operation involving HM Customs, NCIS (seconded Metropolitan Police officer)	Jamaica (3 customs officers, one police officer on rotation)	Drug test using 'ion scan' and urine testing. Intelligence-led and profile-based stops of passengers leaving Kingston and Montego Bay

1.1 National Police Agencies Working Abroad: UK (*cont.*)

Organizations	Locations	Functions
Operation Carib Bridge	Antigua, Barbados, Saint Vincent and the Grenadines and elsewhere in the region	As Carib Bridge, but with fewer dedicated personnel. Mainly implemented by local police officers
Department for International Development Governance Advisors	Jamaica (1, covering Jamaica and the Western Caribbean) Barbados (2, covering Eastern Caribbean/Guyana)	Providing advice on police reform, modernization, etc. Seeking funding for development projects
Operation Trident	UK	UK-based homicide investigators undertaking inquiries in Jamaica and other Caribbean islands.
Police advisors	UK	Officers offering ad hoc advice in relation to firearms training in Guyana and Jamaica, acting as senior investigating officer on alleged extra-judicial killing by police

1.2 National Police Agencies Working Abroad: USA

Organizations	Locations	Functions
Drugs Enforcement Administration (DEA)	Barbados, Jamaica, Puerto Rico, Miami, Bahamas, Dominican Republic, Haiti, Netherlands Antilles	Employs more than 200 agents in over 60 offices around the world
Federal Bureau of Investigation (FBI), Legal Attaché	Barbados, Jamaica	Assistance with legal issues, hostage negotiations, etc
Treasury Department	Barbados	Investigating money laundering
Central Intelligence Agency (CIA)	no access	Intelligence gathering
Department of Homeland Security	no access	Intelligence gathering
US State Department Diplomatic Protection Group	Regional Security Advisor, Guyana	Intelligence gathering, assistance with legal issues, hostage negotiations, etc

1.3 National Police Agencies Working Abroad: Jamaica

Organizations	Locations	Functions
JCF liaison officers	2, based in UK	Jamaica Constabulary Force (JCF) officers based in London undertaking a crime liaison role

1.4 National Police Agencies Working Abroad: Canada

Organizations	Locations	Functions
Royal Canadian Mounted Police	Jamaica	Liaison with regional counterparts

2. Pan-Caribbean Cross-Border Policing Arrangements

Organizations	Locations	Functions
Association of Caribbean Commissioners of Police (ACCP)	Barbados (permanent secretariat). Members include all countries in the English-speaking Caribbean, including mainland Guyana and Belize. Also includes Aruba. Haiti and Cuba are associate members	Established in 1987, has a permanent secretariat in Bridgetown, Barbados. It holds formal meetings of the region's Commissioners twice a year, provides a communications hub, as well as developing training courses, the sharing of good practice and policy development for law enforcement agencies within the region
Regional Drug Squad Commanders' Conference	Revolving secretariat. Includes ACCP police forces	Established in 1993, meets annually
Regional Special Branch Commanders' Conference	Revolving secretariat. Includes ACCP police forces	Established prior to ACCP. Goes back to pre-independence days
Caribbean Ministerial Conference on Regional Law Enforcement/ CARICOM Task Force on Law and Order	Regular informal meeting of CARICOM security ministers	Recommends permanent Committee of Ministers of National Security and Law Enforcement

2. Pan-Caribbean Cross-Border Policing Arrangements
(*cont.*)

Organizations	Locations	Functions
Regional Drug Law Enforcement Training Centre (REDTRAC)	Jamaica—funded by EU, US, Canada, and UK	Anti-drug training centre
Overseas Territories Conference on Law Enforcement (OTRIS – Overseas Territories Information System)	United Kingdom Overseas Territories eg Montserrat, British Virgin Islands, Bermuda, Turks and Caicos, etc	Conference held annually in one of the Overseas Territories
Regional Security System (RSS)	HQ in Barbados covering Barbados and countries of the Organisation of Eastern Caribbean States (OECS)	Formed in 1983 provides links among paramilitary Special Support Units in each country that can be coordinated to respond to civil emergencies
Caribbean Customs Law Enforcement Council (CCLEC)	First signed by 21 countries but now has 36 signatories in the Caribbean basin	Established in the early 1970s as an informal association of customs administrators
Caribbean Drug Coordination Mechanism	Linked to the UN and CARICOM	Information collection and policy making
Regional Information and Intelligence Sharing System (RIISS)	A creation of the ACCP	Intelligence sharing system, build on Interpol (I-24/7) communication system using a 'pointer' to the existence of relevant data (eg a name)
Inter-American Drug Abuse Control Programme (CICAD)	A sub-unit of the Organization of American States	Information collection and policy development
Caribbean Financial Action Task Force (CFATF)	An organization of 30 states of the Caribbean Basin	Established as the result of meetings convened in Aruba in May 1990 and Jamaica in November 1992. Addresses criminal money laundering and the financing of terrorism

Organizations	Locations	Functions
Caribbean Law Enforcement and Intelligence Committee	Puerto Rico	Information sharing
Joint Information Coordinating Centre, El Paso Intelligence Centre (EPIC)	El Paso, USA	Database management
Regional Immigration Officers' Conference	Organized under the auspices of the Organization of Eastern Caribbean States	Information sharing and trust building
Regional Airport Security Officers' Conference	Fledgling organization	Information sharing and trust building

3. Global Policing Agencies

Organizations	Locations	Functions
United Nations Security and Safety Service	UN Headquarters and various other locations	Protects UN buildings and employees, comprised of seconded police officers under central UN control
United Nations Drugs and Crime Programme	Based in Barbados but without personnel for the duration of the research	Information collection and policy development
United Nations Development Programme	Offices in Barbados, Guyana, and Jamaica	Provides resources and advice on governance—supports police reform
International Criminal Police Organization (INTERPOL)	Lyon, Paris. Sub-regional bureau in Puerto Rico. Interpol National Central Bureau is an integral component of each national police force	Formed in 1923, acts as a global intelligence network between autonomous members; membership of 176 countries

4. Private Transnational Policing Agencies

Organizations	Locations	Functions
Securicor, Securitas, Guardsman	In all islands across the region	Uniformed private security guards in private buildings; airport security

Index of Names

Subject Index